Fine Arts of the South Bend Region 1840-2000

Alexis Jean Fournier, *My Bungalow, Blossom Time*

WOLFSON PRESS
INDIANA UNIVERSITY SOUTH BEND

Fine Arts of the South Bend Region

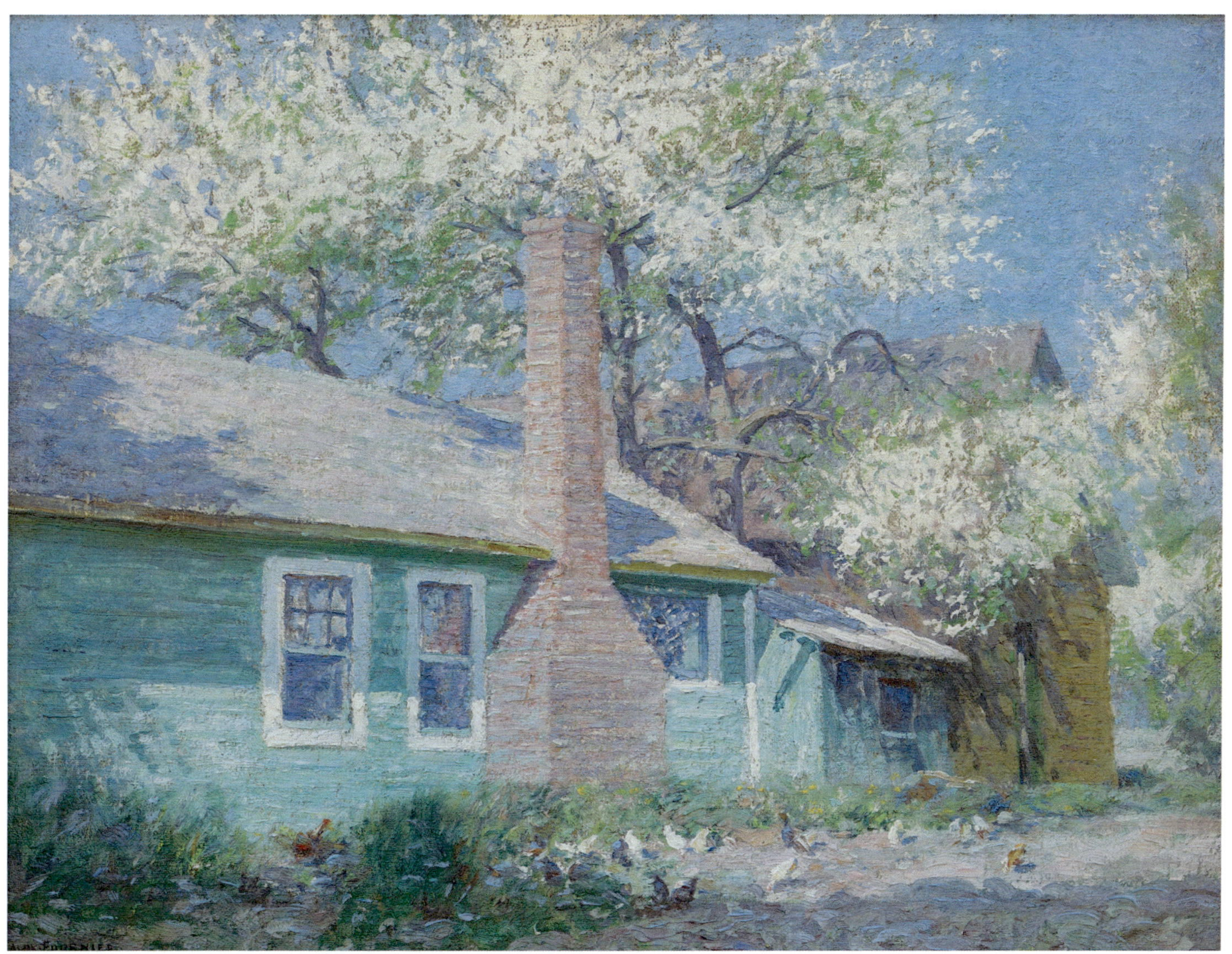

1840-2000

Roger Birdsell, Brian Byrn, Jim Ferm, Patrick J. Furlong, Dean Porter, Marcia Rickard, Susan Visser, and Harold Zisla. Walton R. Collins, Editor

Wolfson Press gratefully acknowledges the artists, family members, friends, collectors, museums, schools, colleges and universities, newspapers, libraries and librarians, archives and archivists, galleries, curators, and fans of the arts without whom this book would not have been possible. Wolfson Press will gladly receive word of any corrections that might be incorporated into the next printing.

Design and editorial team:
David James and Ken Smith.
Cover photography by Peter Ringenberg.

ISBN: 978-1-939674-02-9

Wolfson Press
Master of Liberal Studies Program
Indiana University South Bend
1700 Mishawaka Avene
South Bend, IN 46634-7111
wolfson.iusb.edu

Dedication

Because he has for so many years provoked
our shared reflections and our quest for excellence
in the fine arts, we dedicate this book to Harold Zisla.

Video Interviews

Disc one:

Susan Visser

B. Jane Burns and Brian Byrn

Dea Andrews

Disc two:

Dean A. Porter

Austin I. Collins, CSC

Bill Sandusky

Harold Zisla

Disc three:

Jake (James) Webster

Frederick C. Elbel

Walton R. Collins

Monica Radecki

Table of Contents

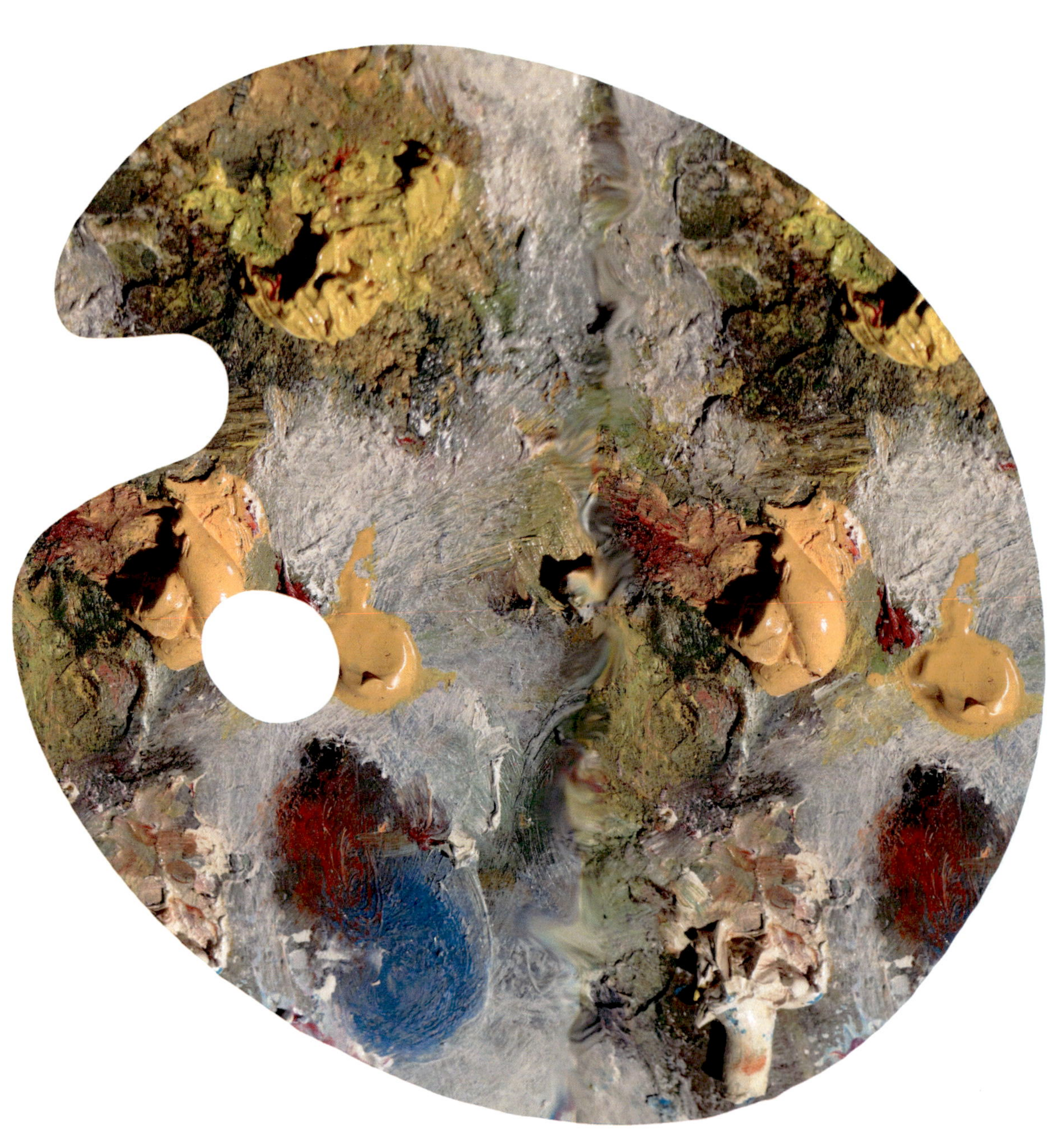

With Gratitude

Over the course of several years individuals and organizations contributed generously, sometimes more than once, to the realization of this project documenting the fine arts history of the region. Members of the book team express their gratitude to:

Anonymous
Ira and Sara Ann Anes
Angel Fund, Community Foundation of St. Joseph County
Frank and Louise Antonazzi
Peri and Beverly Arnold
ArtsEverywhere Fund, Community Foundation of St. Joseph County
Charles and Barbara Asher
Philip and Mary Ashton
Louis and Eleanor Baker
Memory of Anita Beatty
R. Michael Beatty
Aileen Borough
Florence V. Carroll Charitable Trust
Russell Cartwright
Stanley A. and Flora P. Clark Memorial Trust Fund
George and Mease Coquillard
Elizabeth Cullity
Bettie Dippo
June Edwards
Frederick Elbel
Alan and Michelle Engel
Howard and Sondra Engel
John, Anna, and Martha Jane Fields Trust Foundation
Bert and Charlotte Ford
Elinor Gard
William and Leslie Gitlin
Alfred Guillaume and Melanie Smith-Guillaume
Charles S. Hayes
Brian and Carol Hedman
Maury and Candace Hurwich
Muriel Hurwich
Fred Kahn and Marsha Brook
James and Chris Kelly
Kathryn Kramer
Kruggel, Lawton & Company, LLC
Mark and Jessica Kubow
Charles and Dee Ann Mattes
Jeff and Jan McGowan
Janettte Burkhart Miller
Muessel-Ellison Memorial Trust Foundation
Rawson and Chris Murdock
Mendel and Frances Piser
Ernestine Raclin
Ernestine M. Raclin School of the Arts Foundation Board
Maritza Robles
William and Julie Scholl
Tom and Elizabeth Schorgl
Joe Schultz, Northern Indiana Artists, Inc.
Charles and Lynda Simon
Kurt Simon
Richard and Joyce Stifel
University of Notre Dame
Barbara Warner
Steven and Jean Watts
Shirlee Wishinsky
Lester and Frances Wolfson
Harold and Doreen Zisla

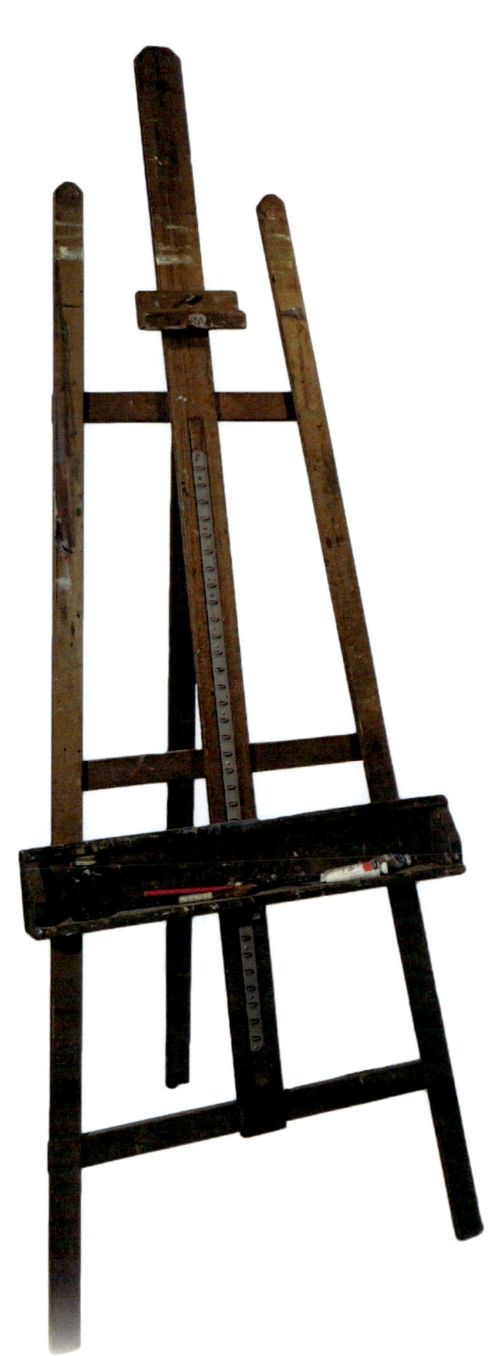

The Story of the Book

A few years ago Michael Beatty and Harold Zisla of Lifetime Education And Research Network (LEARN) became convinced that the time had come for the fine arts community of the region to document its history in a book. LEARN took on that challenge.

The committee members who launched the project were David Bainbridge (Center for History), Michael Beatty (LEARN), Roger Birdsell, Walton R. Collins, Charles S. Hayes, Kim Hoffmann, Ann Kuntz (St. Joseph County Public Library), Cathy McCormick, Dean Porter (Snite Museum, Notre Dame), Harold Zisla (LEARN, IU South Bend). Some contributed their time with special generosity in the beginning, some throughout the project, and some in more than one way. That list starts with, of course, Harold Zisla, and includes Dean Porter (who worked on the project in so many ways), Jim Ferm (who continued to work and help even as he faced increased health challenges), Julie Tourtillotte, and Marcia Rickard from St. Mary's College.

Organizational, staff, publicity, research, and member support came from the Northern Indiana Artists, South Bend Museum of Art, St. Joseph County Public Library, Midwest Museum of American Art, *South Bend Tribune,* Community Foundation of St. Joseph County, Notre Dame Archives, Northern Indiana Center for History, La Porte County Historical Society, and Elkhart County Historical Museum.

The researchers included Janet Beckman, Brandi David, Jim Ferm, Anne Flaig, Kristen Glomb, Jennifer Gregory, Joan Hasse, and David James.

Biographies were compiled by Brandi David, Anne McGraw, and David James.

The main chapters were researched and written by Roger Birdsell, Brian Byrn, Jim Ferm, Patrick J. Furlong, Dean Porter, Marcia Rickard, Susan Visser, and Harold Zisla. The editor was Walton R. Collins.

Video interviews for the DVDs were granted by Dae Andrews, Jane Burns, Brian Byrn, Austin Collins, CSC, Walt Collins, Frederick Elbel, Dean Porter, Monica Radecki, Bill Sandusky, Susan Visser, Jake Webster, and Harold Zisla. The interviews were conducted and edited by R. Michael Beatty. Fundraising assistance, graphic assistance, and video assistance came from Bill Scholl, Steve Liddy, and Matt Gable.

Our thanks to the many people who provided or helped us find images. Major photography was by Peter Ringenberg and David James. The book was designed by Wolfson Press.

Companion exhibits were held at the South Bend Museum of Art and the Ernestine M. Raclin School of the Arts Gallery. Joshua Miller prepared the IU South Bend exhibit, and Kim Hoffmann prepared the SBMA exhibit.

In the final years, the Public Affairs and University Advancement Office of Indiana University South Bend, captained by Ilene Sheffer, committed to the project. Anne McGraw, Michael Beatty, and Ken Smith of Wolfson Press formed the final book committee. Anne McGraw's tireless contributions were essential to the completion of the project. Thanks to all of you and to anyone we might have failed to mention.

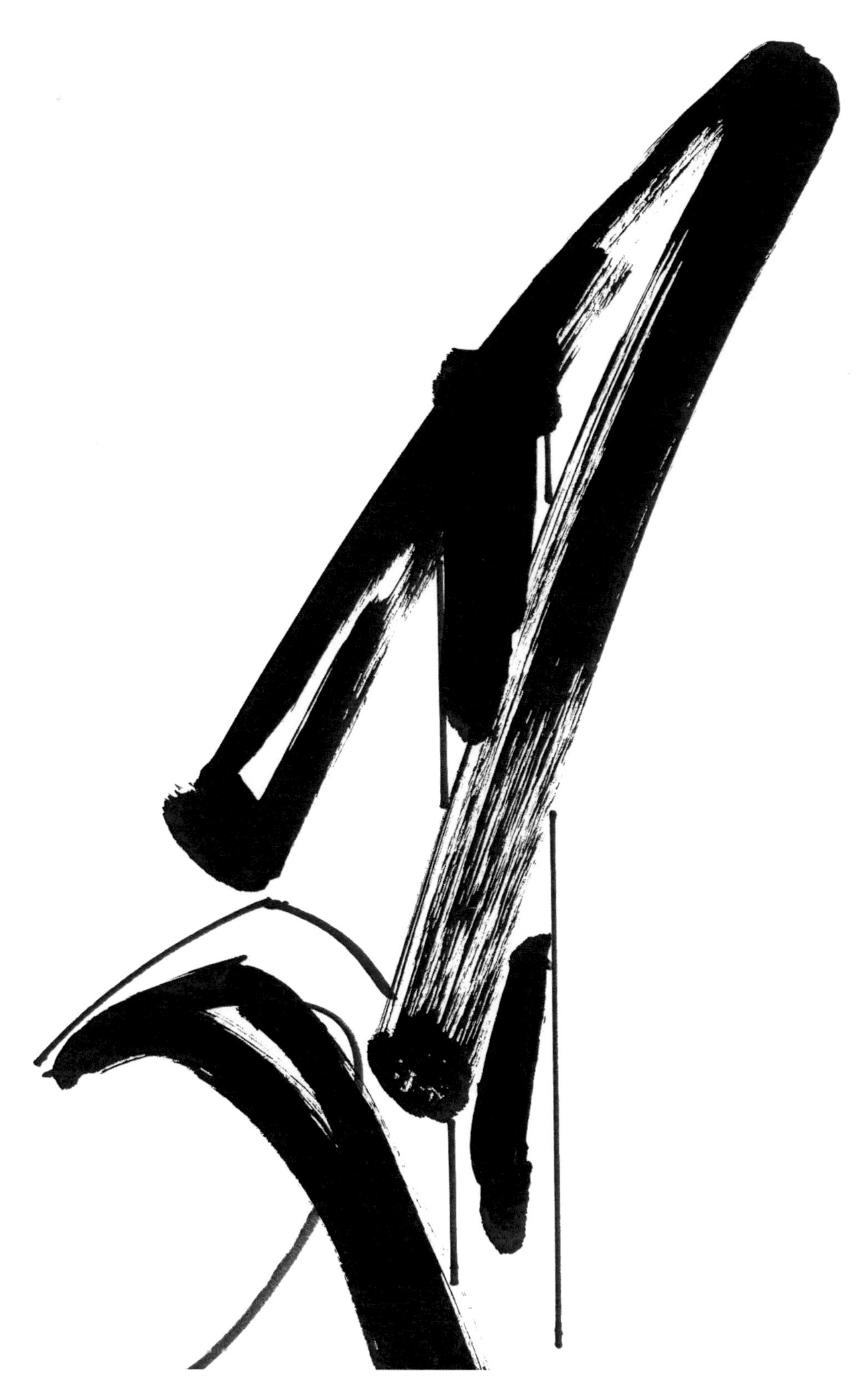

Art in South Bend, A History: 1840-2000

Roger Birdsell

Art as a public artifact reached South Bend when Rev. Edward Sorin, founder of the University of Notre Dame, commissioned a series of fresco paintings to adorn the university's Administration Building and hired an established Italian painter, Luigi Gregori, for the job. Born in 1819, Gregori studied painting in his native Bologna and in Florence before moving to Rome in 1840, where he was employed to restore, arrange and catalogue old master paintings in the Vatican's collection.

Arriving at Notre Dame in 1874, Gregori began the series of 10 large paintings based on the life of Christopher Columbus that line the main entrance hallway of the Administration Building. Clearly reflecting Gregori's Baroque Italian style, the paintings depict Columbus's first voyage of discovery to the New World under the patronage of the Spanish Court. Gregori also painted the frescos inside the Administration Building's Golden Dome cupola, using allegorical figures to depict the disciplines of religion, science, philosophy, history, poetry, music, and fame. Several more Gregori paintings can be seen in Notre Dame's Sacred Heart Basilica, and one also hangs in the old Clem Studebaker mansion, now the Tippecanoe Restaurant, on South Bend's West Washington Avenue. Gregori returned to Italy in 1891, where he died in 1896.

Mark di Suvero: *Keepers of the Fire II.*

The earliest surviving local painting is an 1847 oil portrait of Alexis Coquillard, one of South Bend's founders in the 1830s, commissioned by the sitter. The painter, J. H. VanFlavoran, of whom nothing else is known, is thought to have been self-taught. An oil portrait of Mrs. Coquillard was painted by Alexis Comparet, son of Francis Comparet, another South Bend founder. The younger Comparet studied art in Paris, returned briefly to South Bend and soon moved on to Colorado and later San Diego, where he died in 1906. The two Coquillard portraits are at Notre Dame.

The first artist of record in South Bend was one A. Merine, who advertised his services in the South Bend Free Press in 1841. Another artist, Adolphus Van Sickle, apparently an oil painter and photographer, worked in South Bend in 1848 and again from 1868 to 1874. More is known about the local painter Curran Swaim, a native of Virginia raised on a farm near Fountain City, Indiana. He studied art in New York City and moved to South Bend at the age of thirty. Swaim painted several portraits, including one of Circuit Judge Thomas S. Stanfield, now displayed at the Northern Indiana Center for History. He left South Bend in 1868 and died in 1897 in Missouri. Another early artist was Daniel Kotz, born in a log cabin near South Bend in 1848. He studied art in Chicago and opened a studio in South Bend in the late 1880s, painting a portrait of the wife of former Vice President Schuyler Colfax. He moved to New Jersey in 1890 and became a popular portrait painter on the East Coast. He died in 1933.

Construction of a new St. Joseph County Courthouse in 1900 provided another opportunity for public art. Hans Roeder, a native of Bavaria who decorated wagons and buggies for the Studebaker Company, painted the interior of the courthouse dome. He died in 1930.

L. Clarence Ball, who moved to South Bend in 1880 as a decorator of Studebaker vehicles, eventually became widely known as the city's most prominent artist. Ball was born in Mount Vernon, Ohio, and moved with his family to Goodland, Indiana, at the age of five. He opened a studio in South Bend in 1886, where he gave painting instruction while continuing his own work as a painter of landscapes in oil. During the winters of 1892 and 1893, Ball broadened his horizons by attending classes at the National Academy of Art and visiting galleries and other artists' studios in New York City. His association with the South Bend Engraving Company as a commercial artist began in 1893. Ball maintained a painting studio over a boathouse on Diamond Lake near Cassopolis, Michigan, and wrote poetry. He died in 1915 in South Bend. Several of his landscapes are in the South Bend Museum of Art collection, and one, *Felling the Bee Tree*, hangs in Local History Room of the Saint Joseph County (South Bend) Main Public Library.

Ball's widow, Cora Platz, whom he married in 1884, married another prominent local artist, Alexis Jean Fournier, in 1922. Fournier was born in Saint Paul, Minnesota, in 1865 and moved with his family to South Bend at the age of six months. After brief study at the Minnesota Academy of Fine Arts in 1890, he left for Paris and study at Academie Julian. During his career he painted oil landscapes in a manner reminiscent of the Barbizon School and the French Impressionists. A series of twenty paintings of the homes of Barbizon master painters was Fournier's tribute to his masters. Cora was Fournier's third marriage—he had a son and daughter by his second wife—and she died in 1937. He maintained their home in South Bend until 1944, when he moved to East Aurora, New York, and married for a fourth time. He died in 1948 after a fall on an icy sidewalk.

George Ames Aldrich was a friend and colleague of Fournier's. Born in Worcester, Massachusetts, in 1872, Aldrich studied under John H. Twachtman at the Art Students League in New York City. He then moved to France for some years of study with fellow artists and began devoting his life to landscape paintings in oil. He married the first of his three wives, Eugenie Wehrle, in Paris in 1909 and moved back to New York the next year, later relocating in Chicago. Success in an exhibit of his work in the Oliver Hotel in 1922 convinced him to settle in South Bend, where he married again, fathering a daughter by his third wife, Esta. Aldrich taught drawing at the South Bend Fine Arts Club, lectured with Fournier on landscape painting in 1923 at the Progress Club, and produced picturesque landscapes of France and America for many private patrons until his death in 1941 in Chicago. His paintings are in the collections of the South Bend Museum of Art and the Elkhart Midwest Museum of American Art.

E. E. Whitehill was a student of Aldrich's. Born in 1890 in Peru, Indiana, Whitehill created posters for the Ringling Brothers Circus, which wintered in his home town. He moved to South Bend in 1914, and worked in a variety of media for his clients, including photography. He collaborated with another area artist, John Streibel, illustrating children's books. Whitehill, who died in 1966, was credited with forming a Northern Indiana artists group in 1920, of which nothing more is known.

One day, it was later said, Clarence Ball saw some paintings by Leon A. Makielski and convinced the young man to quit his job as a clerk in the Portage Township Trustee's Office and study at the Chicago Art Institute. Makielski, born in 1878 in Morris Run, Pennsylvania, had been living in South Bend since 1882. He studied at Chicago for a year, and in 1908 he won a traveling scholarship to study in Paris, where he enrolled in the Academie Julian and exhibited portraits at two salons during a four-year stay. In 1915 he was appointed instructor in painting at the University of Michigan's Department of Architecture, a post he held until 1928. Makielski's many portraits—some 160 of Michigan faculty members alone—included prominent local citizens like Albert Erskine and J. M. Studebaker, executed while visiting family members living in South Bend. He also painted landscapes, and some of his works are in the South Bend Museum of Art collection. One of his portraits in that collection is of Muriel (Mrs. Warren H.) Miller, a popular local private art teacher and floral painter. A native of Eaton, Ohio, Miller studied at the Chicago Art Institute and with Makielski and others. She died in 1975 at the age of eighty-eight.

Patrons and Artists

Artists like Ball, Fournier, Aldrich and Makielski relied on sales of their paintings to private collectors for a living. Local individual interest in the arts evolved into group support in 1927 with the organization of a South Bend Chapter of the Hoosier Art Patrons Association. The association had been founded by a group of women born in Indiana and living in Chicago. The women founding the South Bend Chapter elected Mrs. Elizabeth G. Kettering as their president. Chapter meetings with lectures and presentations on art subjects were held in members' homes and later at the Progress Club. The chapter sponsored occasional local art exhibits and supported local artists who exhibited at the annual Hoosier Salon art exhibition, held for many years in Chicago's Marshall Field's department store. (The exhibition moved to Indianapolis in 1944.)

One of the Hoosier Art Patrons' local founders was Ella (wife of E. M.) Morris, who founded the Associates Investment Company, a nationwide enterprise in automobile and other consumer and corporate financing. Morris also acquired South Bend's First Bank & Trust Company. The Morris family was to become became one of the community's primary financial benefactors in the fine arts, music, education and health care.

The Progress Club, founded in 1895 and an affiliate of the National Association of Women's Clubs, supported art in this community starting as early as 1921 with lectures and exhibits in its building on West Colfax Avenue. Other venues for local artist exhibitions during the '20s, '30s and early '40s included the Oliver Hotel, Robertson's Department Store, First National Bank and Union Trust Company, the YMCA and Black Box, a local theater building on South Lafayette Boulevard. Local women of Polish ancestry founded the Chopin Fine Arts Club in 1940, and it too sponsored programs on art and music.

Local artists themselves were organizing for mutual support. Five members of the new Artists' League of Northern Indiana held an exhibition in 1927 in Robertson's Tea Room, and a juried exhibit the following year. One of the exhibitors was Theodora Makielski, sister of Leon Makielski. She opened the Makielski Art Shop on North Main Street in 1911, for many years an informal meeting place for area artists. A native of Poland who attended the Chicago Art Institute, Makielski studied painting with Aldrich and Emile Jacques, chair of the Notre Dame Art Department. She died in 1979 at age eighty-eight.

Another League member was Ludwig L. Blake, a native of Norway who arrived in South Bend in 1913. His Blake Mills manufactured wallpaper. Blake was seventy-five when he began painting. He was noted for his home and extensive gardens on the banks of Juday Creek north of Roseland. His portrait of Jesus Christ was given to the First Methodist Church of South Bend. He hand-carved a large walnut mural with fruits, grains, birds, and cherubs in the Baroque style for display in two local bank lobbies. He died in 1956 at age eighty-six.

Another group of artists that met at Makielski's Art Shop sponsored three events in 1932. A juried spring exhibition awarded prizes to Wilbur West for a sculpture, Beatrice Hartig Zimmerman for an oil landscape, and Vernon Scott for another oil. The group held a "Beaux Arts" costume ball in April in the Oliver Hotel with South Bend Mayor George Freyermuth as guest of honor, and a fall exhibition showed works by twenty-five sculptors and ceramics by West. The Makielski artists organized themselves more formally in 1933 as the Midland Art Academy with the objective of emulating the well-known Brown County school of painters in Southern Indiana. The founders elected Vernon Scott president, Helen Whitlock vice president, Louise Hildreth secretary and Wilbur Kenyon treasurer. Louis Frederick was named business manager. Milton Walton was designated instruction critic, and Rose Zabo chief model.

Midland Art Academy leaders laid out an ambitious program of instruction, with classes meeting on Monday evenings and live model drawing scheduled twice a month. Monthly exhibits of works by members and students were planned, and an annual Fournier Award was established for the most improved student. Annual juried spring exhibitions began in 1934 and continued through 1942. An annual outdoor art fair was inaugurated in 1935 and continued through 1940. "Beaux Arts" balls continued through 1940.

The inauguration of Midland Academy also saw the organization of the Saint Joseph Valley Chapter of the American Artists' Professional League, described as a group of artists seeking a venue for sharing ideas and fellowship. A larger, more permanent local organization emerged in 1942 with creation of Northern Indiana Artists (NIA). Some Midland Academy members subsequently reorganized as the South Bend Art League and sponsored instructional programs under the aegis of the City of South Bend Recreation Department.

NIA charter members were by and large the founders of the earlier American Artists Professional League chapter. The one exception was John DeMan, a partner of James H. Cloetingh in the Cloetingh and DeMan commercial art and photography studio. DeMan had been president of the no longer active Artists' League of Northern Indiana and treasurer of the Artists Professional League chapter. Besides Cloetingh, the NIA charter members were John Bednar, Gertrude Wiser Butcher, Grace Crumpacker, Arthur E. Hartig, Beatrice Hartig Zimmerman, Genevieve "Geni" Hartig Toth, Eugene Kormendi, Elizabeth Kormendi, Theodora Makielski, Harriet Monteith, Edward Reasor, Stanley Sessler, Lester "Bud" Swartz and Wilbur West. The two Kormendi's had not been professional league chapter members. West was elected president, and Bednar chairman of the board of directors.

Cloetingh, born in 1894 in Muskegon, Michigan, moved to South Bend in 1925 and established a studio on East LaSalle Avenue with DeMan three years later. The first photographer to be awarded a Master of Photography Degree by the Professional Photographers Association of America, Cloetingh frequently lectured on photographic techniques. He also painted landscapes and still lifes in oil, later in life turning to abstracts. He died in 1964.

West, born in South Bend in 1912, studied at the Ohio State University, Columbia University and the Chicago Art Institute. He was instrumental in developing an innovative high school art curriculum for the South Bend public schools, where he taught for many years. He also worked as an art appraiser.

Butcher was another South Bend public schools art teacher. Born in 1898 in Jonesboro, Indiana, she moved as a child to South Bend. Following graduation from Central High School, she studied at Ball State University, Columbia, the University of Chicago and the Chicago Art Institute. Her brother, Guy Brown Wiser, was also a successful painter. An aviator in World War I, he became a prisoner after his plane was shot down. He returned to South Bend after the war and worked in the art department of an architectural firm and at the Studebaker Corporation before starting his own commercial art and advertising business. As a painter he concentrated on portraits. Guy later moved to California where he designed movie sets and illustrated books. Guy died in 1983. Gertrude died in 1997 in Mishawaka.

Bednar, born in 1908, was a graduate of Notre Dame where he was an instructor in art from 1940 to 1945. Ordained a priest, he left the priesthood to marry Hermina, a student he met at Notre Dame. They established a commercial art studio in South Bend. John later taught at Indiana University South Bend and the South Bend Art Center. His artistic work included oil paintings, murals and sculpture. Hermina worked in watercolor. The Bednars moved to Madison, Wisconsin, in 1961, where Hermina died in 1984. John died in 1999 in Lansing, Michigan.

Emile Jacques, a native of Belgium born in 1874, arrived at Notre Dame in 1929 to chair the art department. An established painter and art professor, Jacques lost his wife, home and many oil paintings when Germany invaded Belgium in 1914. He immigrated to America in 1923. Besides teaching at Notre Dame, Jacques gave private lessons in a South Bend studio. He drowned in 1937 while swimming near Petoskey, Michigan.

Stanley Sessler succeeded Jacques as chair of Notre Dame's art department, which he joined in 1928. He was born in St. Petersburg, Russia in 1905 and studied at the Massachusetts School of Art and the Courtauld Institute of the University of London. He was a realistic painter of landscapes, still lifes and portraits who exhibited widely and won many awards. He retired from Notre Dame in 1970 and died in 1986.

Eugene and Elizabeth Kormendi were natives of Budapest, Hungary, who immigrated to the United States in 1939 as World War I engulfed Europe. Eugene, born in 1889, studied and executed sculpture in Budapest, Vienna, Rome and Paris, where Elizabeth studied painting under Matisse. Eugene and Elizabeth were married in 1922. Arriving in the United States, Eugene became sculptor-in-residence and professor of art at Notre Dame, and Elizabeth professor of art at Saint Mary's College. Many of Eugene's sculptures are on the Notre Dame campus. Others are at South Bend's Our Lady of Hungary Church and in Fort Wayne. Elizabeth concentrated on religious subjects for her paintings. Her murals can be seen in the Our Lady of the Lake Seminary and Church near Syracuse, Indiana. The Kormendis moved to Washington, D.C. in 1957, where Eugene died two years later.

Arthur Hartig, born in 1879 in Hamilton, Ohio, for many years gave private lessons in South Bend while painting landscapes in oil and watercolor locally and in Brown County. He studied at the Chicago Art Institute and with Jacques and Sessler. Hartig, who died in 1959, was the father of Beatrice Zimmerman and Geni Toth. Beatrice taught art at Penn High School and painted realistic landscapes, still lifes and portraits. She died in 1988. Geni taught at Penn High and in the Mishawaka public schools and was more impressionistic in her paintings. Another daughter, Kathryn Proudfit, a beauty shop operator for many years, began painting later in life. A son, Donald, was a photoengraver.

Harriet Monteith, born in 1903 in Wakarusa, Indiana, gave private lessons in a barn-like building in her back yard. She had studied at the Chicago Art Institute and the Fort Wayne Art School and painted realistic landscapes, still lifes and portraits in oil and pastels. She died in 1975. Grace Crumpacker, born in 1881 in Troy, New York, who also studied at the Chicago Art Institute, painted rural Indiana landscapes in oil and watercolor. She died in 1951.

Vernon Scott, born in 1912 in Portland, Indiana, was a commercial artist and partner in Advertising Artists. He painted realistic urban scenes of South Bend between 1930 and his death in 1980. Edward Reasor was a film director and painter. Lester Swartz was an advertising manager at the Bendix Corporation who took up painting on his retirement.

Northern Indiana Artists held its first exhibition in May, 1942, at the Progress Club, with 35 members entering paintings. While early records indicate a bachelor of arts degree was a membership requirement, NIA quickly adopted an independent jury process as the criterion for membership. NIA became an Indiana not-for-profit corporation in 1946. Its goals were to raise the quality of local artwork and art standards and to give local artists opportunities to display their work in the Michiana community. Meetings were to be held monthly with paint-in sessions, talks and/or demonstrations, and members were to participate in three exhibitions a year.

Over the years, NIA sponsored at least two public exhibits of member works annually, many of them judged by independent jurors. Four cash awards were established for outstanding works. These exhibits had many venues, including the galleries of the South Bend Art Association when it was established in 1947. Some exhibits were jointly sponsored with the Saint Joseph Valley Watercolor Society when that organization was founded in 1958.

The South Bend Art Center

Incorporation of the South Bend Art Association on March 16, 1947, fulfilled a dream of Carlotta Murray Banta, a kindergarten teacher for thirty-five years at Perley Elementary School who dreamed of a community art museum "where beautiful pictures would hang and where little children would come to look and to adorn the galleries with their own precious living images." Mrs. Banta, who had lost a husband, two children, and a sister to early deaths, had a particular love of the engravings of Arthur Rackham, and she collected many of the books the artist illustrated. When she died October 10, 1945, she left her entire estate, valued at about $20,000, to support an art museum, provided that it be initiated within two years of her death. As it turned out, her dream became a reality only through the generosity of Mr. and Mrs. E. M. Morris and the practical support of other community leaders. In the end, surviving relatives successfully contested the Banta estate provision for funding the art museum.

The new museum was connected to another Morris family community benefaction, the E. M. Morris School for Crippled Children. These benefactions began in 1941 when Morris purchased the Clement Studebaker Mansion at 620 West Washington Street for $20,000. The mansion, built in 1889 by the president of the Studebaker Company, then a manufacturer of wagons, housed the American Red Cross chapter during World War II. It was given to the South Bend public school system at the end of the war to be used for special education classes for children with cerebral palsy, polio, muscular dystrophy and other physical disabilities. The school opened in February 1947, with twenty-nine students enrolled in grades one through eight. (The school later was closed and the mansion subsequently became the Tippecanoe Restaurant.)

The Morris gift also provided for the establishment of an exhibition gallery under the auspices of the new South Bend Art Association. The gallery, in two rooms on the second floor of the mansion, opened in May 1947, with an exhibit of sixty paintings from the annual Hoosier Art Salon. The mansion's carriage house was renovated to house an extensive program of classes in various art media for adults and children. The Morris family also donated its own collection of works by Indiana artists, which became the basis of the association's permanent collection. The association also benefited from a new state law allowing the school system to impose a half-cent-annual property tax levy that raised an initial $17,600 to support the association's art programs.

Mrs. Morris was a member of the association's charter board of directors. Dr. F. R. Nicholas Carter, a prominent physician and arts patron, was elected board president. Other charter members included Mayor F. Kenneth Dempsey, School Board President Arthur M. Russell, School Superintendent Frank E. Allen, American Bank President Leon L. Mathews, National Bank Chairman

C. Frederick Cunningham, Studebaker President Paul G. Hoffman, and South Bend Tribune Secretary-Treasurer Franklin D. Schurz. The board hired James Murray Haddow, a native of Scotland who was an instructor in painting and drawing at the National Academy of Art In Chicago, as the association's first director.

Two charter board members were local artists. Basil Greenblatt, born in South Bend in 1904, won numerous awards in commercial graphic design for local business firms. Educated at the University of Michigan, University of Chicago and Chicago Art Institute, Greenblatt used watercolor, pen and charcoal media. He died in 1962. James W. Taylor, born in South Bend in 1902, was a partner in the Carter, Jones and Taylor advertising agency. A graduate of Dartmouth College, he painted landscapes in oil, turning later in life to photography. He died in 1989. Some of his paintings are in the South Bend Museum of Art permanent collection.

James Murray Haddow, a native of Scotland who was an instructor in painting and drawing at the National Academy of Art in Chicago, was hired in September 1948, as the association's first director. He left the following March and returned to Chicago. Greenblatt served as interim director until June, when Reginald H. Neal became the director. Neal was a native of England with a background of teaching and administration in art programs at several American universities. He was a painter in oils and watercolors and a lithographic printmaker. He resigned in 1951 to join the art faculty at Rutgers University.

His successor was Thomas R. Lias, who came from the art faculty at Florida State University. A graduate of Carnegie Institute of Technology in Pittsburgh with a master of fine arts degree from the University of Iowa, Lias served as director until 1957. He died in 1960 in his native Dayton, Pennsylvania. James W. Wicks, born in 1923, served as assistant director during Lias' tenure. A painter who taught drawing, painting and art appreciation at the center, he earned a master of fine arts degree at Indiana University and later worked for many years as an engineer at the Bendix Corporation.

The South Bend Art Association began a decade of growth in 1957 with the hiring of Harold Zisla as its fourth director. Zisla brought a dynamic professional leadership to the association as administrator, fund raiser, teacher and painter. He was born in 1925 in Cleveland, and following service in the Navy during World War II he earned a bachelor of arts degree at the Cleveland Institute of Art and a master of fine arts degree from Case Western Reserve University. He moved to South Bend in the 1950s to take a job as a designer of footwear at Uniroyal, Inc., in Mishawaka.

Under his direction, the association renamed itself the South Bend Art Center and emphasized education as its primary mission. Art classes for children, youth, and adults attracted enrollments that reached around 1,300 annually. The new director established a close collaborative relationship with Martha Carter, the South Bend school system's arts coordinator. Several public school art teachers were engaged as Art Center instructors. Public financial support through paid memberships in the center grew to more than 500, and a foundation was established to accept larger endowed gifts. The center sponsored a popular art film series and lectures by art historian Catherine Evans and other museum directors and artists. Looking back years later, Zisla said he strove to develop the Art Center as an "important community center" rather than an art institution. He wanted it to be "a place where people were comfortable using the facilities because it was that kind of institution rather than a lofty elitist kind of place."

Zisla inherited an annual spring juried exhibition of works by Indiana and Michigan artists, including purchase prizes chosen by outside art professionals. In 1959 the exhibition was renamed the Michiana Local Biennial to distinguish it from the Michiana Regional Biennial, launched in 1960. The Local exhibition, for artists living within a 150-mile radius of South Bend, offered more opportunity for inclusion of these artists. The Regional exhibition, for Indiana and Michigan artists, was later expanded to cover a nine-state area. The Regional biennial continues; the Local biennial was discontinued in the mid-1980s.

A 1962 fire, probably started from a ceramic kiln, destroyed the renovated carriage house with its classrooms, studios and offices. Most of the permanent collection survived, but several of the paintings required restoration at the Radecki Galleries, which were opened in 1957 by Roman J. Radecki, a South Bend native born in 1914. Radecki was a sculptor who died in 1988. His daughter Monica and two sons, Martin and Ron, became art conservators. With the loss of the Carriage House, the Art Center trustees approved rental of an empty YWCA building at 121 N. Lafayette Blvd. as the Art Center's new, if temporary, home. The building's small gymnasium served as the exhibit gallery.

Under Zisla's leadership the Art Center attracted a strong instructional faculty. One of these teachers, Zygmund S. Jankowski, had been a founder of the Barn School of Art in 1952. This school conducted classes and held exhibits in an old barn behind the residence of Doctors Gordon and Gladys Frith on West Washington Ave. The school closed with the migration of some of its teachers to the South Bend Art Center's carriage house facility a block away. Besides Jankowski, other Art Center teachers of that period included Joseph Wrobel, Gertrude Harbart, Edward E. Harding, Edward Herrmann, Robert Kuntz, H. James Paradis, Marion R. Pilarski, Alonzo H. Stivers, Robert W. Thomas, David Sanders, and Kay West.

Jankowski, a South Bend native born in 1925, served in the Navy during World War II after graduating from Washington High School. He studied at the California College of Arts and Crafts in Oakland after his discharge from the Navy, then returned to South Bend and supported himself through commercial art for the next few years. A prolific expressionistic painter in both oils and watercolors with a preference for landscapes, Jankowski exhibited widely and influenced many artists as both teacher and painter. Sales of his serious paintings enabled him to abandon commercial work. He was apt to attach humorous titles to many of his paintings. He maintained a summer home in Gloucester, Massachusetts, and moved there permanently in the 1970s. He died in 2010. His son Coy Jankowski is a painter in South Bend.

Herrmann, born in 1914 in Fort Wayne, came to South Bend in 1943 with Raymond Loewy Associates to work on designs for postwar Studebaker cars. He opened his own design consulting business in 1958. Largely self-taught, Herrmann the painter worked extensively in both oils and watercolors. His work became more expressionistic and abstract over the years. He opened a studio/gallery in South Bend in 1969, but moved to Estes Park, Colorado in 1975 where he opened a studio/gallery that featured Rocky Mountain National Park landscapes. After a few years in Arizona, he moved back to Estes Park.

Harding worked in the Studebaker design department and later moved on to open his own commercial art business. Born in 1929 in Leiters Ford, Indiana, he earned bachelor's and master's of fine art degrees at the University of Michigan. A printmaker as well as a painter, Harding using the tusche method of painting grease on stones to produce lithographs. In 1975 he accepted directorship of a new commercial art program at the South Bend Campus of Indiana Vocational Technical College (Ivy Tech) while maintaining his own studio at his rural home near North Liberty. Harding died in 1993 shortly after retiring from Ivy Tech.

Kuntz was a sculptor who also worked in the Studebaker design department. He owned a local woodworking shop. The native of South Bend, born in 1929, graduated from Riley High School and studied at the School of the Chicago Art Institute and Indiana University South Bend. He often used discarded auto parts in his metal sculptures. Kuntz taught at Saint Mary's College and Goshen College, and received commissions for public sculptures in the South Bend area. His large steel *Trilithon* stands in front of the Morris Performing Arts Center.

Harbart was a lifelong resident of Michigan City, where she was born in 1908. She studied at the School of the Chicago Art Institute and in New York and Provincetown, Massachusetts. One of her teachers was Charles Burchfield. Harbart produced mixed media abstract paintings and taught during the winters in Tucson, Arizona, as well as at the Art Center and the Dunes Art Foundation near Michigan City. She died in 1999.

Paradis, born in 1924 in Rice Lake, Wisconsin, graduated from John Adams High School, earned bachelor's and master's degrees in education from Indiana University, and taught art at Washington High School for a number of years. He was a ceramicist whose works won widespread recognition. He became a professor of art at Saint Mary's College in 1966 and later was chair of its fine art department. Upon retirement he moved to California.

Pilarski, born in 1928 in South Bend, also taught at Washington High. He earned a bachelor's degree at Indiana University and a master of fine arts degree at Notre Dame. He died in 2002. Stivers and Thomas, both born in 1931, were other art teachers in the South Bend public schools who earned master's degrees at Notre Dame.

The ceramics program begun by Paradis at Washington High School continued under Tom Meuninck. Born in 1943, Meuninck also taught at the Art Center. His *Patchwork Pond*, an abstract mural of ceramic panels, is in the main lobby of Teachers Credit Union's downtown South Bend building. His ceramics are in the collections of the Art Center and the Midwest Museum of American Art in Elkhart.

James C. Borden, born in 1928 in Indianapolis, became a popular local portrait painter and influential Art Center instructor. He studied at the American Academy of Art in Chicago as well as with Zisla and

Jankowski. Borden for many years worked in his family-owned South Bend restaurant. He moved to Vermont where he recently died.

An older influential artist and instructor was Edward Basker, a co-founder of the Barn School. Born in 1908 in Hammond, Indiana, he was a graduate of Central High School who was largely self-taught. As a youth he worked as a window designer at Robertson's department store. He later started a commercial advertising display business. He was primarily a watercolorist who painted many scenes of the Notre Dame campus. He died in 1972.

Colleges Nourish the Arts

While South Bend's Art Center flourished as a public, community-based institution, expanding programs at Notre Dame, Saint Mary's College and Indiana University South Bend gave an important added dimension to local visual arts during the second half of the 20th century.

Rev. Theodore M. Hesburgh, president of Notre Dame from 1952 to 1987, supported the strengthening the university's visual arts programs. Expansion began in 1952 with the opening of O'Shaughnessy Hall, a gift of Ignatius A. O'Shaughnessy of Minneapolis. The building housed the college of arts and letters, new arts classrooms and studios, and 16,000 square feet of exhibit space in five galleries. The galleries provided greater accessibility to the school's growing permanent art collection, which had been displayed previously on the top floor of the library (now the school of architecture building).

The next important Notre Dame art commitment was the appointment in 1955 of the internationally renowned sculptor Ivan Meštrović as professor of art. The appointment was recommended by Art Department Chair Rev. Anthony J. Lauck, himself a sculptor. Notre Dame constructed a new sculpture studio adjacent to O'Shaughnessy Hall for Meštrović. He was born in 1883 in Croatia, where native villagers financed his apprenticeship to a stonecutter in Split; the quarry owner recognized the youth's talent and sent him to Vienna for further study. Meštrović later moved to Paris, where he was a protégé of Auguste Rodin. He visited the United States in 1920, and the trip resulted in a commission for the equestrian Native American sculptures that stand in Chicago's Grant Park. Following World War II, Meštrović immigrated to the United States and joined the art faculty at Syracuse University. He worked at Notre Dame until his death in 1962. Several of his large-scale sculptures are on the Notre Dame campus.

Meštrović attracted a number of other sculptors to Notre Dame. Joseph Turkalj (1924-2007), also a native of Croatia, worked under Meštrović and remained at Notre Dame until 1965, when he left to join the Gilmour Academy of Art faculty in Cleveland. Turkalj's bronze *Moses* sits near Notre Dame's Hesburgh Library. Theodore Golubic (1928-1998), a student at Syracuse, also worked under Meštrović at Notre Dame and later taught in Missouri and New Mexico. His *Crucifixion* is at Little Flower Catholic Church in South Bend. Waldemar Otto (1929-) succeeded Meštrović as head of sculpture at Notre Dame, returning to Germany after two years. His *Jeremiah* sits between Grace and Flanner resident halls on the campus.

Konstantin Milonadis, born in 1926 in the Ukraine, came to Notre Dame in 1959 after studying at the School of the Chicago Art Institute and earning a master of fine arts degree at Tulane University. He used small wire to create moving constructivist kinetic sculptures, one of which is in the Snite Museum's permanent collection.

Rev. Austin Collins, a Notre Dame graduate with a master's degree in fine arts from Claremont University in California who has served as art department chair, created large outdoor sculptures, installations, and liturgical pieces. His *Steelworkers Hill* can be seen on Holy Cross Hill at the Notre Dame campus.

Moira M. Geoffrion became the first full-time woman faculty member of Notre Dame's art department in 1977. She combined tree limbs, other wood, handcrafted paper and white space to create her mixed-media installations. She left Notre Dame in 1986 to head the University of Arizona art department in Tucson.

David Hayes, a Notre Dame graduate with a master of fine arts degree from Indiana University, created *The Descent of the Holy Spirit* sculpture on the outside sacristy walls of the university's Moreau Seminary. His large abstract steel *Griffon* perches outside the Snite Museum. Hayes studied under sculptor David Smith and maintains studios in Connecticut and Paris, France.

Thomas Fern, born in Minneapolis in 1921, joined the Notre Dame art faculty in 1967 and later chaired the department. With art degrees from the University of Minnesota and a doctorate from New York University, he is known for his large-scale portraits in oil.

Robert Leader was born in 1924 in Cambridge, Massachusetts, and was wounded as a Marine fighting on Iwo Jima during World War II. He studied art at the Boston Museum of Fine Arts, Yale University, and the University of Illinois, and joined the Notre Dame faculty in 1953. A painter in oils, Leader is known for his liturgical works and stained-glass designs. His windows can be seen in South Bend's St. Matthews Cathedral and Notre Dame's Sorin Hall Chapel. Leader died in 2006.

Don Vogl, born in 1929 in Milwaukee, taught at Notre Dame from 1963 to 1994. He studied at the University of Wisconsin, the School of the Chicago Art Institute, and Cleveland Art Institute. He is a painter in oils and mixed media whose commissions have included paintings at Purdue University, Saint Mark's Church in Niles, the Immaculate Conception Church in Hartford, Michigan, and the Stevensville, Michigan, Methodist Church.

Two more recent Notre Dame art faculty members are Douglas Kinsey and Rev. James Flanigan. Kinsey, a graduate of Oberlin College, where he also taught, has a master of fine arts degree from the University of Minnesota. Father Flanigan is known for large-scale drawings depicting human sufferings, particularly of AIDS sufferers and victims of wars and massacres.

By the end of the 1970s, Notre Dame's permanent art collection had grown to more than about 4,000 objects, many of them donations from private collectors. The collection moved into a new home in 1980 with completion of the $2 million Snite Museum of Art, a gift of Fred B. Snite of Chicago and his family. Under the direction of Father Lauck and then Dean Porter, the Snite acquired a significant collection ranging through Old Master drawings, paintings illustrating the history of Western Art, pre-Columbian native American art, an important collection of Western American Art, and selected works of twentieth-century American artists. The Snite, with a collection of about 26,000 objects, has benefited from an advisory council of private collectors and a growing endowment.

Father Tony Lauck was born in Indianapolis in 1925. His sculpture of *Our Lady of the University* is on the mall leading from the end of Notre Dame Avenue north to the Administration Building. He died in 2001.

Dean Porter, born in 1939 in Gouverneur, New York, has undergraduate, master's and doctoral degrees from the State University of New York at Binghamton. He came to Notre Dame in 1966 as curator of the permanent collection and served as director of the Snite from 1974 until his retirement in 1999. He pursues an artistic career in oil and acrylic paintings and woodcut prints.

Saint Mary's College began a new era in the fine arts with the 1957 opening of the $2 million-plus Moreau Hall and O'Laughlin Auditorium, fulfilling a vision of Sister Madeleva Wolff, the president of the Catholic women's college from 1934 to 1961. Moreau Hall provided classrooms and studios for expanding art, music and theater programs. Art exhibits were accommodated in a small gallery and adjoining theater-foyer.

Sister Rose Ellen Morrissey, born in 1921 and a graduate of the college, was chair of the art department and director of the gallery at Saint Mary's for many years. She studied art in Chicago and at Harvard University, and produced her own art in many media. Sister Rose Ellen died in 1995. Two other Holy Cross nuns taught art at Saint Mary's for many years. Sister Mary Edna Orzechowska (1892-1973), a native of South Bend, painted in oils, watercolors and frescos. Sister Marie Rosaire Blatterman (1905-1967) was a printmaker for whom the Moreau Hall gallery was named.

Norman Laliberté, who was to become an internationally recognized painter, printmaker and sculptor, joined the Saint Mary's art faculty with the opening of Moreau Hall and departed in 1962. A French-Canadian born in 1925 in Worcester, Massachusetts, Laliberté grew up in Montreal where he studied for a year at the Academy of Fine Arts. Moving to Chicago, he earned degrees in visual design and art education before coming to Saint Mary's. He left the college to teach at the Rhode Island School of Design. His designs of colorful banners later helped cement his artistic reputation. A major gallery owner described his work as "utterly childlike, yet thoroughly sophisticated."

Two more recent art teachers at Saint Mary's are Julie Tourtillotte, associate professor, and her husband William. Both are graduates of the Cranbrook School of Art near Detroit. Bill, a printmaker and illustrator, also taught at Notre Dame and Indiana University South Bend. He was curator at the South Bend Museum of Art for ten years. Julie uses stitching, embroidery, dyed fabric, and photos to create mixed-media pieces.

Indiana University conducted a few university-credit evening classes in South Bend's Central High School as early as 1933. By the mid-1950s the presidents of Indiana and Purdue Universities decided to develop a network of two-year colleges across the state. (They soon became four-year, degree-granting institutions.) As a result, Indiana University's new Indiana University South Bend campus opened in 1961 with completion of Northside Hall on the north bank of the St. Joseph River east of the city center. Lester M. Wolfson arrived on the campus in 1964 as its director. (The title was later changed to chancellor.)

Wolfson, who retired in 1987, gave high priority to fine arts programs, and in 1966 he hired Harold Zisla as department chair to develop an expanded visual arts curriculum. The university acquired and renovated a former tool-and-die company building next to Northside Hall, and within it established art classrooms, The faculty was expanded. Zisla taught painting, drawing, and art appreciation. William Fabrycki was hired to teach design, and Zygmund Jankowski was added as a part-time adjunct painting instructor. Joining the full-time faculty in 1971 were Harold (Tuck) Langland and Anthony (Tony) Droege, who were to stay on until retirement in 2003 and 2008 respectively.

Langland, born in 1939 in St. Paul, Minnesota, received his bachelor and master's degrees from the University of Minnesota. He is a prolific sculptor who receives many commissions for works in bronze. His *Violin Woman* stands outside South Bend's Morris Civic Auditorium. *Educators* sits in Mishawaka's Kate's Garden. *Crossroads*, by the campus fountain, is one of six of his works at IU South Bend.

Droege, born in 1943, received his degrees from Pennsylvania State University and the University of Iowa. His oil paintings include portraits and still lifes and are noted for their exuberant use of color.

Alan Larkin, a native of Minnesota born in 1953, joined the IU South Bend art faculty in 1977 as an instructor in drawing and printmaking. He also paints in oils. Ron Monsma, a native of Columbus, Ohio, and Riley High School graduate, studied at IU South Bend and then joined the faculty. He paints primarily in pastels, producing still lifes and landscapes that have been described as ambiguous, moody and dramatic.

Zisla later described the IU South Bend studio program as "largely oriented to representational art, emphasizing craft and technique, especially in sculpture and printmaking, rather than experimentation." Zisla retired from IU South Bend in 1989. His own paintings, primarily in oils, have moved over time from the impressionistic and figurative to the abstract. Many of Zisla's earlier paintings are concerned with imaginative literary and philosophical portraits. His paintings are in many local private collections.

While institutional art programs were expanding, local artists continued to band together informally for inspiration and support. Kathy Reddy White, a South Bend native with a master of fine arts degree from Notre Dame, was a catalyst for the organization, in 1984, of the Aquinas Studios and Art Gallery. Located above the Aquinas Bookstore at Michigan and Monroe Streets, the studios provided space for some twenty local artists. Reddy White said participating artists welcomed the opportunity to explore visual images beyond traditional genres in their paintings, and to be part of group exhibitions. Aquinas flourished for five years. Reddy White and her sister Patty Reddy later opened the Circle Arts Galley on East Colfax Avenue.

Another venue for the visual arts was the former Colfax Elementary School building on Lincoln Way West, acquired by the South Bend Heritage Foundation in the 1980s. A National Endowment for the Arts grant funded studios for artists working in the building for a few years. The center continues to provide space for local artist exhibits. 1979 saw the establishment in Elkhart of the Midwest Museum of American Art by Dr. Richard and Jane Burns for the acquisition and exhibit of American art beginning with their collection of nineteenth- and twentieth-century paintings.

Photography as an art form beyond its commercial application attracted many practitioners over the years. Camera clubs were organized, and photography classes offered. Three influential photographers and teachers in the 1980s and '90s were Todd Hoover, an art teacher at Riley High School; James (Jack) Kapsa, an art teacher at St. Joseph's High School; and Steve Moriarty, Notre Dame assistant professor and photography curator at the Snite Museum.

South Bend Museum of Art

With the departure of Zisla in 1966, the Art Center went through a number of directors. Whitney Sevin was there for a year, followed by Jesse (Jay) Wright. During Wright's tenure, the Women's Art League was founded in 1969 "to increase the effectiveness of the Art Center in its endeavor to further the appreciation of the visual art in the community." The League (renamed the Art League in 1995) sponsors lectures, exhibits, and volunteer services, and raises money for the museum, principally through the annual Garden Walk started in 1989.

Vincenzo Mangione became the center director in 1970 and served until 1976. He was a native of Italy who studied in Europe before moving to South Bend in 1968. When Mangione left for the Michigan City Art Center in 1976, John Surovek became director for two years. During these years, the directors debated, sometimes heatedly, proposals to identify and finance a larger, more permanent home.

The actual vehicle for a new Art Center building evolved through the City of South Bend's ambitious "cultural center" downtown redevelopment project. Under the leadership of Mayor Jerry J. Miller and Common Council President Peter J. Nemeth, who succeeded Miller as mayor, the city proposed in 1972 to clear a wide swath of older buildings along the St. Joseph River for a cultural center campus. The project would cost $5 million, including $1.25 million in federal funds. Art Center participation became possible in 1974 when the local Clark and Muessel-Ellison Foundations committed $1 million for construction of a new Art Center building.

Center Board President Andrew W. Nickle, an attorney, negotiated the 1976 Occupancy Agreement with the city, by which the Clark and Muessel-Ellison grant helped finance the construction of what was to be named the Century Center. Designed by the New York architectural firm of Philip Johnson and John Burgee, Century Center contained 32,000 square feet of space for Art Center classrooms, studios, offices and galleries. The multi-purpose building also included a large convention center, a performing arts theater and exhibit space for the city-owned Studebaker National Museum vehicle collection.

Under the occupancy agreement, the Art Center became an autonomous lessor of Century Center with full control of its own programs and activities. The Art Center paid its share of Century Center utility and security costs, and provision was made for continued civil city financial support of the Art Center budget. The Art Center board under the leadership of Nickle and Ray Larson, with a major lead gift from Barbara K. Warner, raised more than $350,000 in additional funds to equip its new space. The Art Center celebrated the move to its new home in 1978 with a major loan exhibition of twentieth-century American Masters, and an inaugural poster designed by the artist Robert Indiana.

With the move, the Center's curator, Thomas Schorgl, became its new director. Schorgl was a graduate of the University of Iowa with a master of fine arts degree from Miami University of Ohio. He resigned in 1981 to start an art gallery in Mason City, Iowa, and he subsequently served as executive director of the Indiana Arts Commission (1983-93) and director of the Cuyahoga Falls, Ohio, arts and culture program. Judy Oberhausen succeeded Schorgl as curator and remained in the position under directors John Brice and Brooks Joyner. She became acting director when Joyner resigned in 1986.

The Century Center board of managers and the Art Center board appointed a Committee for Art in Public Places, which commissioned a sculpture from the internationally known Mark di Suvero. With financing through a grant from the National Endowment for the Arts and local contributions, *Keepers of the Fire* was placed in 1980 on a plinth where the dam on the St. Joseph River makes a right angle to create the East Race that once powered the machinery of factories. The large bright-orange steel sculpture centers on a girder shaped like a bow. The sculpture commemorates the Potawatomi Indian Nation people who were on the land before the arrival of European settlers.

The Art Center joined the art departments of IU South Bend and Saint Mary's College and Notre Dame's Snite Museum in 1984 as sponsors of a major retrospective exhibit of George Rickey entitled *The Return of the Native*. Rickey was born in 1907 in South Bend and moved to Glasgow, Scotland, when his father, manager of the Singer Sewing Machine Cabinet Plant in South Bend, was appointed manager of the Singer factory in Glasgow. Educated at Balliol College and the Ruskin School of Drawing at Oxford University, Rickey returned to the United States in 1930. He taught at Indiana University in Bloomington and other schools and turned from painting to sculpture, the medium in which he made an international reputation. His outdoor abstract metal constructions allow movement by passing air currents. Rickey died in 2002.

With the move to the Century Center, the Art Center trustees redefined its mission. It now included "development of an awareness of the visual arts through a focus on American art, especially regional contemporary art and historical Indiana art." The mission statement also acknowledged the importance of education through "studio art classes, school and community outreach and museum tours." In 1987 the center received accreditation from the American Association of Museums and hired a new director, Susan R. Visser. Visser received her undergraduate degree in art and education from Marietta, Ohio, College and a master's degree in art history from the Ohio State University. She worked as a registrar at the Columbus, Ohio, Museum of Art from 1976 until 1985, when she became coordinator of exhibitions and registrar at the Terra Museum of American Art in Chicago. She worked briefly at the

Chicago Historical Society before accepting the Art Center directorship.

The Center trustees in 1992 approved changing the name from South Bend Art Center to South Bend Regional Museum of Art to reflect its recent accreditation. (The name was shortened in 2008 to South Bend Museum of Art.) The mission was refined in 1994 "to better reflect the museum's focus on public participation and inclusion."

The museum's physical space was renovated and enlarged by 6,000 square feet with a 1996 addition to the Century Center. This work was financed with a $600,000 bond issue and an $800,000 capital campaign that included major gifts from June Edwards, for whom the wing is named, Barbara Warner, the Weikamp Family, and the Carmichael/Raclin Family. The addition included the large new Carmichael Gallery for the permanent collection. The Regional Biennial exhibit continued in the Warner Gallery, along with traveling and other special exhibits. Three other galleries became venues for faculty, student and selected local artists' exhibits. The museum mounted twenty-three separate exhibits in 2000.

Under Visser's leadership, the museum continued to expand and strengthen its collaborations and partnerships with other community institutions. The 1990s, for example, saw a Holocaust Exhibit with Temple Beth-El and twenty other community partners, and a Latin American Exhibit in cooperation with the Latino community and Memorial Hospital. Art classes for neighborhood youth were instituted at the Charles Martin Youth Center.

In the year 2000, the South Bend Museum of Art enrolled 1,070 students in art classes taught by a faculty numbering thirty-three. There were 51,402 visitors to the galleries, plus 5,000 students and teachers in tour groups. The staff of seven full-time and thirteen part-time members was assisted by more than 225 volunteer workers and thirty-three docents. Paid museum memberships attracted a record 1,020 individuals. The board of trustees had thirty-three members. Fund raisers included 9,157 people attending the four "Meet Me on the Island" summer events combining the visual and musical arts. The year saw $742,653 in museum operating expenses.

By the beginning of the 21st Century the visual arts in the area had expanded well beyond the Notre Dame campus and the work of early portrait painters. Art was well established in public and private school curricula and in local and regional higher-education institutions. A 2010 survey counted thirty-seven public and private galleries and museums in South Bend and Mishawaka. Nearby communities in Indiana and Michigan supported additional venues. Opportunities abounded for the viewer and patron on the one hand, and the creative painter, photographer, sculptor, and ceramicist—whatever the media—on the other.

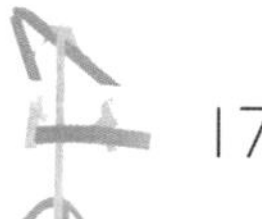

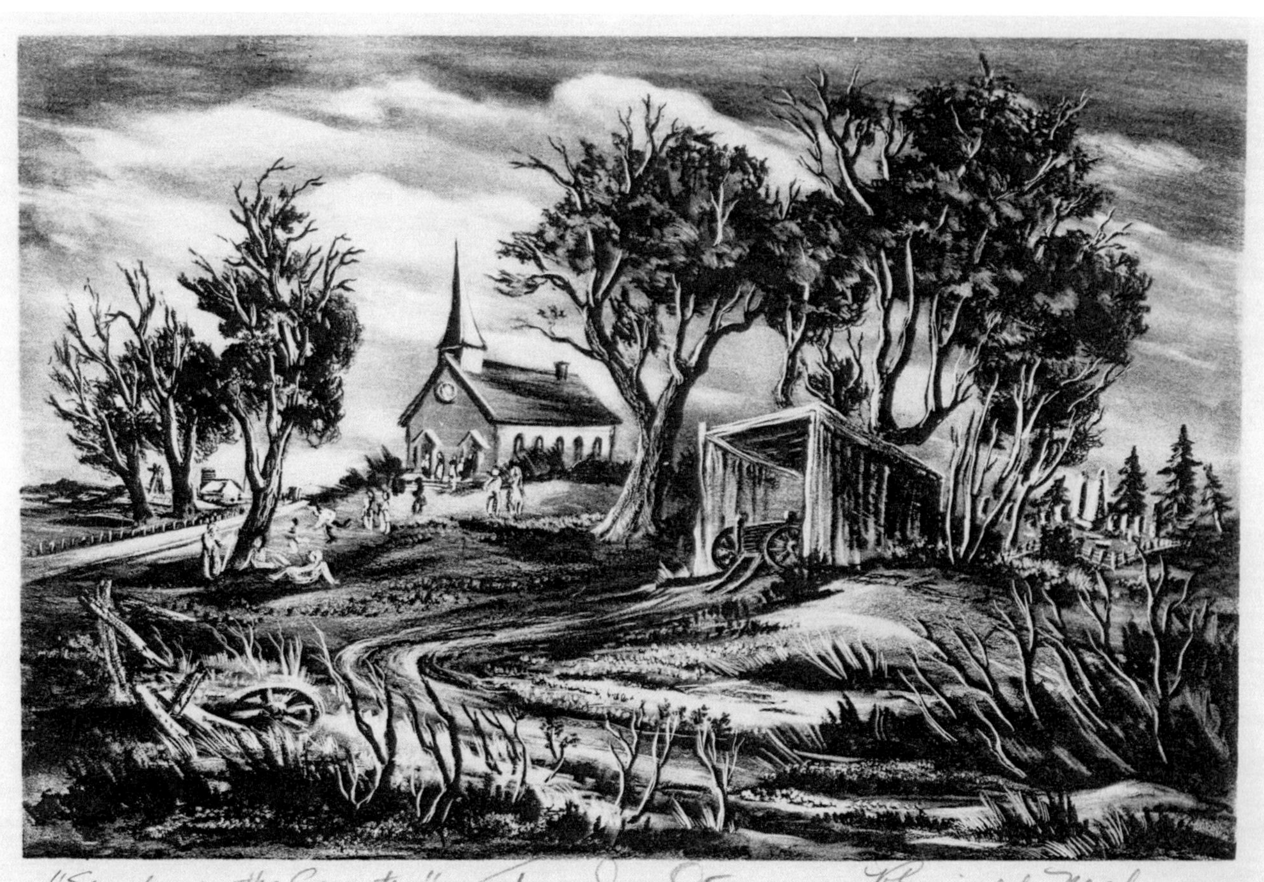

"Sunday in the Country" To Joe Otis Reginald Neal

The Community and the Arts: An Overview

Harold Zisla

During my sixty years in South Bend there has been incremental growth and increasing sophistication about the arts. More people are painting and drawing, and there seems to be more activity in the visual arts. It's not a continuum, but I think that it does have a wholesome aspect.

I rate some art that has been purchased as very substantial. This is not a community with outstanding collectors, but a few collections are noteworthy. South Bend has certain characteristics that are much more based upon its history, economics, ethnicity, and the structure of the community, culturally, than on art itself. South Bend is ultimately reflective of these elements whose priorities deal with more pragmatic realities. Thus, art is not a priority. A cursory glance at the *South Bend Tribune* or watching local television would clearly reflect the character of this community.

The South Bend Museum of Art and the Snite Museum at Notre Dame are the major art organizations in the community. I think IU South Bend has also come along as a force through its fine arts department and its new gallery. In addition, the two big amateur art organizations, Northern Indiana Artists and the Saint Joseph Watercolor Society, have both been healthy over many years, and a lot of the people are involved through both organizations. On the other hand are many people who are not associated with any group.

Doing art is more the dominant art activity locally, while seeing art, or consuming it, is not as important. I am, however, pleased that academic institutions continue to budget for art even though other matters are deemed of higher priority.

Many community members have contributed to the fine arts. June Edwards, who came on the scene within the past 10 or 15 years, has donated a good deal. There have been other figures over the years—Jerry Crowley, the former president of O'Brien Paints, for example; and people like Phil Welber, who was the owner of Robertson's department store, and Jimmy Peacock, a realtor in town. Bob Fischgrund and George Coquillard and many others have participated as board members and were really interested in doing a good job. Generally speaking, my evaluation would be that there's a positive attitude toward art but not an overwhelming numerical response. And to say it bluntly, the money was never forthcoming, although I believe it was there, and still is. In every instance of a cultural institution, adequate funds surface as key to real aesthetic growth or progress. Nelson Rockefeller, a board member of the Museum of Modern Art, once said a board member should have three attributes: money, money, money.

There have been a few notable collectors in the area. Fred Baer, a local attorney, collected known artists and had a small collection that was very good. He got a lot of stuff from going to New York and from auctions. He had superb taste and knew what was going on, in a sense, beyond what South Bend normally considered art. I think he gave some pieces to the Snite and some to the community.

Reginald Neal, *Sunday in the Country.* In the collection of the Art Center, 1955.

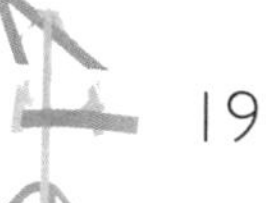

Currently Charlie Hayes collects local and midwestern art, a great deal of it "Brown County art." Personal taste and sophistication looms large in collecting art or anything else. The key to influencing taste is the director or curator or acquisition committee of an institution, and this should be a guiding principle if the institution defines itself as a "museum." As a community, I don't think ours is one that is really phenomenal artistically, but it's good, it's solid and it's growing. The balance of what people need and what they want is tricky. The director of any art institution needs to be more of a sociologist or psychiatrist or historian than an art specialist.

The proximity of Chicago and its Art Institute absolutely has an effect on the community. That's where people go to see not just contemporary art but a good deal of art history. Even so, I don't think it changes art tastes locally. People just go up there and 'oooh' and 'aaah' at being in a major museum, but they don't change their opinion about owning art or about the artists who do art. You have to be a serious student of art history to feel this thing that's called "art," and still it is not possible to define it. Our proximity to Chicago means that people tend to go there or to New York galleries when they want to purchase art. That makes it difficult to have a homegrown art industry here. I would say on a scale of one to ten, we're probably a five or six. The "solution" lies, I truly believe, in education about art and in emphasis on art history, not studio or the manipulation of art materials. Obviously this is very controversial and I doubt if it will ever happen.

My impression is that buying art is not something that's done here in South Bend, although that would probably be true in any community. Other things are consumed: TV sets and cars, for example. Even within the larger arts community, I think other arts are consumed much more than the traditional arts. I mean music and theater. Theater has had one person propel its success, and the same was true for music. The South Bend Symphony has had unusual support over many years and the *South Bend Tribune*, an important supporter, has helped the symphony's success. Art has not had that kind of dynamic.

When you talk about the art world out there in the big cities, you're talking about something that is totally different than what exists in South Bend. I'm not saying that South Bend is primitive or unsophisticated, but it is at a level far below what exists in New York or Rome or Chicago or elsewhere. Art here has not advanced aesthetically in tandem with art in the national or international movements. It hasn't gotten into really challenging kinds of images that are congruent with what is occurring in the big scenes. Even in the universities, as far as I know, there is not a push into avant garde, experimental art. The art here is good, solid art, and there are some people who paint very, very well and are accomplished but have modest reputations because there's just not the opportunity to move into the bigger scene as there is in larger communities. Do we get what we deserve? What a community emphasizes is what a community projects. To my way of thinking all art is local and in transition, as is every other human agency.

The di Suvero sculpture, *Keepers of the Fire*, is an important part of the art of this community. There was some money available, a grant through the federal government for a community that wanted to put up a sculpture. Tom Schorgl, who became the director of the Art Center during this process, was a supporter. A committee was formed; Fred Baer, Dean Porter, Andy Nickles, and some others—knowledgeable people. They consulted with various people—I was one—and talked about what they might do. There were some goofy ideas proposed: a huge fish with a Studebaker on top of a hat, and all kinds of weird stuff.

Their choice, Mark di Suvero, is one of the important sculptors of the last half of the twentieth century. He's internationally known and historically well represented in books. They talked him into doing *Keepers of the Fire* and he did a superb job. Symbolically it's kind of a herald that relates to the Indian heritage that existed here. It is, arguably, the greatest piece of art in the community, but is not fully appreciated by many people here and has created heat and anger.

So be it. That it was controversial reflects the community. If art is not representational or naturalistic or recognizable, if it does not have a story to it and the content is not easily absorbed, then it's controversial. When I came into the Art Center there was political stuff that existed. Someone who was vociferous in the community thought that modern art was Communist-inspired. That created some problems for me, nothing major, but there were problems. There was an element that felt modern art was not American, that it was foreign and was not patriotic, and all of that is a part of what this community is about.

But now a lot of it is accepted, a lot more than was then, and some experimental art is creeping into the system here. I think the community is growing little by little into something that may, in 30 or 40 years, produce something totally different. For a key difference, compare it to Columbus, Indiana, where one person who was the president of a major company brought in some really outstanding art. They had a very wealthy institution sponsoring all that and someone who really had a vision for the community and the resources to make that happen.

We didn't have that. In our case, nice people, good people, intelligent people, simply stopped at a certain ceiling. They had the wherewithal, but they didn't have the passion, and so we don't have a community that reflects something that's really, really unique.

"Art" can be defined in many ways, and so can its implications. Certainly, enlightenment and pleasure are components, and in our free-market, capitalistic, entrepreneurial society, economics looms large. The cost of art (not necessarily the value) has risen astronomically, and therefore local art institutions simply cannot be "in the market," nor can they encourage potential donors to buy quality work by artists of note.

How is Michiana doing as an art community? I believe there are more people now who are painting and drawing. There seems to be more activity in fine arts, in the visual arts. There are a few galleries in the area. There are a lot of people who seem to be interested in art. It's not a continuum but it is a community, and as a community it has a kind of wholesome aspect relative to visual arts. I think Notre Dame and the Snite museum, Saint Mary's, IU South Bend, Elkhart's Midwest Museum, the South Bend Museum, a couple of the galleries, all show that the community has moved up over the years.

My feeling philosophically is that it's the community that should be reflected in its art, rather than something historical or something international, even though the art might be less important or less significant than the great works of art. The great works are off the market anyway—you can't afford them. Even the Snite, which probably has a fairly good purchasing budget, can't afford to buy major works. Somehow the community is, indeed, reflected in the art, its level, its quality, its volume, and the respect it receives.

The impression I have given in these remarks has the merit of presenting some of the problems, but they are ongoing and many of those involved in academia, in the art institutions, and various others with vested interests, in my opinion, are well satisfied with the state of art in this area. Are there frustrations? Of course, but my guess is that they will always be there. Is art a dynamic force here? I would be hard put to say yes, but that is no doubt true of every community, large or small.

The Art Center—South Bend Museum of Art: the Early Years

Over the years there have been a number of community leaders who were prompted by—or perhaps pushed by—the late Ella Morris. People like Jimmy Taylor, who was a painter and an advertising person. They found out there was a state law that stipulated that communities of over a hundred thousand were allowed a small amount of the tax dollar for the arts. It was just a fraction but it was enough to get started.

Ella Morris owned what is now called Tippecanoe Place, though it was then the Morris School for Crippled Children. The Art Center board worked with her and they bought a collection of ten paintings. Jim Taylor selected them, and he had a very good eye and bought very, very good paintings. They were mostly landscapes by well-known midwestern artists, most from Brown County. Rooms were refurbished in the main building of Tippecanoe Place to display these paintings.

Behind the main building was a carriage house that became the first Art Center. The display walls were taken down and everything was transported there. Classes were begun, and a program evolved. The center added a film series, local exhibitions, and other refinements of the facility.

That started it going and they hired a full time director who was here for a couple of years and then left to go to an academic teaching job. James Haddow was hired, and then Tom Lias, who was my predecessor; I came in 1957. Lias did much to get a program moving and to refine the facilities. I believe that he achieved much toward making the Art Center a really effective working cultural institution.

Art in the South Bend schools was very dynamic in those days. When I was Art Center director, Dr. Martha Carter and her assistant, Ruth Simmons, were in charge, and we had a very close relationship. Initially, the school corporation budget gave us half of the arts funds and the city gave half, so there was that tie-in. I made a point of allowing the art teachers to use our facilities for their meetings. I felt that the major aspect of the institution should be educational, and that exhibiting works of art was only one part of the program. I invited teachers to bring students in on field trips, and part of our legal responsibilities was to have visits by South Bend Community School Corporation students.

So my relationship with the schools was very strong. Then came Ken Geoffrey as director of art for South Bend, and although his field was music, he made sure we always had two South Bend School Corporation members on our board. Alex Jardine, the school superintendent, was one of them and was very effective in helping us. Because our budget was modest, the school corporation was cooperative in things like sending over carpenters and painters and plumbers and electricians as we needed them, and that meant a great deal to us in saving money and establishing a relationship. I still believe that the success or failure of art in any community lies in cultivating responses from the young—that is where real achievement takes place.

We also had relationships with other art teachers in the community, which was very helpful. We brought them to the Art Center and did everything we could to entice various other groups that were participating in some kind of art activity. Notre Dame was always a presence. They had a substantial studio art department, and of course they built the Snite, which played a big role in the art community. Dean Porter, who was the director, was very aggressive in getting community people involved in the Snite. That's unusual for a university art gallery.

Our quarters when we were in the carriage house were modest. Tom Lias had done a good job of rehabilitating part of the building, but it was still a carriage house and not really a museum facility. The fire in 1962 had destroyed virtually everything, but we saved most of the paintings and refurbished and conserved and cleaned them, and that became the foundation of the collection. We received a very substantial insurance settlement that became the Art Endowment Foundation. If there had not been a fire, my guess is that the Art Center would still be in the Carriage House.

But the fire was just an interruption. We moved our quarters to the former YWCA building, and we set up classes and an exhibition schedule. The YWCA wasn't really a heck of a lot better than the carriage house as far as facilities went, however, and we needed new quarters. But we stayed there till facilities opened up at the present Century Center.

When I was at the Art Association, there was nothing competitive among the institutions. We understood each of our uniquenesses, and there wasn't much overlap. We borrowed work from Notre Dame and showed it in our gallery. We had a thing called masterpiece-of-the-month, and Notre Dame was very cooperative in loaning us works. I think our relationship was fine. Later on the Snite museum decided it wanted to pull people from the community and so the relationship with the Art Center changed. Many, many people of South Bend have dual memberships.

The Art Center was comfortable, and I think still is, with its role in the community. It's defined differently with the growth of the institutions like IU South Bend, Saint Mary's, as well as Notre Dame. At one time there was a Michiana Arts & Sciences Council, an overarching entity, but it had very little effect and eventually disappeared. It could have defined and assisted various cultural art situations to achieve a more unified progress and one of increasing audience.

When I was director of the center, several artists taught there who were important in the community. They were part of the reason we had a very successful dynamic teaching situation. There were Zyg Jankowski, Ed Herrmann, and Joe Wroble. There were Dave Sanders, Gertrude Harbart, and Ed Harding. These people among others were effective artists in their own right and they taught classes and had followings. When I left the Art Center there were 1,300 students taking classes, and we had a very robust children's program that I personally emphasized because I thought that they would be the ones who would establish an art environment here.

We also tried to have exhibitions that would entice people to think about owning art themselves, and I think it worked. I would get stuff from galleries in New York and Chicago and from traveling salesmen who would come through, and I'd make sure people were aware of that. It worked fairly well, and things bought then are still in local homes now. I felt, and still feel, that the community, people's homes and everyday lives somehow should be enhanced by bringing art, however defined, into their lives. Today, with technology supreme, much can ensue in spreading culture. But it is local or regional art that creates a wholesome, lasting situation—much else dissipates, and empty boosterism is not real progress.

One of the activities I inherited at the Art Center was an exhibition called the Michiana Regional Show, a two-state, competitive show. We brought in a jury, and artists paid a small fee to submit two works. Some entries were accepted and some were given awards, but many were rejected. The director before me, Tom Lias, had some purchase awards, and that work became part of the Art Association's collection. But that was controversial because the jurors rejected a lot of local people. It created quite a situation, though narrow in its scope.

That was in the mid '50s. We brought in "name" people to jury the exhibitions. I remember I had the temerity to write to Andrew Wyeth and ask him to come, and he wrote back saying he had been having problems with health and so he couldn't make it but he wished us good luck. We had other jurors who were collectors or academics or well-known artists. Jack Tworkoff was teaching down in Bloomington, and he came up and juried a show, as did Joshua Taylor, who was well known, and Henry Koerner, a major twentieth century painter. These were super people, but I felt the show was not working in a public-relations-positive way, so I made it a biennial show and I added a Michiana local show that was open to artists within a hundred miles. It was still juried, but more local people got into it, so it was, I think, more effective as a signal of our desire to service this particular community, which was our defining mission.

At one time these shows created a lot of activity and interest. You could mount a good exhibition in those days, but the character of museums and galleries has changed so much now that I guess the definition of art has become something that should not be competitive. Chicago, for example, used to have a very large show called the *Chicago Vicinity Show*, which included our whole area, but they dropped it. Major museums like the Carnegie Institute don't have competitive shows any more; now the curators go out and select work and award exhibitions or prizes to certain artists, but it is no longer something competitive. The South Bend Museum of Art still has a competitive show, and Elkhart also has one, and they're very happy with that and they define it according to their own purposes.

If I were still involved actively, I doubt very much whether I would have a competitive show. I think I would select artists by traveling to their studios and choosing works for exhibition. The ideal is solo shows, several works by one artist, rather than group shows, but this is a personal prejudice. Art should not be competitive, and by its nature isn't. I cannot justify competitive art exhibitions philosophically. But I feel art institutions should constantly reexamine their programs for refinements that are congruent with changed conditions that make the institution a contributing force along with other cultural forces in the community.

I always felt that if the community didn't have money to build a collection for the museum or the Art Association, why not bring in works that would entice people to buy them and keep them in their homes? Eventually, I hoped, these works would end up in the museum collection. So I would go to New York and visit the galleries and select work that I thought was saleable but also of a high caliber, and we had that kind of show. The other kind of show that I thought was really important was a collectors' show; modest as the available material was, still I think it gave people a sense of pride to know that the local art museum or art center would show whatever they had collected, and that might inspire other people to collect.

I also felt that because the Art Association was a public institution, we should reflect that, and so we always showed Northern Indiana Artists and St Joseph County Watercolor Society art without commenting on any of the quality, but as a public service. I felt also, and still feel, that it's a regional museum and thus should show material that is available locally, notwithstanding the fact that there might be some stuff that is less of the caliber that would be shown at the major museums in Chicago or New York. So we had a series of exhibitions drawn from various institutions and artists locally, going up into Western Michigan, Kalamazoo, Michigan State, and down into Bloomington and the Herron and various institutions that had people who were creative artists.

In all of this I should emphasize that I'm not in any way criticizing what has come after my directorship because there are other definitions that are perfectly valid, and an institution must make judgments relative to every aspect of its operation as the director or the executive committee determines. In a real sense, an art institution is a history museum, and future generations should know the art history of past periods.

As far as the Art Museum is concerned, they still have a dynamic program that has matured over the years and has a very good reputation. They're in the cultural scene and, I think, very effectively. After I left as director, things were unstable for some time—a short period when Tom Schorgle was director and Judy Obenhauser was curator was a high point of that era—and now with Susan Visser's long tenure as director there has been much stability and notable progress.

What I'm trying to say is that there was a community aspect I really attempted to foster. I tried to define the Art Center as an institution in South Bend rather than just an art institution. People were comfortable using the facilities because it was that kind of institution rather than a lofty elitist kind of place. My tenure is dull history and is little remembered, but I know that there are still effects from that tenure today. Modest perhaps, but there.

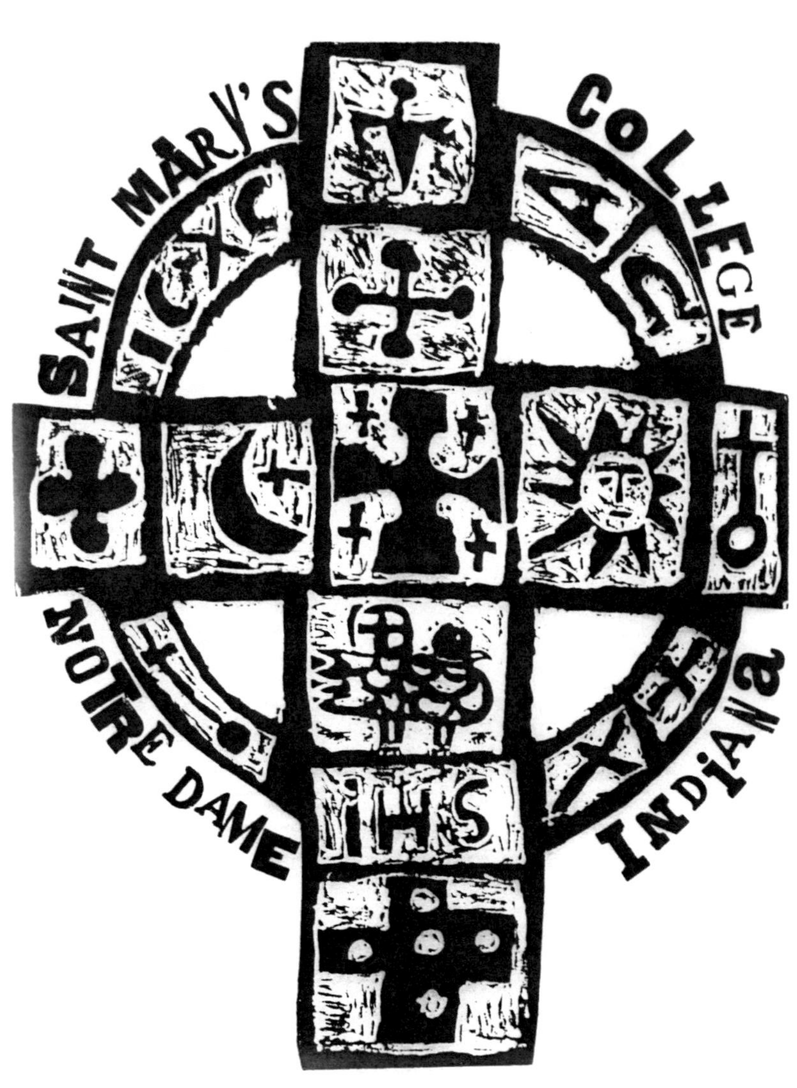
SAINT MARY'S COLLEGE
NOTRE DAME INDIANA
IHS

Art at Saint Mary's College, 1844–Present

Marcia Rickard

Saint Mary's College was founded in 1844 by the Sisters of the Holy Cross who came to northern Indiana from Le Mans, France. These sisters initially cared for the priests at the University of Notre Dame, but soon began teaching children and determined that their true mission was to teach young women. Saint Mary's College was established first in Bertrand, Michigan, and moved to its present location in 1855.

The Nineteenth Century

Art was an important and very early part of the curriculum at Saint Mary's as described in an unpublished paper (1971), "Early History of the Art Department," by Sister M. Anastasia, CSC (Congregation de Sainte-Croix). Tradition has it that two art teachers were brought from Canada. Archival records confirm that Sister Emily Rivard, CSC, who was from Canada, went to Nerinx, Kentucky, to study art with the Sisters of Loretto. Later, in 1853, she accompanied Sister M. Angela Gillespie, CSC, the director of the college in its formative years, to France where she continued her art studies. Mother Angela visited galleries in Europe and became a member of the Arundel Society, which provided yearly copies of prints of world masterpieces to the college. Upon her return in 1854, Sister Emily Rivard became the first head of the art department. Sisters continued to teach art at the college until the end of the twentieth century with Sister Cecilia Ann Kelly's retirement. Great care was taken to ensure that they were professionally trained, with many doing graduate study at premier institutions.

Art was part of the early curriculum and reflected the expectations of the day for a well-educated woman. An 1850 college publication, *Prospectus*, listed the fees for a five-month session as follows:

Drawing and painting–water colors	$6.00
Drawing and painting–oil	10.00
Flowers (artificial flower-making)	3.00
Fruits	3.00

Given that the cost per session for board and tuition was $35.00, these fees seem quite high.

By 1860 the first college *Bulletin* listed the fee for oil painting as $30 per annum, while that for "Board, laundry, and instruction in the usual branches of an English education" was $100. By 1873-4, there was an announcement in the *Bulletin* that fees had been reduced to $20.00 "in order to encourage pupils to get a thorough artistic education." Modern art students can sympathize.

The 1867-68 *Bulletin* announced the opening of the School of Design, with "efficient teachers in all the various departments of Drawing and Painting." Enrollment in art in 1873-74 was 40 students out of the total 149 at the college; by 1899-1900 there were 44 art students among a total enrollment of 153. After moving from Bertrand to the current site of the college in 1855, plans were drawn for a building to house a "School of Design." This only took form, however, a century later when Moreau Center for the Arts was finally realized. In the meantime, art classes were held in Bertrand Hall (now

Norman Laliberté, *Poster.*

a part of the Convent), which also housed a gallery.

One of the more interesting and influential figures to become part of the Saint Mary's College Art Department in its early years was Eliza Allen Starr (1824-1901). She was born in Deerfield, Massachusetts, to a prominent Unitarian family, but converted to Roman Catholicism in 1854. (Her niece, Ellen Gates Starr, was co-founder with Jane Adams of Hull House in Chicago.) Starr established a studio in Boston where she taught in private schools. Eventually she moved on to Brooklyn and Philadelphia, finally settling in Chicago in 1856 where once again she set up a studio and gave private lessons, held lectures on Renaissance artists, wrote and published poetry, and wrote and illustrated essays on art in magazines and books. Her two-volume *Pilgrims and Shrines* and *Three Keys to the Camera della Segnatura* (by Raphael) were illustrated histories of Catholic monuments. She received a medallion from Pope Leo XIII for *Three Archangels* and *The Guardian Angels in Art*. She was the first female recipient of the Laetare Medal from the University of Notre Dame in 1885 and was awarded a gold medal for work as a teacher of art at the World's Columbian Exposition in 1893.

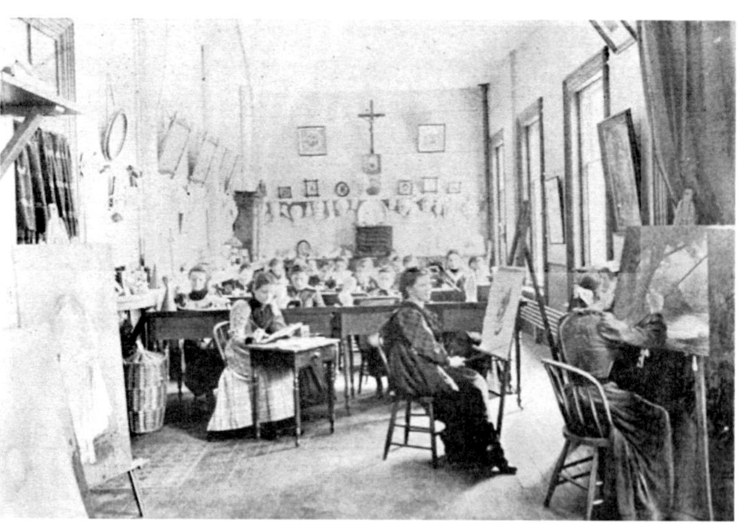

Bertrand Hall Studio.

In 1871, Eliza Allen Starr's studio was destroyed in the Great Chicago Fire. In that same year she was invited by Mother Angela to teach at Saint Mary's College and would remain in residence for five years. Even after her return to Chicago in 1877, she continued to visit and teach at SMC. She may have been the first lay teacher of art at the college.

Starr was very active in the women's movement of the late 19th century. "Women in Art" was a published version of a lecture she presented at the World's Columbian Exposition in 1893. She never compared female to male artists as a means of legitimating their status and competency because, she averred, they already have legitimacy. She placed needlework, often associated with "women's work," on the same level with painting and sculpture, never demoting it to "craft." And she stressed the need for equal art education for women at the best art schools in Europe and America.

Starr's pedagogy is grounded in the French Beaux Arts tradition, with its emphasis on a strong foundation in drawing, including the figure, before the use of color. This would include drawing from the model (probably clothed at this time) and plaster casts. (Photo above: art class in Bertrand Hall from 1893 *Chimes*, the college's annual student literary and art magazine, first published in 1892 and still continuing today.) The influence of transcendentalism, especially Emerson, is evident by Starr's grounding her studies in nature. "Never copy;" she wrote, "always look to nature and study the natural sciences."

Starr's influence and professionalism were carried on by her students, Sister M. Aquina Kirwan, CSC, and Sister M. Marietta Egerton, CSC, who became head and assistant head of the Art Department in 1892. Both of them also studied with Luigi Gregori at Notre Dame.

The relationship with the University of Notre Dame art faculty was a close one in the late nineteenth century. Gregori (1819-96) who painted the murals in the Notre Dame Administration building and in the Basilica, taught Saint Mary's students and sisters, who in turn became influential teachers and administrators at the college. Jobson Emilien Paradis, who was himself a pupil of Gregori at Notre Dame, had studied in Paris at the Ecole Nationale Superieure des Beaux-Arts before returning to Notre Dame to teach in 1900. He taught at Saint Mary's as well, and was a strong influence on teachers of art at Saint Mary's, notably Sister M. Immaculata Duchene, CSC, who had a long teaching career as well as being head of the department.

The Twentieth Century

The 1920s saw a turn to more professionalism in the art curriculum. Saint Mary's College was approved as a teacher training center by the State of Indiana, which included art education for both elementary and high school. The bachelor of fine arts (BFA) degree was offered for the first time in 1924-5. The *Bulletin* for that year outlines the program: English, 10 hours; language, 12 hours; history, 4 hours; philosophy, 16 hours; education, 13 hours; fine arts, 65 hours; religion, every semester.

Art history was introduced into the curriculum in 1914. In addition to the Arundel Society collection of prints of masterpieces begun by Mother Angela, the college acquired the Dusseldorf Collection of engravings for teaching art history in 1902. A 1905 gift by Reverend John A Zahm, CSC, of an oil copy of Murillo's *La Niña* (*The Immaculate Conception*) is still visible in Le Mans Hall. Thanks to the upheavals of World War II, European scholars and art historians flocked to the U. S. Otto von Simson fled Germany and taught art history at Saint Mary's for two years, followed by Bruno Schlesinger, who fled Austria to begin a decades-long career at the college, eventually establishing the Christian Culture Program (Humanistic Studies today). Art history has been a major concentration since the 1970s.

The long-held dream of creating a state-of-the-art building for the arts was finally accomplished under the leadership of Sister Madeleva Wolff, CSC. Moreau Hall (now Moreau Center for the Arts) was completed in 1956. The building still houses art studios, classrooms, and Moreau Art Galleries (MAG) as well as O'Laughlin Auditorium, Little Theater, music and theater classrooms and practice rooms. Sister Madeleva commissioned Jean Charlot to design and paint fourteen frescos for the front of O'Laughlin even before the building was completed.

Charlot (1898-1979) was born in France and studied at the Ecole des Beaux-Arts in Paris before moving to Mexico in 1920, a time when the government there was commissioning large-scale mural projects for public buildings by artists such as Rivera, Orozco, and Charlot. Charlot moved to the United States in 1929, and forged a varied and prolific career as a muralist, printmaker, ceramist, illustrator, and author. He eventually settled in Honolulu, where he taught at the University of Hawaii for decades, but occasionally gave summer classes in true fresco painting at Notre Dame. It was during one of those residencies, in 1955, that he was commissioned by Sister Madeleva to create a series of murals celebrating the arts. The series of four-foot-by-four-foot frescos were set in aluminum frames for later insertion into the façade of O'Laughlin because the building was still incomplete in the summer of 1955. The subjects include allegories of ceramics, needlework, drama, painting, dance, music, poetry, and a portrait of Sister Madeleva as Saint Hilda of Whitby. Charlot was awarded an honorary degree by the college the following year, at which time Sister Madeleva prevailed upon him to paint another fresco at the entrance of Little Theater, *The Fires of Creation*. The frescos have recently been restored.

The 1950s and '60s saw the arts flourishing in its new building under the art department leadership of Sister Marie Rosaire, CSC. Among the many artists to visit Saint Mary's during this period was Andre Gerard, a French painter who studied with Rouault in his youth. In addition to his murals featured at the Paris International Expo, 1937, and the New York and San Francisco World's Fairs of 1939, he experimented with a technique of painting directly on seventy-millimeter film (as long as ninety feet). These transparent images were then projected as a hand-painted film. His *Passion of Christ* and *Sermon on the Mount* were shown at Saint Mary's in 1960 and were subsequently donated to Sister Madeleva and the college by alumnae. He returned in 1963 for an exhibition of his paintings and silk screens in Moreau Hall.

Norman Laliberté (1925–) joined the faculty from 1957-1962 after completing his studies at the Institute of Design at Illinois Institute of Technology. A prolific and energetic artist/teacher, he organized jubilant liturgical processions about campus accompanied by painted and printed banners. The college maintains a sizeable collection of his work from this period. Laliberté went on to establish a distinguished international career with work in major collections around the world. The college awarded him an honorary degree in the 1980s.

Joseph Jachna (1935–) also studied at the Institute of Design, IIT, in the 1950s where he worked with photographers Aaron Siskind and Harry Callahan. He taught at Saint Mary's in the early 1960s, but returned to teach at his alma mater. He, too, developed an international reputation with work in prestigious collections and received numerous awards. He was followed by one of his students, Barbara Blondeau (1938–1974), who taught photography at Saint Mary's from 1966–1968 while working on her MS at the Institute of Design. This was a period of great experimentation when she developed long photographic strip prints reminiscent of the Midwest landscape itself. Blondeau had a one-woman exhibition of her work in 1967 at the college.

The 1970s were both tumultuous and gratifying, beginning with the merger/non-merger between Saint Mary's and Notre Dame. The initial agreement to unite with the "school across the road" was cancelled, and

Saint Mary's College remained an independent women's Catholic college while Notre Dame began accepting women for the first time. To distinguish its own identity from that of Notre Dame, the art department applied for and won national accreditation from the National Association of Schools of Art and Design (NASAD) in 1974, for both its BA and BFA degrees. Sister Rose Ellen Morrissey, CSC, chair at the time, was deeply committed to the organization and to the excellence in teaching that NASAD represents. The Department remains active in the organization and still holds national accreditation for both degrees in the areas of art history, ceramics, painting, printmaking, fibers, sculpture, photography, and new-media studies.

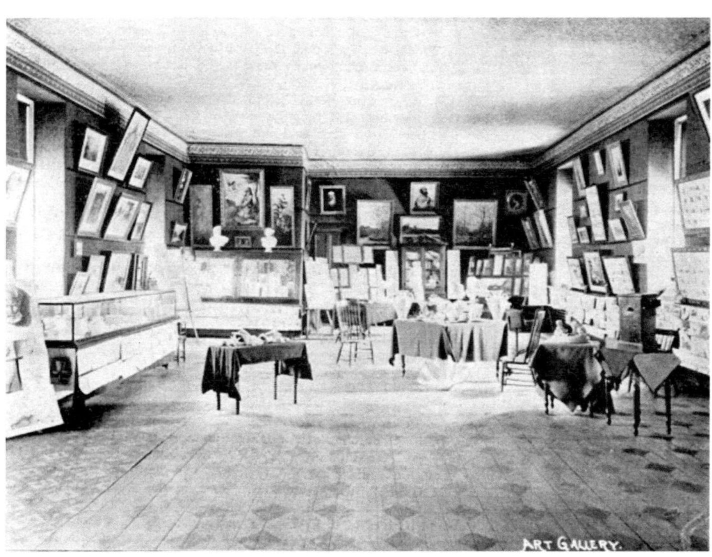

Bertrand Hall Art Gallery.

The 1970s also saw the founding of the Saint Mary's Rome Program, which included a strong art component from its inception. H. James Paradis, art department chair, was instrumental in the program's founding, and Sister Cecelia Ann Kelly, CSC, and Billy Ray Sandusky both taught in Rome and on the home campus. The Rome Program is still active and thriving. The month-long London Summer Travel Program also included courses in art taught by department faculty. This program continued until recently.

The art department also created an intensive two-week summer art camp for college students at Redbud Trail Camp in Buchanan, Michigan, in the 1970s. Courses for college credit were taught by department faculty until the 1990s. The Fine Arts Camp for children is taught annually in the summer at the college.

Moreau Art Galleries

Saint Mary's maintained an art gallery from its early years in Bertrand Hall. The *South Bend Tribune* regularly covered the annual student exhibitions at the college in the 19th century. Students also exhibited off-campus at the World's Columbian Exposition in 1893, and won awards at the Annual Competitive Exhibition for Art Students in Philadelphia.

Moreau Art Galleries (MAG) present professional and educational exhibitions of contemporary art that are challenging and innovative in both content and media. Exhibitions serve as a teaching tool for the department of art and reflect the needs, interests, and concerns of students. Portfolio reviews require every art student to exhibit a selection of her work every semester in the gallery for review by the entire faculty. A juried exhibition of student work takes place every summer. Individual senior comprehensive exhibitions are the culmination of every student's study in the department and provide the opportunity for students to hang their work in the professional setting. Student work is also exhibited on a rotating basis in the Marilou Eldred Gallery in the Student Center on Saint Mary's College campus.

MAG has been the site of hundreds of exhibitions showcasing contemporary artists (up to nine each year). Recent exhibitions echo the changing themes in the global art world. Contemporary social issues, many pertaining to women—such as eating disorders, sexual stereotyping, environmental degradation, cultural identity, immigration, and the empowerment of women—are some of the issues addressed by MAG. The exhibitions support the educational objectives of other departments at Saint Mary's College and serve as cultural and intellectual enrichment for the entire Saint Mary's community. They encourage the community-at-large to become more aware of the important role the arts play in education and the general enhancement of everyday life that the visual arts provide.

The gallery has been the centerpiece for multicultural and cross-disciplinary exhibitions and intellectual events. For the 125th anniversary of the college in 1968-69, for example, an important semiotics symposium, *Language, Symbol, Reality*, with speakers such as Meyer Schapiro, S.I. Hayakawa, Paul Ricoeur, and Roman Jakobson, was complemented by *Sign, Signal, Symbol*, an exhibition of works ranging from Durer to Dali. This was followed by an exhibition of Robert Indiana graphics that accompanied a summer institute, *The Dynamics of Creativity*.

For the 150th anniversary of the college (1994–95) the theme, *Honoring Tradition, Pioneering Change*, utilized the quilt as a metaphor for the unity of the whole college arising from its many and varied parts. The gallery was the site of historic as well as contemporary quilt exhibitions. Quilts also reflect the long tradition of fiber arts at the college, from embroidery classes in the nineteenth century to courses in sustainable textiles taught by Julie Tourtillotte today.

Doug Tyler, professor of photography, holography, and new media, organized the International Congress on Art in Holography in 1990, accompanied by an exhibition of prominent international holographers. This was followed by *Leading Lights: Women in Holography*, an exhibition featuring works by women in this cutting edge technology. The intersection of science, technology and art has been featured in other exhibitions as well.

MAG has also participated in community collaborations—with Notre Dame's Institute for Latino Studies, for example, and with the South Bend community's George Rickey exhibitions in the early 1990s. A local museum consortium of nine museums and exhibition spaces, including Saint Mary's, organized coordinated exhibitions and programming on shared themes in the 1990s as well.

Visiting lecturers and artists-in-residence have been a regular part of the curriculum since the earliest days of the college. Artists often accompany their work to MAG exhibitions and speak at the openings. Artists-in-residence are invited every semester, for a few days to longer stays, to work with students. Some of these artists have been Margo Hoff (1979), Houston Conwill (1983), and Judy Chicago. Speakers as varied as

Miriam Schapiro (1995), Rudolph Arnheim (1978), and John Stilgoe (1994) have enlivened the art environment. Regular field trips, often sponsored by the student Art Club, to Chicago, Indianapolis, Toledo, and elsewhere, amplify the campus curriculum.

The Past Meets the Future

The fine arts at Saint Mary's College have always been an integral part of the college and the community. The current faculty—Julie Tourtillotte, Doug Tyler, Billy Ray Sandusky, Krista Hoefle, Sandi Ginter, and Tiffany Johnson-Bidler—continue to contribute to the creative vitality of the college. Painting and drawing are still a part of the curriculum, as are ceramics, fibers, printmaking, sculpture, photography, and art history. Now there are new art forms, such as digital media, holography, and video, as well as more interdisciplinary initiatives. Saint Mary's College has come a long way from artificial fruit and flower making. The art department develops students able to adapt to future needs, to see the possibilities of art in a constantly changing global environment.

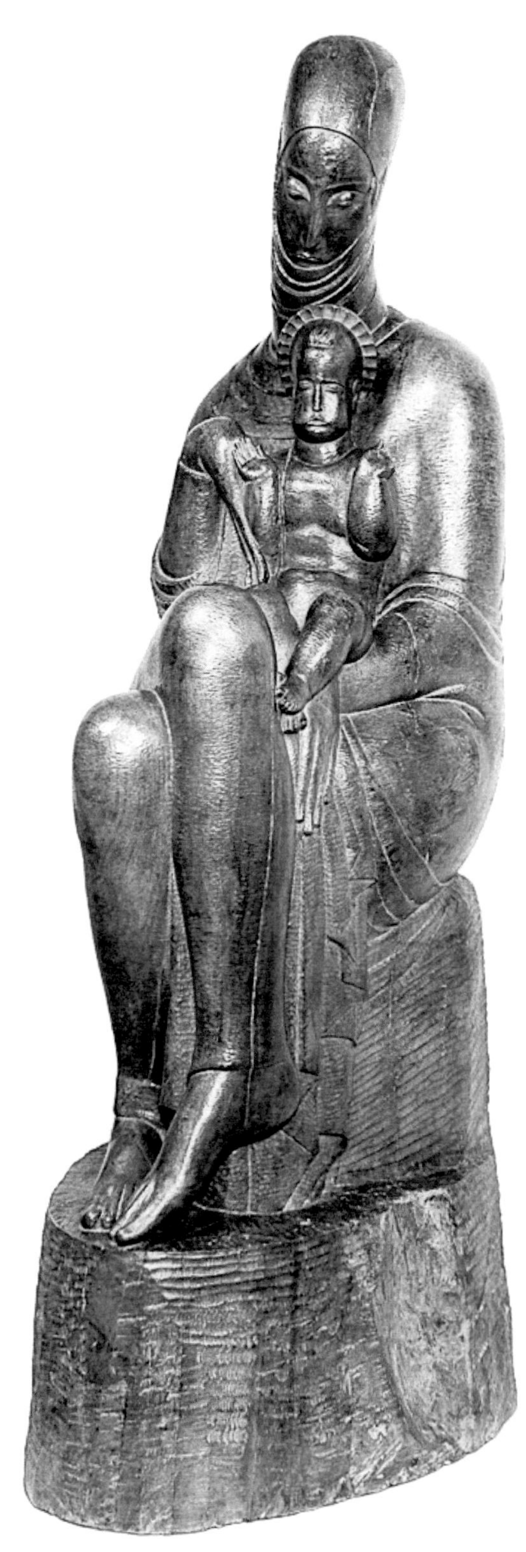

University of Notre Dame

Dean A. Porter

The University of Notre Dame is celebrated for courses in theology, business, and law, among others. Seldom, however, is it applauded for its Department of Art, Art History and Design, even though it has achieved a wonderful reputation nationwide. It has achieved excellence in studio art through inspiration by leadership with vision, a dedicated faculty with a fertile imagination, and bright, adventurous students.

These participants achieved success in spite of inadequate physical facilities and levels of funding. Historically, studio faculty have been compelled to work in facilities that were designed for other purposes. The O'Shaughnessy Hall facilities quickly proved to be too small to accommodate a growing department. Graduate students occupied houses on or near the campus. When the Joyce Athletic Center was completed in the early 1960s, the Art Department made a plea to postpone the scheduled demolition of the old Field House and open space there for studio courses. Still, the department required more space, this time for industrial design courses that were burgeoning in size. In the 1960s, the attic in O'Shaughnessy Hall was retrofitted to house this program, and it remained there until the 1990s.

When the wrecking ball finally caught up with the Field House, the department again went looking for space, finding the old Chemistry Building available but not without costly retrofitting. While all of this work was under way, the art history program, including the slide room, remained in O'Shaughnessy Hall. Even with all of these changes, artists working in studio were cramped. Again the wrecking ball was cheated when a steel/aluminum building owned by the Congregation of the Holy Cross, called "The Annex," was saved and three priests occupied the building.

Even the geographical location of Notre Dame has placed the art department in a difficult position: historically, artists want to be located in large, culturally active centers. However, in 1842, when Father Sorin was looking for a place to establish Notre Dame, he probably wasn't concerned with the location and proximity to great art centers as much he was with the beauty of St. Mary's and St. Joseph's Lakes. Even in the dead of winter, in an untamed wilderness, he saw a future for his new university. This required courage, wisdom and an enormous amount of faith.

Notre Dame's first Artist-in-Residence, Luigi Gregori, arrived from Rome in 1874. Father Sorin wanted an Italian painter who would create the decorations for Sacred Heart Church as well as paintings of other themes and individuals of consequence. Gregori had served as a conservator to the Vatican as well as a portrait painter. If Father Sorin was looking for support for his new university from Rome, the hiring of Gregori must have pleased Pope Pius IX. The artist came with high praise as Pius IX insisted that Sorin, "Take Gregori. He is just finishing some work here. You will find him and his work thoroughly satisfactory."

Gregori was a mature 55-year-old religious artist of modest talent who had developed a pseudo-Renaissance style of painting, one that could easily produce the type

Ivan Meštrović, *The Ashbaugh Madonna.*

of images and iconographic program Sorin was seeking. A great admirer of the Renaissance painters, notably Perugino and Raphael, Gregori was well versed in their styles and compositions. Sorin concluded that the partnership of artist/patron was precisely what Notre Dame needed, and in July 1874, Gregori signed a contract as Notre Dame's first Artist-in-Residence. He was to paint fourteen panels, the Stations of the Cross, and "was to be paid $1,000 a year" or "its equivalent in scudi." Furthermore, he was "to teach art to students." A guaranteed salary of $1,000 was a handsome amount in 1874. Besides his work for Notre Dame, Gregori could spend time satisfying private commissions, some of which were in response to *his* ideas, not contractual dictates.

Gregori likely followed nineteenth century traditions in teaching theory, figure drawing, and painting, usually from plaster casts or semi-clothed, live models. He also had a collection of his personal drawings, and some two hundred, largely nineteenth century Neapolitan pen and ink studies, which could be used in classroom demonstrations.

During his seventeen-year stay at Notre Dame, Gregori became the center of attention when he painted murals for Sacred Heart Church, as well as the Columbus cycle for the vestibule and the dome of the Main Building. He also created easel work, some sixty portraits of American bishops, as well as commissions for local patrons. By the time he returned to Italy in 1891, he left an impressive legacy.

According to Fred Beckman, James Warden followed Gregori, directing the art program until 1919. "He is given credit for [establishing] the basic art courses and a sequential curriculum in studio arts."

By 1917, Notre Dame was building art collections but they were sadly lacking in quality. Reverend Dom Gregory Gerrer, a Benedictine priest from Shawnee, Oklahoma, came to Notre Dame to care for the collections while teaching art. Gerrer also became Notre Dame's first museum director, a position that consumed much of his time. In the early 1930s, the directorship was turned over to a Chicago dilettante, Maurice Goldblatt, and he held the position until Father Lauck became director of the Art Gallery in 1962. I succeeded Lauck in 1974, and Charles Loving followed me in 2001.

Ernest Thorne Thompson arrived on campus in 1922, becoming chairman and continuing to develop the art curriculum. In 1930, Professor Stanley Sasha Sessler, a Russian painter, joined Thompson and Gerrer, and began his forty-year stay. Sadly, Thompson decided to go to New York City to study. According to an article in *The Scholastic*, friends felt the department could ill afford to lose an educator who showed "exceptional promise and considerable achievement." By the late 1920s, the art department offered a bachelor of fine arts [BFA]. To graduate, a student had to take 133 hours, including a total of sixty-two hours in Art 1, 2, 3, and 4. Catholics had to take an additional eight hours in religion. A student could receive private instruction for a fee of fifty dollars.

Artists with national reputations came often to Notre Dame. One such was Charles Emile Jacques, who, succeeding Thompson, taught painting and chaired the department. Jacques was a well-established artist by the time he left his native Belgium for America in 1923 and settled in Oregon. Before arriving here in the early 1930s, Jacques established an art department at Columbia

University. During the Depression, he had forged a distinguished career working in an American Impressionist style, and for a few years Notre Dame was fortunate to have an artist of his talent and reputation. Unfortunately, Jacques' career came to a tragic end when he drowned in 1937.

Jacques was succeeded by Francis Joseph Hanley, a graduate of the Rhode Island School of Design, who taught painting until 1942 when he enlisted in the navy. Shortly after returning to Notre Dame, he was attracted to Hollywood and the silver screen. Rather than working at the easel, the handsome Hanley became a supporting actor of some note.

Besides teaching figure drawing and beginning painting, Stanley Sessler served as the chairman of the department. During the early years, art was taught in the upper level of the Main Building, where it remained until the opening of O'Shaughnessy. By that time, the top floor of the Main Building was deemed unsafe, yet it had proved to be an ideal setting for artists who, after climbing four flights, could work and learn in the loft-like space. The ceilings were high and the illumination was good, some coming from clerestory windows. Photographs taken during figure drawing classes, show partially clad models, often male, posing. White plaster castes, popular teaching tools in the late nineteenth century, were also evident and remained in the classroom well into the twentieth century.

In 1940, a year after he earned his MFA from the School of The Art Institute of Chicago, Father John James Bednar joined the department, adding sculpture to the curriculum. The Hungarian sculptor Eugene Kormendi also joined the faculty and worked with Bednar in the sculpture program for nearly two decades. The Hungarian-born sculptor having done commissions on two continents, arrived in America in 1939. Besides receiving awards in exhibitions for his sculptures, he created a portrait of President Harry S Truman. Notre Dame was unquestionably attracted to Kormendi because of his religious sculpture, often heroic-size images of the Blessed Virgin and Child. His twenty-two-foot *Christ the Light of the World*, located in front of the NCWC Building on Massachusetts Avenue in Washington, D. C., may well be his masterpiece. In many respects, his sculpture anticipated the work of another sculptor who would arrive on the Notre Dame campus in 1955, Ivan Meštrović. The work of both Bednar and Kormendi can be found at several locations on campus.

In the 1930s and '40s, faculty came and left, often after a few years. Bednar left the Holy Cross order in 1945. In 1951, Kormendi declared, "Notre Dame has a very good atmosphere and spirit about it and I am quite content here." He was to remain in South Bend until his death in 1959.

In 1946, Frederick S. Beckman, a design specialist, joined the faculty, soon becoming a vital force in the department's growth. He began as an instructor and, over the next fifty-five-plus years, built an ambitious industrial design program that knew few equals. In 1953, Robert Leader joined the department; a graduate of Yale University, he taught advanced painting, while Stanley Sessler handled beginning courses. Leader also created a large number of handsome stained glass windows, fitting neatly into the Notre Dame mission of quality religious as well as secular art. When he wasn't teaching in the studio, he taught art history to as many as 600 students each semester, and his Art Traditions course became legendary.

The photography program began when Richard Stevens moved from the humanities in the early 1960s, bringing his talent and camera. For nearly thirty years, until retiring in 1998, Stevens created and developed an excellent photography program. What little time he had after personally building three photography studios and darkrooms as the department moved from one facility to the next, he developed handsome collotypes. He was also instrumental in the early growth of the Art Gallery's photography collection. From the early 1960s to the present, Stevens, Richard Gray and Martina Lopez have created a quality photography program.

Father Anthony J. Lauck

With the life-long commitments of Sessler, Beckman, and Leader, new leadership was found in a man of the cloth. Anthony J. Lauck, a Holy Cross priest, studied at the John Herron in Indianapolis, the Corcoran in Washington, D. C., Alfred University, Art Students League, and Columbia University, all New York, and Cranbrook Academy, Detroit. He also studied under some of America's most important figurative sculptors—including Ivan Meštrović at Syracuse University. The soft-spoken sculptor created wonderful stained glass windows of faceted glass. With the assistance of two CSC priests, Greg Green and James Flanigan, his windows in Moreau Seminary are among America's most beautiful.

Father Lauck continued what Bednar and Kormendi started in sculpture. When the department moved to O'Shaughnessy Hall, he found studio space in the Architecture Building and the basement of O'Shaughnessy Hall. Unfortunately these studios were severely limiting in size, handicapping him when he attempted to work in large scale. That and inadequate lighting were serious handicaps that even the most talented educator would have difficulty in overcoming. Two small kilns, inadequately vented, also limited the student. Yet Lauck, like all who taught in the department, overcame restrictions.

When Father Lauck felt the program needed a fresh, creative mind, he turned to those who could help him most and gave new life to the tradition of sculptors who also happened to be members of the Congregation of Holy Cross. Fathers James Flanigan and Austin Collins transformed a campus featuring stock religious images to what is today – in the process of becoming a beautiful sculpture garden with objects created by innovative sculptors working in contemporary styles regardless the subject matter.

O'Shaughnessy Hall

Nineteen fifty-three was a year of celebration with the opening of the O'Shaughnessy Hall College of Arts and Letters. The art department and gallery were no longer squirreled away in some obscure location. Thanks to the generosity of philanthropist Ignatius O'Shaughnessy, Father Hesburgh dedicated a modern, up-to-date facility. Besides classroom space, the building included an art gallery, a facility which was to become an important factor in art students' education. Father Hesburgh quietly became a strong advocate of art on the campus. Under his leadership, the new age of art at the university began.

In O'Shaughnessy Hall, art students enjoyed spaces conducive to creativity. The gallery, located down the hall from the classrooms, became the center of activity. Besides exhibitions of Meštrović's sculpture, solo shows by members of the art department, emerging artists, and loan shows, speakers such as Frank Lloyd Wright, Marisol Escobar, George Segal, Richard Hunt, and Cristo, all attracted large crowds. In 1965, the distinguished Russian painter Marc Chagall was given an honorary doctorate, the first artist to be so honored by Notre Dame. Most importantly, an annual student show, considered by many to be the Art Gallery's most exciting exhibition, was showcased.

"The Maestro"

Father Hesburgh, following the recommendation of Father Lauck, persuaded the internationally known Croatian/American sculptor, Ivan Meštrović, to leave Syracuse University and join the Notre Dame faculty. Like Father Sorin before him, Hesburgh was looking for an artist to accept the position of Distinguished Sculptor-in-Residence. In Ivan Meštrović, he found a sculptor who was capable of completing ambitious projects stressing religious subject matter. In Meštrović's *Pieta*, on permanent view in The Metropolitan Museum of Art since 1947, Father Ted undoubtedly saw the icon of twentieth-century American religious sculpture. That sculpture needed a permanent home in an environment sympathetic to religious sculpture. At Notre Dame the *Pieta* is now the destination for the thousands.

Meštrović tolerated contemporary movements in art while seeking an environment which that appreciated his classical style, where the human form was allowed expression through bodily contortions and not surgical alterations. Equally important, the sixty-five-year-old artist, working in the fading years of a colorful career, needed a modern studio, and Notre Dame was the answer to that need. He moved to the Midwest in 1955, splitting his time between teaching and working in a new studio.

Dubbed "the Maestro," Meštrović enjoyed celebratory status. While teaching, he created *Christ and the Samaritan Woman at Jacob's Well*, located in front of O'Shaughnessy Hall; a wood relief of *The Last Supper* for the North Dining Hall; and a bronze *Mother and Child* for the Lewis Hall Courtyard, among other works. Until his death in 1962, the Meštrović studio was the scene of spirited activity. He did his own work in the morning, and after lunch and a siesta he taught students. Professor Edward Fisher once wrote, "If one Notre Dame professor is remembered it will be Ivan Meštrović."

In 1984, the munificence of Notre Dame alumnus Russell G. "Pete" and Jeanne Ashbaugh enabled the University to possess the largest collection of sculptures and drawings by Meštrović in America—over 300 works. With Father Hesburgh as its principle patron, art became a topic of conversation and visual excitement on the campus.

Art Department Growth

Stanley Sessler set a pattern that continues today—faculty members who came to Notre Dame as young, aspiring artists and remained until retirement. They excelled as artists, and the 1960s saw the emergence of the art department as a major school in the College of Arts and Letters. Father Lauck was able to expand the staff, hiring Don Vogl, John David Mooney and myself. Thomas Stern Fern came to Notre Dame from Berea College, and Douglas Kinsey from the University of Minnesota.

Fern, with a doctorate in education from New York University, was a painter/administrator hired to succeed Father Lauck and chair the department. He revolutionized the department's philosophy. Prior to his arrival, it subscribed to a predetermined, sequential course of study and the philosophy that one program fits all. Instead of following an inflexible program, students were now allowed to select courses they thought would best serve their needs. A student might take advanced painting before taking beginning drawing, for example. The program produced interesting results and students with fine careers, but after several years the department reverted back to its earlier course of study.

Vogl, a recent graduate of the School of the Art Institute of Chicago, brought a new level of creativity to the campus. A talented artist with a fertile imagination, he was the department's most inventive and prolific teacher from 1963 to 2003, exploring idea after idea in oil, acrylic, pen, wood, and any material available to him. During his years at Notre Dame, he created thousands of paintings, drawings, graphics and sculptures.

Douglas Kinsey, working in a figurative tradition, stressed the use of nineteenth-century painting techniques; he focused on critical social conditions facing mankind worldwide in the twentieth century. No teacher had a greater effect on students. A master draftsman and painter, Doug worked his canvases to effectively reflect his feelings on a specific subject matter. For over thirty years, Notre Dame students were fortunate to work with three master painters—Robert Leader, Don Vogl and Douglas Kinsey.

The art department's programs were so successful that the small classrooms in O'Shaughnessy Hall could no longer satisfy student needs. As a consequence, students in the master of fine arts program found studio space in small houses, scattered on and around the campus, that were owned by the university. Unfortunately, having students working in separate spaces was problematic, though it did not destroy one of the qualities that characterized the department, the spirit of camaraderie.

The Old Field House

The university attempted to solve the problem of scattered art students by postponing demolition of the Field House and opening it to the art department. This couldn't have come at a more propitious time. The structure offered space for classrooms as well as studios for faculty. The only drawback was the university's refusal to put any money into the decaying building. It had to be used as was—leaking roof, dirt floors, a hardwood floor that was once the university's basketball court, an inadequate heating system, and other problems too numerous to describe.

In 1974, Moira Marti Geoffrion joined the faculty, in part due to Notre Dame's decision to go co-educational. She was an effective educator in the classroom, in her studio, and eventually as department chair. As a sculptor, she worked in vinyl, collaborating with the local company Uniroyal. In 1986, after a successful stay at Notre Dame, she moved to the University of Arizona-Tucson, to become head of its art department.

When Bill Kremer joined the faculty in 1973, the department took on yet another new look. While ceramics had been taught for years, students usually created small utilitarian objects. Kremer brought national attention to ceramic sculpture and Notre Dame. During his first summer, given $500 by Chairman Fern, Bill built forty wheels, constructed kilns with recycled firebricks, and poured a concrete floor. Granted, the students still learned how to throw a pot on Kremer's wheels but, they now also had the opportunity of creating large-scale sculpture made of clay.

Even with its huge, cavernous space, the Field House presented Kremer with problems. He had to find a space to accommodate ceramics that was not under a rotting roof. He also had to jury-rig a heating system so that classes could be held during Northern Indiana's frigid months. Eventually the Field House could no longer be saved and the art department again packed up its equipment and all those makeshift potters' wheels and the salvaged firebricks, and moved to another hand-me-down space, the old Chemistry Building. Studio arts would continue to survive and flourish, but only with the imaginative efforts of faculty and students.

Kremer again rose to the occasion. On his home grounds in Edwardsburg, Michigan, Bill created the walk-in ND wood-fired anagama kiln. This kiln attracted Notre Dame students and ceramic sculptors nationwide to fire their clay vessels and participate in exhibitions and symposia at Notre Dame. America's most important ceramic sculptors travelled to Notre Dame and Kremer's home. In fact, in 2001, the godfather of ceramic sculpture, Peter Voulkos, created his last major sculpture, fired in the Kremer's ND kiln.

Isis Gallery

Even students joined the department's efforts to secure space for their programs. In the late 1960s, a period of turmoil and student unrest nationwide, they sponsored a program to express their grievances with the department. Curiously, with the entire art faculty seated on the stage "on trial" to field questions, the art department was never discussed. Rather, the students expressed their dissatisfaction with the Art Gallery and its offerings. After much discussion, Father Lauck designated one of the Art Gallery's smaller galleries exclusively for student use. It was an invitation to the students to mount exhibitions, which they felt were of relevance to them. Despite that gesture, the students failed to follow up with the Art Gallery. Instead, they found a space and named it Isis Gallery, and for more than thirty years, it served them well. For the first time in the long history of the university, students had a space where they could exhibit their art as well as that of artists *they invited*. Ultimately Isis moved to Riley Hall of Art. Appropriately, Isis was the name of the Egyptian goddess of death and resurrection.

While the students enjoyed Isis Gallery, an annual student exhibition featuring undergraduates and MFA students proved to be one of the highlights of the Art Gallery and the Snite Museum of Art. Annual faculty exhibitions were also featured until the late 1990s.

Industrial Design

Industrial design, under Fred Beckman's leadership, became a major course offering. In fact, few programs graduated a higher percentage of students whose careers were directly shaped by their majors. For years, a huge percentage of industrial design's students ended up in Detroit, working for Chrysler, General Motors and or Ford. With the increasing number of students signing up for industrial design courses, Beckman had to find a larger space for classes. Because of the students' projects, designing automobiles including full-scale models, the space had to be reserved for industrial design only. He examined the attic in the south wing of O'Shaughnessy Hall and with generous grants from Chrysler created "The Loft." The space had the desired effect of bringing a large number of students together, as team after team worked on projects that would end up in Detroit.

Fred elevated the industrial design program to one of consequence. With his connections in Detroit, he was of the conviction that the department should provide courses that would insure employment for its graduates. Students majoring in design, with a broad educational background in the humanities and other disciplines, enjoyed more avenues of employment, particularly for those seeking positions of leadership in the corporate world. Fred was also instrumental in initiating computer-generated art. With John Sherman at his side, a computer lab became as important to students as any painting, sculpture, or graphics studio.

When the decision was made to move to the Chemistry Building, Fred, with his experience, was well qualified to make decisions that would affect the department for the next several decades. He decided to create a low-tech interior, based on an Art Deco style. The building, renamed Riley Hall through a $500,000 gift from the family of Radwan and Allan Riley, New York, solved some of the department's needs. Beckman also renamed the department the Department of Art, Art History and Design, a change that reflected the diversity that characterized the department and, of course, the growth of industrial design. Yet even with another hand-me-down facility, the classes were squeezed into small, restricting space. While studio was taught in Riley Hall, art history and the slide room still used space in O'Shaughnessy Hall. Having the entire department under one roof remained a problem.

Fred hired talented faculty to teach classes specializing in the design of transportation products, energy-saving devices, furniture, and ordinary household objects such as toys. By the mid-1970s, the Industrial Design Program was attracting attention nationwide. Besides Chrysler, Ford, General Motors, and Armco Steel, other corporations were inviting Notre Dame to participate in their programs to create more effective products. In 1975, the Notre Dame program was fully accredited by the Industrial Designers Society of America.

To meet the demands of industrial design classes, Beckman hired some excellent faculty—notably George Tistan, Paul Down, John Caruso, Derek Chalfant, John Sherman, and Robert P. Sedlack. Each designer had his field of specialization. Tistan worked with automotive designs; Sherman is in charge of the computer lab and teaching graphic design; Chalfant furniture design; Sedlack publications design; and Down is director of the Design Program and National Education Chair of the Industrial Designer Society of America.

Late in Fred's career, he turned to steel sculpture. Following the examples set by Father Collins and a host of other sculptors, he travelled to K & M Manufacturing in Cassopolis, Michigan, to mine steel "drops" that K & M were not using. Fortunately, Michael McGloughlin, owner of the firm, was a Notre Dame graduate who adopted the art department. Beckman believed that his sculpture "represented an emotional liaison with the spirit of the ever present and continuing modernist movement."

For years, the studio faculty was made up of males only. In 1974, after Moira Geoffrion became the first tenure-track female in the department, painter Maria Tomasula came aboard. Since 1991 her images of gravita have attracted national attention. Her intensely colorful, handsomely painted themes of morality evoke viewer response, which is both fascinating and arresting. Since 1994, she has been the Michael P. Grace Professor of Arts and Letters.

Two printmaker/photographers, Jean Dibble and Martina A. Lopez, extended the medium of photography to express their ideas. Their work often marries photographs to other media. Dibble came to Notre Dame with an impressive background, studying and working in some of America's finest printmaking programs. She transformed Notre Dame's printmaking program from one taught part time by painters into an even stronger major. Lopez, with an MFA from the School of the Art Institute of Chicago, is enjoying a distinguished career at Notre Dame; she held the Michael P. Grace Chair in the College of Arts and Letters from 2002 to 2005. Her highly refined, provocative work is involved with the human experience as she explores nineteenth century, highly refined, provocative images though the use of digital imagery.

The Annex

In the mid-1990s, two Holy Cross priests—Fathers Flanigan and Collins—recognized the need for an adequate space in which to create their sculpture. The Congregation for Holy Cross owned Holy Cross Seminary whose principal building was razed. Eventually, the order was given to demolish a steel and aluminum structure that had been part of the original compound. However, Father Collins saw a space, called "The Annex," where he could create his large totems of steel, Father Flanigan his large and bold religious images, and Father Martin Nuygen his wall-sized portrait watercolors. The CSC priests finally had a cavernous space that would accommodate art of any size. They had come a long way from the closet-like space in the basement of O'Shaughnessy Hall. In the great tradition, which has marked the art department, three priests have adapted space that once accommodated a basketball court, and later a storage facility, to wonderful studios where, in a relaxed atmosphere, art is created, taught and celebrated.

The sculpture program born during World War II was now flourishing under three other CSC priests, Collins, Flanigan and Lauck. In 1986, I decided that the Snite Museum of Art needed a large sculpture for the main entrance. After considering several internationally known sculptors, we reasoned that the honor of the commission should go to one of the art department's graduates, David Hayes, Class of 1963. The appearance of the twenty-nine-foot *Griffon* influenced a host of commissions, purchases and gifts of modern and contemporary sculpture for the Notre Dame campus. Funding for *The Griffon* was made possible by the Humana Endowment for American Art, a fund which was established by another Notre Dame alumnus, William Ballard. This fund also enabled the museum to acquire sculptures by Theodore Rozak, Deborah Butterworth, Richard Hunt, and Stephen De Staebler, among others.

From the earliest days of sculpture on campus, the university's museum directors have enjoyed cooperative efforts with members of the studio faculty. Father Lauck, followed by me and currently Charles Loving, brought sculpture to the exhibition galleries as well as to strategic locations on the Notre Dame campus. This cooperative spirit began with exhibitions of Meštrović's sculpture. From 1966, the three museum directors were also responsible for exhibitions and the acquisition of sculptures by Richard Hunt and George Rickey. Exhibitions of ceramic sculpture were also common. When Chuck Loving was appointed director of the Snite Museum of Art in 2001, he also assumed the title Curator of American Sculpture. Since the beginning of the twenty-first century, ceramic sculpture has flourished, evident in the Museum's exhibitions and collection's growth.

For two years, August 1995 through July 1997, Notre Dame exhibited thirty outdoor sculpture created by twenty-five different artists. The campus, once known for its "religious statues," became a beautiful sculpture garden through the cooperative efforts of priests and the directors of the Snite. In 1995, the Campus Sculpture Committee, working with Father Austin Collins, organized the University Public Sculpture Project. While many of the sculptures were placed on a two-year loan, others were either purchased or gifted by the artists and patrons.

With Loving working in close cooperation with members of the department, collections of modern and contemporary sculpture have been attracted to Notre Dame. Besides acquiring individual pieces by significant sculptors, the Snite retained Michael Van Valkenberg Associates , landscape architects, to design a sculpture park on an eight-acre campus site. For years there had been discussion of establishing a Theodore M. Hesburgh sculpture garden, one not too dissimilar to the Franklin Murphy Campus Sculpture Garden on the campus of UCLA. Whether it is named after Father Hesburgh or some other benefactor, the sculpture park has been given an excellent head start.

Notre Dame's Art Museums

Notre Dame's art museum came of age in the 1950s, the Golden Age of Collecting, with the appointment of Father Hesburgh as Notre Dame's president. While Father Ted never spoke of the art collections as a top priority, he quietly and without fanfare influenced the growth of the university's permanent collection from one of embarrassment to one that was highly respected nationwide. Quality attracts quality. Father Ted brought the Fisher collection of Renaissance and eighteenth-century masterpieces to Notre Dame in 1953, and in the early 1960s major collections of Western art were donated to the Art Gallery by Father Ted's friends. By the 1960s, the Art Gallery possessed the finest collection of Western art of any university museum in America. It boasted of paintings, sculptures and drawings by Frederic Remington, Charles Marion Russell, Thomas Moran, Walter Ufer, Victor Higgins, and others.

However, Western art was not to be the Father Lauck's focus. He opened the entire world to Notre Dame's collections: Pre-Columbian, African, Oriental, Medieval, Modern. He was a generalist, and for over a decade he developed the beginnings of fine collection representing virtually every culture. With a paltry acquisitions budget, he had to develop a legion of benefactors, and it wasn't before long before collectors from New York to Chicago and points west became supporters of the Art Gallery. Father Lauck was interested in creating a catholic collection of quality and he succeeded. He created a firm foundation for the directors who followed.

His greatest contribution was creating an advisory council, a team of experts, friends and collectors from across America, to work with a hand-picked professional staff. This team set the foundation for the opening of the Snite in 1980. In 1974, Lauck retired but continued working closely with me, his successor. We were joined by Stephen B. Spiro, one of the country's most talented curators, and it wasn't long before the Snite Museum could boast of exceptional collections: most noteworthy the Butkin collection of French oil sketches and Feddersen collection of Rembrandt etchings.

I hired two talented curators, Douglas Bradley and Stephen Moriarty, both Notre Dame alumni. It wasn't long before that Bradley built a collection that would fill one sculpture case into an entire gallery of Pre-Columbian objects of exceptional quality. Moriarty, not to be outdone, expanded a collection of photographs from one in 1974, which came to the collection accidentally on the mount of a nineteenth century photograph, to well over 10,000 today.

In 1986, Jack Reilly, an alumnus, was introduced to the Snite Museum, and over the next quarter of a century, guided by Spiro, he funded the acquisition of a wonderful collection of Old Master and twentieth-century drawings. With the opening of the museum, benefactors donated higher quality objects, and for the first time the curators were able acquire specific objects. Basically, after 1979 the collection was selected by museum professionals.

Every museum moves in a direction that its directors consider consistent with university priorities. For over a hundred years, the main emphasis at Notre Dame was on religious art. From the 1950s and Father Lauck's directorship on, the Art Gallery sought to form a broad general collection whose major emphasis was on quality. From the 1970s until 2000, the emphasis was to "narrow the gaps" with the highest quality objects, "adding strength to strength."

Contemporary American sculpture, a passion of three museum directors and several members of the art department, has flourished and today is one of the main focuses in the Snite Museum and on campus. Richard Hunt was given the first of three solo exhibitions in 1966, long before he was honored by the Art Institute of Chicago. George Rickey first came to Notre Dame in 1974, and in subsequent years was honored by solo exhibitions. Today, both sculptors hold honorary degrees from Notre Dame, the place to visit if a scholar wants to study their art and archives.

Charles Loving is also committed to creating the pre-eminent collection of Latino art while placing a strong emphasis on outreach programs. Art students are playing an incredibly active role in the museum's scholarship. Success in the arts at Notre Dame has resulted from the support of many. Few universities can boast of such a sustained move towards excellence for over 170 years.

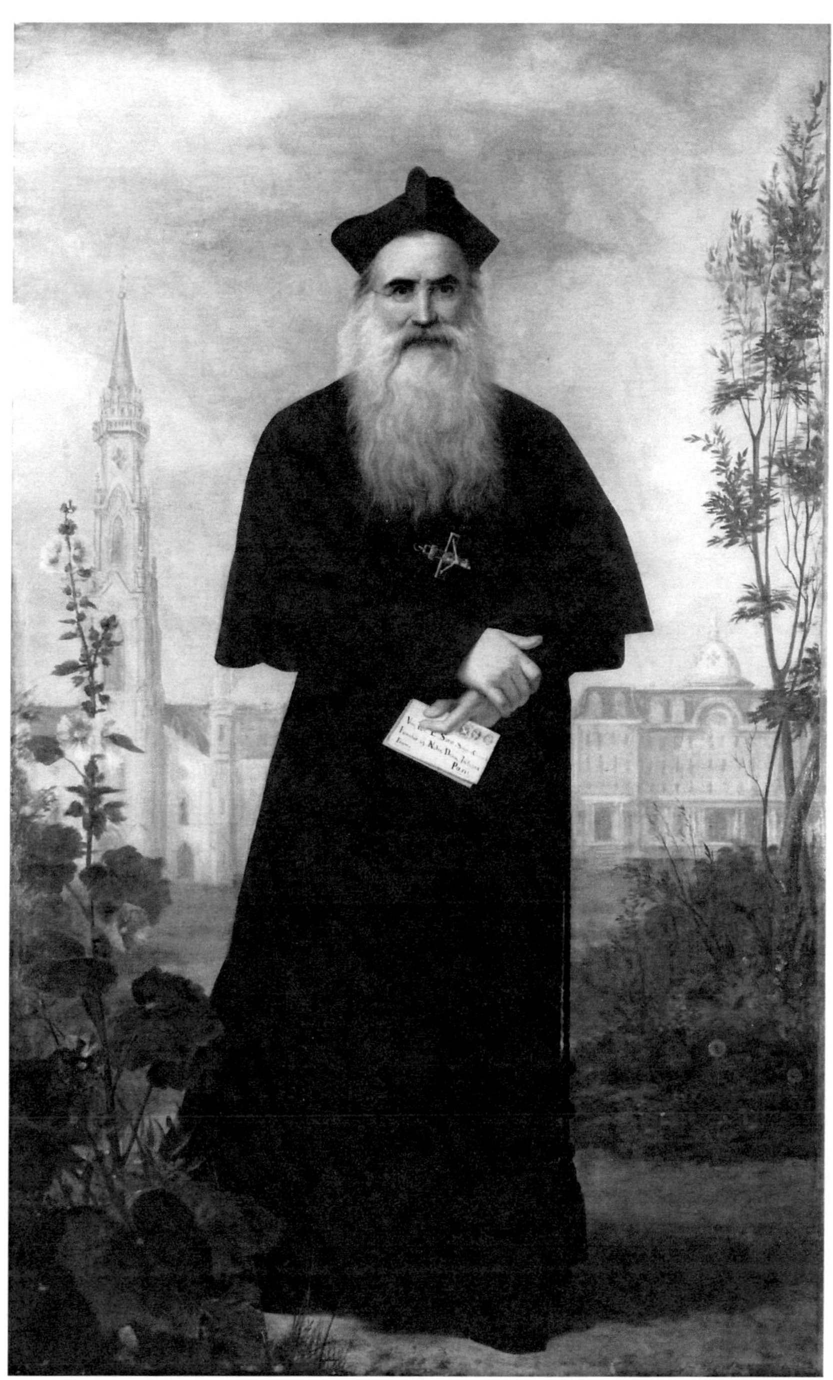

Luigi Grigori, *Father Sorin,* 1875.

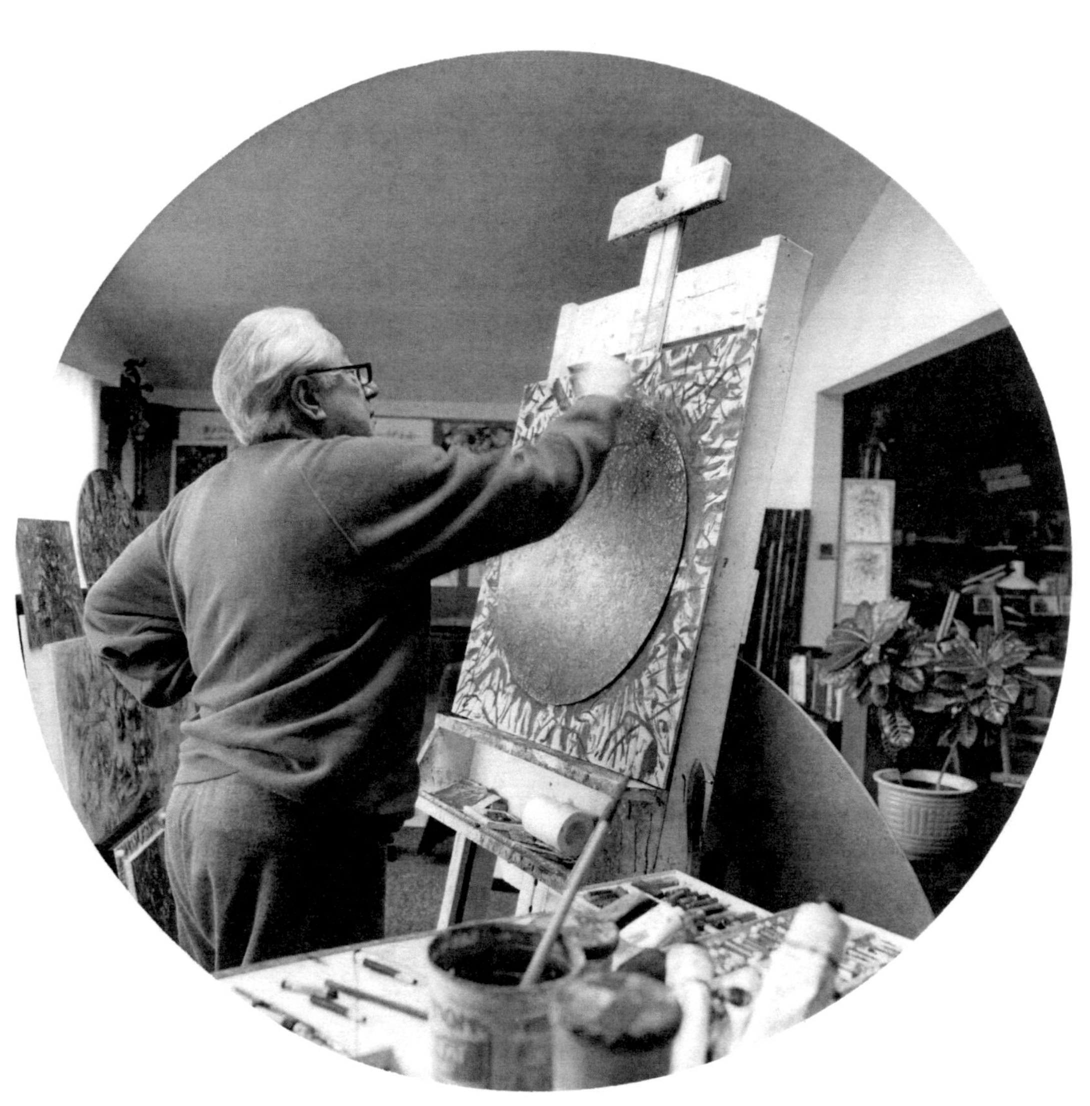

Fine Arts at IU South Bend, 1961-2000

Patrick J. Furlong

Before the Second World War, the Indiana University extension program in South Bend offered art appreciation and art history classes, as well as occasional courses in design. All classes were located at Central High School in downtown South Bend, and taught in the evening by part-time faculty. When the South Bend-Mishawaka Campus moved to Northside Boulevard in the fall of 1961 its new building included appropriate studios for design and painting classes, but there was only limited provision for sculpture. Classes were offered in art appreciation, design, drawing and oil painting, taught still by part-time faculty until the fall semester of 1964, when Matthew Zivich was appointed as instructor in fine arts. He had just received his MFA degree from IU's home campus in Bloomington and taught a remarkably wide range of classes, including art appreciation, design, drawing, film making, painting, and sculpture. Zivich was well recommended by his graduate professors in Bloomington, but he was a disappointment for South Bend.

Harold Zisla came to the university in 1966, after a varied career as an industrial designer for Ball Band shoes in Mishawaka and nine years as director of the South Bend Art Center. Zisla was hired by Lester M. Wolfson, the recently–appointed dean of the campus, soon to become chancellor of the re-named Indiana University at South Bend, generally known, then, as IUSB. Together Zisla and Wolfson worked to build a strong fine arts program, a partnership that flourished until Wolfson's retirement in June of 1987.

Zisla's early years as department chair were troubled by the first tenure and reappointment cases at IU South Bend to become a subject of legal dispute. Zivich and William Fabrycki, an assistant professor of painting, sued the university after being turned down for permanent positions. Fabrycki held a master's degree from Ball State University and had previously worked for the Lafayette Art Center and later taught at Saint Mary's College. He was hired by Zisla in 1967.

The two young artists won their case before the federal district court in 1970, as their cause attracted favorable attention from *The Preface,* the student newspaper, but much less attention from the *South Bend Tribune*. Indiana University appealed the lower court's decision and eventually prevailed before the Seventh Circuit Court of Appeals in Chicago. Zivich and Fabrycki departed quietly for teaching positions elsewhere. With two faculty positions to fill for 1971, Zisla grasped the opportunity to reshape the department to emphasize figurative art. The basis of instruction at IU South Bend now followed the classic late Renaissance technique of drawing the human figure, but this was not a common practice in American university art programs of the early 1970s. Remarkably for such a conservative community as South Bend, there were never any public objections to the use of nude models, both male and female. Anthony Droege was hired first, to teach painting, and he recommended his colleague Harold Langland (always called Tuck) for the position in

William Healy, *Bringing About (Harold Zisla).*

sculpture. They had taught together for three years at Murray State University in Kentucky, and came to IU South Bend for the opportunity to shape a new program. Alan J. Larkin joined the department in 1977 to teach drawing and printmaking. These four artists had their professional differences, of course, but they each remained in the department until retirement. "We always respected each other," Droege remembers, and "we were in agreement about what should happen in the classroom." Their chief difficulty was the university's tight budget, particularly during the recession years of the early 1980s. Studio space and lighting was the problem for the painters, while Tuck Langland struggled for years to obtain off-campus facilities suitable for casting bronze. University architects in Bloomington had difficulty understanding why Larkin needed reinforced flooring for heavy presses and lithography stones. Money to pay models was a constant concern.

Students at IU South Bend during the 1960s and '70s were all commuters and most of them worked, many of them full time. A large number of the traditional age students in their late teens and early twenties were the first from their families to attend college, and they were joined by substantial numbers of mature students in their thirties, forties and fifties. All faculty members recall that there were never any problems with the wide age range among the students in their studios. Zisla in particular, who began his own career in industrial design, sought to help younger students to develop skills which might prove helpful in finding employment. The department had no difficulty attracting students for either lecture or studio classes, and in fact often faced a shortage of studio space. A good number of fine arts students, particularly the more mature, were more interested in learning to improve their skills for painting and sculpture than they were in completing a bachelor's degree. Although all the faculty members believed firmly in the importance of drawing the figure, they carefully avoided any pressure on students to produce figurative work. Zisla's own painting, in fact, became increasingly abstract.

Students remember a friendly and open relationship with the faculty and with one another. Unlike the students in majors which emphasize lectures, laboratories, and written assignments, fine arts students work chiefly in studio classes. Their classes sometimes run as long as three hours, and of necessity they can view one another's work in progress. Faculty move from student to student, making comments and suggestions, and students to make comments and suggestions to their fellow students. In most university classes students speak rarely, most often to ask or to answer a question of their teacher. Such limits apply in an art history class, but not in the studio. At the end of the semester, art students joined to clean the studio and to celebrate afterwards that their work was done. As one student from the mid-1970s remembers, fine arts at IU South Bend was "a strong, solid program." It was not always entirely serious, however. On at least one occasion, a nude female model streaked across the room during an art appreciation lecture. The large class, mostly young freshmen, were at first startled and then broke out with cheers.

Although the faculty artists at IU South Bend each exhibited their work from time to time, the absence of gallery space on campus until the early 2000s limited their opportunities. On two occasions they exhibited jointly off-campus. Their first show appeared at the South Bend Art Center in 1973, called *Artist and Model: Three Views*, featuring portraits of one another and their wives. In 1980-1981 the enlarged department featured *Four Figurative Artists*, a traveling exhibit of forty works displayed at five galleries in Indiana and Michigan. There is no photographic record of either exhibit, but the Indiana Arts Commission sponsored a booklet called *Four Figurative Artists* that includes eight full-color illustrations.

Over the years the department employed a number of part-time and full-time art history teachers, but not until the arrival of Benjamin Withers in 1994 did anyone remain long enough to achieve tenure. Withers had just completed his PhD at the University of Chicago and IU South Bend was his first teaching position. Zisla and Langland also taught art history classes. A full time faculty position in graphic design was added in 1997, with the appointment of Karen Ackoff. She holds an MFA from the Rochester Institute of Technology and before coming to IU South Bend taught at the University of the Arts in Philadelphia and worked for ten years as a scientific illustrator at the Smithsonian Institution in Washington. Courses in photography were becoming more popular with students, but not until the appointment of Susan Moore in 2003 was there a full-time professor of photography.

The Department of Fine Arts was organized as an academic department with Harold Zisla as chairman in 1968, within what was then called the Division (now the College) of Liberal Arts and Sciences. The department could now award a bachelor of arts degree with a major in fine arts, a traditional liberal arts program with extensive general educations requirements. A campus reorganization in the spring of 1990 created the Division of the Arts, bringing together fine arts, music, speech and theater, under the leadership of Dean Robert Demaree. The existing departmental structure was eliminated, although there was no change in course numbers or course titles. Art appreciation, for example, was still called FINA H100. After several years of discussion, university and state officials finally authorized IU South Bend to award the bachelor of fine arts degree in 1994. This permitted students to take more credit-hours for studio work and diminished the general education requirements. The BFA degree quickly became more popular among IU South Bend students, because it offered better preparation for a career in fine arts, as well as admission to graduate programs leading to the master of fine arts degree at IU Bloomington and other large campuses. Students interested in art history continue to enroll in the traditional BA program.

Although no longer an academic department, fine arts remains a vital program at IU South Bend, within what is now (2014) known as the Ernestine M. Raclin School of the Arts. The program has grown beyond its early emphasis upon painting and sculpture, but most of its students still follow the centuries-old tradition of beginning their study of art by drawing the human figure from life. Students from all of the fine arts programs as well as students from many other majors in Liberal Arts and Sciences and the School of the Arts continue to study art history, ranging from ancient Egypt and China, through classical Greece and Rome, medieval Europe and the Renaissance into the incredible varieties of modern and post-modern art on a global scope. International study is becoming more popular among IU South Bend students, among them growing numbers of fine arts majors. With the completion of the Arts and Education Building in 2013, the fine arts program at IU South Bend now at long last has adequate studio space and ample gallery facilities for exhibits featuring its own students and faculty.

Northern Indiana Artists

Jim Ferm

The core of the group of professional artists who formed Northern Indiana Artists, Inc. (NIA) in 1942 was made up of members of the Midland Academy of Art. They met in a gallery above the Makielski Art Shop, 117 North Main Street, South Bend. This nucleus and other interested artists in the area became the thirty-four charter members. A clipping from the March 14, 1942, *South Bend Tribune* announced the beginning of NIA.

Wilber West was elected president at a subsequent meeting in the home of Mrs. W. A. Butcher, 802 South Ironwood Drive. Other officers were Lester Swartz, secretary; John Bednar, CSC, chairman of the board of directors; and Herbert Trottnow, Mrs. Charles H. Bulloch, and Mrs. John C. Lavengood, directors. Northern Indiana Artists was chosen as the name for the group, whose objective was to promote exhibitions and artwork in the city.

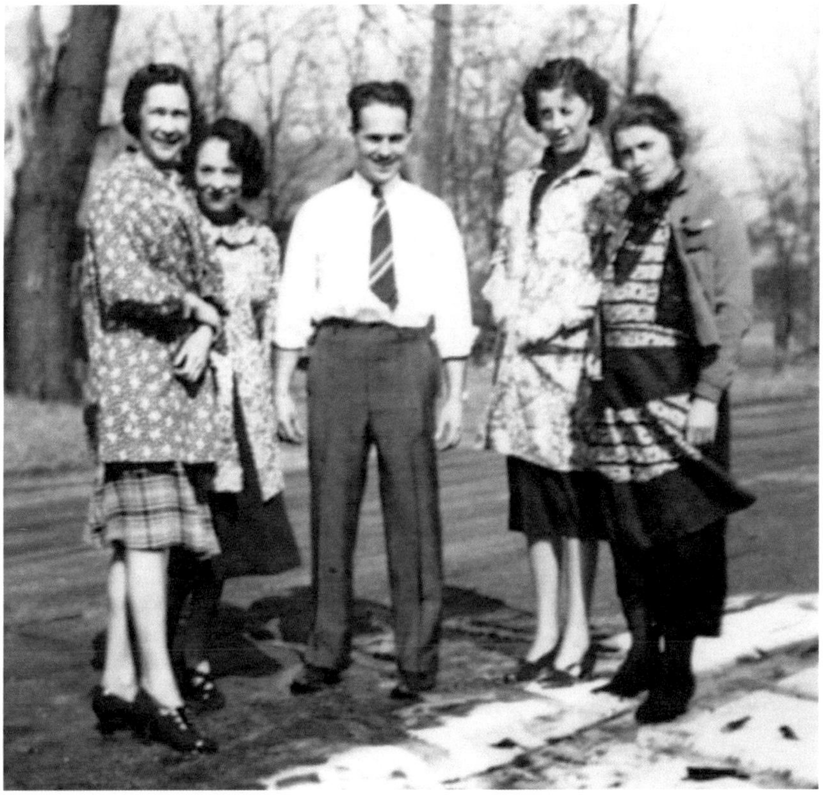

Wilber West was an art teacher at Riley High School and later became the head of the department of design at Kent State University in Ohio. Later still he was the head of the art department at Cornell College in Mount Vernon, Iowa, from which he retired in 1974. He returned to South Bend after retirement.

NIA held an exhibit at the Progress Club in May 1942 at which all thirty-four charter members exhibited. The group exhibited three more times at the Progress Club in the 1940s, as well as five times in the Mezzanine Galleries of the Oliver Hotel and three times in the YMCA. The Oliver Hotel was the site of many NIA exhibitions over the years. The last show there was in November 1956.

South Bend Tribune photo: Core artists of Midland Academy and charter members of Northern Indiana Artists: from left to right; Beatrice Hartig Zimmerman, Inez Walker, Lester Swartz, Harriet Monteith, and Theodora Makielski.

In 1952, ten years after that first meeting in the Makielski gallery, three NIA members organized an art school in the "barn" of Doctors Gordon and Gladys Frith at 501 West Washington Avenue. The organizers were H. Stanford Barret, Zygmund Jankowski, and Edward Basker. Other NIA members joined these three, and the Barn School flourished for several years. It closed when many instructors left to teach at the newly organized South Bend Art Association.

The *Tribune* carried an article on June 27, 1982, that celebrated NIA's fortieth year and perfectly defined the organization.

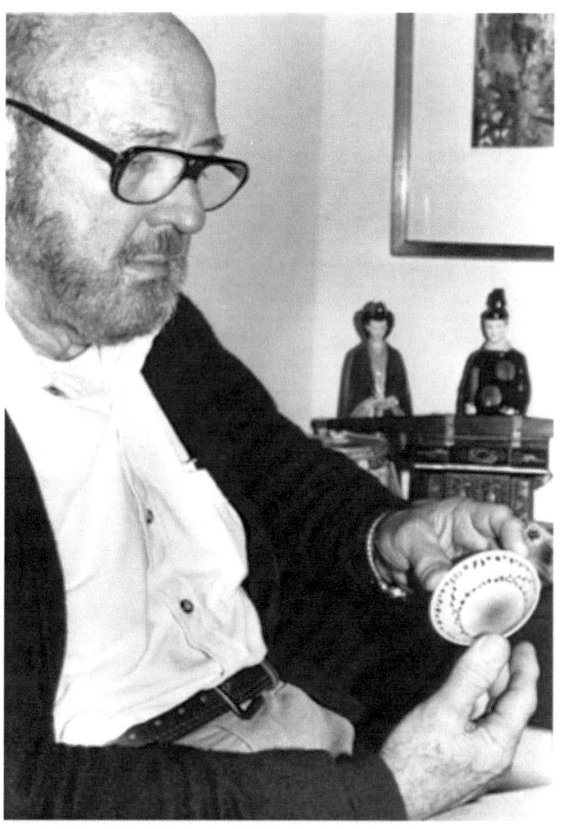

Wilbur West, first Northern Indiana Artists president, carefully displays a blue ceramic dish he entered in an international competition show in Alfred, New York, in 1933.

"Pioneer South Bend 'Artists Colony' Starting Fifth Decade"
Linda Bloom, *South Bend Tribune*

There was a time, older artists in the area recall, when anyone who took art seriously, especially as a career was considered an oddball by the general public. These were the days before art leagues and government endowments, before the South Bend Art Center and the numerous art galleries that have sprung up throughout Michiana.

For the most part, artists were still categorized as Bohemians who spent much time starving in a garret somewhere in Paris.

"Art wasn't promoted in the way it's been promoted since the Second World War," said Wilbur West about that time in the early 1940s. "The artists still were suffering from stigma. You couldn't be an artist and live in a community like any other family did."

Yet there were artists in the South Bend community longing for company and support. So, in 1942 they banded together to form Northern Indiana Artists and named West as their first president. This year, the NIA is celebrating its 40th anniversary. The annual NIA exhibit opens today in Century Center.

West pinpoints the Makielski Art Shop at 117 N. Main as the original meeting place for what would become the NIA. Theodora Makielski, he explained, would introduce the artists to each other. "Teddy was always interested in meeting the artists and having them come in," he added.

West, who was a Riley High School art teacher at the time, joined some other artists on outings to paint together. The group soon decided to organize. "At the outset, there were only a few of us ... who got it started," he said. There was a desire on the part of those people to have a group of people with whom they could talk and communicate about art.

According to its constitution, the purpose of the NIA, which was incorporated in 1944, is "to promote contemporary creative art, to raise the quality of work produced and the art standards of our community, to sponsor exhibits of members' work and to hold meetings of members for mutual benefit gained through discussion, lectures, workshops, inspirational seminars and social contacts."

Selection of members was and continues to be through the use of a jury. The juries, which are held in spring and fall, inspect three or more paintings of a prospective member and decide whether the artist qualifies for membership. Those who do not pass can become associate members and try again later.

Bea Hartig Zimmerman remembered the original members being social companions as well as colleagues in art. "We used to have potlucks on Sundays and visit each other's houses," she said.

Mrs. Zimmerman, her sister, Geni Hartig Toth, and their father, Arthur Hartig, all were charter members of Northern Indiana Artists. Both women, following in their father's footsteps, had been painting since their teens and continue to do so today, although Mrs. Toth is no longer a member.

Many of the 34 original members are no longer living. A few former members either live out of town or are no longer active in the group. Ed Reasor, for example, joined the NIA because he saw it as a way to continue his art training after high school. He left the group to attend Indiana University, became an art teacher and was co-founder of the Indiana Art Education Association.

West left the organization in 1945 when he moved to Kent State University to head the department of design there. Later he was head of the art department of Cornell College in Mount Vernon, Ohio, where he retired in 1974 because of health problems. West is now back in South Bend and hopes to get involved in the arts community here again.

In addition to exhibits, NIA sponsored other activities, such as the Beaux Arts costume ball, which began in the 1950s. Violet Petersen, who was NIA president in 1956, helped plan these balls. Members dressed up and drove through town in convertibles to advertise the dance. The balls were not necessarily fund-raisers. "They were more to get people involved in the arts," Mrs. Peterson recalled. "[Art] was not a popular thing. We couldn't get anybody to pay attention to us." Around that time, the NIA also sponsored "art marts" to gain visibility. "The art fairs were simply a means of getting your work out and selling it," Mrs. Petersen said.

Drs. Gordon and Gladys Frith became involved in painting and the NIA when Violet Peterson and several other artists asked if they could use the couple's property as a meeting place. "They found we had a loft in our garage that had a lot of space in it," Frith said. Then the artists insisted that the

Friths take lessons. "We started dabbling and enjoyed it and just kept it up for a number of years," Gordon Frith said. He added that Stan Barrett, a Notre Dame instructor, was especially helpful to them.

Mrs. Petersen, who started painting seriously in 1950 "when I saw the work of Zygmund Jankowski and Steve Glovna," gradually stopped painting after returning to work as a guidance counselor at Clay Middle School. She retired in 1979.

Gladys Frith, a clinical psychologist with the South Bend school system, gave up painting because of a hip malady. Her husband, Gordon, a retired physician, put down the brush in favor of lapidary, the cutting and polishing of semiprecious stones, in 1980. Several of his paintings adorn the walls at St. Paul's Retirement Community.

Today's NIA consists of about 130 members of all age groups. The organization continues to have occasional potlucks and bus trips, as well as maintaining the discussion meetings mentioned in the original purpose. "We have artists come in and give demonstrations and lectures—both from the group and outsiders."

The Northern Indiana Artists have exhibited at least seventy times before this article was written in 2012. NIA held only one exhibit per year from 1977 to 1991. We shared the Warner Gallery with the St. Joe Valley Watercolor Society those years and had some great shows. Many of our members were also Watercolor Society members in that era, as is true today.

Personal note:

I was elected president in 1991 and the following year I presided over NIA's next milestone. For our 50th anniversary, we asked for extra space at the yearly combined show in the Warner Gallery to permit a retrospective show of charter members. We were given a nice space that we were able to fill with art loaned by friends and relatives of charter members, as well as by some charter members themselves who were still living. We asked the charter members to attend the reception if possible, and we gave corsages to those who did to identify them. I can remember only two of the seven original members that made the reception. Wilber West was in a wheelchair. Genevieve Hartig-Toth was spry and her mind was sharp.

The same year, NIA opened a "Christmas" store in a vacant space at Scottsdale Mall. We called the store "NIA Artworks." Utilities were provided, and the rent was a small percentage of sales. The store was so successful we opened one the following year.

We have exhibited in many venues and enjoyed many informational presentations through the years. The organization has fostered many endearing friendships and enhanced the careers of countless members. NIA is strong today, and I believe it will remain so in the future. Those charter members created something precious.

The club meets the second Sunday in January, March, September, and November. A social get-to-gather is usually scheduled in May. For more information visit our website, nia-art.org.

The NIA mission statement:

Northern Indiana Artists, Inc. (NIA) is a non-profit organization dedicated to the promotion of contemporary creative art. The NIA strives to raise the quality of work produced and the standards of the community.

NIA has been active in Michiana for over seventy years. Its membership is composed of area artists who have passed an independent jury process.

NIA sponsors exhibits of members' works and holds meetings for the mutual benefit gained through discussion, lectures, inspiration, scholarships and social contacts. NIA awards scholarships to deserving and emerging artists.

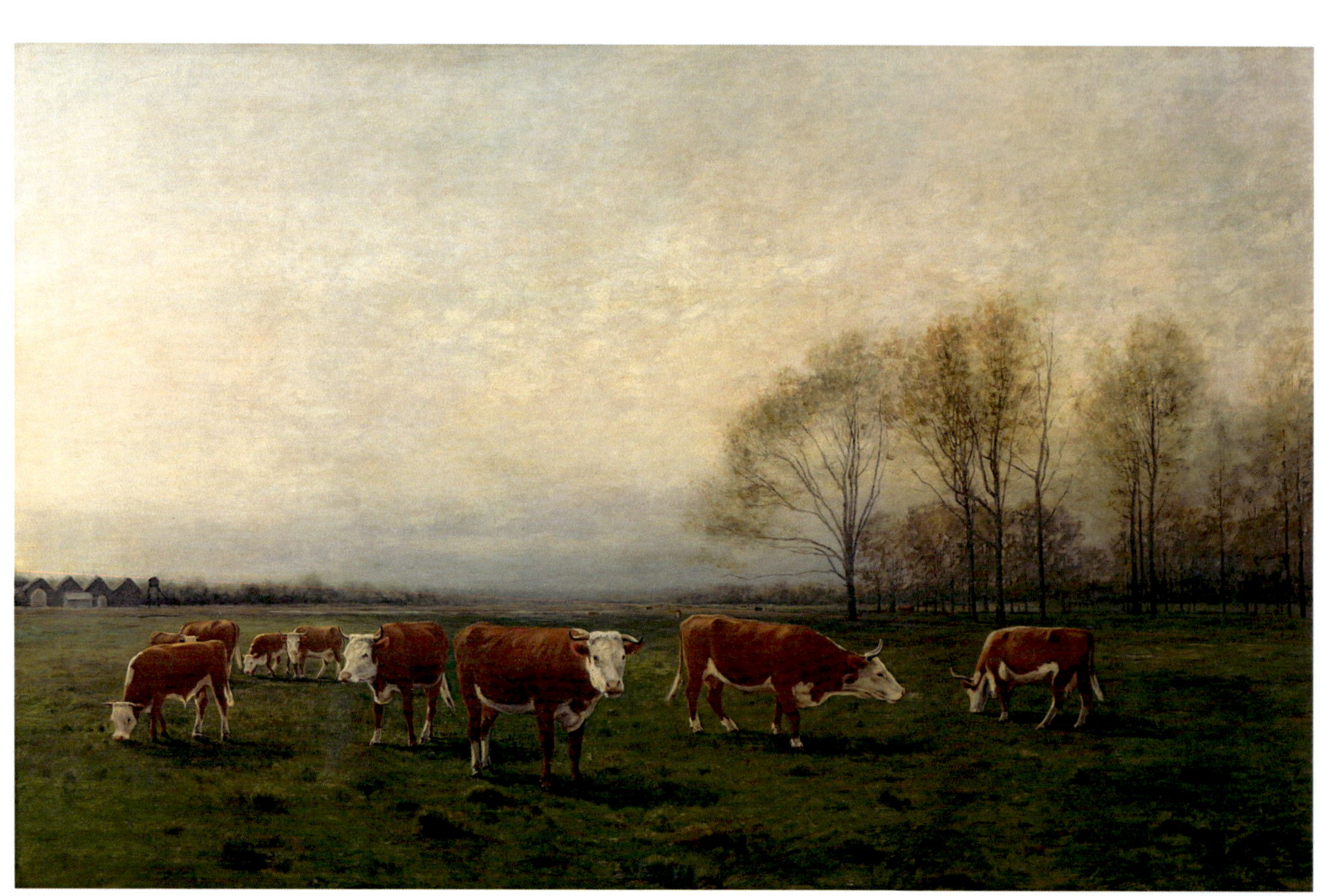

The Midwest Museum of American Art

Brian Byrn

The history of the Midwest Museum of American Art begins with the building's previous owners. The St. Joseph Valley Bank in Elkhart had grown through mergers by the time it was decided to build its newest and grandest facility in 1922. The building was designed and constructed by Johnson Brothers, as one of the building's cornerstones indicates. The St. Joseph Valley Bank made 429 South Main Street its home for the next fifty-three years under the leadership of such men as John W. Fieldhouse, C.D. Greenleaf, Clarence Ziesel, and Lewis Armstrong.

The facade of the bank, with its Corinthian columns and neoclassical style of architecture, has remained virtually unchanged. In 1959, Wiley and Associates contracted to redesign the building's interior and add more space to its north and west sides. Perhaps it was at this time that the turret used to support the Gatling gun, which was employed for security in the 1930s, was removed so that the roof could be extended over the new office spaces. Legend has it that even the bank president's office housed a shotgun just above the 1922 state-of-the-art vault. John Dillinger remained an ever-present threat in the minds of the employees throughout this time period. The vault's unique design was taken seriously and insured that this safe could not be cracked.

Inside, the ceiling was lowered to add more efficiency to the structure's heating and air conditioning. The magnificent gilded moldings and ornate wrought-iron skylight (which reflected a Louis H. Sullivan influence) were covered over and seen no more. Instead they were replaced with two modern architectural domes that today add to the mystique of the museum's main gallery. On either end of this grand hall, the walls gently curve down to an undulating edge of a lower ceiling. Continuously formed fluorescent lighting placed both inside the domes and running along the edge of the curving portion illuminate the ceiling with a quiet elegance.

In 1973, the St. Joseph Valley Bank had outgrown its renovated facilities. As Lewis Armstrong retired after 38 years, the bank moved to the opposite corner of the block in a modern structure designed by the architectural firm of Skidmore, Owings, and Merrill. The retired building that once held great assets was sold to a South Bend industrialist named C. J. Wood. The building sat empty from 1974 to 1978 and Wood eventually planned to sell it to the City of Elkhart to be torn down and replaced with a parking lot.

Except for a brief stint in 1976, when the building was used for Republican Headquarters, it sat unnoticed until two Elkhart citizens came forward with a dream—and a plan.

Dr. Richard D. and Jane Burns had been residents of Elkhart for ten years by the time they found the St. Joseph Bank building. They had chosen Elkhart as the community to start a new orthodontic practice while Dr. Burns was finishing his stint in the air force, stationed in Japan. Starting in 1968 through 1978, Dick and Jane Burns acquired a modest collection of American art—modest only in terms of numbers, and then only when

---

Daniel Kotz, *Studebaker Farm.*

compared to collectors such as the Gettys, Hearsts, and Chryslers, whom they often bid against at auctions. Important works by Burchfield, Rothko, Pollock, De Kooning, Hartigan, Reid, Blakelock, and Rockwell were acquired and eventually brought to Elkhart and exhibited at the museum. Some of these works formed the core of today's permanent collection.

The Burns's personal art collection was one of extreme quality and engendered deep personal satisfaction. The couple enjoyed collecting art with their family of four children in mind and with philanthropy as a guiding force. The collection became their passion to share with friends and a broader public. Collecting American paintings and sculpture was never intended to be an ego boost, nor was their eventual dream of founding a museum characterized as an ode to vanity. The Burns family tended toward the educational. When they settled on American art as a main theme, it was due primarily to the lack of interest shown by most institutions and other collectors of the day.

The Burnses began to travel to New York and Chicago and all points in between to visit auctions and museums. They saw great success for public institutions in larger cities and felt that a similar situation could arise in a town of, then, 41,000. Their dream arose from a want and a need to provide a similar experience for their community as well as to share with the public the educational values and expressive nature of an American fine art heritage to include works by artists from the golden age of American illustration.

In 1978, Dr. Richard D. and Jane Burns, after some discussion with friends and associates, formed the Midwest Museum of American Art Foundation, a not-for-profit, 501(c)(3), public trust. The Board of Trustees became the governing body over the institution, establishing the policies and mission of the museum. The building was securely purchased and interior renovation began. One year was the time-frame given to complete gallery facilities, hire professional staff and begin programming—one year before the institution would take its place among the ranks of the Indiana's finest public museums and become its premier museum of American art.

The task was not impossible one, but if it had not been for the organizational prowess of Dr. and Mrs. Burns and the commitment to the idea of an American art museum by a newly appointed advisory board, perhaps the dream would have failed. Charter members who became Society of Associates members came forward with contributions. One of the first benefactors of the Midwest Museum of American Art was Dorothy Greenleaf Boynton, daughter of the former bank president C. D. Greenleaf. Today, one of the main floor galleries is named in her memory. Another of the museum's first supporters, Barbara McClelland Kirk, was a woman of boundless energies and enthusiasm for the institution. The second floor gallery (renovated in 1984) bears her name as a memorial from friends and family as her final bequest. Carolyn Keefe of Houston, Texas, came forward (in the 1990s) donating monies to secure to galleries in honor of her parents, the late Mary Jane Parmater (Keefe) and Paul D. Keefe. And most recently contributions were secured from the late Pat Warner to commemorate her memory and that of her late husband, Russell Warner.

As for donations of art, the museum received its first major gift from Mr. and Mrs.

William E. Fackert, Jr. Fifteen pastel drawings and one oil by the Indiana artist Glen Cooper Henshaw remain the core of the Midwest Museum's interest in early artists from Indiana. The Fackerts, like so many of the charter members, remained ardent supporters throughout their lives.

May 5, 1979 was the inaugural opening of the Midwest Museum of American Art. The renovation was complete and the new interior boasted five galleries that would host a myriad of traveling exhibitions for the next two years. The museum became a crossroads of exhibits from the Smithsonian Institution traveling west, as well as exhibits from the Western Association of Art Museums going east. The value of these brief "stop-overs" ranged in the millions. The Midwest Museum was off to a running start with exhibits changing monthly, Sunday afternoon concerts, children's and adult classes, lectures, films, and performances. The "dream" had become a reality.

Five full-time staff members were hired as the first director, Mark Meister, came on line from Ann Arbor, Michigan. Michael Flannagan was hired as curator of exhibitions. Karen Karmel was hired as curator of education. Two other administrative assistants were hired as well. This staff changed temporary or traveling exhibits monthly, with little attention given to a permanent collection. Slowly though, a collection began to form with work donated or placed on extended loan. These pieces were generally shown in the small "vault" gallery on the west end of the Main Gallery (Richard D. & Jane Burns Gallery). As time progressed, the curators moved on to other positions—Flannagan at Northern Illinois University's Swen Parson Galleries, and Karmel at the Toledo Museum of Art. Eventually too, the director moved on, leaving an assistant curator and an administrative assistant to run the museum. This inadequacy in staffing resulted in Jane Burns, a founding trustee, stepping in as a caretaker to the directorship while the board searched for a replacement.

Unfortunately, in 1981 the economic outlook was dim due to a national recession and a replacement was not found, so Mrs. Burns stayed on as acting director. In October of that year, she met a young artist just beginning his career. Brian Byrn was a graduate of Indiana University who had moved to Elkhart in May from Southern Indiana. His BA in Fine Arts degree along with his real-world working experience caught her eye as she read his résumé, found in a file after he dropped it off in hopes of finding a volunteer position. The attention paid to Byrn was furthered by his winning the Best of Show award in the 3rd Elkhart Juried Regional competition. It seemed to be the right match, and Byrn was hired as Curator of Exhibitions & Education—a position he has retained for thirty years. Mrs. Burns too stayed on for thirty years as director, and together they developed many important programs and exhibits for the public.

Burns and Byrn were joined over the years by several administrative assistants that included Trudy Basquin (eight years), emerging from the ranks of charter docents, and Martha Culp (a retired banker), who worked for fourteen years as administrative assistant. It is noteworthy that outside of their accumulative experience, both director and curator went on to further educate themselves. Jane Burns graduated from Goshen College in 1990 with a degree in business and a major in marketing. Brian

Byrn, while sent by the director continually to professional workshops on conservation, museum education and grants writing, finished a master's degree in education in 1996 from Indiana University South Bend that emphasized art. Most recently Stacy Jordan, another IU grad and former intern, joined the staff as assistant curator, providing important technical support to the institution's website and other digital maintenance.

The museum staff has created a sound foundation of changing exhibits, educational programs, a docent program, public outreach, an outstandingly successful annual competition, and a continually-growing permanent collection of now over 3,000 works in all media. In addition, the temporary exhibitions created or managed by the team of director and curator resulted in many instances of national recognition. Some of these exhibits included *Behind the Lens, The Photographs of Linda McCartney*, a major exhibit of Ansel Adams photography, Norman Rockwell paintings and drawings, cross-cultural materials such as Roy Rogers/Dale Evans memorabilia, and even *The Art of Antique Toys*. Exhibits from the Smithsonian and other traveling shows continued to pass through the museum galleries until to date they have exceeded two hundred. Thousands of visitors have participated in viewing these exhibitions and taking in the educational programming created for them.

Today, the Midwest Museum passes its thirty-fourth anniversary with great hope that the future will shine as brightly as the steel vault door that still adorns the main gallery. While the round steel portal tells the story of a time of a different kind of prosperity in the magnificently restored building, the permanent collection of the Midwest Museum of over 3,000 objects prospers with approximately 850 works of art on display on any given day, plus an American coin collection of 4,000 pieces. With the seeds planted by citizens of Elkhart, the collection as a whole has been formed by more than 400 sources from across America and represents approximately 800 artists over a 180-year period (1830-2012).

The Midwest Museum of American Art continues to be an important asset to the community and the state of Indiana as it defines what is now called the Arts & Entertainment district of downtown Elkhart. With the restoration of the Lerner Theater, downtown Elkhart has become a destination of culture for the people of Michiana and all those who visit it from afar.

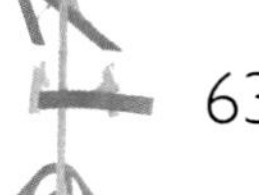

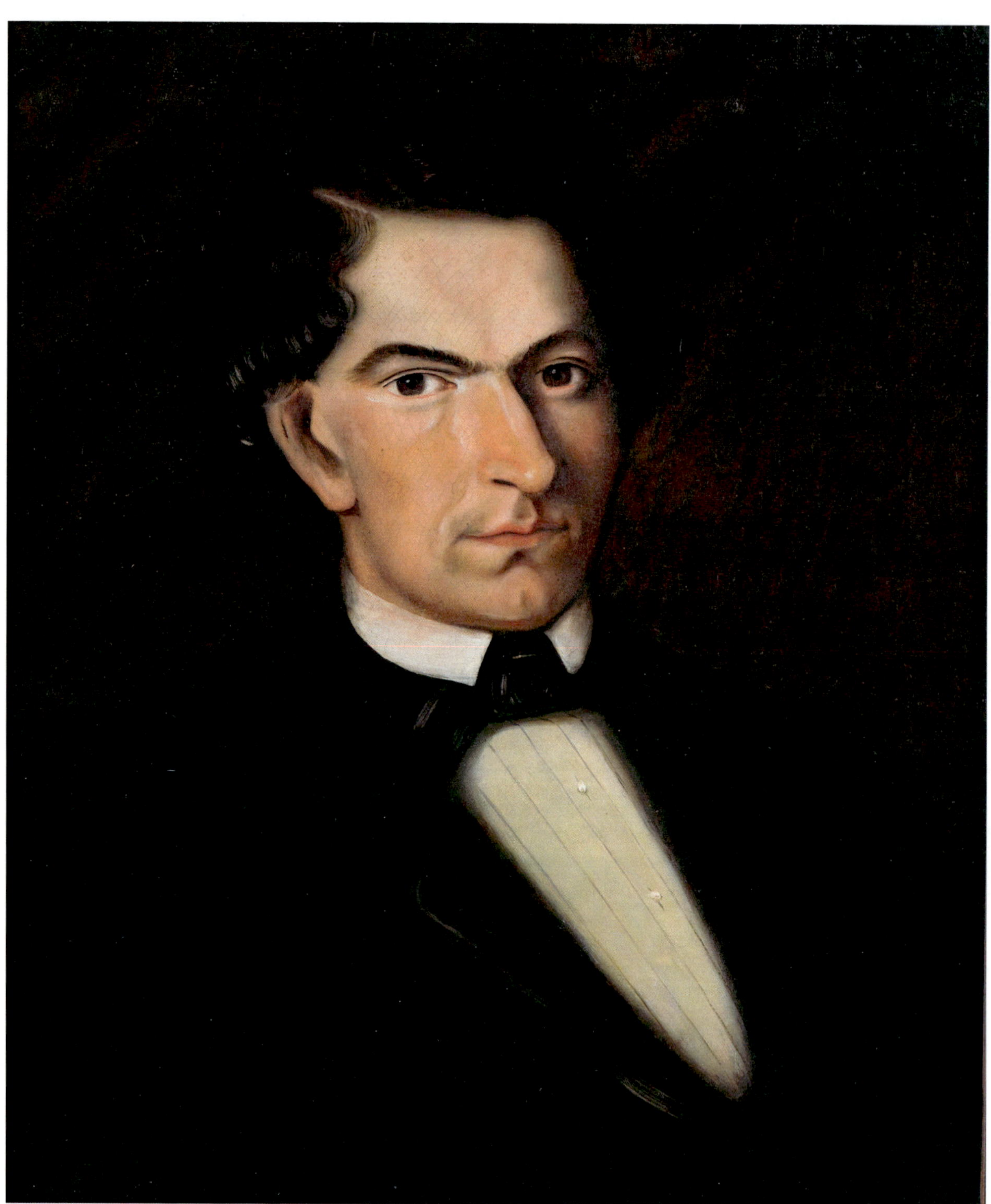

South Bend Museum of Art: A Brief History, 1947–2000

Susan Visser

The South Bend Museum of Art (originally known as the South Bend Art Association and subsequently as the South Bend Art Center and the South Bend Regional Museum of Art; called "the museum" for this essay) has provided cultural leadership in the South Bend/Mishawaka community since 1947. A community art museum had been the long-time dream of Carlotta Banta, a local kindergarten teacher. Miss Banta gave the first signs of life to a museum through her will, in which she requested that her life savings be used to build an art center. Although her bequest was contested in the courts and the designated funds were not used to establish a museum, Banta's wishes provided the impetus for other sympathetic community leaders to help realize her dream. In 1947, two years after her death, the South Bend Art Association was created.

The second floor of a local school and the carriage house of Tippecanoe Place, a historic mansion, were used for the purposes of the newly founded organization. The museum had its official opening on February 10, 1948. A month later, Mr. and Mrs. E. M. Morris donated an art gallery, located in the mansion itself, to the museum. It was an intimate gallery designed to show the works of Indiana artists. Mr. and Mrs. Morris also donated their collection of works by Indiana artists, which formed the basis of the museum's permanent collection.

Over one hundred students enrolled for the first session of art classes, and the museum's growth accelerated as more people became involved in its life. Over time, the activities were adjusted, shaped and altered to fit the needs of the community. In the late 1950s it was evident that the growth of the museum required an expansion program. The demand was for an enlarged and enriched program in the visual arts. In June 1962, a disastrous fire, which left the carriage house charred beyond repair, ended the hopes of expansion. In September 1962, the museum relocated to a former YWCA building. It was thought to be a temporary home, for the board hoped to soon erect a new building specifically designed for art activities. The museum remained there until 1978. During this time, the museum's programs and community involvement continued to grow.

The Art League, a support group established with the purpose of increasing "the effectiveness of the [museum] in its work of developing an appreciation of the visual arts within the community" was established in 1969. Over the years the Art League provided invaluable volunteer support for the museum and, later, began raising monies to support museum exhibitions, educational programs and additions to the permanent collection. The Art League continued its important work into 2000.

The museum's tradition of hosting biennial exhibitions—competitions featuring the work of local or regional contemporary artists—was started in the 1960s. Although the format of the biennials changed from time to time over the years, these exhibitions were always strong and served to support the efforts of the regional artists' community. They were also a primary source through

---

Anonymous, *Portrait of Adolphus Eberhart.*

which the museum was able to build its permanent collection. By way of community solicitations and, later, through the generosity of the Art League, annual purchases were funded. For this reason the museum's collection is a fine document of local and regional art through the years.

Collection growth has been also supported through gifts to the collection and through memorial contributions. In 1993 the Harold Zisla Acquisition Fund was founded by friends of Mr. Zisla to honor his tenure as executive director of the museum from the mid-1950s through mid-1960s, as well as his contributions as a professor of art at Indiana University South Bend. The focus of the Zisla Fund was the purchase of works by artists from Indiana and Michigan. This fund grew steadily through contributions in honor of Mr. and Mrs. Zisla and became an excellent source of funds for acquiring the work of significant local artists.

In the early 1970s the museum was offered an opportunity to have a new facility of its own. A downtown center was proposed that would function as an arts and convention complex and would house not only the museum, but also a performing arts theater, the offices of the local arts council, and a branch of the Studebaker National Museum. The construction of the cultural/convention complex, to be called Century Center, was funded with a combination of private and public resources. The City of South Bend made a commitment to the museum to pay for the annual costs associated with occupying its space in the new building, including maintenance and utilities. The museum undertook a successful fundraising campaign to fully equip the new facility. In 1978 the building was completed and the museum moved into its new home. The museum's 32,000 square feet in Century Center would allow allowed for expanded programming and gave the institution a more prominent community role in presenting a full range of educational programs in the visual arts.

The inaugural exhibition for the museum's new space in Century Center opened on January 14, 1978. The exhibition, *European Paintings from the Collection of Richard S. Zeisler*, featured an outstanding selection of works on paper on loan from a New York collector. The works ranged in date from 1916 to 1972 and included such European luminaries as Picasso, Delaunay, Dubuffet, and Miro. As stated by Andrew W. Nickle, then President of the museum's Board of Trustees, "This exhibition of paintings from the personal collection of Richard S. Zeisler is intended to evidence a commitment our institution is making for the future."

In early 1977, the museum administration and board of trustees teamed up with the Century Center board of managers to appoint a community committee to explore the idea of placing a kinetic sculpture on a cement pad in the river adjacent to the Century Center complex. Thus, the Art in Public Places Committee was formed. Working with staff members of the Michiana Arts and Science Council, museum staff members submitted a grant to the National Endowment for the Arts. NEA funding as well as local grants from the Clark and Muessel-Ellison Foundations and private contributions made it possible for the Committee to move forward with the sculpture commission. The artist Mark di Suvero was selected. The work he created for the site, *Keepers of the Fire*, was completed and installed in 1980 and still stands on the site, a major example of twentieth-century contemporary sculpture.

Two important school programs were also started in the 1970s: Museum Morning and the Docent Training Program, both collaborations with the Snite Museum of Art at Notre Dame, enabled fifth graders from South Bend, Mishawaka public and parochial schools to tour both museums in one morning. Fifty volunteers received ongoing training at both museums related to collections, exhibitions, and art history. Their primary task was to lead tours for the Museum Morning programs.

By the mid-1980s the museum had clearly defined its mission statement, which included the development of an awareness of the visual arts in South Bend through a focus on American art, especially regional contemporary art and historical Indiana art. The mission also acknowledged the museum's importance as an educational center through programs such as studio art classes, school and community outreach, and museum tours. In 1987 the museum achieved accreditation by the American Association of Museums.

In 1985 the museum embarked on another partnership with area schools, teachers, and students: *Scholastic Art Awards*, a national competition that recognized junior and senior high school student achievements in the visual arts. Started in 1923, the *National Scholastic Art Awards* program became the largest and oldest juried exhibition of its kind in the U.S. Works in the museum's regional exhibition represented students in grades 7-12 from seventeen surrounding counties in Indiana and Michigan. Award-winning work from regionals was sent to New York City for the nationals, where scholarships were awarded to the winners.

An exhibition of national significance in 1985 showcased the work of sculptor George Rickey. Rickey was born in South Bend in 1907—the son of a mechanical engineer who worked for Singer Sewing Machine Company. The exhibition, *George Rickey in South Bend*, was a partnership among the museum, the Snite Museum of Art at the University of Notre Dame, Saint Mary's College, and Indiana University South Bend. Large-scale sculptures by Rickey were placed throughout the community and on the campuses of the college and universities, enlivening the city. The project was a significant step in the museum's history of community collaborations.

Program expansion in the late 1980s and 1990s stressed accessibility, both within the museum's facility and in the community at large, and became particularly successful through collaborations with other institutions. In 1990 the event *Meet Me on the Island* was begun as a partnership with WVPE Public Radio and Century Center. The series was held on four Friday evenings during the summer and featured art exhibitions and jazz concerts on the island in the Saint Joseph River adjacent to the museum. Then, in 1998, the museum formed a partnership with the Center for the Homeless, offering an art component for its Starting Over/Stepping Higher program. Other community collaborations included community murals and annual Kwanzaa and Day of the Dead celebrations.

In keeping with the collecting, exhibiting, and educational focuses, and to reflect its AAM accreditation as a museum, the museum underwent a name change in 1992 to become the South Bend Regional Museum of Art. The museum's mission was revised in

1994 to better reflect its focus on public participation and inclusion.

A renovation and expansion completed in 1996 added 6,000 square feet to the museum facility, including a Permanent Collection gallery, improved retail space, and an entrance rotunda. Gallery and work spaces were also reconfigured to provide a better flow of space for the public and improved work areas for the staff. The construction, again funded by a combination of public and private funds, also provided a new gallery, The Crowley Community Gallery, which featured educational or didactic exhibitions and showcased local artists' groups.

The grand reopening of the museum's expanded and renovated spaces was celebrated on March 16, 1996 with the Warner Gallery exhibition, *The Intuitive Edge: Midwest Folk and Outsider Art*. The exhibition was organized by then Museum Curator, Leisa Rundquist, and showcased works by self-taught artists and traditional American arts. As stated by Susan Visser, Executive Director of the Museum at that time, "The works of these artists embody the sentiments of our country, our region. They speak of its people, its history, its cultural traditions, its struggles, its growth. We are proud to share this body of work with our regional audience."

In its most ambitious partnership to date, the museum hosted the exhibition, *Imagining the World Through Naive Painting*, from March 27 to May 9, 1999. Organized and circulated by Meridien International, it featured naive paintings from 17 countries, including: Argentina, Brazil, Chile, Colombia, Costa Rica, Cuba, The Dominican Republic, Guatemala, Haiti, Honduras, Mexico, Nicaragua, Panama, Peru, Spain, Uruguay, and Venezuela. The exhibition would be the centerpiece for a celebration of Latino culture, which would include art, music, dance and food.

The museum convened a group of Latino community members as an advisory committee that was representative of the multiple Hispanic cultures existing in the community. The large scope of the project was made possible by a corporate partner, Memorial Hospital and Health System, which served as the major funding source and also participated in the planning process by assigning two staff members to the advisory committee.

In keeping with the missions of both the Regional Museum and Memorial Hospital, the intentions of this project were to convey and celebrate the rich traditions of the Hispanic community, demonstrate the variety of traditions within this community, and initiate a dialogue about the role of art in our everyday lives. Programming included the *Imagining the World* exhibition, two companion exhibitions and four events which that featured culture-specific food, dance and music. Community response to the celebration was overwhelmingly positive. The four events brought in audiences that had never before been to the museum.

In early 1999, the museum started work on a project, which would come to fruition in 2001 and would be the largest community collaboration ever undertaken by the museum. From March 4 through May 13, 2001, the Kurt and Tessye Simon Fund for Holocaust Remembrance and the museum would host an art exhibition entitled *Witness and Legacy: Contemporary Art about the Holocaust*. This collection of visual works would serve as a foundation for a united, community-wide remembrance of the Holocaust through the arts and humanities. Through these visual experiences, the artists and the audience would be compelled to understand how the Holocaust happened and what it has done to our humanity.

A steering committee composed of representatives from twenty organizations in the South Bend/Mishawaka area collaborated throughout 1999 and 2000 to create an exciting, powerful, community-wide event. Each organization would present an event particular to its discipline that would be accessible to youths and/or adults with lessons of prejudice awareness and the consequences of apathy in society. The varied platforms included history, art, drama, dance, film, symphonic and choral music, religious heritage, and broadcast media. The programs of *Witness & Legacy* and *In Unison* (the name of the overall collaboration) were developed with the intent to foster a deeper knowledge of the Holocaust, promote tolerance in the community, and encourage a greater understanding of our neighbors.

The years leading up to 2000 brought with them a chance to refine the museum's programs and its administrative process. The museum was awarded American Association of Museums re-accreditation in 1999. The process of re-accreditation focused museum board and staff members on the core values of the museum. It encouraged them to look forward and take measures to assure that the museum would remain strong and viable for future generations. Moving into the new millennium, the museum offered a broad portfolio of programs.

Exhibition programming provided opportunities for regional, emerging and established artists while also supporting area youth and artists' groups. The Art League Gallery presented four solo and two-person exhibitions by Midwest artists annually. In-house organized traveling and competitive shows in the Warner Gallery offered historical and contemporary exhibitions and introduced new and challenging art forms. In the Crowley Community Gallery the museum featured exhibitions that supported educational purposes or showed the work of local artists. The museum was interpreting exhibitions for visitors through brochures, catalogues, wall text, reading tables, gallery guides, tours, and hands-on and art-making areas.

Through its collecting program, the museum continued to conserve a rich visual arts heritage. The collection consisted of 900 works from the nineteenth century through the present and was dedicated to significant American artists and trends, especially from Indiana and the Midwest. The museum's historical work provided context to its contemporary exhibitions and provided a cornerstone for ongoing school tours. Works by Indiana and regional artists constituted approximately 750 of the 900 objects.

Teaching programs provided instruction in all artistic mediums for children, teens and adults. Five sessions of classes were offered annually. A faculty of area artists shared their passion and expertise with a wide range of students and created a sense of community, cultural dialogue, and peer group support.

The museum's strong school programs provided depth and supplemented classroom teaching for area schools. Sculpture Quest included a docent-led tour of the current featured exhibitions and a related hands-on art making activity and discussion. Museum Morning and the Docent Training Program continued to thrive and evolve.

Community outreach was equally strong. Starting Over, Stepping Higher continued to be a successful partnership with the Center for the Homeless. This daylong workshop provided guests from the center with the opportunity to make art, tour the exhibitions and explore new methods in looking at art. Meet Me on the Island was well established as a key community event and the museum sustained its support of the *Scholastic Art Awards*. Community art projects were pursued in the varied forms of murals, gardens and installations.

A solid base of support for the museum was in evidence at the turn of the twenty-first century. This included a growing financial base, member base, student enrollment, and community involvement, as well as its traditionally strong programs. The elements were aligned to assure that the museum would thrive, grow and sustain its important arts educational programs for generations to come.

Note: In 2008 the South Bend Regional Museum of Art changed its name to the South Bend Museum of Art.

Mark di Suvero, *Keepers of the Fire I.*

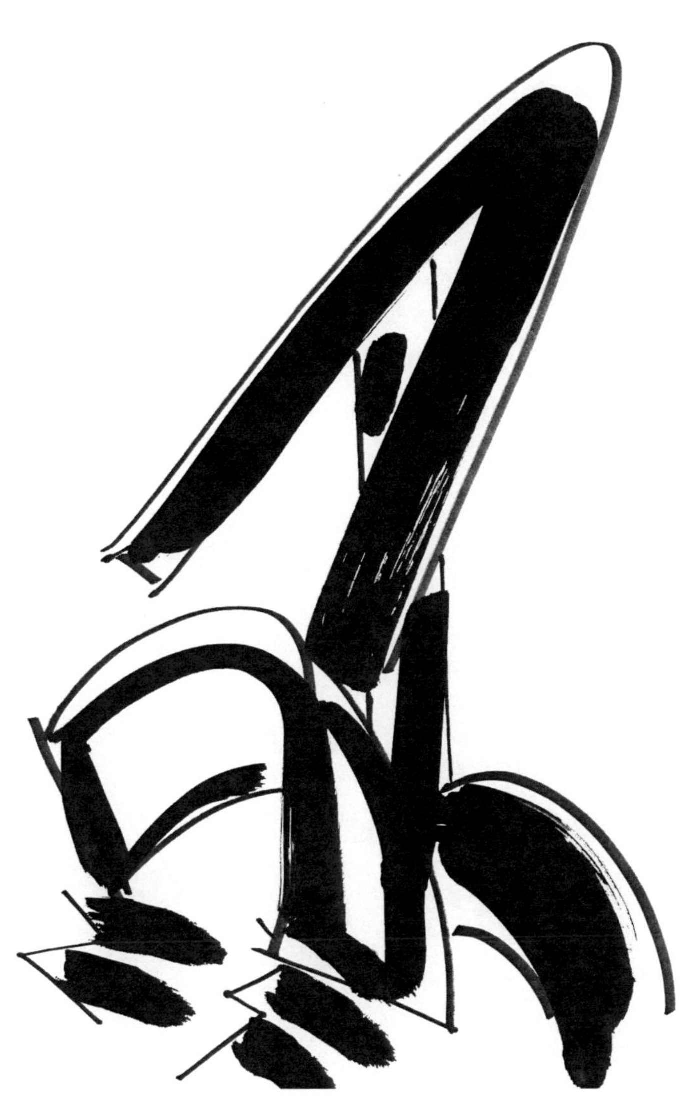

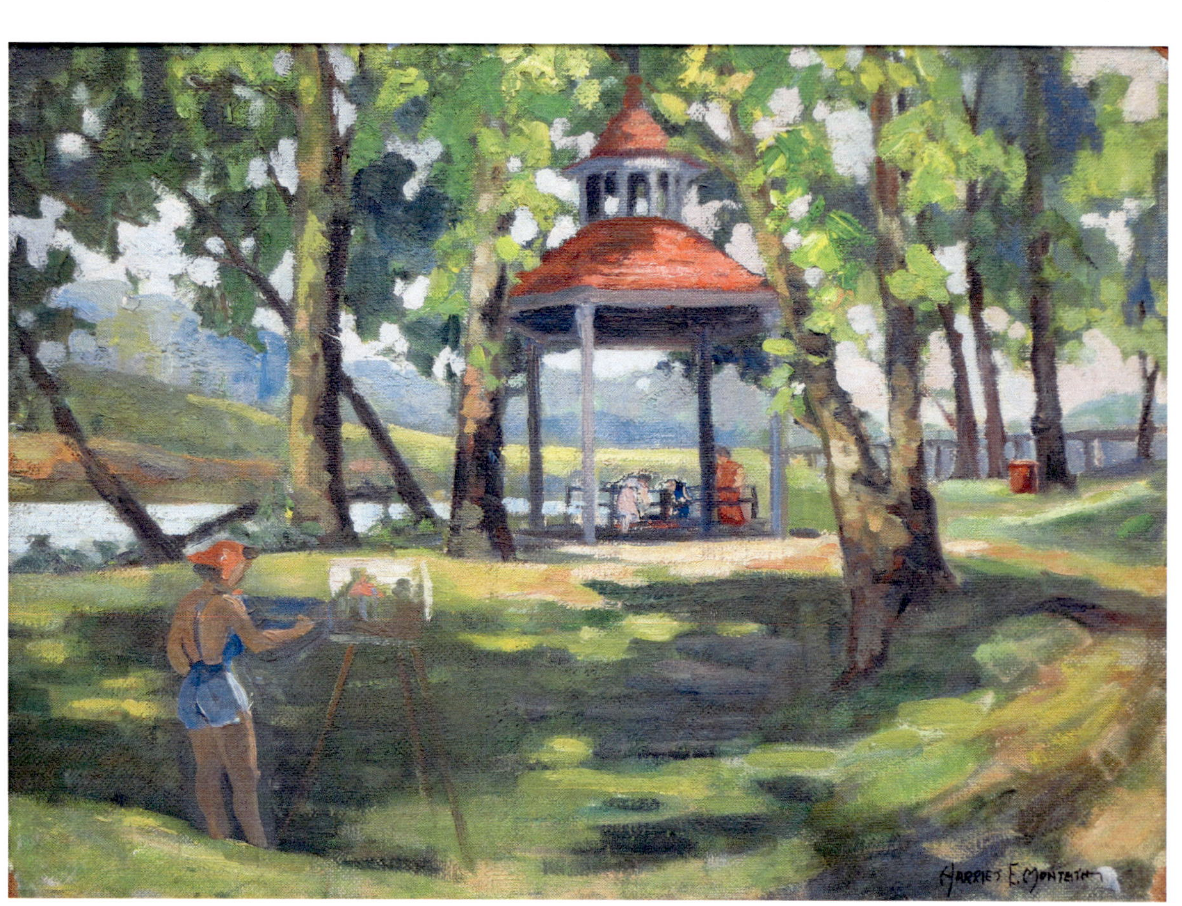
HARRIET E. MONTEITH

A Gallery of Artists

Harry Ahn was born in 1937 in Korea. He studied at the M.S.Harris Studio School of Art in Toronto and at the Shou-Ra-Bul College of Arts in Seoul, Korea. Ahn has shown many of his large-scale oil portraits across the globe and is a member of many organizations, including the International Art Club, the Northern Indiana Artists, Oil Painters of America, and the New York Society of Portrait Artists to name a few. Ahn taught at Andrews University.

George Ames Aldrich was a prolific painter of landscapes, perhaps best known for his paintings of Normandy and Brittany. Few facts have been verified about Aldrich's early years beyond being born on June 13, 1872, in Worcester, Massachusetts. He may have attended the Massachusetts Institute of Technology for architecture since its influence can often be seen in his work. However, it is known that he attended the Art Students League of New York before traveling Europe and studying at the Académie Julian as well as the Académie Colarossi and the American Academy at Rome. He painted many impressionistic scenes of rural French villages and rivers that very closely matched Norwegian artist Frits Thaulow's style, with whom Aldrich claimed to have studied. In 1917 he returned to America and took residence in Chicago where he displayed many of his works. The dunes along Lake Michigan in northern Indiana proved to be a regular destination for him and he soon gained a following in South Bend. From 1922 until 1926 he lived in the city and focused on the St. Joseph River and Juday Creek as his favorite subjects. Aldrich completed a few industrial scenes as well as settings in Chicago, one of which became a prizewinner in the 1929 Hoosier Salon exhibition. He remained in Chicago and continued to paint until his death in 1941 at age 68.

Harriet E. Monteith, *Painting at Island Park.*

David Edgar Allen was born in Terre Haute in 1950 and began painting at fifteen. Before too long, he found himself studying and drawing influence from Harold Zisla at Indiana University South Bend. Although Zisla's style wasn't quite realistic, Allen found himself creating realistic landscapes of the city of South Bend. He was particularly interested in the west side of the city and it was there that he focused on the most. The scenes were often painted at night and created a mysterious view of the area, but what was so important was that Allen often chose exceptionally ordinary scenes to portray—railroad tracks, blocks of houses—rather than the exquisitely beautiful or the decrepit. He also created linoleum block prints and abstract paintings, but was most known for the landscapes. In 2002, Allen was a co-founder of the Studio Arts Center where he taught drawing, painting, and making woodcut prints. Additionally he has taught at the South Bend Museum of Art, and managed the New Gallery. He currently resides in South Bend.

Janet Stewart Allen, born in 1904 in Mansfield, Ohio, came to South Bend as a girl and spent much of her life in the area. She began studying art while at Central High School and went on to study at several more schools including National Park College in Maryland, the Chicago Academy of Fine Arts and the School of Industrial Arts in Philadelphia. She

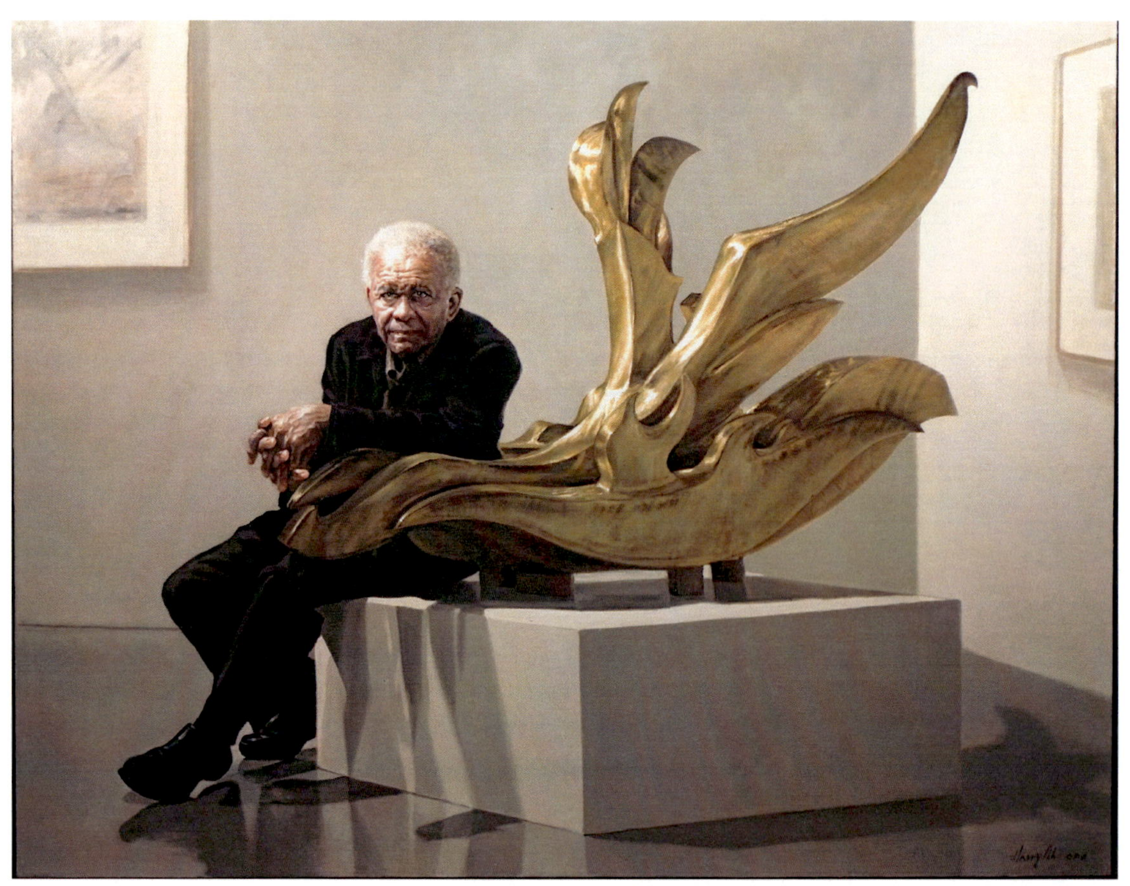

Harry Ahn, *The Sculptor Richard Hunt.*

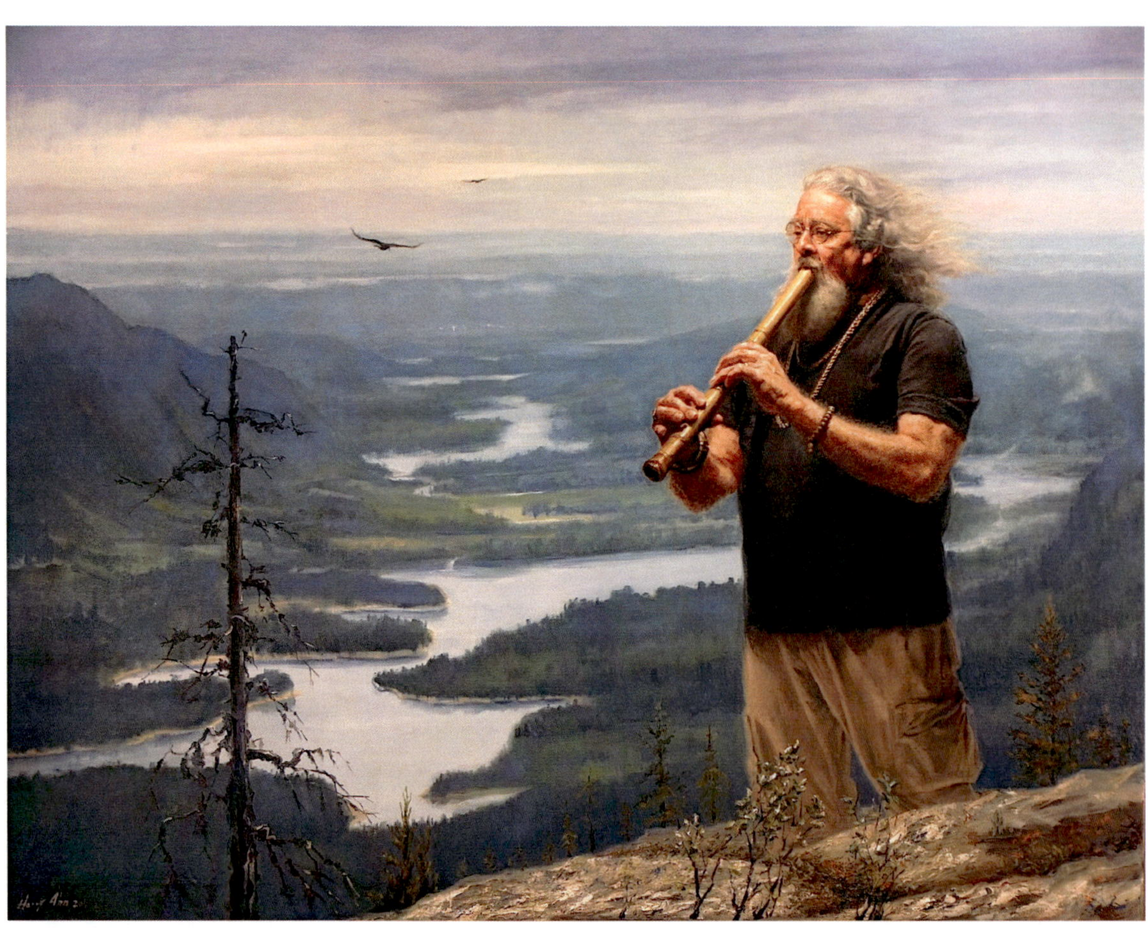

Harry Ahn, *Serenity.*

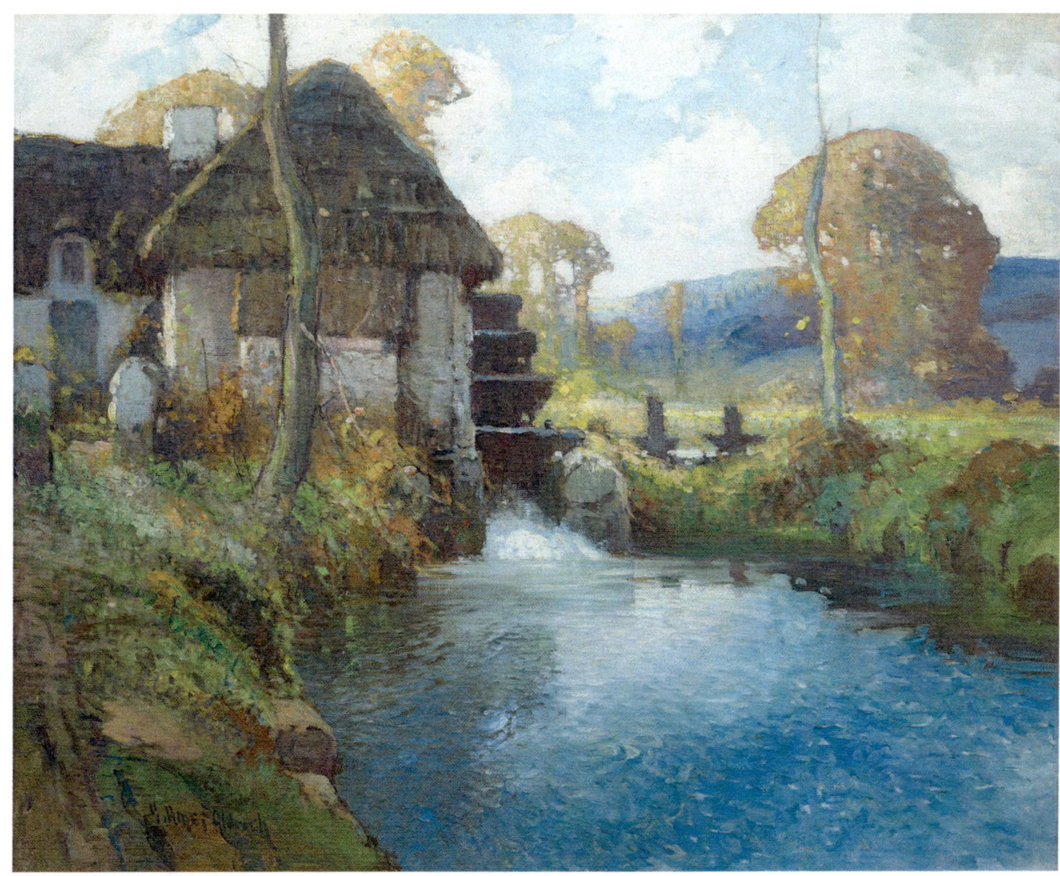

George Ames Aldrich, *Brittany Mill.*

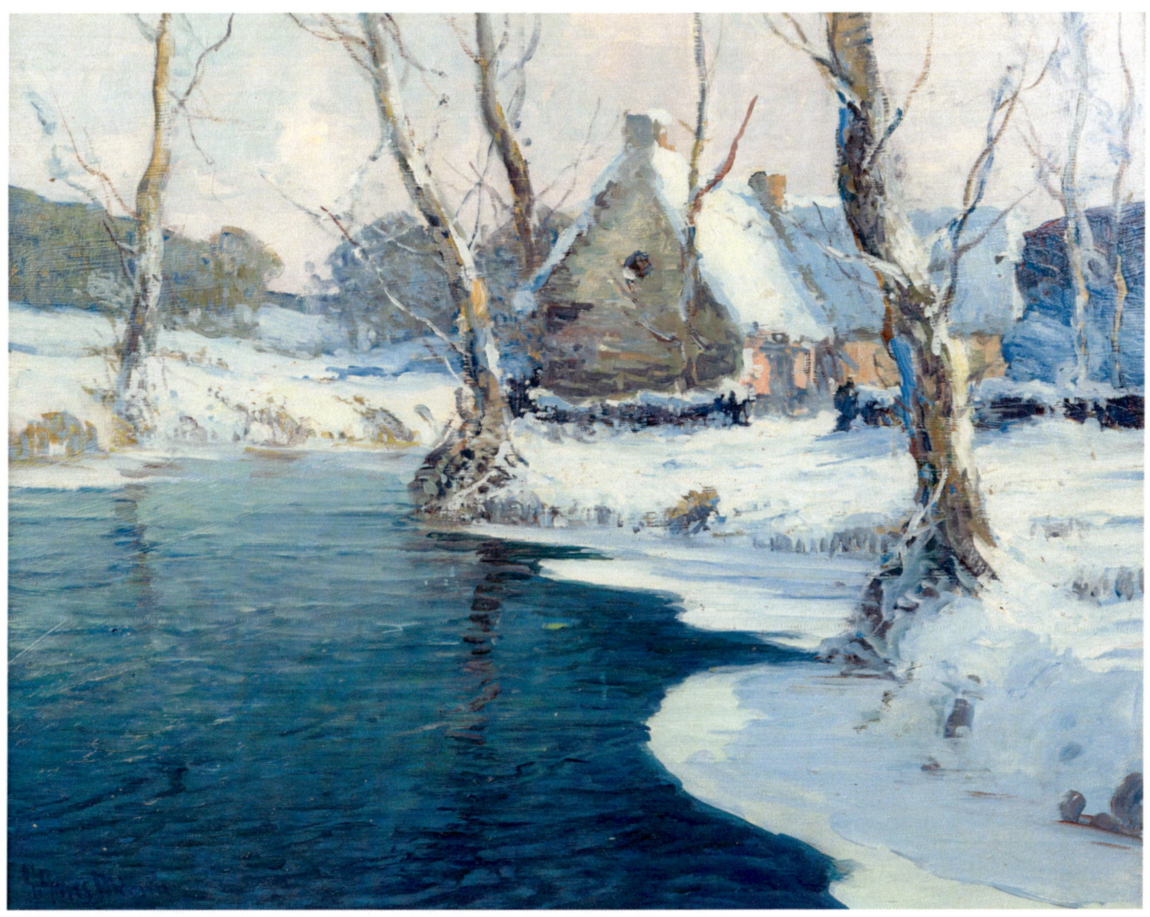

George Ames Aldrich, *Winter River.*

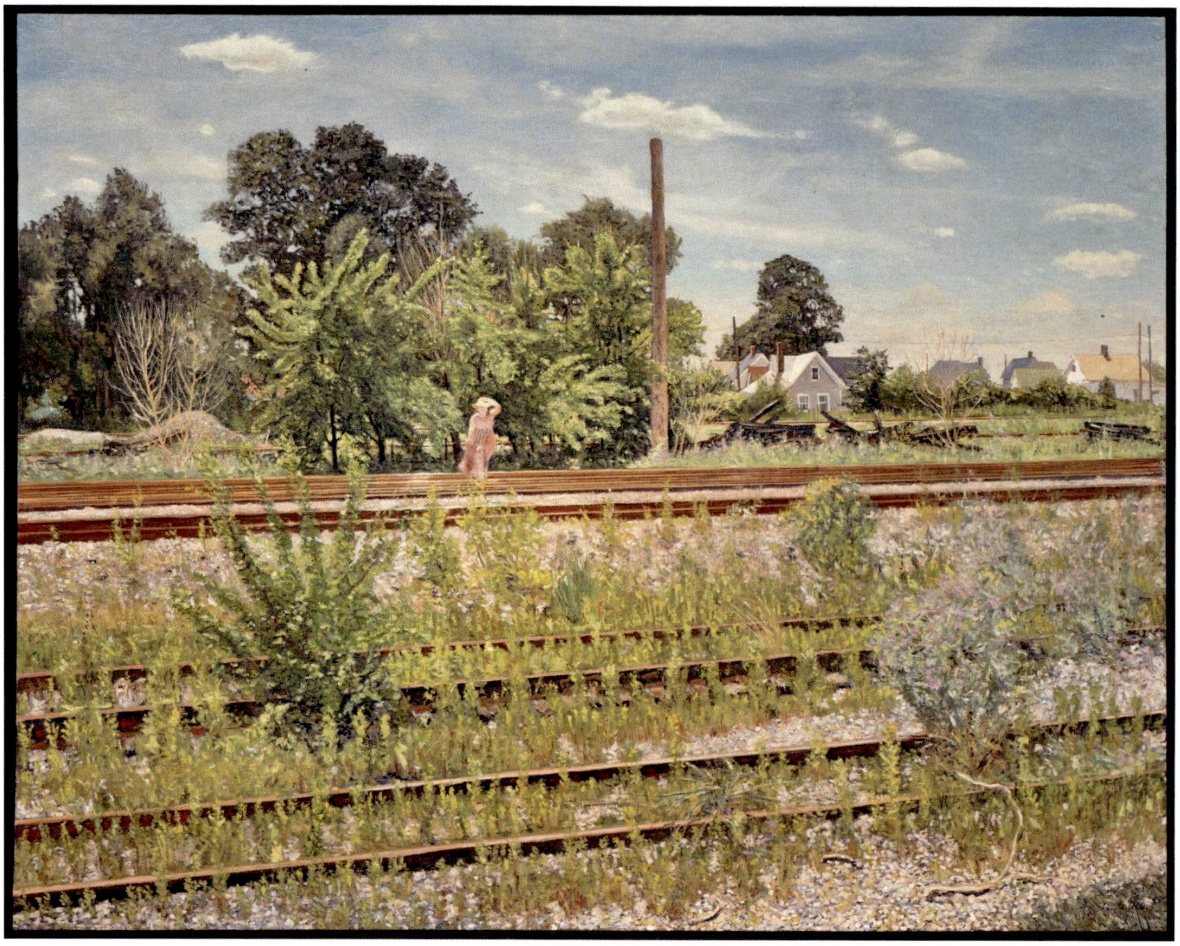

David Allen, *Debbie Crossing the Tracks, South Bend.*

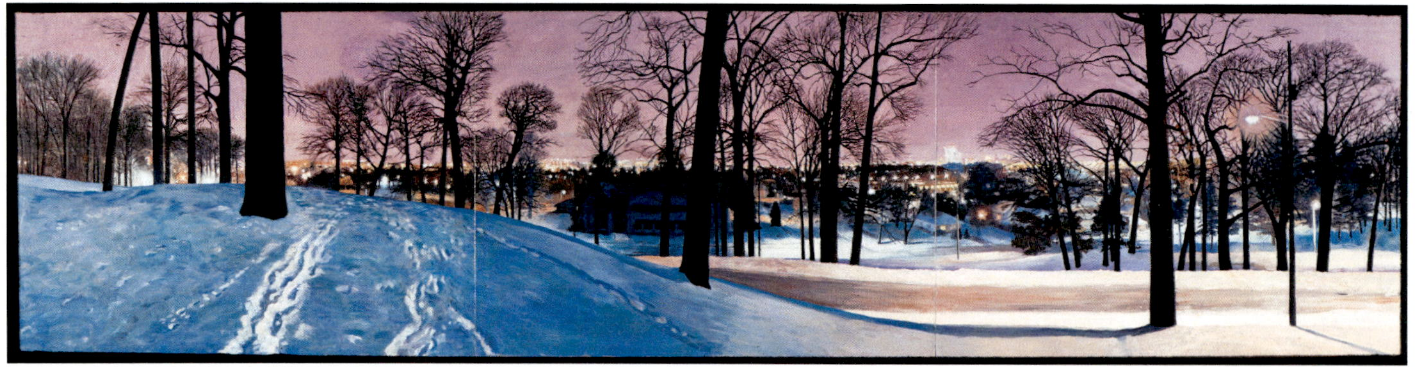

David Allen, *South Bend From Rum Village Park In the Snow.*

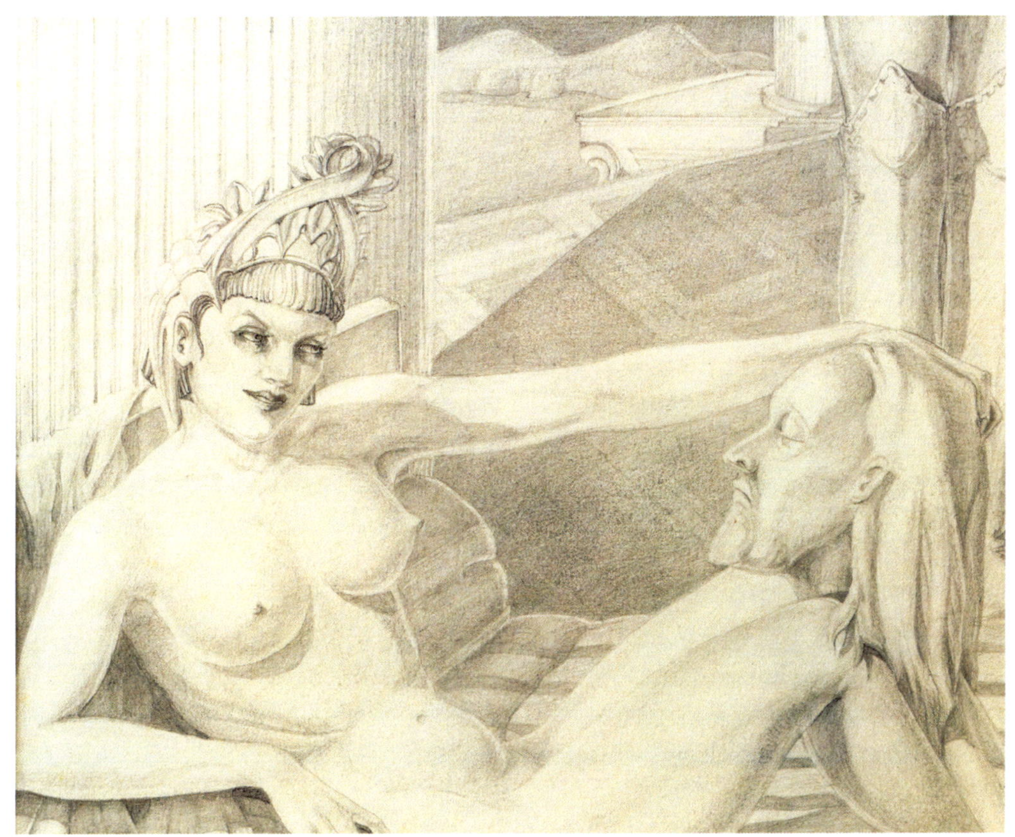

Janet Stewart Allen, *Salome.*

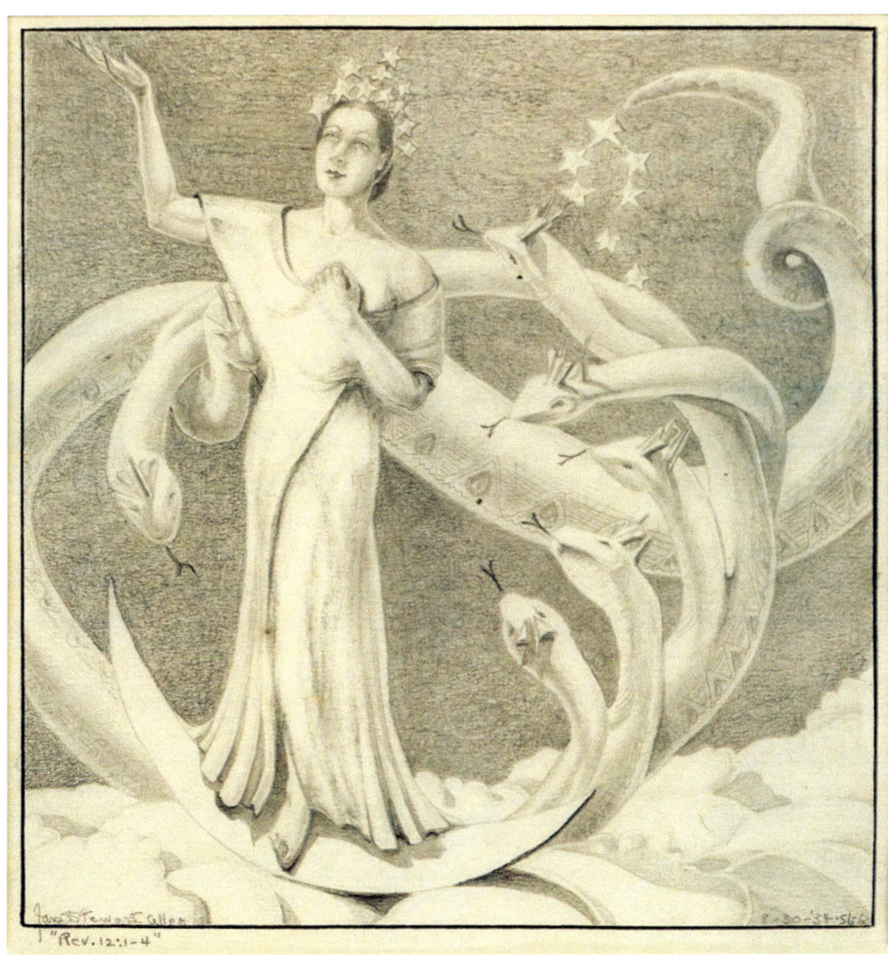

Janet Stewart Allen, *Revelation.*

also studied with Harold Zisla and Stanislaw Szukalski. She used watercolors to create realistic portraits, and in 1989 had an exhibit at the 1989 Annual Northern Indiana Artists and St. Joseph Valley Watercolor show at the South Bend Art Center. Unfortunately, she passed away only two weeks before the opening. Her life in South Bend extended well beyond her artistic contributions; she was the first woman to run for mayor of South Bend and received several "Woman of the Year" awards from the South Bend Chamber of Commerce in addition to serving on the South Bend Art Center Board of Trustees.

Jack Appleton was born in Chicago on December 27 in 1932, raised in South Bend, and has spent much of his adult life in the area as well. Jack studied at the American Academy of Art in Chicago, the Southport Art Center, as well as studying from the Famous Artists Course. He also spent time at Indiana University. Through his studies he acquired a keen sense for landscape watercolor and gouache paintings. He worked as a commercial artist, but also created many fine pieces for exhibition. His most accessible and well-known works are pictorial paintings done across the University of Notre Dame campus. This series depicts some of the key locations on campus such as the Grotto, the Sacred Heart Basilica, and the Golden Dome during the various seasons. Appleton has also been featured in many publications from the *South Bend Tribune* to *Famous Artist* magazine.

L. Clarence Ball's oil and watercolor paintings often depicted shepherds, sheep, and rural landscapes. Ball was born in Mount Vernon, Ohio, in 1858 and attended the National Academy of Design from 1892-1893, but was largely self-taught. Following this interval Ball moved to South Bend where he began his art career painting scenes on the sides of wagons for the Studebaker company. This job led him into the larger realm of art and in 1911 three of his pieces were chosen for exhibition by the American Watercolor Society. Ball used impressionism as a method to explore and document the natural beauty of Indiana as he focused on the Kankakee and Saint Joseph rivers. His interest in the local landscape made him a popular figure in the community and his sudden death in 1915 shocked the area. Before his death, Ball taught several students, including Leo Makielski. One of his most famous works, *The Felling of the Bee Tree*, was gifted to the city of South Bend and currently hangs in the downtown library. Other famous works include *On the Kankakee River*, *Autumn Uplands*, and *Approaching Storm in the Kankakee*. His works have been exhibited at the St. Louis World Fair in 1904, the John Herron Art Institute in Indianapolis, as well as the Art Institute in Chicago.

H. Stanford Barrett was born in Binghamton, New York, in 1909. He studied at several art schools in France including the Académie Julian and the Académie de la Grande Chaumiere as well as the Slade School of Art located in London. He also studied in America at the Art Students League of New York. The first stage of his career was based in Los Angeles where he primarily painted portraits and landscapes. While there he enjoyed success and participated in several exhibits throughout the state. During the 1930s he relocated to South Bend, Indiana, where he taught architecture for the University of Notre Dame. He also joined the Northern

Indiana Artists and was a founding member of the Barn School of Art with Zygmund Jankowski and Edward Basker. The school was very successful for years, until teachers began teaching at the recently established South Bend Art Association, now known as the South Bend Art Museum. Barrett passed away in 1970. His son is the noted American sculptor, Bill Barrett.

Edward J. Basker began his artistic career doodling on butcher paper from the local shop. He was born in 1908 in Hammond, Indiana. This modest beginning developed into the exquisite artwork the surprisingly self-taught Basker created. Although he was offered a scholarship to the John Herron Institute, he turned down his chance for formal art school to help support his family. As the years went on, however, he continued to study and doodle by himself and adopted realism as his own while working to support his family. Basker's primary tools were pen and ink until the mid-1930s when he was able to study for a short time in New York. During this period he became familiar with watercolor in an attempt to refine his overall style. As his style improved, his art became well known and he taught at the University of Notre Dame during the summer, as well as the Barn School of Art that he co-founded in 1952 with H. Stanford Barrett and Zygmund Jankowski. His art was exhibited several times from 1954 to 1966 at the Hoosier Salon and he received the Ernest M. Memorial Award in 1965 and 1966. His subjects often included Lake Michigan and the surrounding beaches, though he focused on landscapes in general as can be seen in *Fog Road*, and *Sand Creek*. Some of Basker's work resides in permanent collections at Indiana University, Detroit Museum of Art and Montreal Museum of Art. Basker passed away in South Bend, in 1972.

R. Michael Beatty was born in South Bend. Early local influences include Harold Zisla and Beatty's uncle, H. James Paradis. He attended Indiana University, Bloomington where he graduated with a bachelor of science in fine arts education, and the Pratt Institute in New York. Beatty started as a writer and printmaker and was heavily influenced by the conceptual movement of the 1970s, which developed his art into a form of visual writing/concrete poetry. The resulting works functioned both as prints and as published works in periodicals. In 1974 he received local, South Bend, recognition when his conceptual piece *Woman* was awarded first place, prints, in the Michiana Biennial Competition. Simultaneously, Beatty was also expanding into video and interactive video. He was one of the founding board members (vice president of communications and editor of the newsletter) of the national Interactive Video Association, headquartered in Chicago. He was also a staff member of WNIT-TV (the local PBS affiliate) from the mid-1970s through the mid-1980s. While there, Beatty played a significant role in the promotion and support of the arts in the Michiana area. He produced and hosted a weekly television program on the arts as well as producing regular art related specials. These programs emphasized and introduced local arts and artists to a broader television audience. In the mid-1980s Beatty began using photographs as part of his printmaking process. In the 1990s he began creating mixed media work utilizing photography, printmaking,

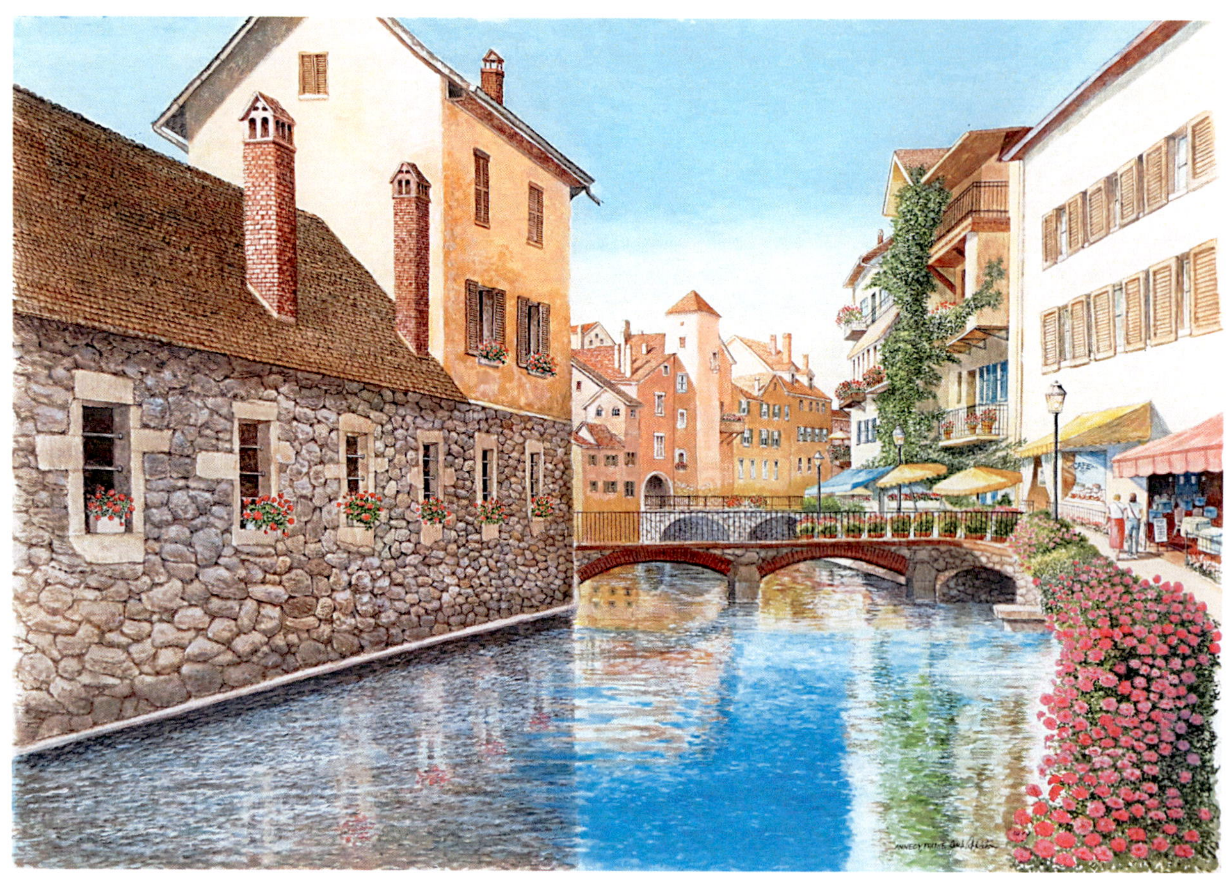

Jack Appleton, *Annency, France.*

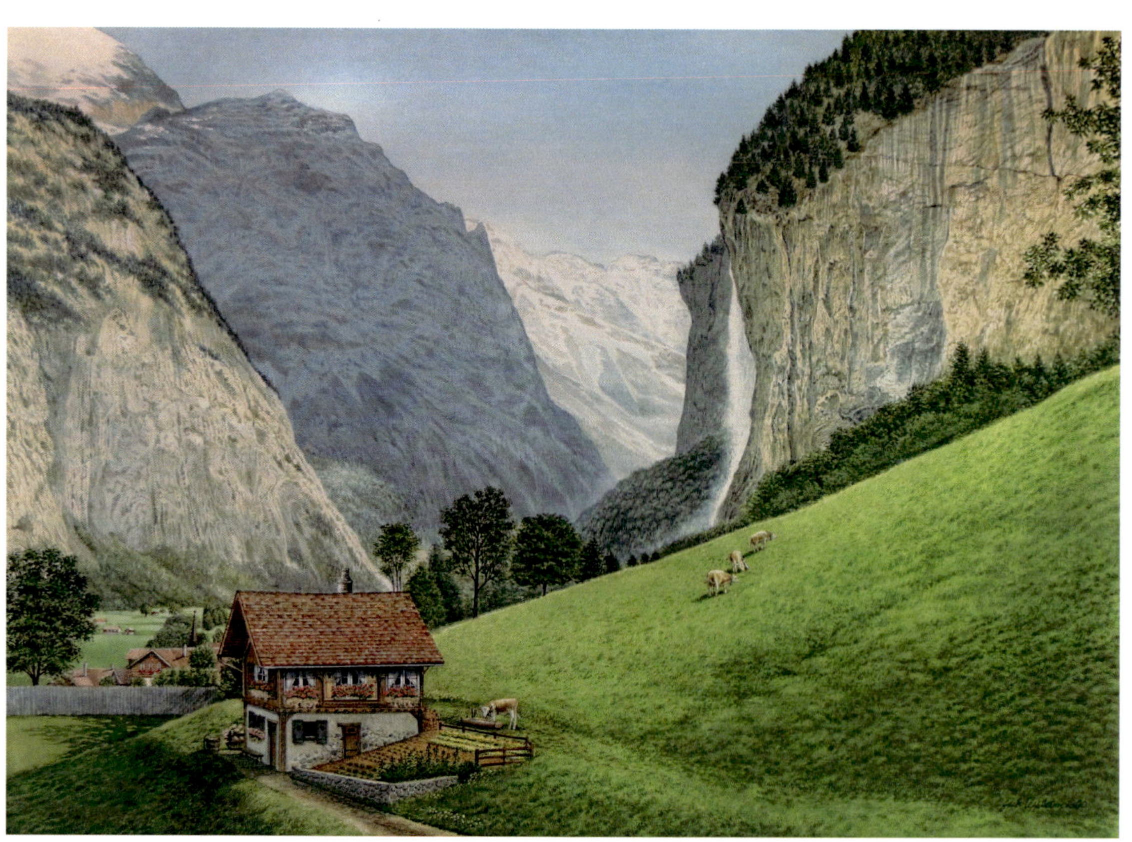

Jack Appleton, *Staubbach Falls in Lauterbrunnen Valley, Switzerland.*

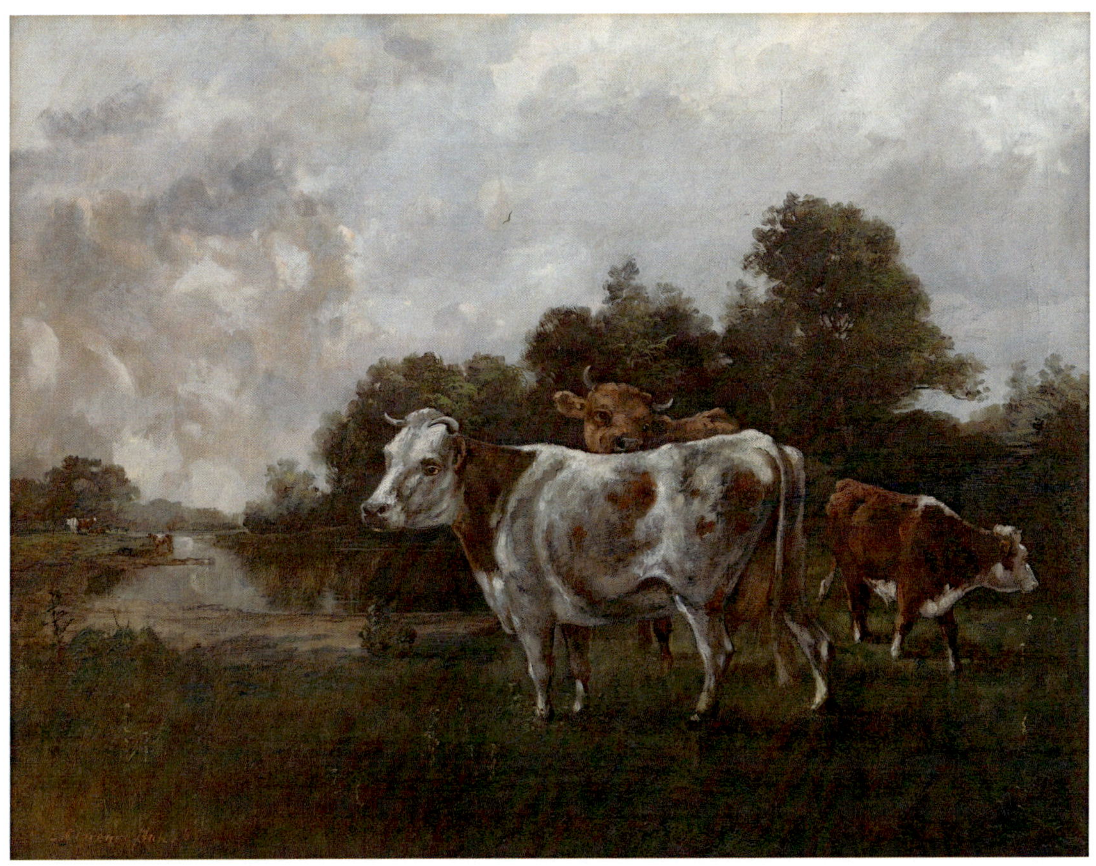

L. Clarence Ball, *Cows.*

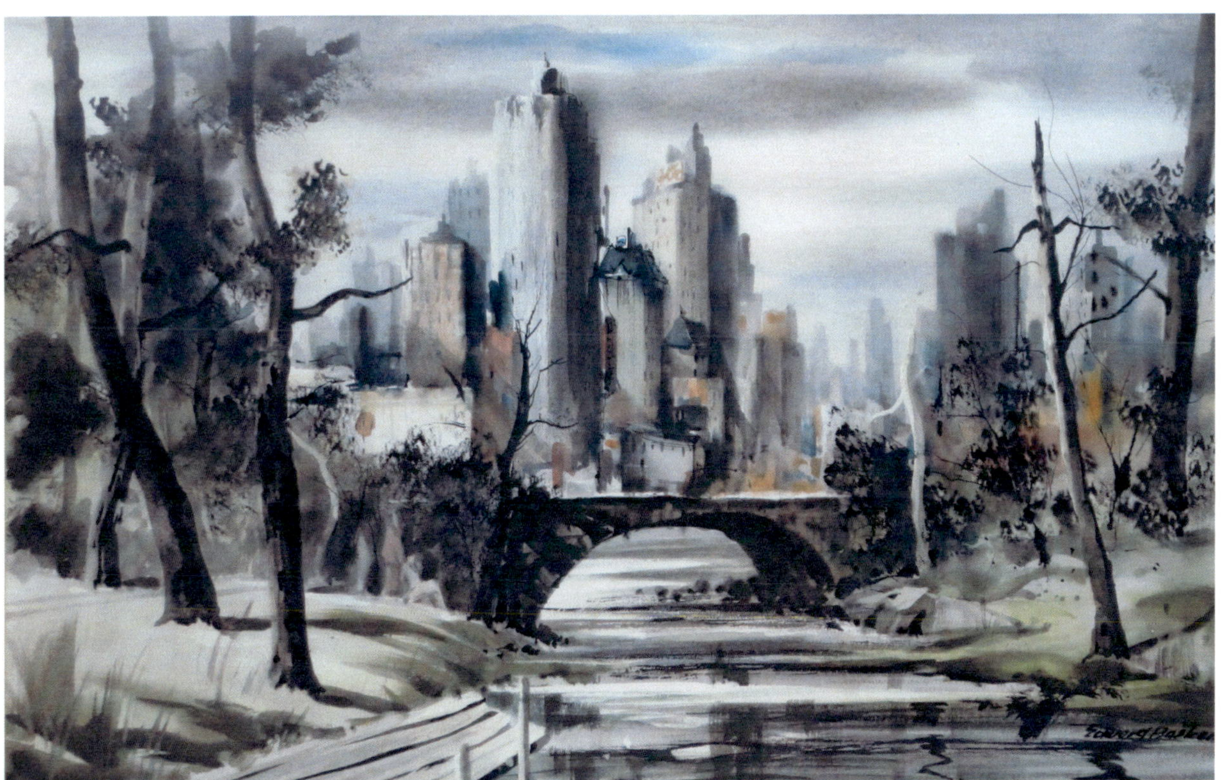

Edward Basker, *Central Park, New York.*

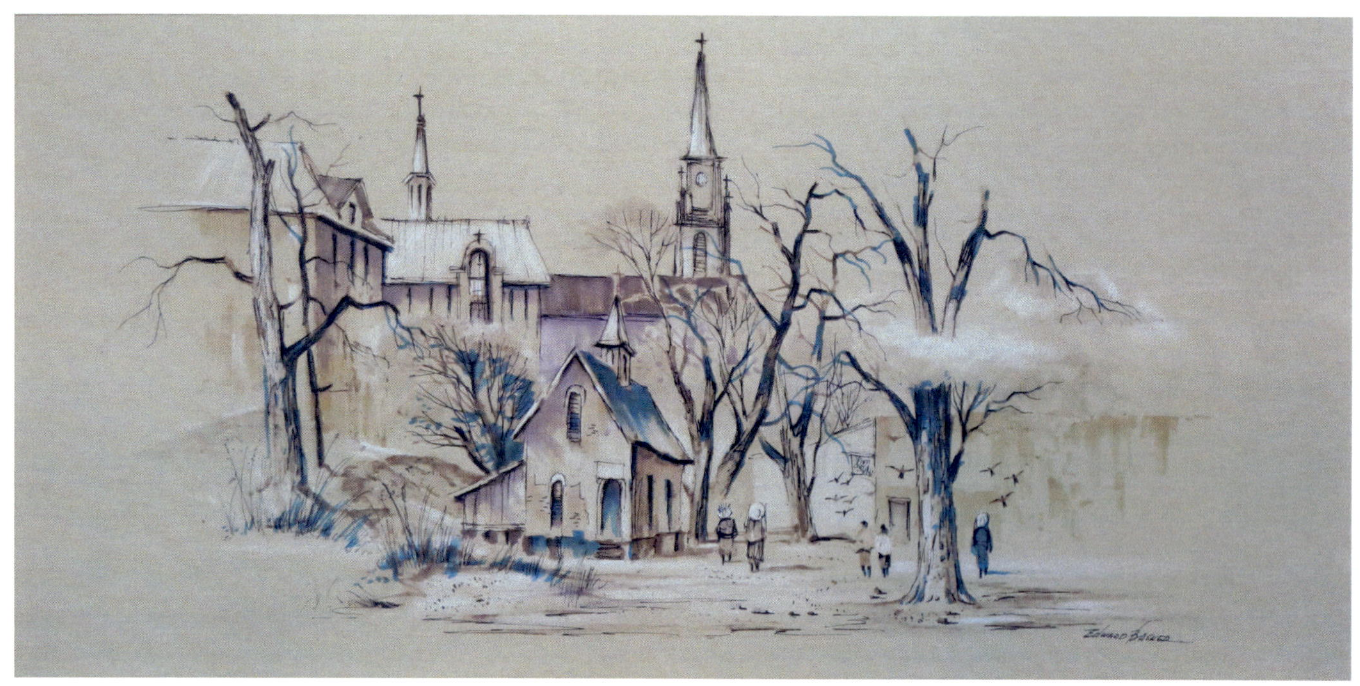

Edward Basker, *Notre Dame.*

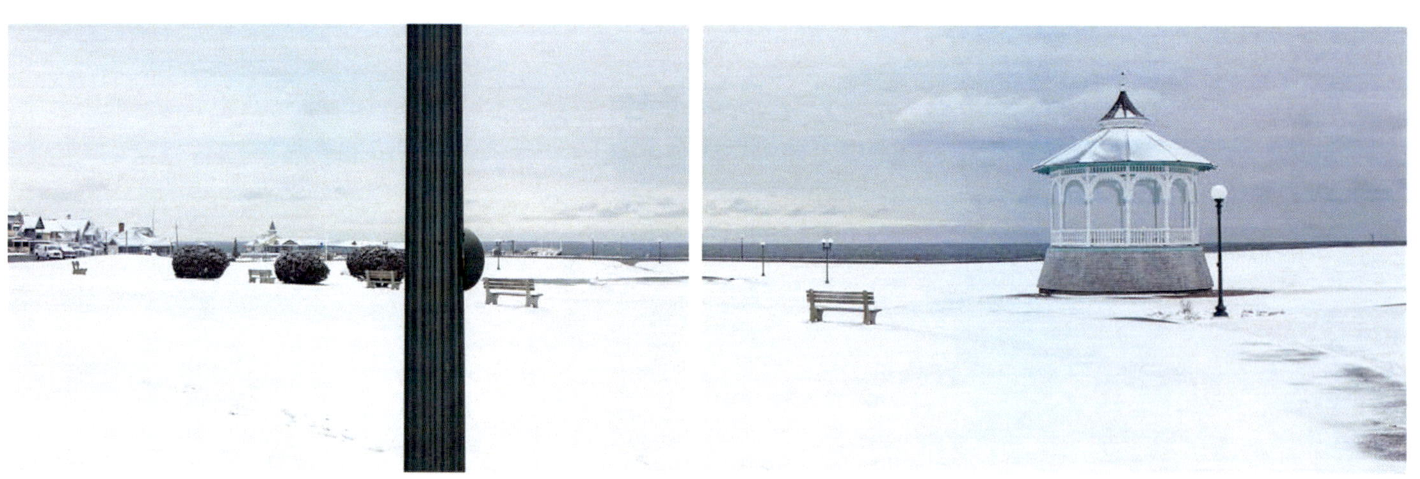

Michael Beatty, *Gazebo.*

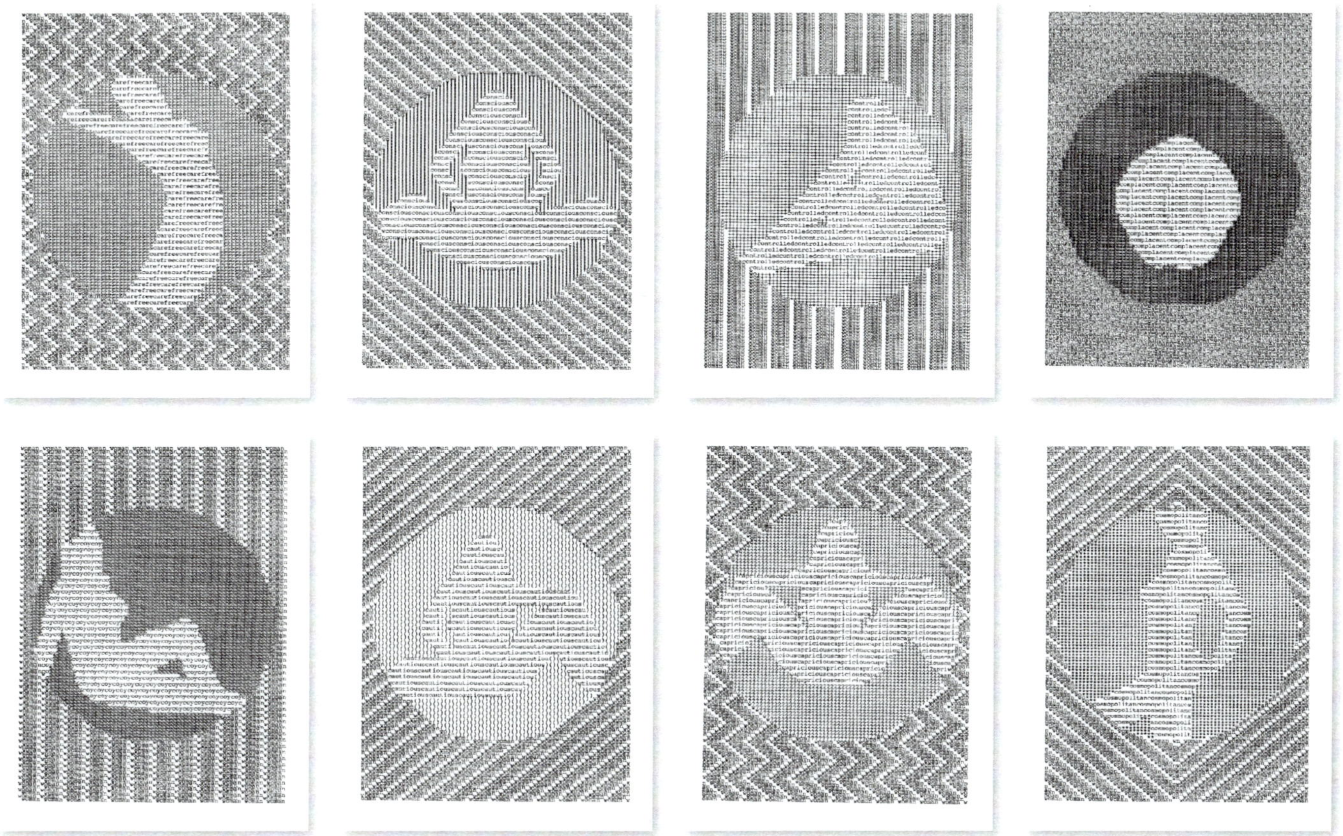

Michael Beatty, *Woman: Carefree, Conscious, Controlled, Complacent, Coy, Cautious, Capricious, Cosmopolitan.*

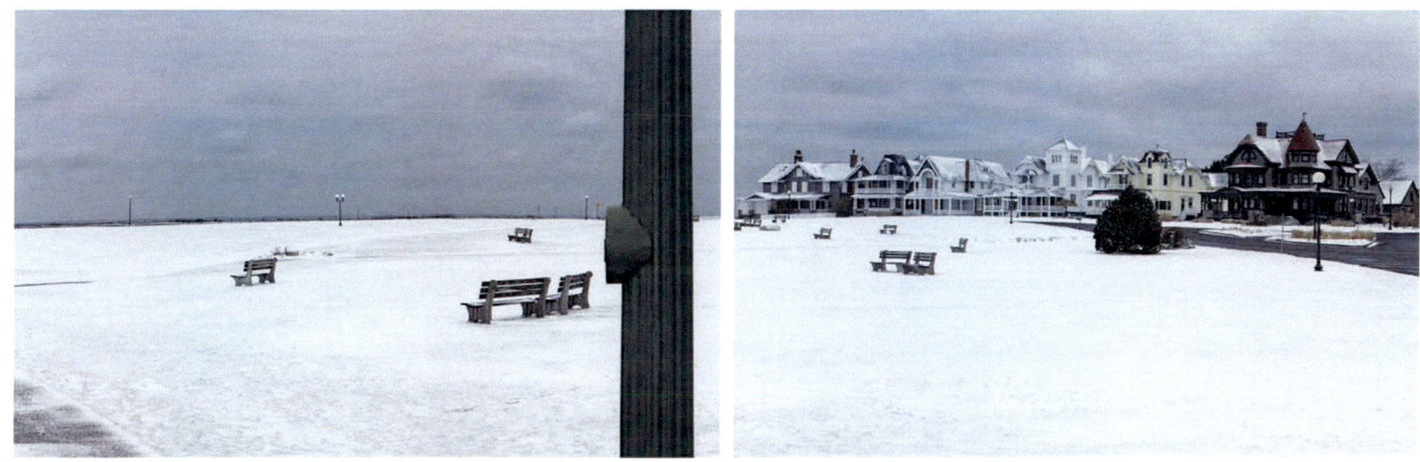

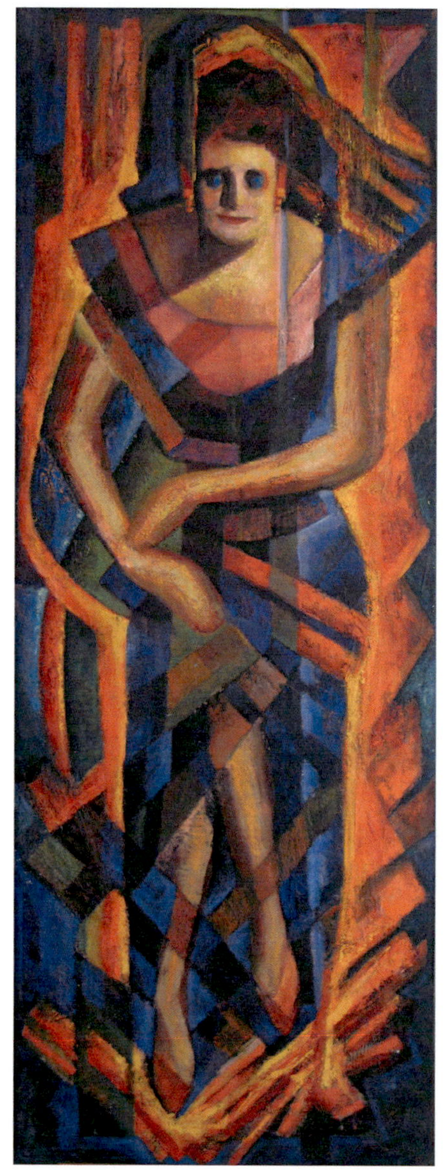

H. Stanford Barret, *Theodora Barret*.

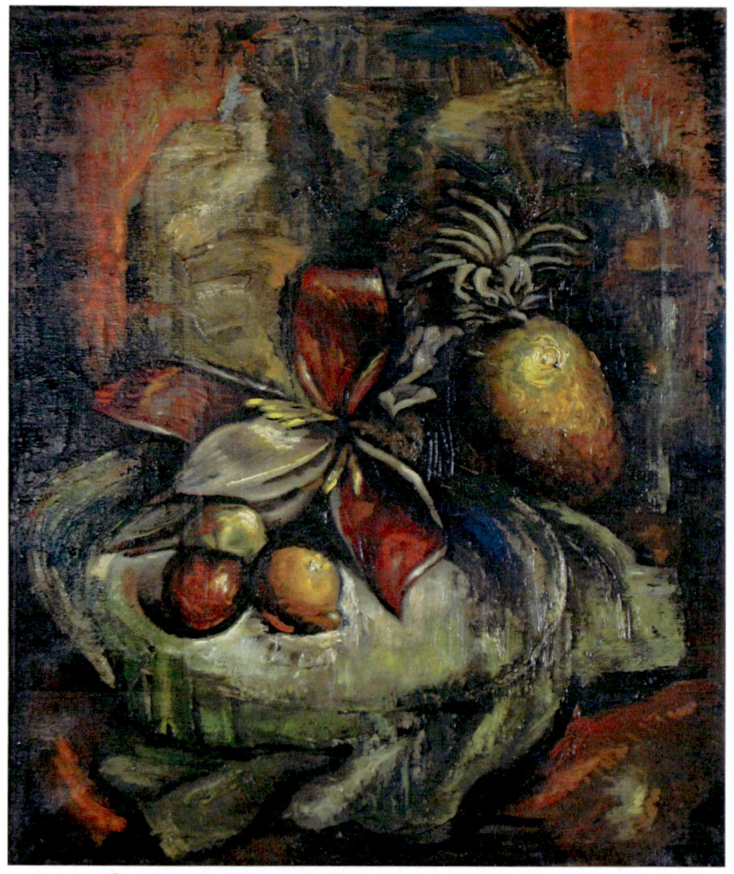

H. Stanford Barret, *Stillife*.

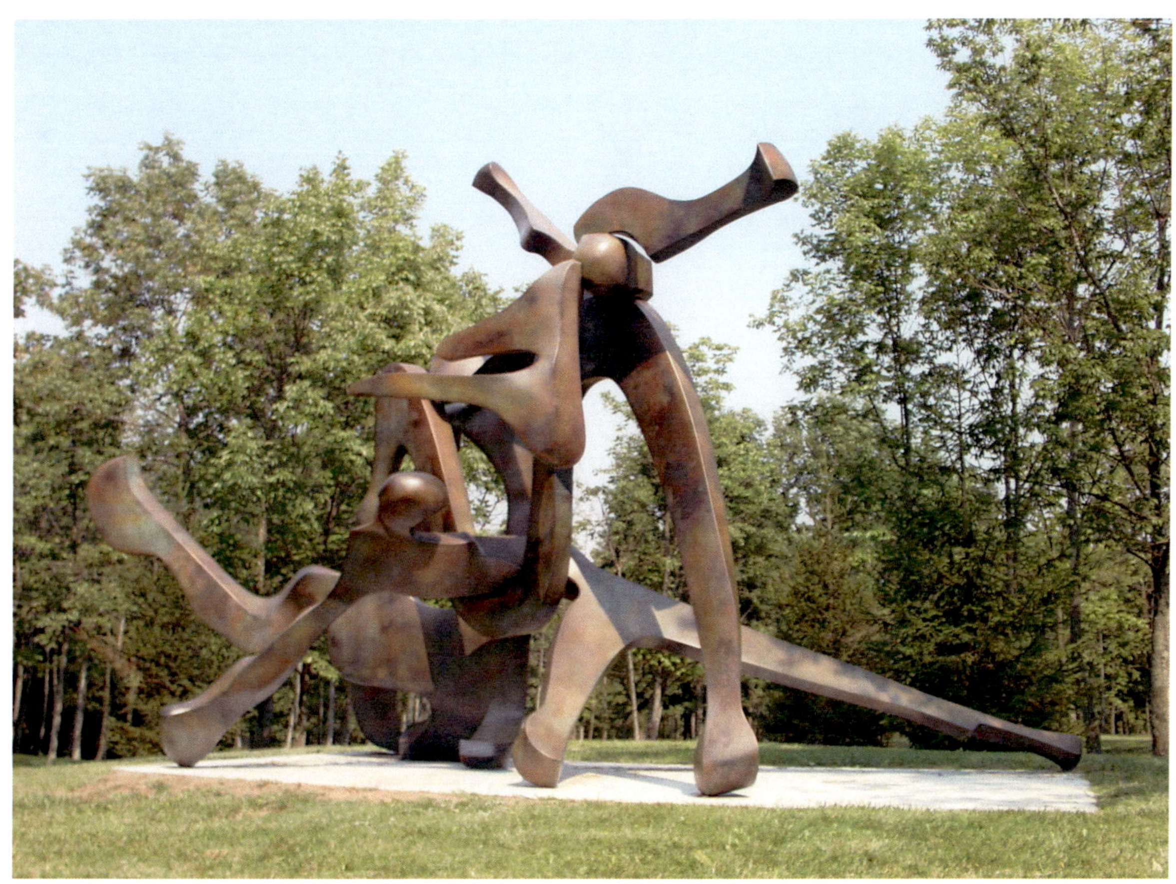

Bill Barret, *Melinda At the Beach.*

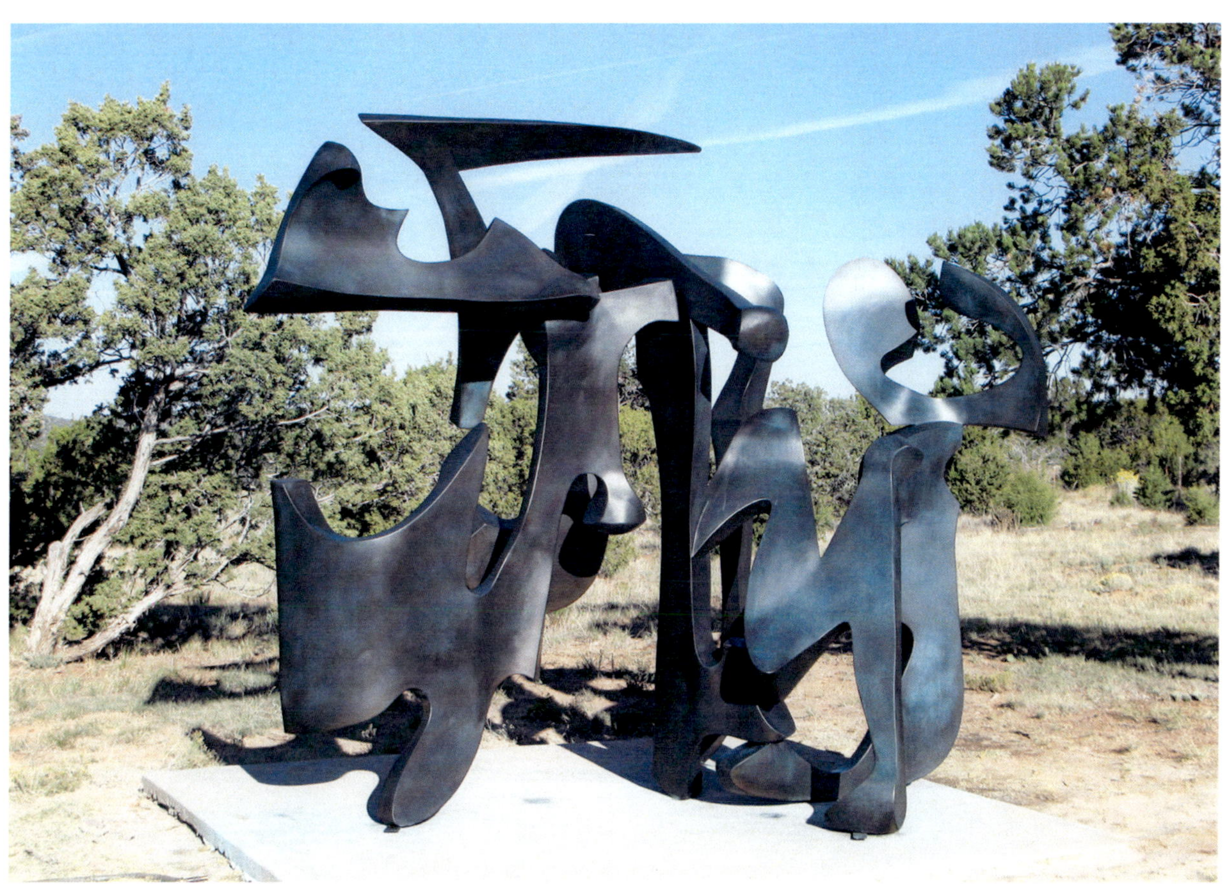

Bill Barret, *Bravura.*

encaustic (wax) processes, and other techniques and materials. Through the end of the century, this two-dimensional work continued in tandem with his media work. Related honors include: George Foster Peabody, Chicago Emmy, CPB Special Achievement awards, and recognition at the New York International Film and Television Festival and the Chicago International Film Festival.

Sister Marie Rosaire Blatterman was born Eleanor Mary Blatterman on May 19, 1906 in St. Louis Missouri. She joined the sisterhood at Saint Mary's College in 1934. Before giving her final vows she attended many different schools to focus on design and printmaking. Beginning at St. Roch's, she eventually went on to receive a bachelor of arts from St. Mary's in 1928 as well as a master's from Pius XII in Florence. She continued with graduate work in Chicago, Cleveland and Notre Dame. She joined the faculty at St. Mary's a short time before taking her vows and was also very involved with the Northern Indiana Artists, the South Bend Art Center, the College Art Association as well as the Catholic Art Association. While with St. Mary's she served as the chairman of the Fine Arts Department. She continued with St. Mary's until her death on March 4, 1967. In recognition of her service, a sub-gallery within the Moreau Center for the Arts on campus was named after her.

David Blodgett and **Linda Crimson** began their accomplished careers as muralists more as a happy accident than by planning it. The couple received their bachelors of arts degrees from Indiana University South Bend before moving on to the University of Oregon for masters of fine arts in 1977. Just one year later, while Blodgett was acting as a visiting artist in North Carolina and had nothing to do, the couple began painting their well-known murals. Individually, the two have different mediums: Blodgett has always been a naturalist painter, while Crimson focused more on sculpture. They returned to their alma mater of IU South Bend to teach their respective mediums, but before long they were working together to create large murals in both private and public buildings. Many of their works reside in libraries and on the sides of buildings, such as at Horizon School in Granger, as well as on the exterior of buildings in downtown South Bend and in the Bittersweet Branch of the St. Joseph County Public Libraries. Together, they have painted over 150 murals and show no sign of slowing down any time soon.

James C. Borden, born in Indianapolis in 1928, probably launched his artistic career as a young boy when he drew a picture of a robin pulling a worm out of the ground. His father saw the drawing, was impressed, and from that point on he never stopped drawing. He continued to learn by himself until he attended art classes at John Adams High School in South Bend and eventually the American Academy of Art in Chicago. He also studied with local artists such as Harold Zisla, Zygmund Jankowski, and Stanford Barrett. Through this education he became a well-known portrait artist who used oil and watercolor paints. For a number of years he was as an editorial cartoonist for the *South Bend Tribune*. Jim taught at the South Bend Art Museum for more than thirty years, and also at Fernwood in Niles. He also worked for years in community theatre creating and painting sets. One of his most famous works was a series of portraits that included Abraham Lincoln, Robert E. Lee, Ulysses S. Grant, Sitting Bull, and George Custer, that was accepted by the United States Veterans Administration and presented at the White House in 1976. This was one big factor in his nomination for the South Bend Hall of Fame, which he was inducted into in 1994. A number of years ago he relocated to Middlebury, Vermont. Jim Borden died in December of 2013.

James Cloetingh was very familiar with midwestern America; he was born in Muskegon, Michigan in 1894, spent a few years in Dayton, Ohio, and passed away in South Bend, Indiana in 1965. Following his 1925 arrival in South Bend, Cloetingh opened a commercial art and photography studio in 1928 known as Cloetingh and DeMan Studios. He gave many lectures on photographic technique and was the first person to receive a masters of photography degree by the Professional Photographers Association of America, Cloetingh also considered himself a realist landscape painter. His work has been exhibited at the Royal Academy in London and he has headlined two different one-man shows at the Hackley Art Gallery in Muskegon, Michigan.

Austin Collins, CSC, creates large outdoor sculptures and installation pieces, often with themes of social and political concerns and opinions. He earned his bachelors of science from the University of Notre Dame, followed shortly by a master of fine arts from Claremont Graduate University in California. He currently works as a professor of sculpture at the University of Notre Dame, where he has also acted as the chair of the Art Department. Additionally, Collins has curated many local exhibits, such as a 2011 exhibit at Fernwood Botanical Garden and Nature Preserve. His works can be found across the country, and IU South Bend received *Temple XX*, for display as a two-year loan. Overall, Collins has participated in more than 130 exhibitions, some solo and some group; he currently resides in South Bend and continues to work for the University of Notre Dame.

Alexis Comparet, born in 1856, is one of the earliest artists from this area with surviving artwork. He was born in South Bend, and studied at the Académie Julian in France under Benjamin Constant in 1874. He was exceptionally proud of his French heritage and education and later in life would change the spelling of his last name to "Compera" to reflect the French pronunciation. Upon returning to the United States, he studied with the early Colorado painter, Harvey Young, and honed his craft as both an impressionist and a realist. While many of his paintings were landscapes and portraits, he also completed a few mystic paintings. Alexis moved to Colorado for his health and took a teaching position at the Colorado Academy of Design for a period of time before moving to San Diego, where he passed away in 1906.

Carl Benton Compton created strikingly realistic landscapes and human figures throughout his life. He was born in 1905 in Westerville, Ohio and studied at a plethora of schools including several European institutions such as the Academy Colarossi and the Academy de la Grand Chaumiere. He also studied at several schools in the United States, specifically the Art Institute of Chicago and the University of Notre Dame. During

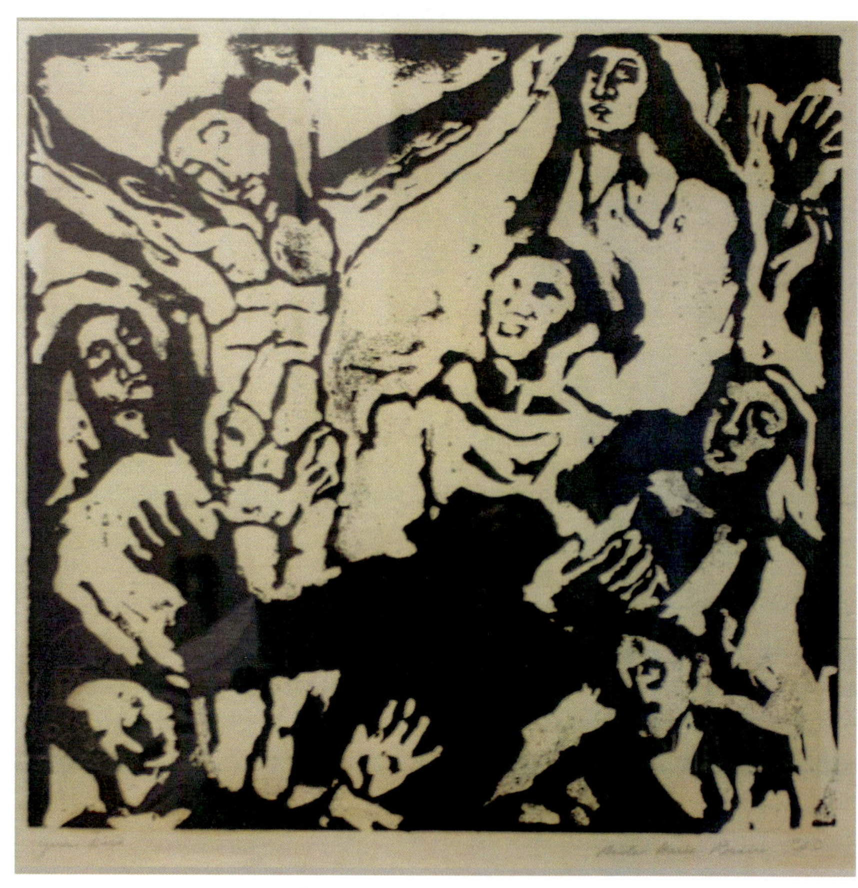

Sister Marie Rosaire Blatterman, *Jesus Dies.*

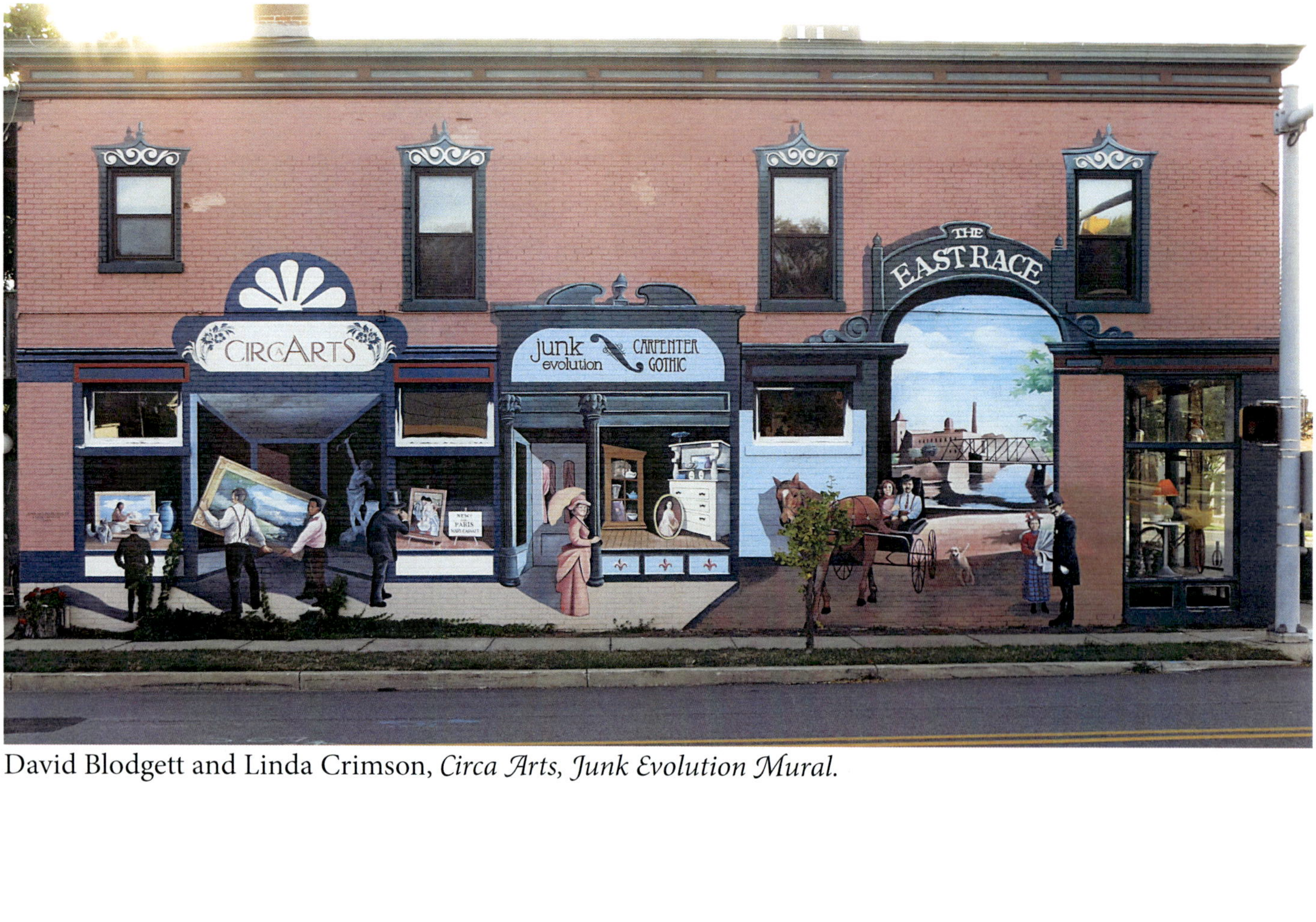

David Blodgett and Linda Crimson, *Circa Arts, Junk Evolution Mural.*

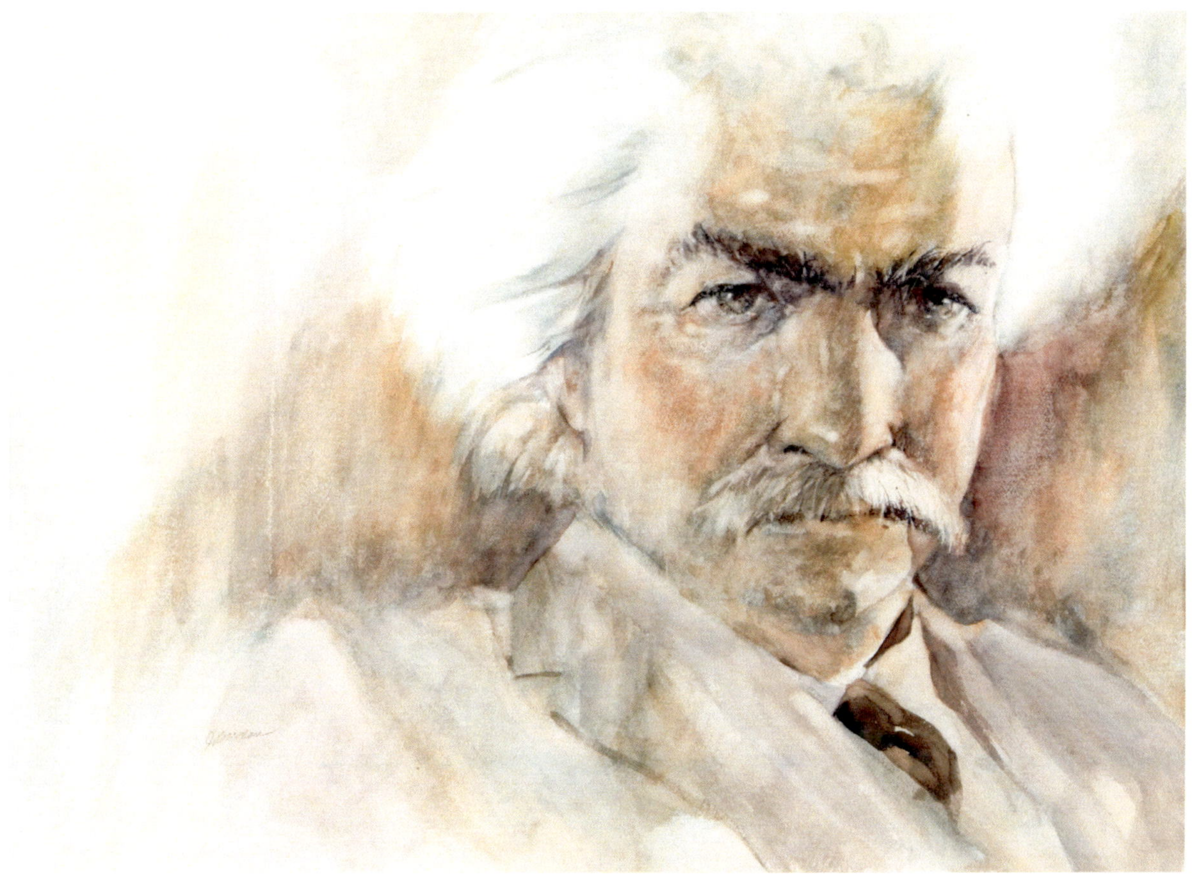

James C. Borden, *Is It Mark Or Is It Albert?*

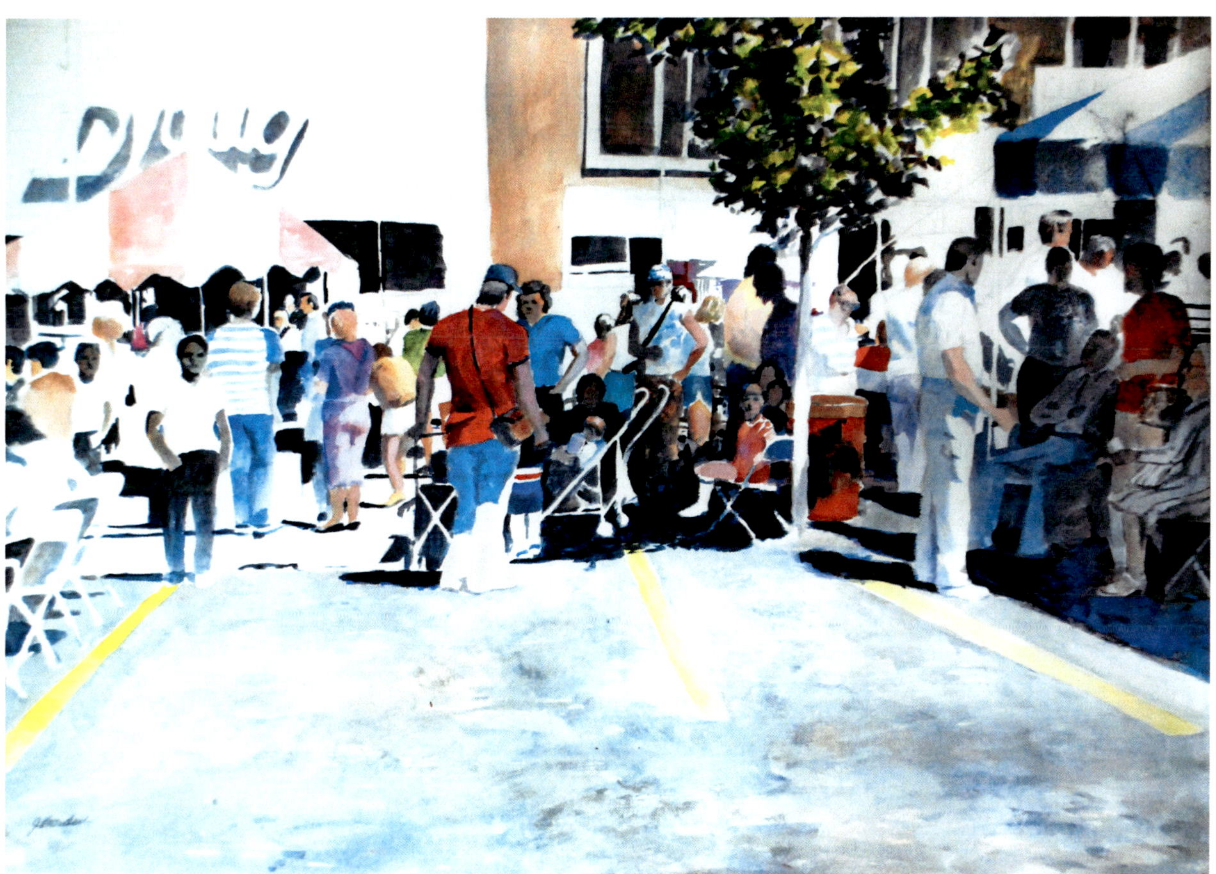

James C. Borden, *Family Outing.*

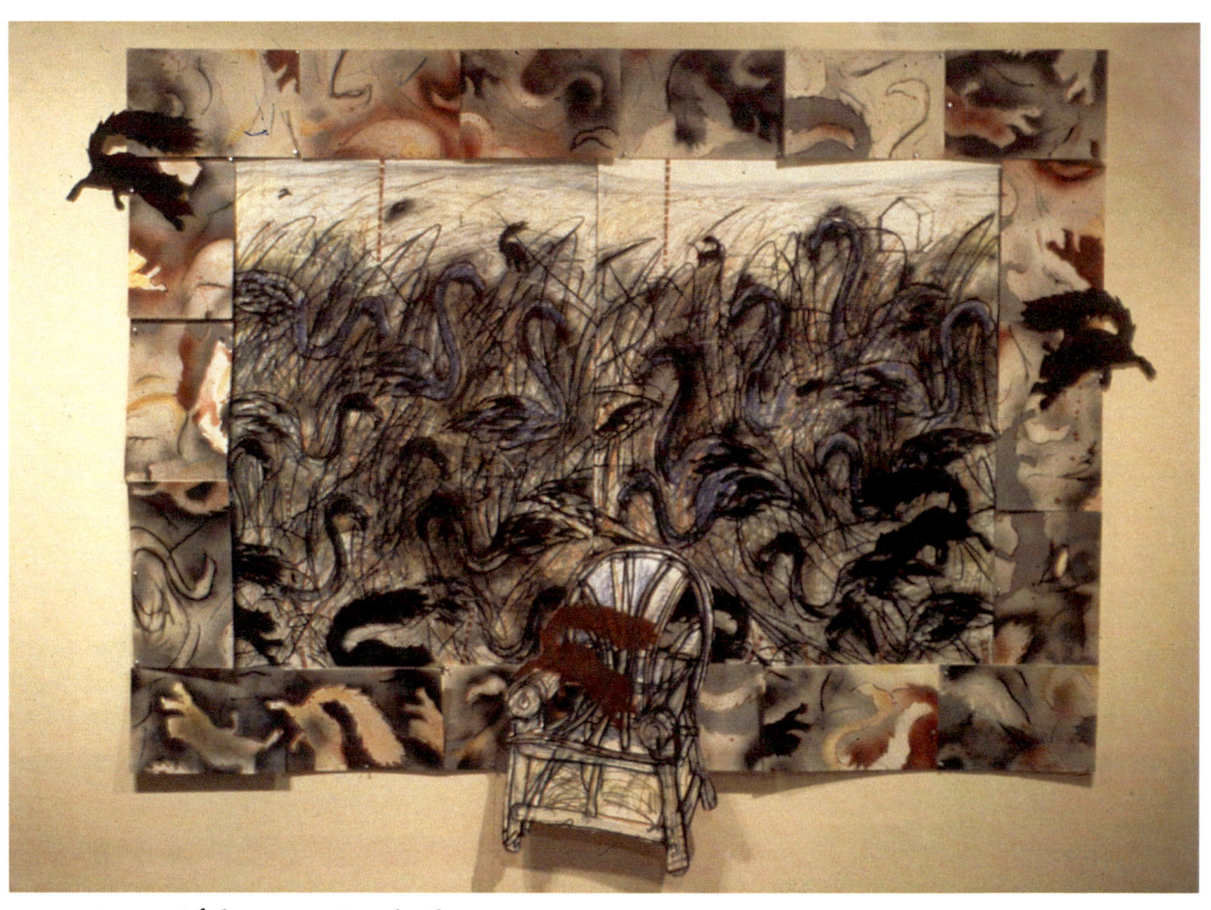

Brian Byrn, *Midwestern Beach Chair.*

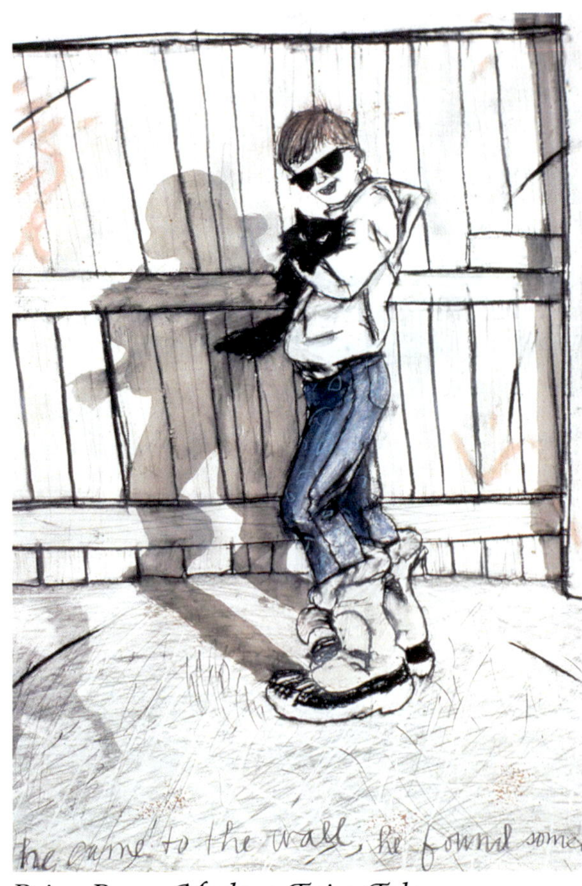

Brian Byrn, *Modern Fairy Tale.*

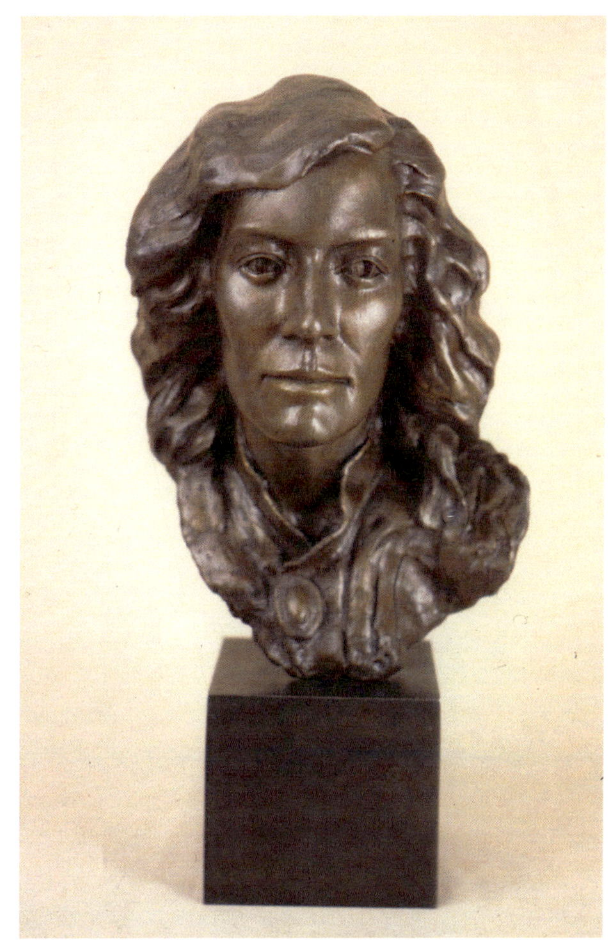

Linda Crimson, *Judith Guevara.*

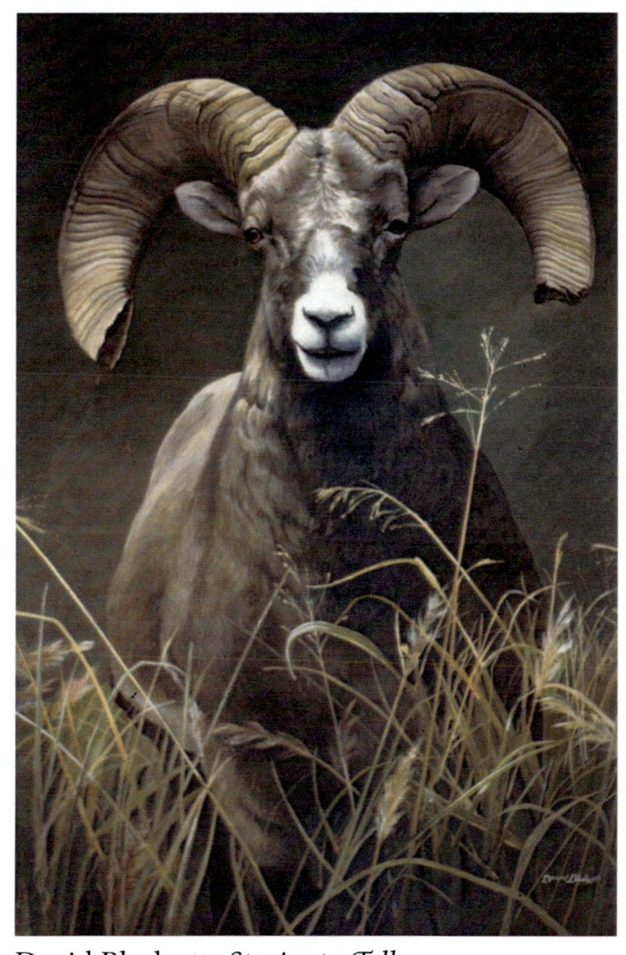

David Blodgett, *Stories to Tell.*

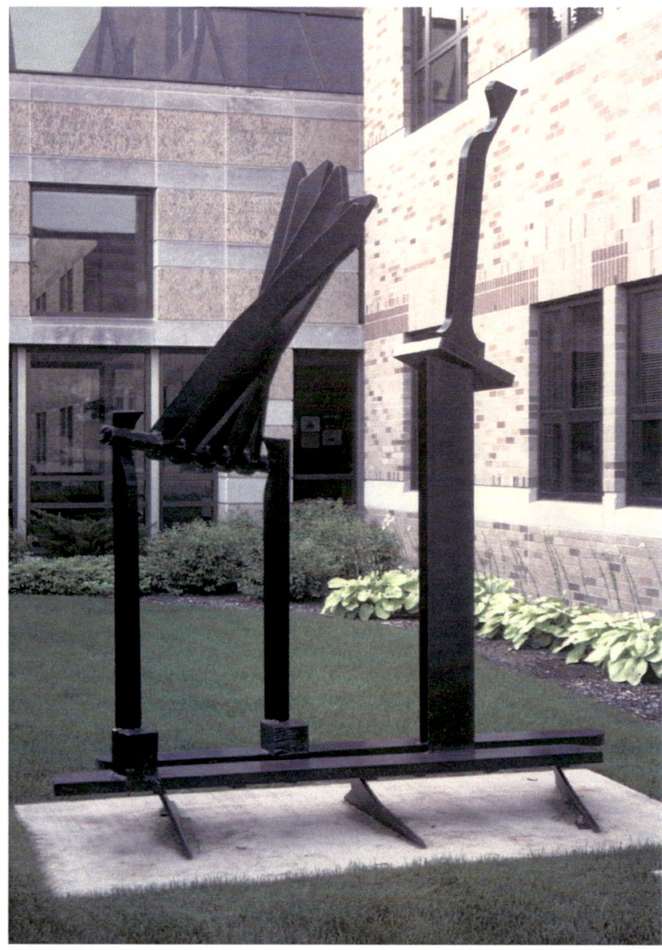

Austin Collins, CSC, *Cages of Soweto X*.

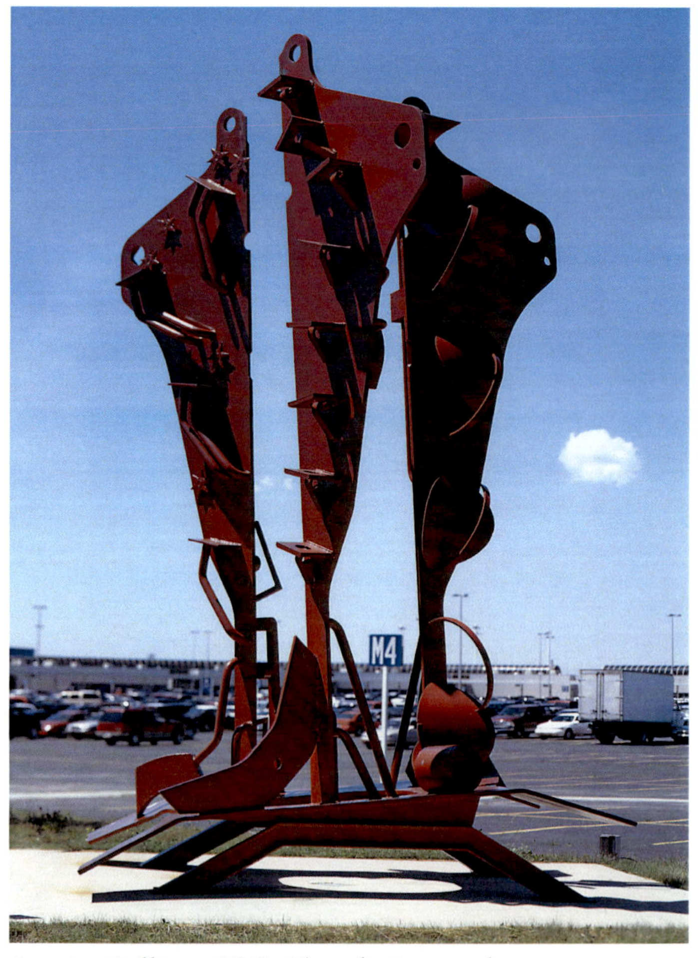

Austin Collins, CSC, *Temple Carousel*.

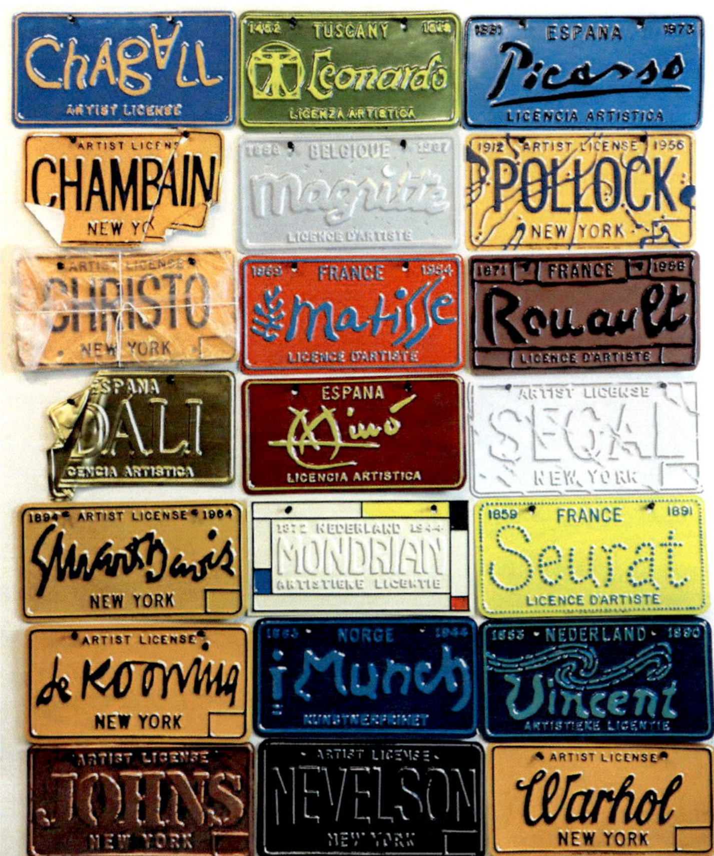

Greg Constantine, *Artist Licenses.*

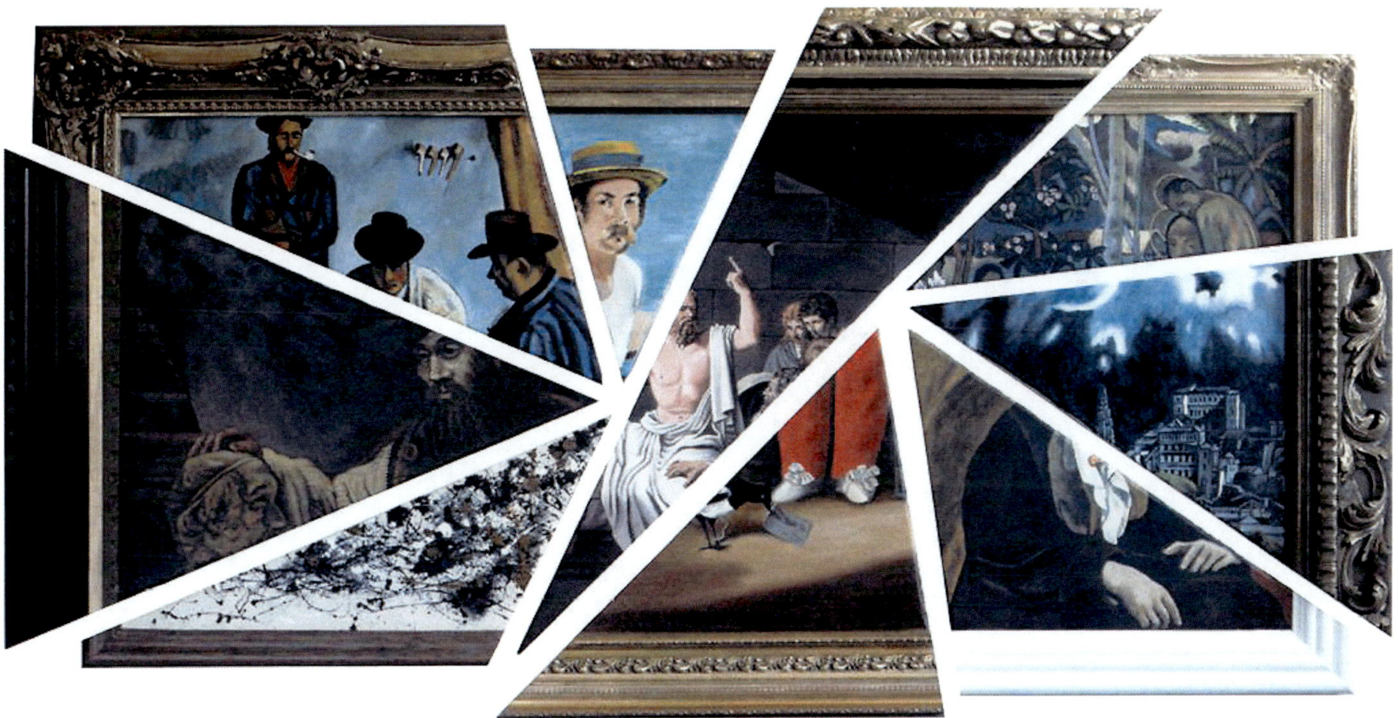

Greg Constantine, *New York Metropolitan's Greatest Hits.*

the 1930s he taught at Midland Academy and hosted a radio show in South Bend in 1936. After several years in the Midwest, Compton relocated to Texas where he taught at North Texas State Teachers College; he would eventually find himself teaching in Mexico as well. His exhibitions spread across the United States, from New York to Pennsylvania, from Illinois to Texas. In 1981, he died in Denton, Texas.

Greg Constantine, born in Windsor, Ontario, Canada, in 1938, became a naturalized United States citizen in 1976. Before gaining his citizenship, Constantine came to the U.S. and received his bachelor of arts from Andrews University in 1960 and a master of fine arts from Michigan State University in 1968. His proficiency was in acrylic painting with quite a bit of experience in drawing as well, creating mod-figurative imageries and abstractions. His first exhibitions took place during the late 1960s and early 1970s, first in group shows but he quickly began exhibiting alone. In 1973, he took a job with his alma mater, Andrews University, where he acted first as a professor of drawing, painting, and art history followed by being appointed as the Artist-in-Residence and Research Professor of Art in 1996. While teaching, Greg also began writing and creating entertaining art history books. The first series focused on great artists and their imagined adventures to the large cities of the United States, such as *Vincent van Gogh visits New York* (1983), followed by *Leonardo visits Los Angeles* (1985), and *Picasso visits Chicago* (1986). He retired from Andrews in 2006, but began publishing again in 2009, this time focusing on famous artists as children. Overall Greg has participated in over twenty solo exhibitions and more than sixty group exhibitions. He currently resides in Berrien County, Michigan.

Mary Dance was an award-winning watercolor landscape artist who also worked as a commercial artist. She was active in area arts organizations as a member of the Hoosier Salon, a board member of the South Bend Art Center, and a member and president of the St. Joseph Valley Watercolor Society. Dance won the Hoosier Salon Juried Show twice. She has also exhibited at the Indianapolis Museum of Art, the Penrod Society and the Holiday Inn Invitational for Michigan Lakeland Painters. In 1975 she had a solo show at the South Bend Art Center. She was educated at Saint Mary-of-the-Woods College and Ball State University, and completed a BFA at Indiana University South Bend.

Mark di Suvero's sculpture *Keepers of the Flame* is a local landmark worthy of its continued attention from locals and sightseers. Born in China in 1933 as Marco Polo di Suvero, he began going by "Mark" after immigrating to California with his family in 1944. He received a bachelor of arts in philosophy from the University of California Berkley in 1957 and later moved to New York. This move centralized him with the abstract expressionist art movement, which he explored through sculpture. Initially, di Suvero used mostly found objects like scrap metal and railroad ties. Following a tragic accident where he was partially crushed by an elevator, he was told he would never walk again. However, after years of physical therapy he regained the ability to walk and the sheer size of his art reflects this extraordinary achievement. His current works are monumental and are often found in outdoor public areas in addition to those in private galleries around the world. Some of his most famous works include *Joie de vivre*; *Motu viget*, which is also referred to as the *di Suvero swing*; and *The artist's tower of protest*. Di Suvero has won several awards in recognition of his artistic achievements, such as the International Sculpture Center Lifetime Achievement Award in 2000, the Heinz Award for Arts and Humanities in 2005, and the National medal of Arts in 2010. He is also a founding member of several galleries, including Park Place Gallery and ConStruct. Di Suvero currently resides in New York with his second wife and his daughter while maintaining three studios worldwide and continuing to create massive steel sculptures.

Theodore "Ted" W. Drake became one of the most widely known artists from the area despite a short-lived formal art education that took place only at Elkhart (Indiana) High School. Born on September 2 in 1907, Ted grew up in Bremen, Indiana. His formal art education took place only in high school, but this did not deter him from expressing his artistic talents. As a child, the first drawing he could remember creating was of a leprechaun, which would eventually become his most well-known creation. While in high school, he worked for the New York Central Railroad lines in Elkhart until his position as an iron molder was eliminated during the Great Depression. In 1942 he enlisted in the navy to assist in the war effort. His art became well known among his fellow officers as a result of a weekly newspaper he provided illustrations for. When he returned home in 1946 Ted would claim that it was his time in the navy that truly made him an artist. It wasn't long after returning home that he began working with Franklin Burr Tillstrom as an illustrator for the *Kukla, Fran, and Ollie* show, a children's puppet-based television program. The professional relationship lasted until the '50s, when the Kuklapolitan show no longer needed an illustrator. Ted's artistic career continued, though, and he went on to create two of the most well-known sports team logos—Notre Dame's "fighting Irish" Leprechaun in 1964 and the Chicago Bulls' bull in 1966. Both logos are still used today. Ted passed away on May 25, 2000.

Nancy Swan Drew is a one-woman wonder, an expressionistic artist, colorful in more ways than one. Born in Royal Oak, Michigan, in 1948, Nancy has had a full and adventurous life and artistic career. As a young girl, she was first inspired by her kindergarten teacher, who doubled as her grandmother because of how much time they spent inside and outside of the classroom creating arts and crafts. She studied for several years at the Cranbrook Art Program, where teacher Glen Michaels became a role model. In 1968 she graduated from the University of Michigan with a bachelor of fine arts and pursued graduate studies at the University of Notre Dame. Nancy's first solo exhibit took place in the 1970s and she's been busy ever since. In addition to painting and exhibiting, Nancy hosted National Public Radio's *Art Talk* program, and was an artist for the *Chicago Tribune*'s syndicated strip *A Fine Line*. She also creates greeting cards, designs clothing and writes books--thirty and counting. One of her favorites, *Be Your Own Angel . . .* (2005), does more than describe her experience with breast cancer; it has provided many women suffering from the disease with hope and

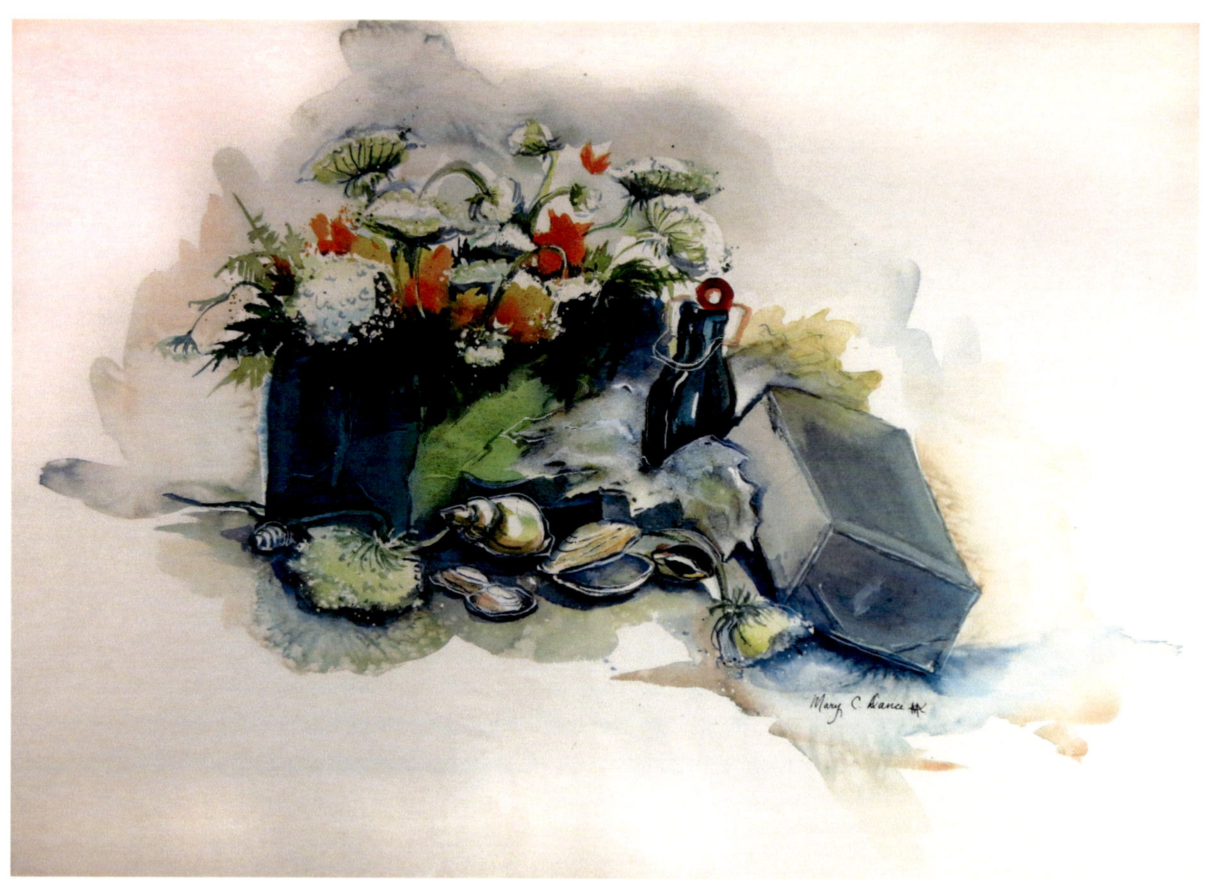

Mary Dance, *Still Life*.

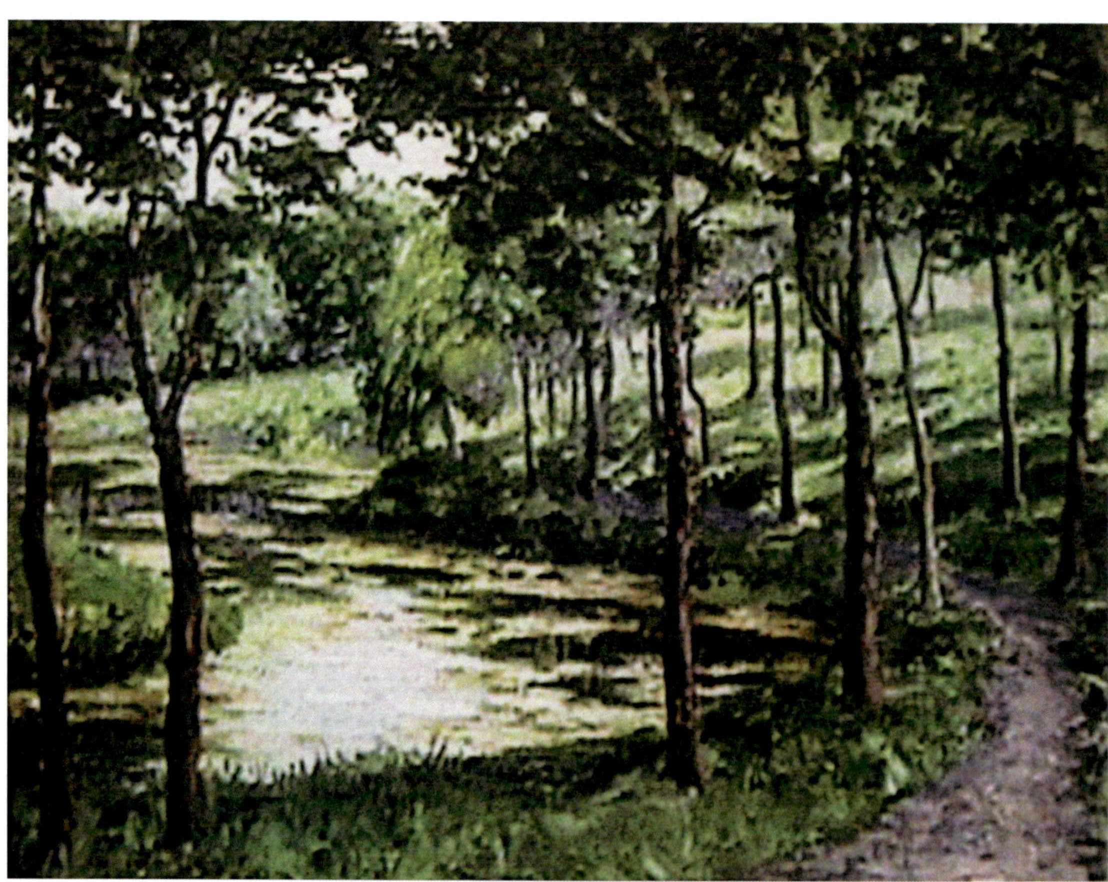

Anna Maria DuChene (Sister Immaculata, CSC), *Woodland*.

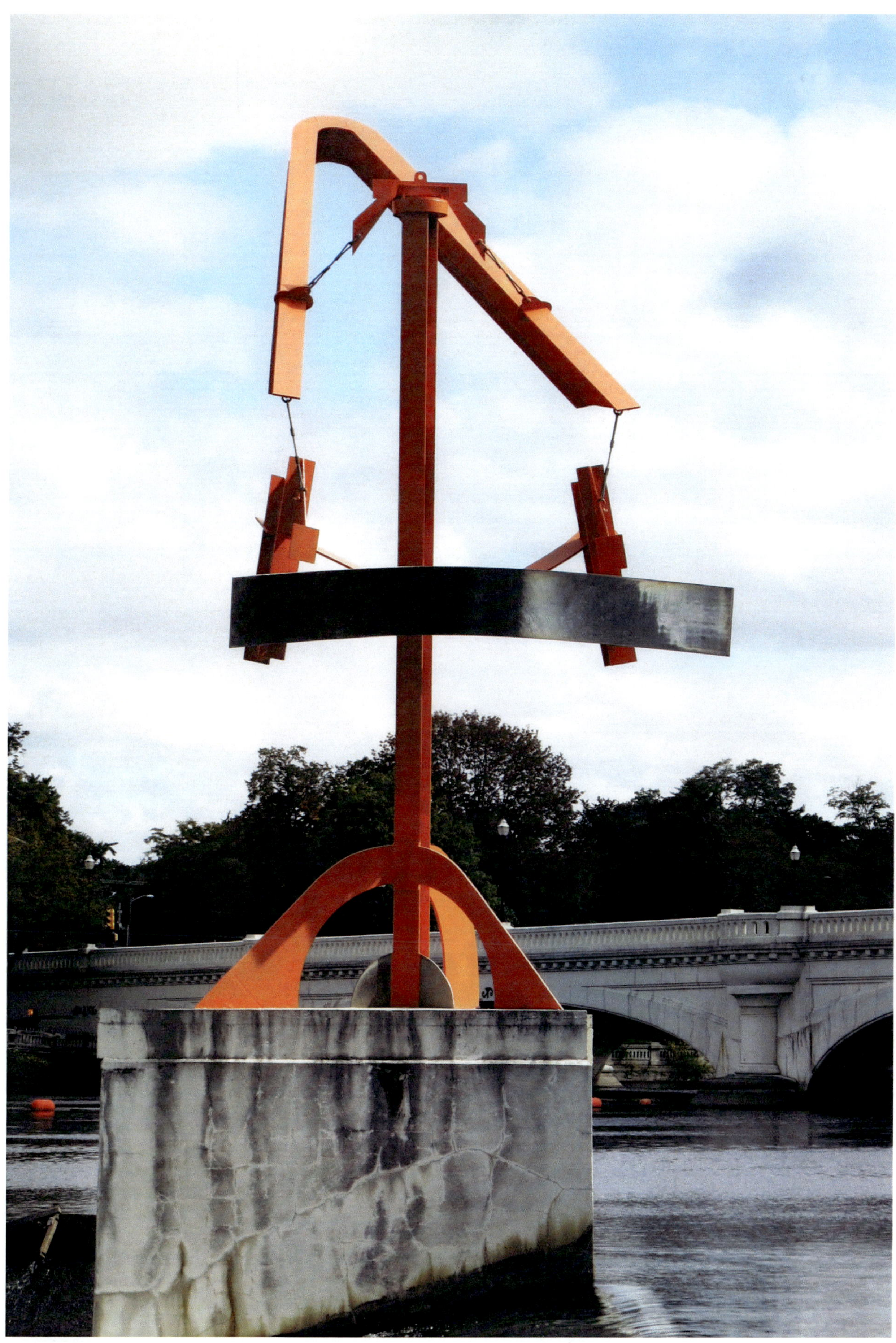

Mark di Suvero, *Keepers of the Fire*.

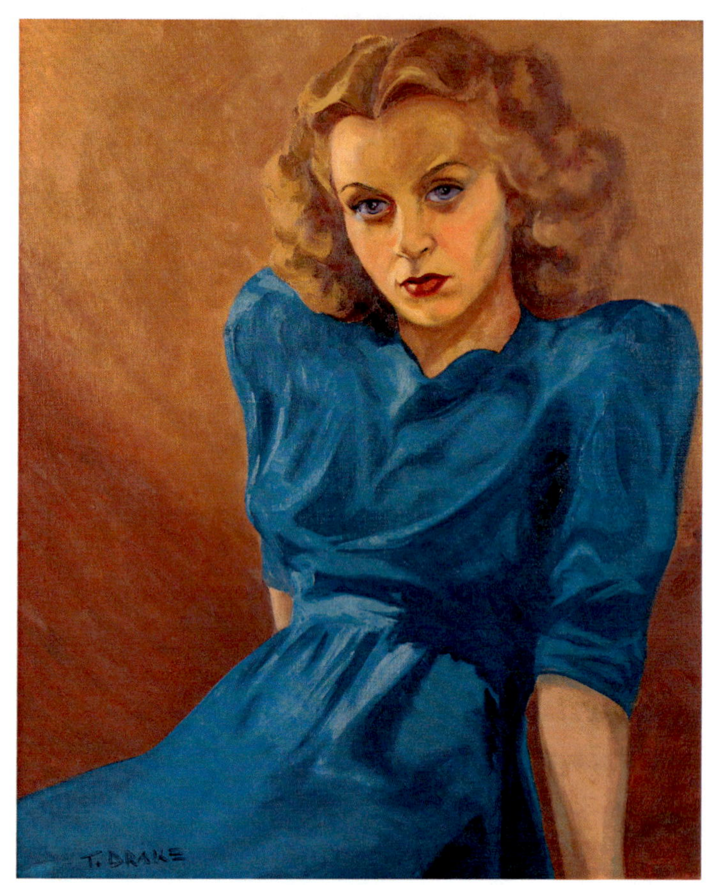

Theodore W. Drake, *Portrait of Elizabeth Lennox.*

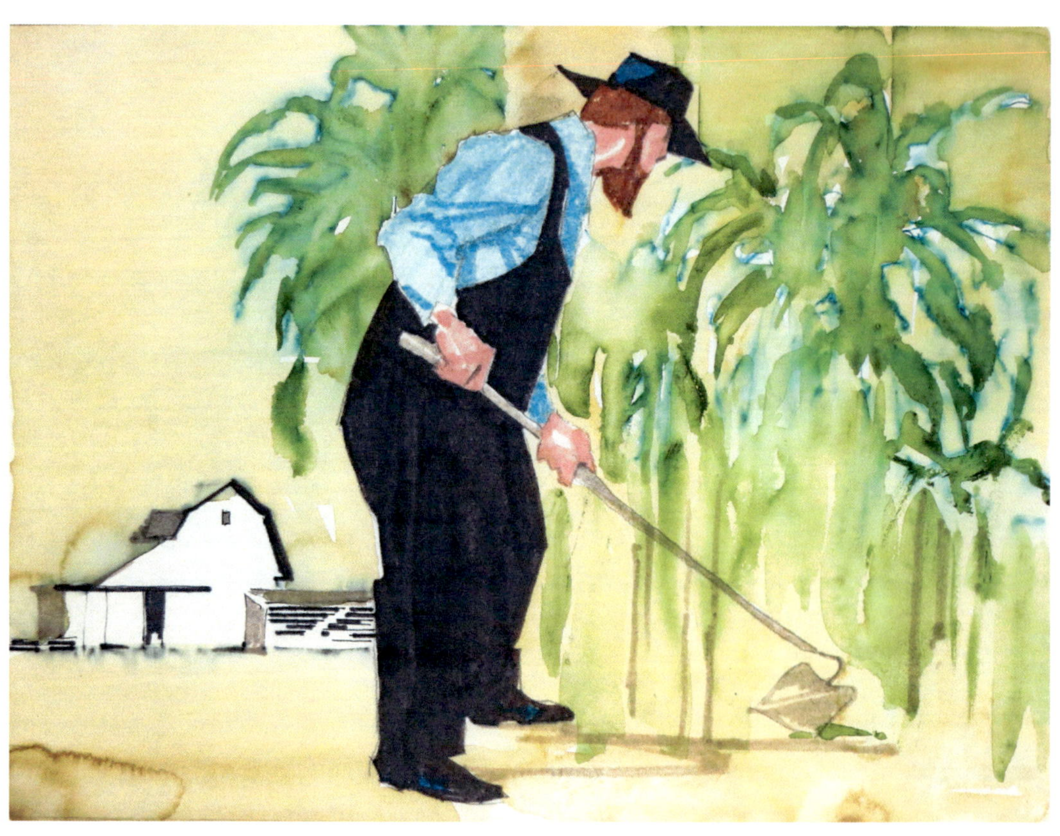

Theodore W. Drake, *Farmer Hoeing.*

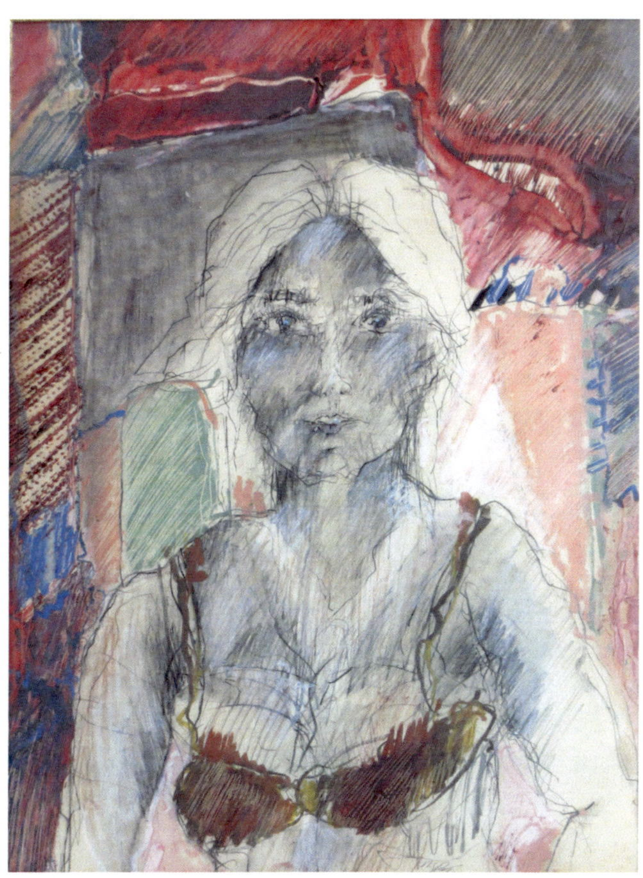

Nancy Drew, *Untitled.*

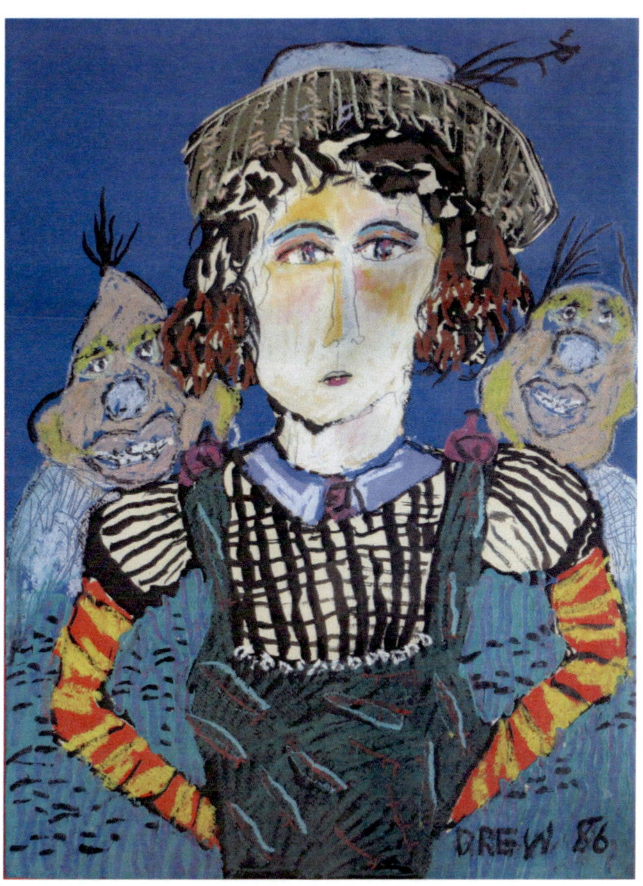

Nancy Drew, *Untitled.*

strength. The book shares her personality and artistic style. Nancy currently lives in Michigan with lots of family to love.

Anthony Droege's inspiration for his paintings has long been personal nuances. Born in 1943 in Philadelphia, Droege received a bachelor of fine arts from Penn State in 1965, and both a master of arts and a master of fine arts from the University of Iowa. Following graduation, he took a position with Murray State University for a short time, from 1969-1971, before coming to Indiana University South Bend. He remained here, becoming the chair of the Visual Arts Department in 1995, until he retired from that position in 2008. While at IU South Bend, Droege continued to paint and exhibit, primarily locally and primarily still lifes and abstract expressionist paintings based on the motions of dancing. Although he is retired, Droege continues to be involved in local art.

Anna Maria DuChene, later known as **Sister Immaculata, CSC**, was born in 1872 in Cacheville, California. She studied across the United States, beginning with Saint Mary's College at Notre Dame, and eventually traveling to Baltimore, Cape Cod, and Washington, D.C. She returned to St. Mary's, where she taught and became involved with exhibitions. Many of her paintings were of landscapes, including three of her most well known pieces, *Still Life*, *The Pond*, and *Cyclamen*.

Oscar William Fackert was born in Jersey City, New Jersey, in 1891. He specialized in painting the human figure; his painting *Red Kimono*, won an honorable mention at an art show in Kansas City. He also painted landscapes and designed tapestries. He exhibited around the Midwest, including at the Art Institute of Chicago, the Hoosier Salon, at Marshall Fields in Chicago, and Grand Beach in Michigan. Oscar passed away in New York in March 1939.

Thomas S. Fern was best known for his large-scale oil portraits. He studied at the University of Minnesota, where he received both his bachelor of fine arts and a master's degree; he received a PhD from New York University. In 1967 Fern took a position in the art department at the University of Notre Dame and he would eventually serve as the Department of Art chairman. In 1988 he moved to Venice, but while in the Midwest he participated in a series of exhibitions and served on a number of committees. He had exhibits at the South Bend Museum of Art, the Midwest Museum of American Art located in Elkhart, as well as the Snite Museum of Art at Notre Dame, and Purdue University in West Lafayette. He also served on the South Bend Art Center's board of trustees, the Indiana Committee for the Humanities and the South Bend Visual Arts Program.

James Flanigan, CSC, entered the Holy Cross Seminary in 1949 and recently celebrated the fiftieth anniversary of his ordination. He received his master of arts degree from the University of Notre Dame, and a master of fine arts from George Washington University. Although Father Flanigan joined the seminary early, it wasn't until 1962 that he began to create and teach art at Notre Dame. He is known primarily for sculptures, such as the statue of Brother André Bessette on Notre Dame's campus, currently positioned outside the Eck Visitor's Center. Flanigan also created large-scale charcoal drawings in addition to the sculptures. Typically, he exhibits locally; in December 1994 he had a solo exhibit at the South Bend Museum of Art. He taught sculpting and drawing for over forty years, retired from teaching in 2006, but still resides in the seminary at Notre Dame and continues to create artwork.

Alexis Jean Fournier's relationship with Brown county of Indiana began following his marriage to Cora May Ball in 1922. He was born in St. Cloud, Minnesota in 1865 and began painting at a young age. He had sold several paintings by age 16 despite very little formal training beyond a short time at the Minneapolis School of Design under Douglas Volk. In 1890, Fournier enrolled at the Académie Julian in France. There he embraced the French Barbizon style; he has since been considered one of the last great French Barbizon painters. Only a few years later in 1893, his panoramic mural *The Cliff Dwellers* was part of the Columbian Exhibit at the World's Fair. This was a huge turning point in his career and the financial success of this exhibition helped fund Fournier's many expeditions abroad. In 1913 Fournier began to associate himself with a group of Impressionist painters from Brown county in Indiana, which led to a shift away from French impressionism and instead to the prominent regional style. His marriage to Mrs. Cora Mae Ball cemented his ties to the local area and he maintained a winter home there. *Between Showers* (1934), painted in Indiana, won the Thomas Butler Outstanding Landscape in Oil award at the 10th Annual Hoosier Salon. Following his wife's death, Fournier relocated his primary studio to East Aurora, New York. Although he visited the area only irregularly, he was welcomed fondly upon every return until his death in 1948, after slipping on ice, at age 82.

Moira Geoffrion was born in Olney, Maryland, and is widely known for her unique styles of drawing and sculpting. She received her bachelor of fine arts from Boston University and later worked towards her master of fine arts at Indiana University but finally received one in sculpture from Southern Illinois University. Geoffrion took a teaching position with the University of Notre Dame in 1974. She remained there until 1986, when she left South Bend to take a position with the University of Arizona. Sculpting was her initial passion, but had to switch to minimal drawing following surgery on her hands. Eventually, she was able to journey back into sculpting. Her later exhibits, both drawings and sculptures, utilized white space. This was extremely apparent during her final local exhibit in 1986 at the South Bend Museum of Art. Although she left the area in 1986, Geoffrion continues to create and exhibit her artwork in Arizona.

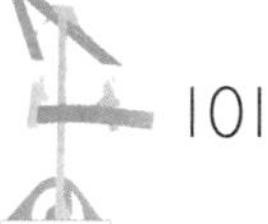

Richard Gray has been involved in the art world for more than 30 years, and has spent much of that time exhibiting his photography. Born in 1954, Gray began his college career at Illinois State University and received a bachelor of science in graphic arts in 1976, followed a master of fine arts a few years later in 1982. He also studied at the Rochester Institute of Technology and earned a master of fine arts. Through these programs, he grew as a photographer and soon began teaching classes such as photographic practice, studio lighting, and contemporary issues at the University of Notre Dame. He has also

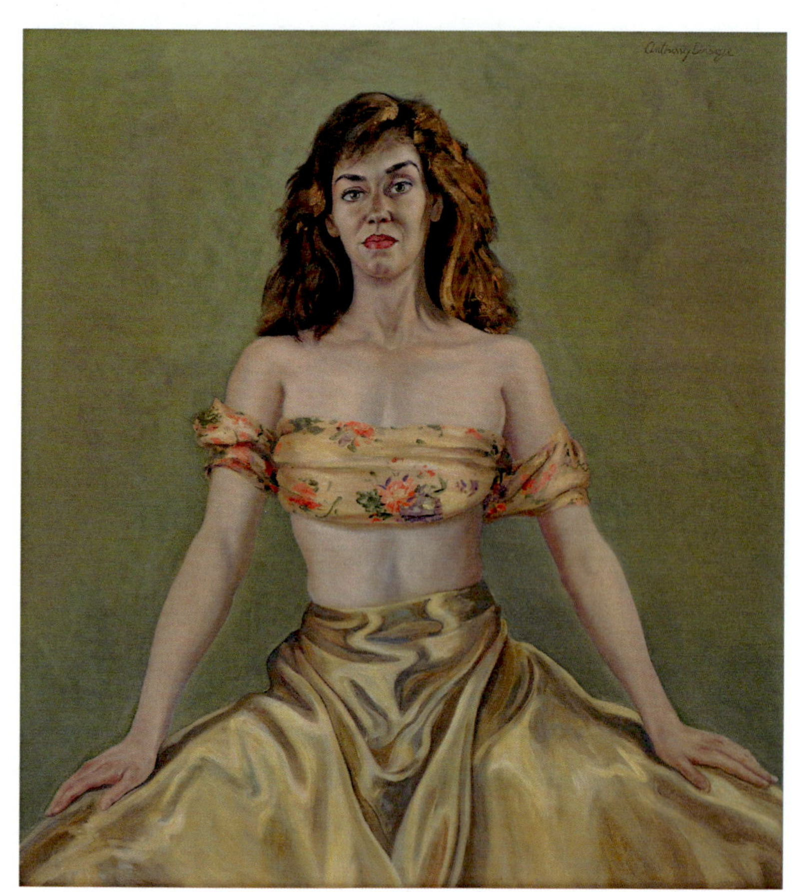

Anthony Droege, *Anette.*

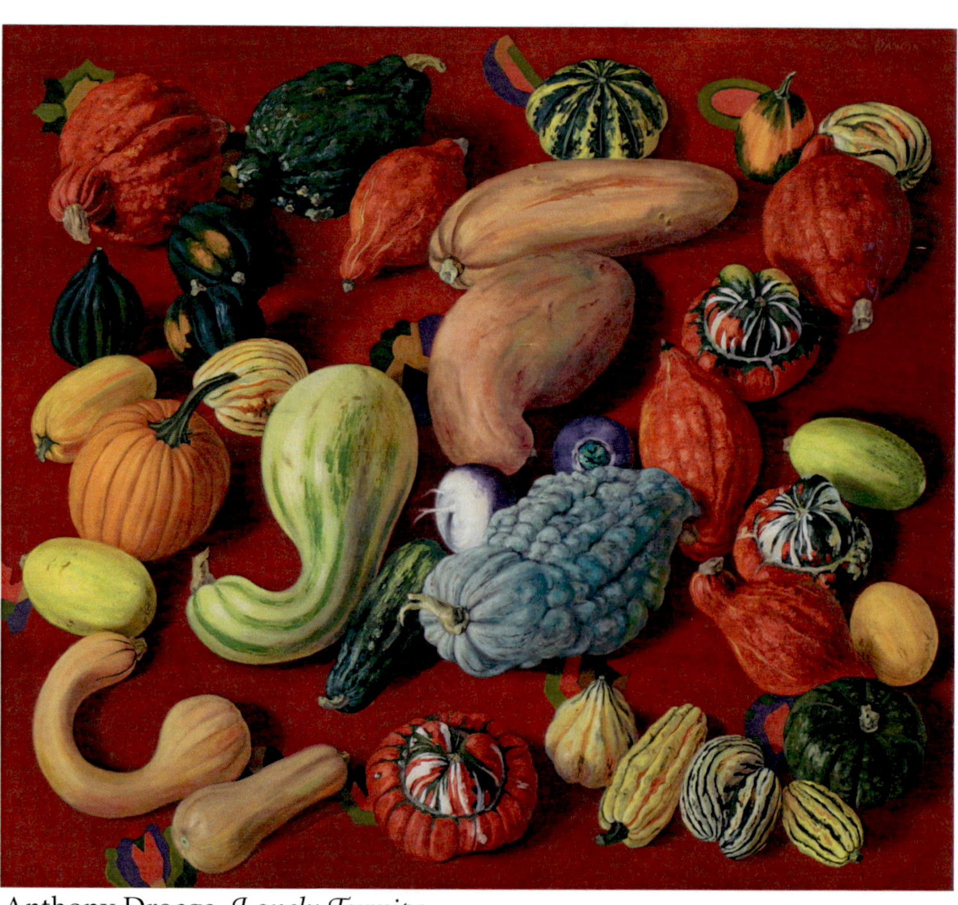

Anthony Droege, *Lonely Turnips.*

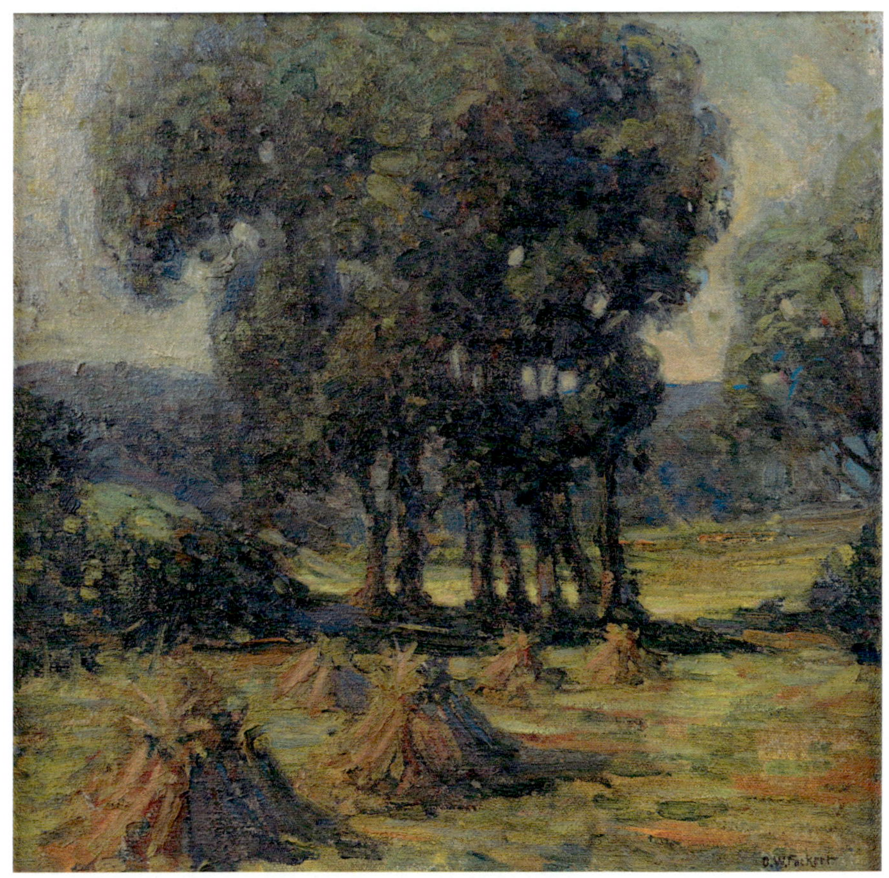

Oscar W. Fackert, *Landscape with Haystacks.*

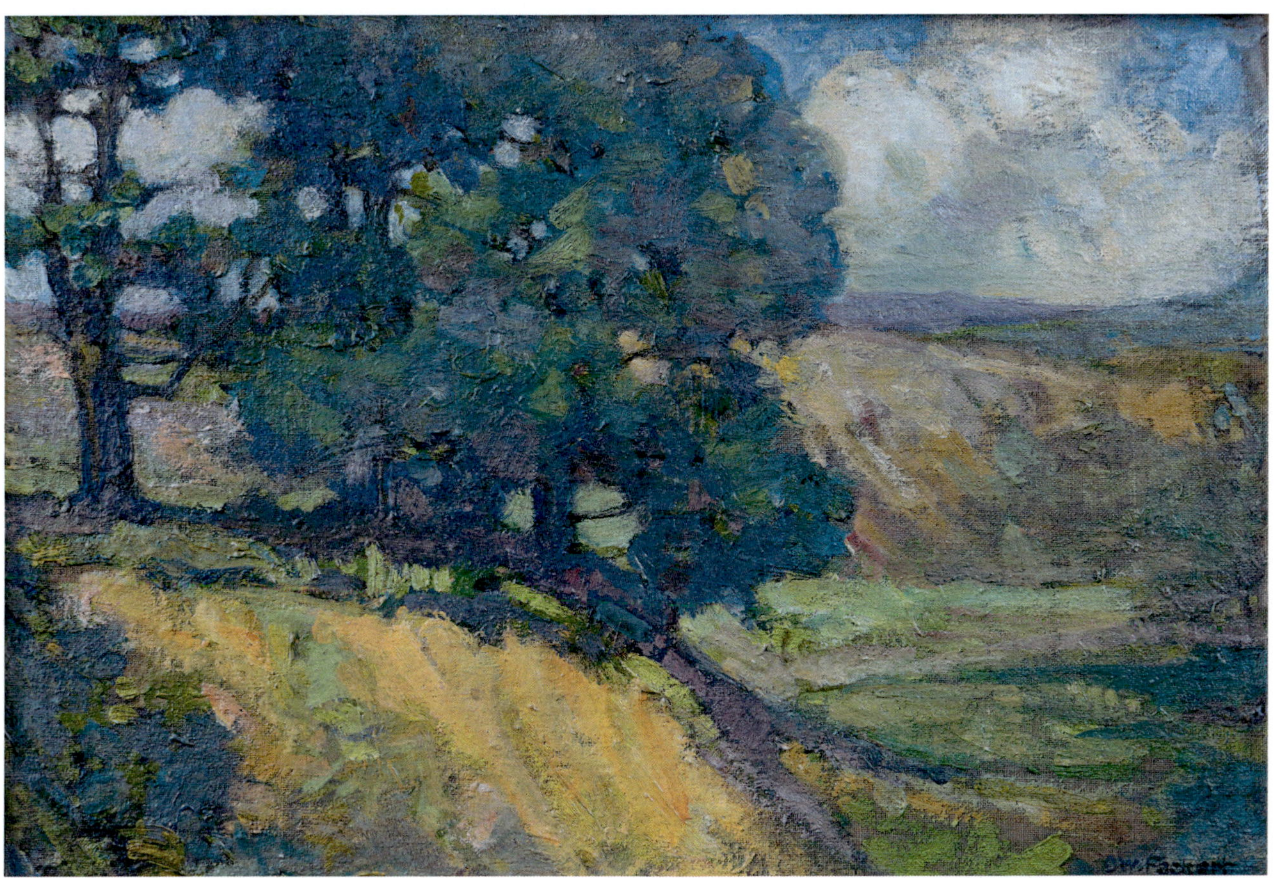

Oscar W. Fackert, *Midsummer.*

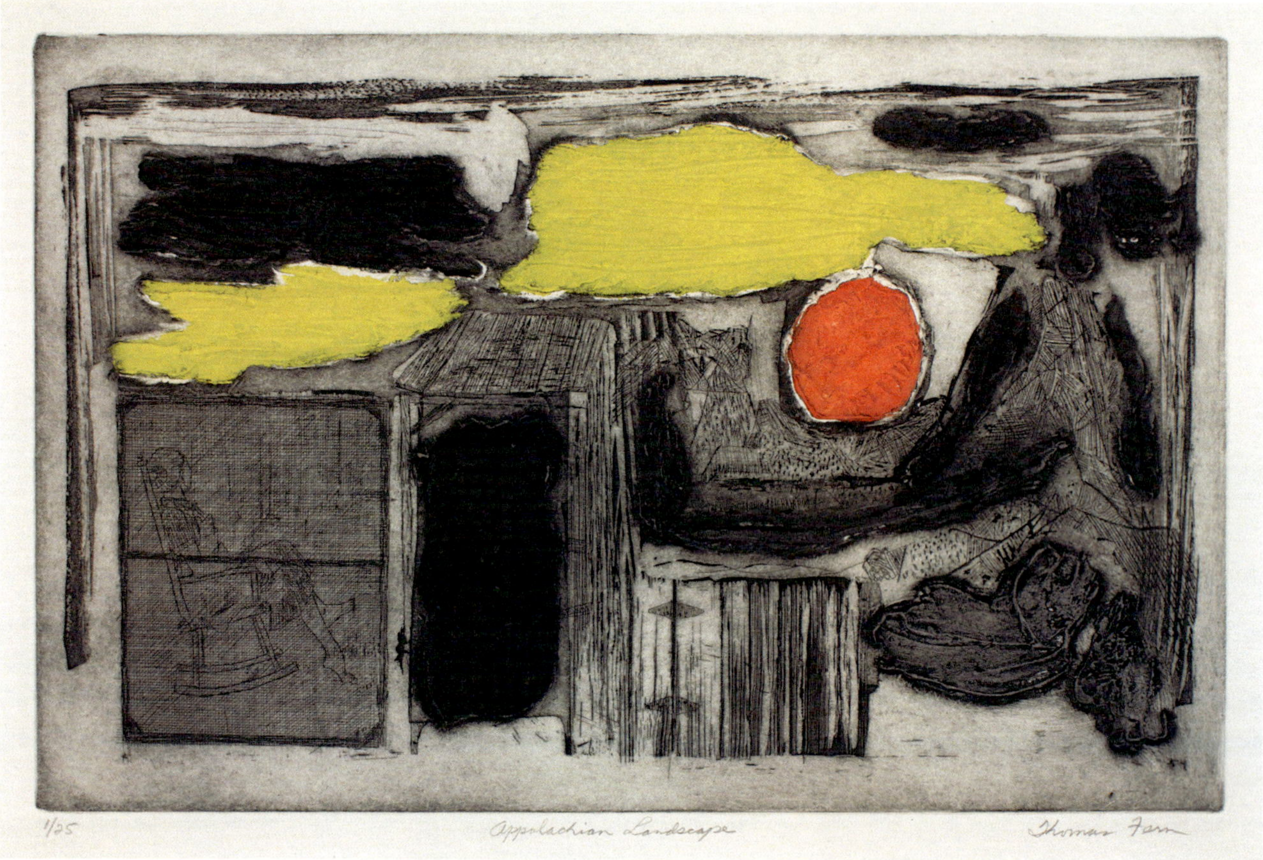

Thomas S. Fern, *Appalachian Landscape.*

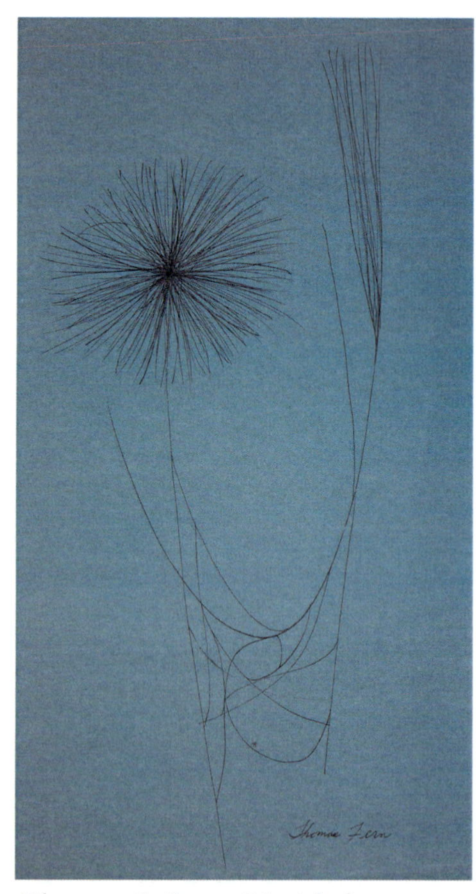

Thomas S. Fern, *Untitled.*

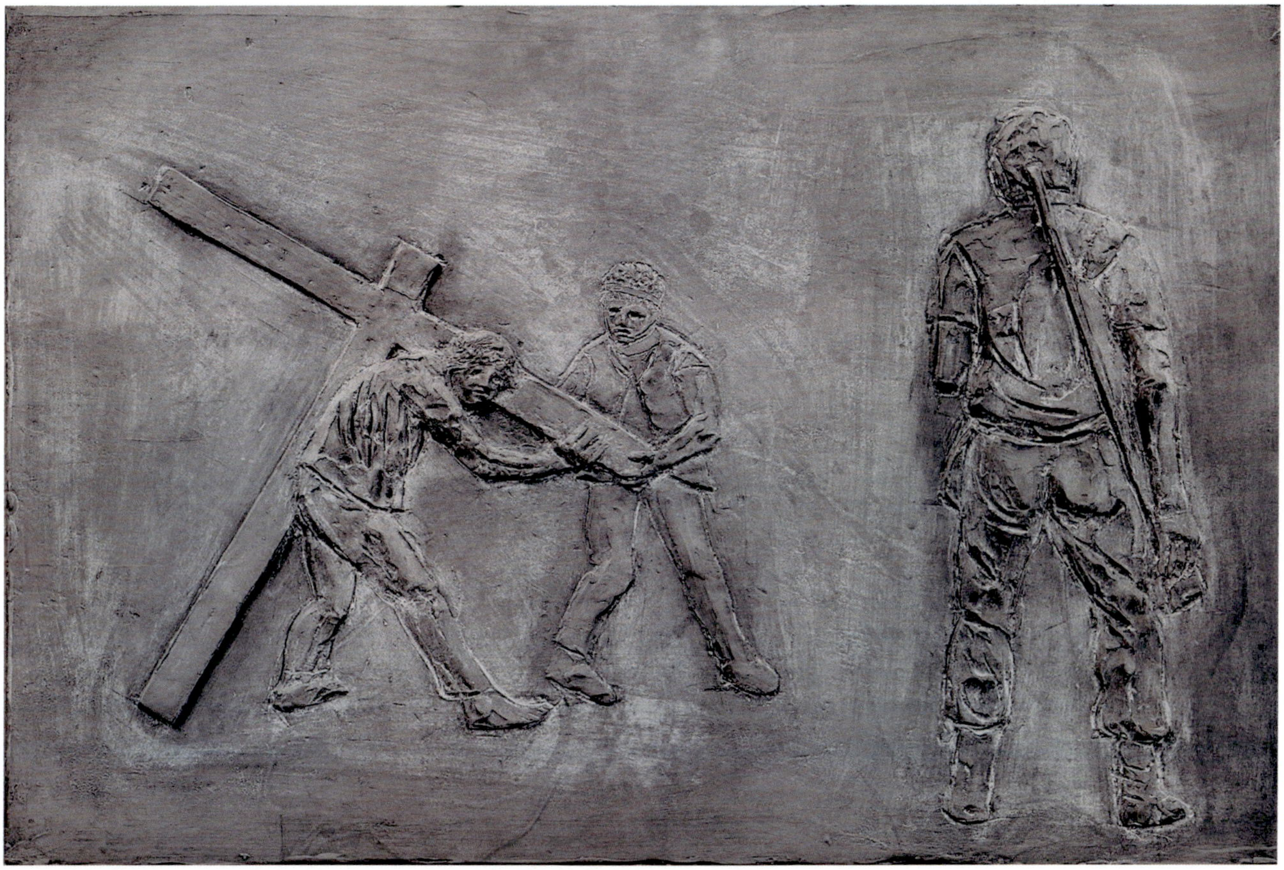

James Flanagan, CSC, *Simon of Cyrene Helps Jesus Carry the Cross.*

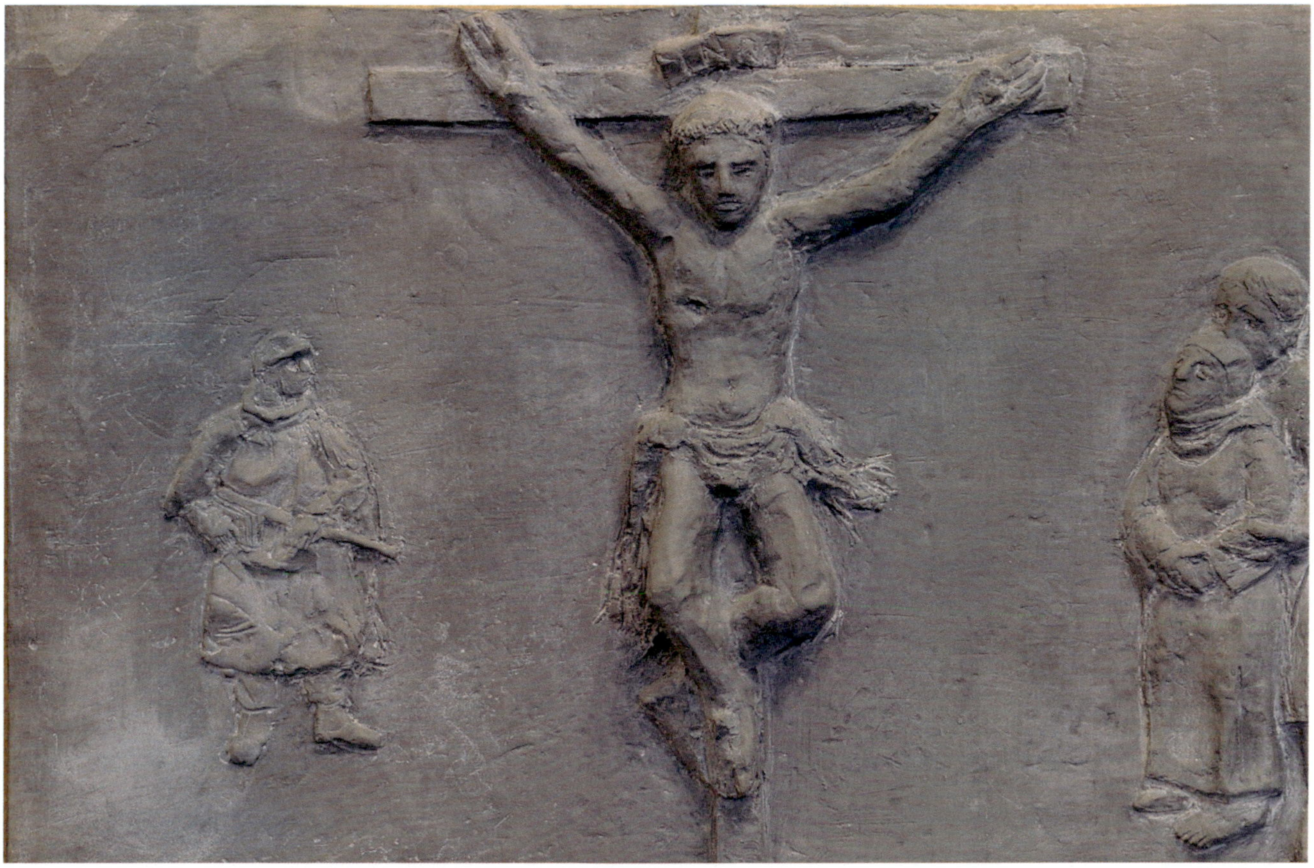

James Flanagan, CSC, *The Crucifixion.*

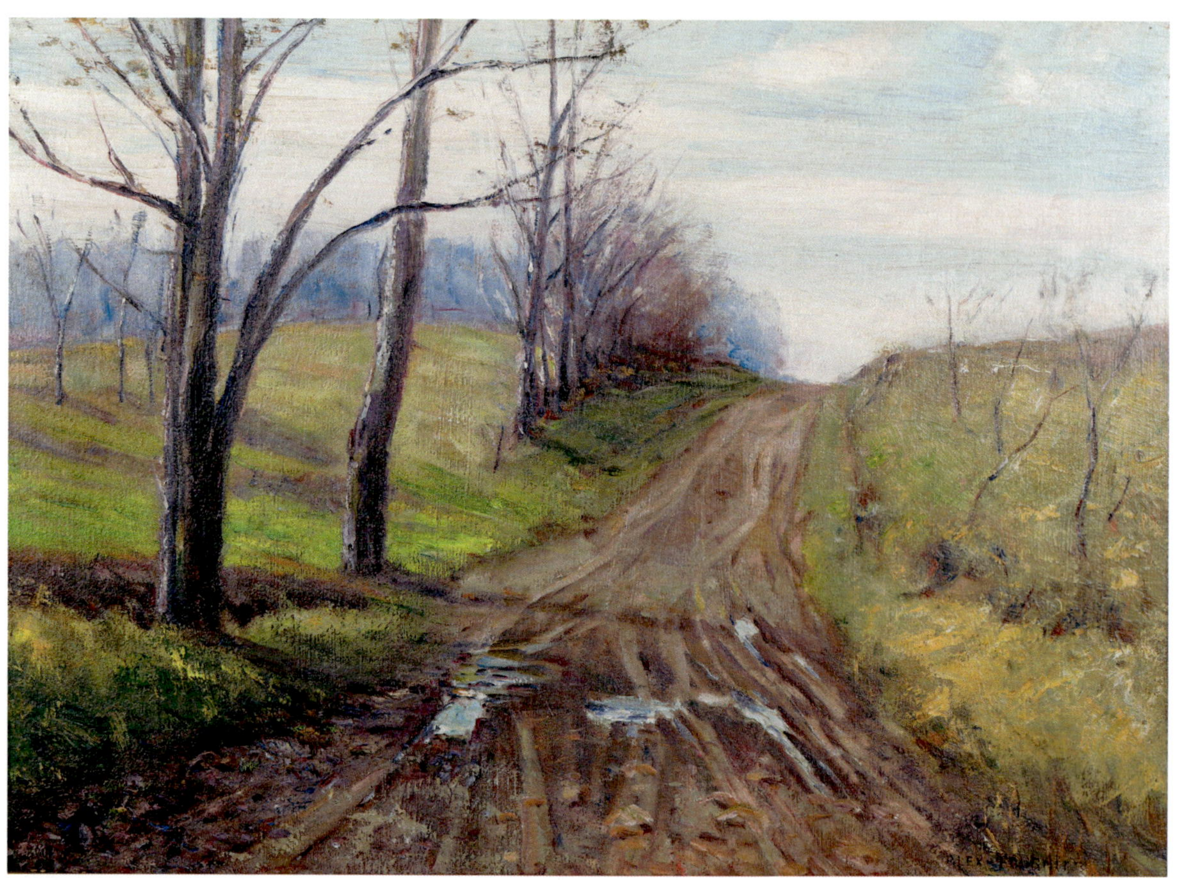

Alexis-Jean Fournier, *Path Through the Landscape.*

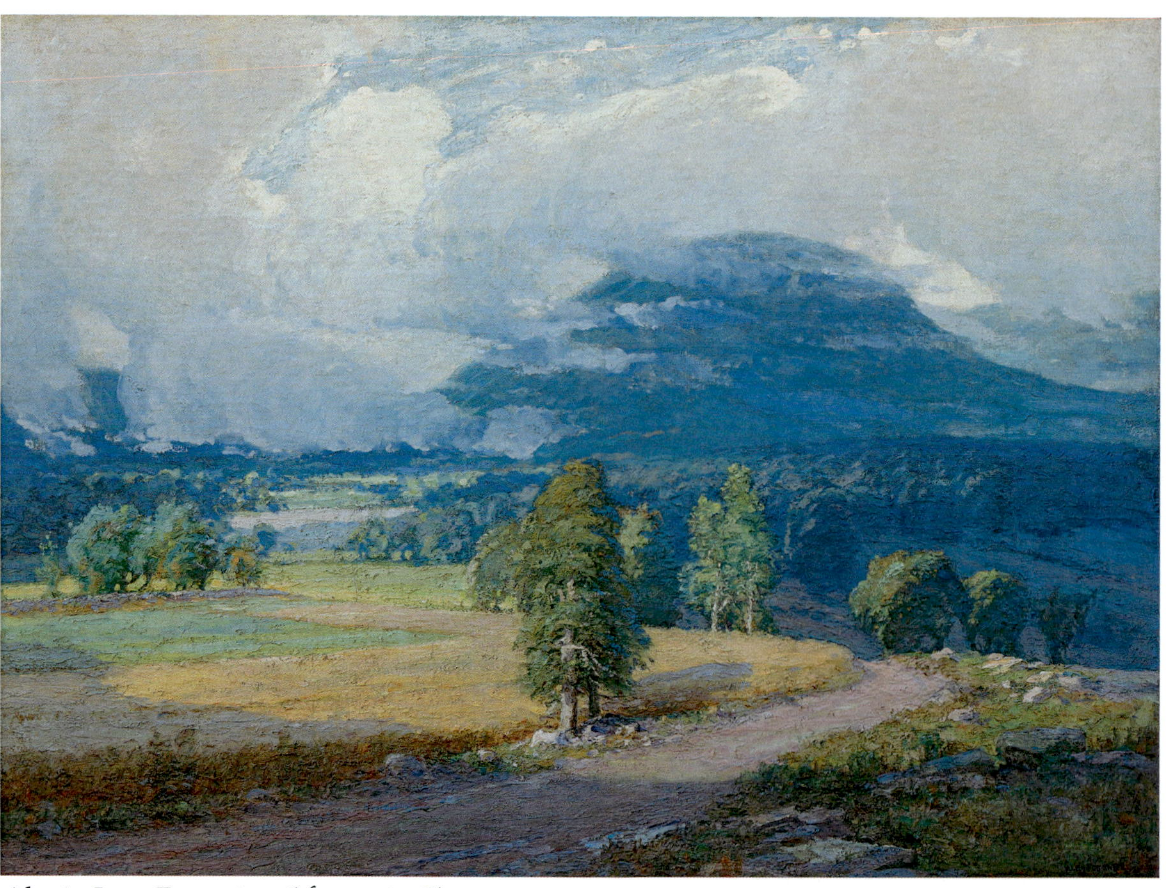

Alexis-Jean Fournier, *Mountain Trees.*

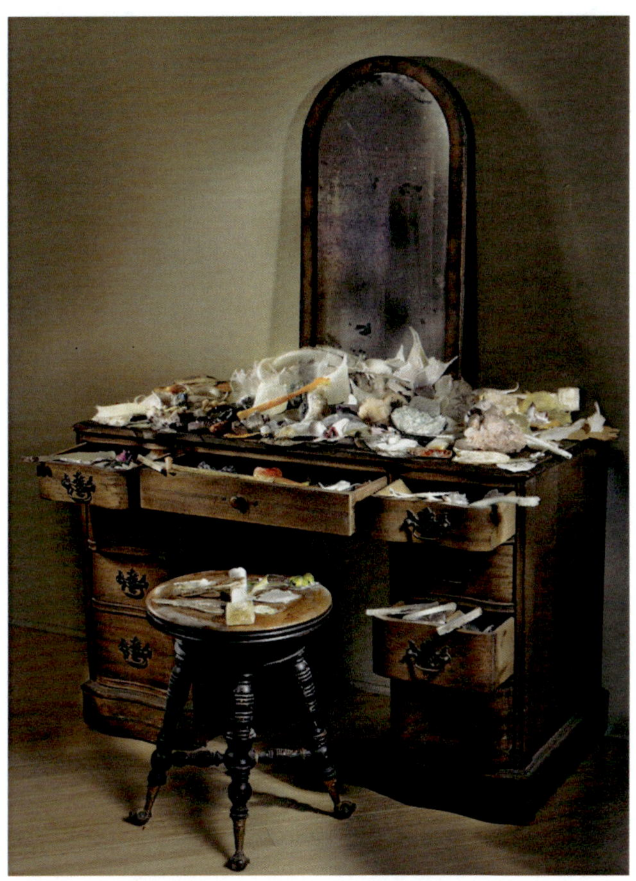

Moira Geoffreon, *Gertrude's Desk.*

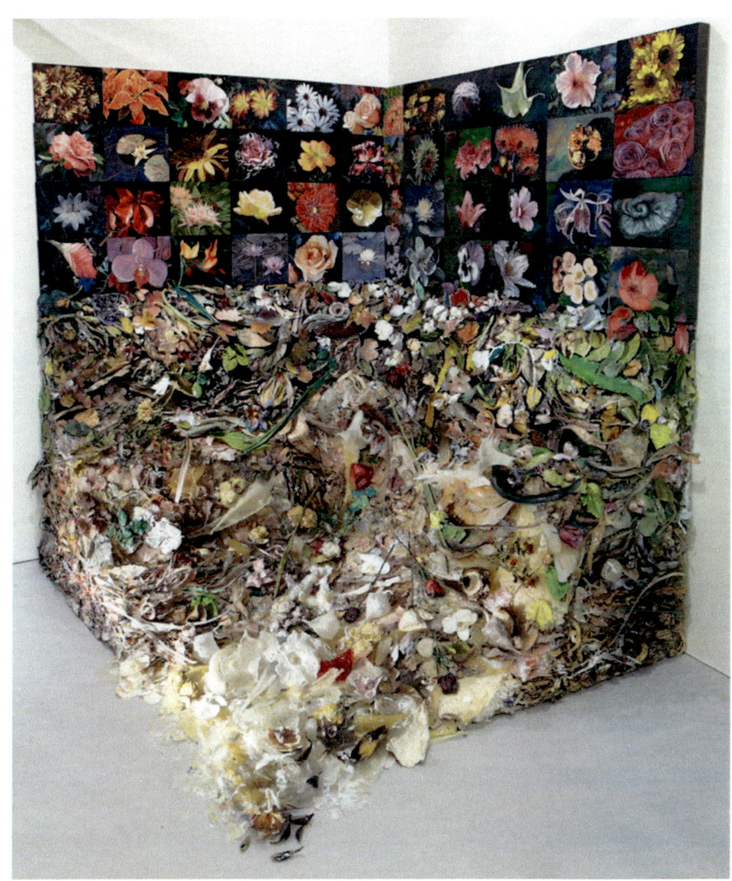

Moira Geoffreon, *The Disappeared.*

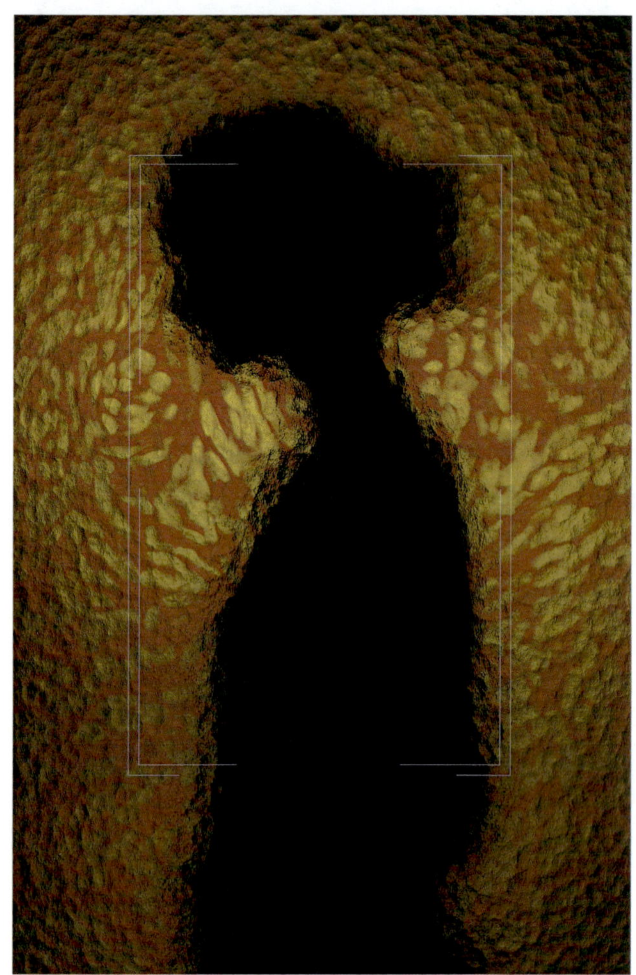

Richard Gray, *Witness 5*.

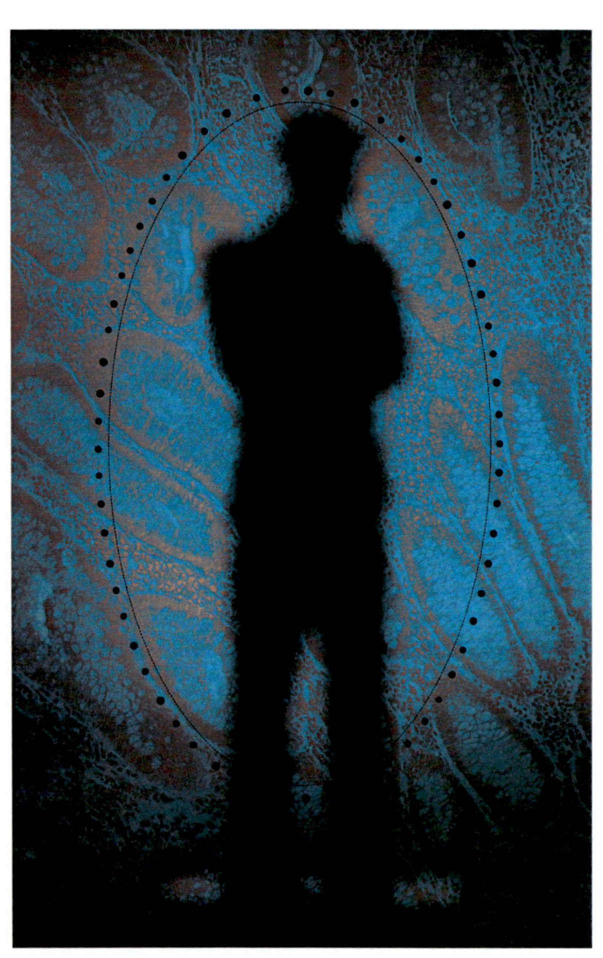

Richard Gray, *Witness 9*.

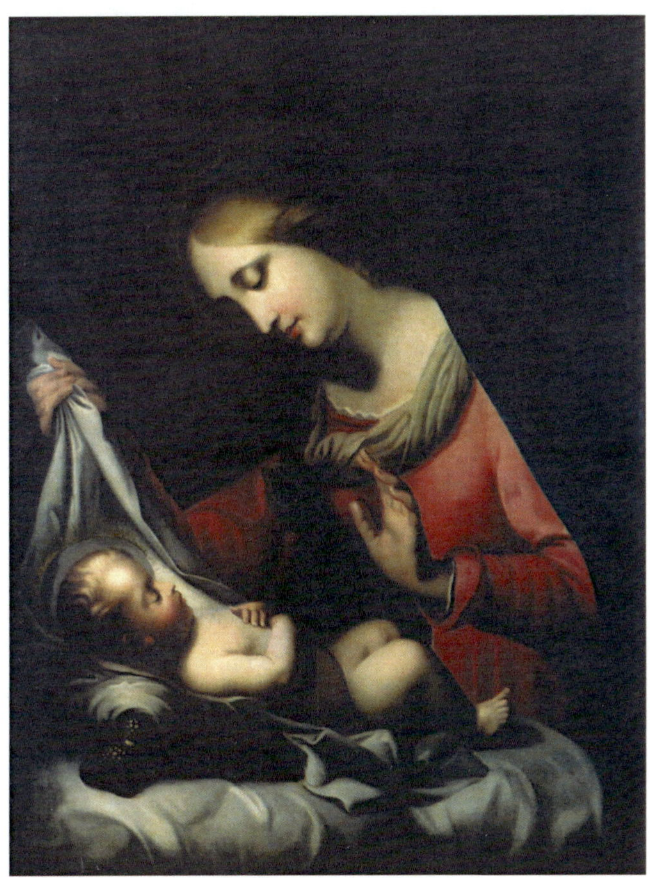

Luigi Grigori, *Madonna of the Veil.*

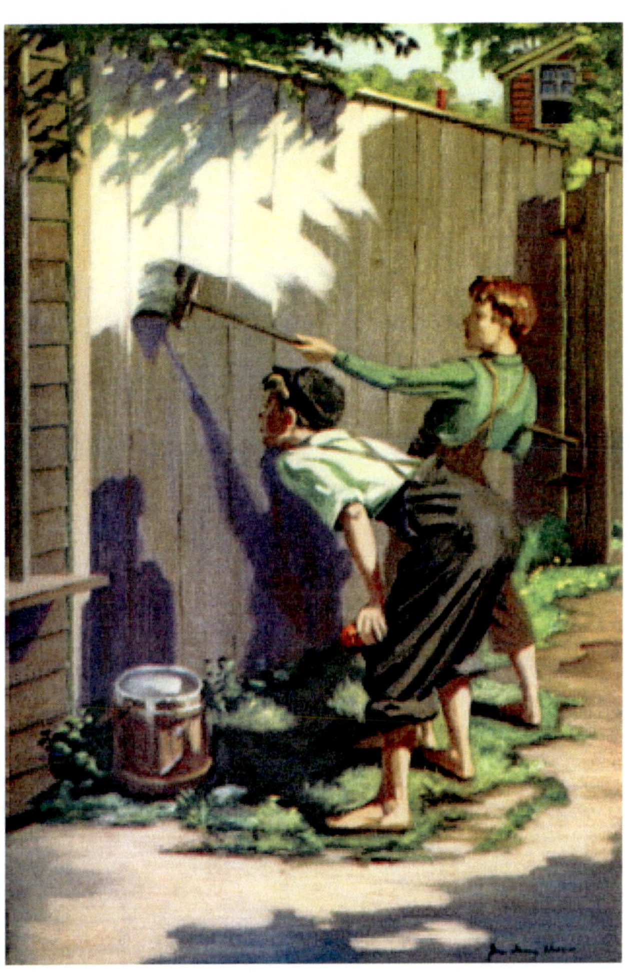

James Murray Haddow, *Whitewashing.*

served as director of the Center for Creative Computing, again at Notre Dame. Gray has also been involved with the nation-wide Society for Photographic Education (SPE) since the 1980s where he acted as the chair and has served on the SPE board since 2004. On a more local scale, he has also served on the board of trustees for the South Bend Museum of Art. His work has consistently shown his interest in human identity, which can be seen throughout many of his works. Gray currently resides in South Bend, Indiana, and continues to work for the University of Notre Dame.

Luigi Gregori, Italian by birth, but Hoosier by association, was born in Bologna, Italy, in 1819. Much of his schooling occurred in Europe where he apprenticed to Giovanni Battista Frulli, served Prince Pignatelli of Monteleone, and eventually enrolled at Academia di San Luca in 1840 where he studied beneath Tommaso Minardi. Under Minardi, he became familiar with Renaissance style art and neoclassicism. Following his education, Gregori was hired as an artist in residence at the Vatican by Pope Pius IX where he was commissioned to create portraits. However, due to Pope Pius IX's focus on restoring and maintaining classic art, he created little and instead became a specialist at restoration. Following a visit to the Vatican in 1874 by Father Edward Sorin of Notre Dame, Gregori and his family relocated to northern Indiana where he often had a plethora of creative projects to keep him occupied, starting with designing the Sacred Heart Church, currently known as the Basilica of the Sacred Heart. He was also commissioned to paint a series of fourteen Stations of the Cross to depict Christ's journey to Calvary, as well as the *Life of Christopher Columbus* mural cycle in the Administration building. He only resided in America for 17 years and returned to Italy in 1891 with his daughter. Luigi Gregori passed away in Florence, Italy in 1896 at 77 years of age.

James Murray Haddow came to the United States in 1926 from Scotland, his home country, and promptly began studying American art. He had previously studied at Strathaven and Pollock Shields Academy in Scotland. Upon arriving in America, he took to studying at the National Academy of Art as well as the Art Institute, both in Chicago. For a short period of time, Haddow was a resident at the Tree Studio Building and Annexes, also in Chicago. In addition to these experiences, he worked as a drawing and painting instructor at the National Academy of Art in Chicago and was a member of the Chicago Galleries Association. He also served as president of the Chicago Painters and Sculptors Group. From 1947-1949, he found himself engaged as the first director of the South Bend Art Association.

The **Hartig** family proved that artistic talent can run in the family genes. **Arthur** and two of his daughters **Beatrice (Hartig-Zimmerman)** and **Genevieve (Hartig-Toth)** all painted oil landscapes. Arthur was born in Hamilton, Ohio, in 1879. Before his children were born Arthur studied at the Chicago Art Institute under Stanley Sessler and Emile Jacques, the latter of whom his children studied with as well. Beatrice, the eldest daughter, was born in 1904 in Chicago while Genevieve, locally referred to as Geni, was born ten years later, in 1914. Beatrice received a four-year scholarship to use for her high school education majoring in art at the Chicago Art Institute. All three family members studied under Emile Jacques and Stanley Sessler of the University of Notre Dame. Geni also attended Ball State in 1940. Following the girls' marriages, they continued to paint and embrace art on a local level. In addition to exhibiting art at the Hoosier Salon, Beatrice owned her own gallery in Osceola. Later, Geni helped establish the art department at Penn High School, where she became an art teacher. Geni also submitted many small paintings to the Caspari Card Company in New York for use as greeting cards. Beatrice was a librarian, music teacher, and church organist for thirty years. All three family members were members of the St. Joe Valley Chapter of the American Artists Professional League in 1936; Arthur and Beatrice were also members of the Midland Academy of Art in South Bend. Arthur passed away in 1959, Beatrice in 1988, and Geni in 1997.

Edward Harding was an important area figure as a fine artist and arts educator. Born in Leiters Ford, Indiana on April 21, 1929, Harding earned an MFA at the University of Michigan, where he learned stone lithography. Harding was a lifelong artist, working as a printmaker, and as a painter in watercolor, oil and acrylic. Shortly before his death, the South Bend Regional Museum's Warner gallery held a retrospective of his "en plein air" watercolors which were painted throughout the midwest, the East coast, Arizona and California. Harding was a member of the Michigan Printmakers Society, the Washington Print Society, and the American Watercolor Society. He taught at several colleges and universities, Culver Academy, and the South Bend, Niles, and Bremen art centers. Harding was chairman of the Visual Communications Department at Ivy Tech Community College of South Bend from 1970-1992. Harding passed away on July 29, 1993.

William Healy is best known for his stark photographic works, but he also uses oil paints and pastels. He is a member of the Northern Indiana Artists and acts as the board president of Fire Arts, Inc. For several years, Healy has taught a class at Indiana University South Bend on Sunday nights called the Life Drawing Group, where artists gather and use models to focus on drawing the human figure. In 2009, he won an award for his pastel drawing *Sweet* at the NIA membership show. Healy resides in South Bend.

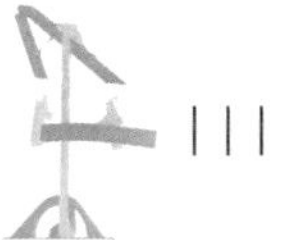

Edward E. Herrmann was a native Hoosier, born in Fort Wayne on August 23, 1914, and spent much of his life in Indiana. He attended school as a mechanical engineer at three different institutions including Purdue University, Indiana State University, and Pennsylvania State University. In 1943, he moved to South Bend and joined the Studebaker Corporation in Automotive Styling and Design. Herrmann eventually progressed to become the manager of interior design and color for both Raymond Loewy Associates and the Studebaker-Packard Corporation. Although he had never attended formal art classes, he began joining workshops and worked towards honing his artistic abilities. He primarily used watercolor or acrylic paints to portray realist and naturalist landscapes. After leaving the industrial world in 1958, he opened his own design consulting firm called Herrmann Design Consultants and taught art there for 16 years until 1974. Herrmann also began lecturing and teaching art workshops at the

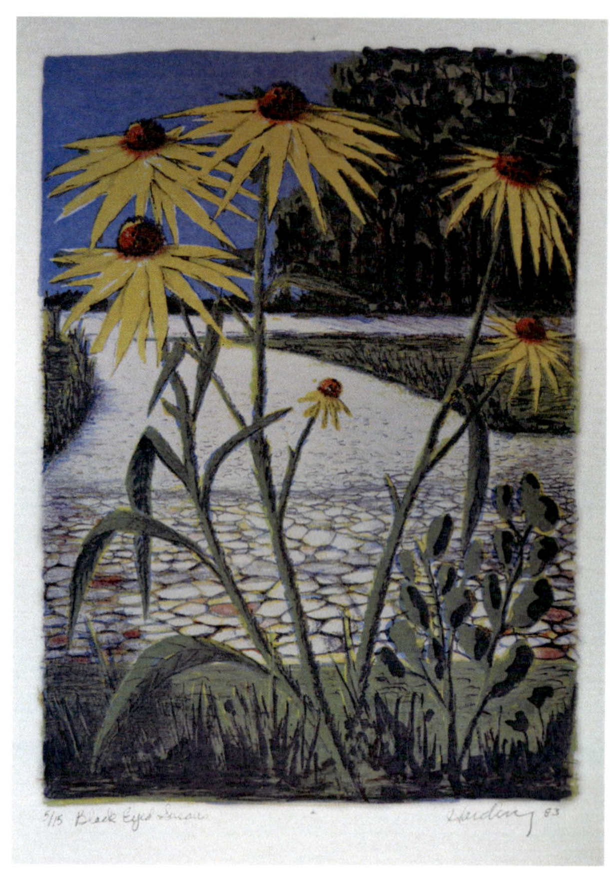

Edward Harding, *Black-Eyed Susans.*

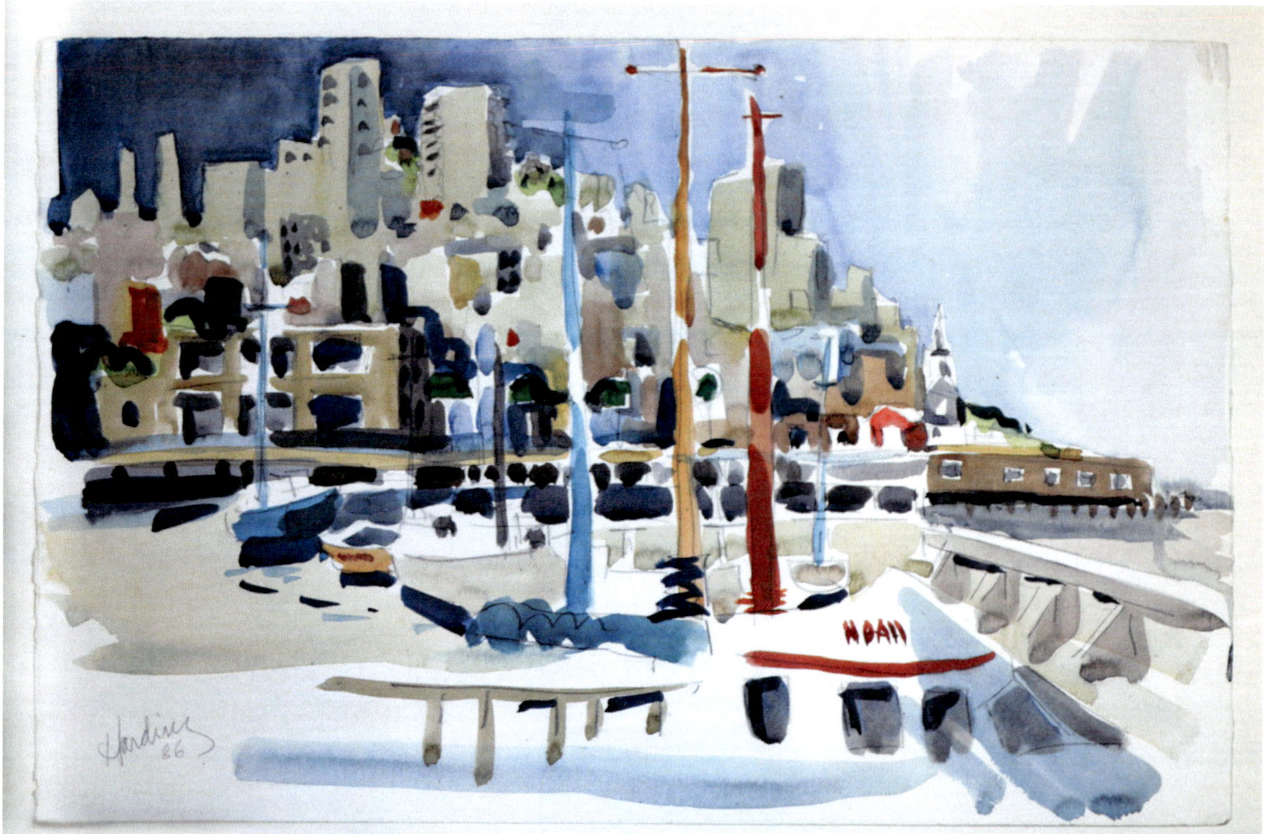

Edward Harding, *San Francisco Harbor.*

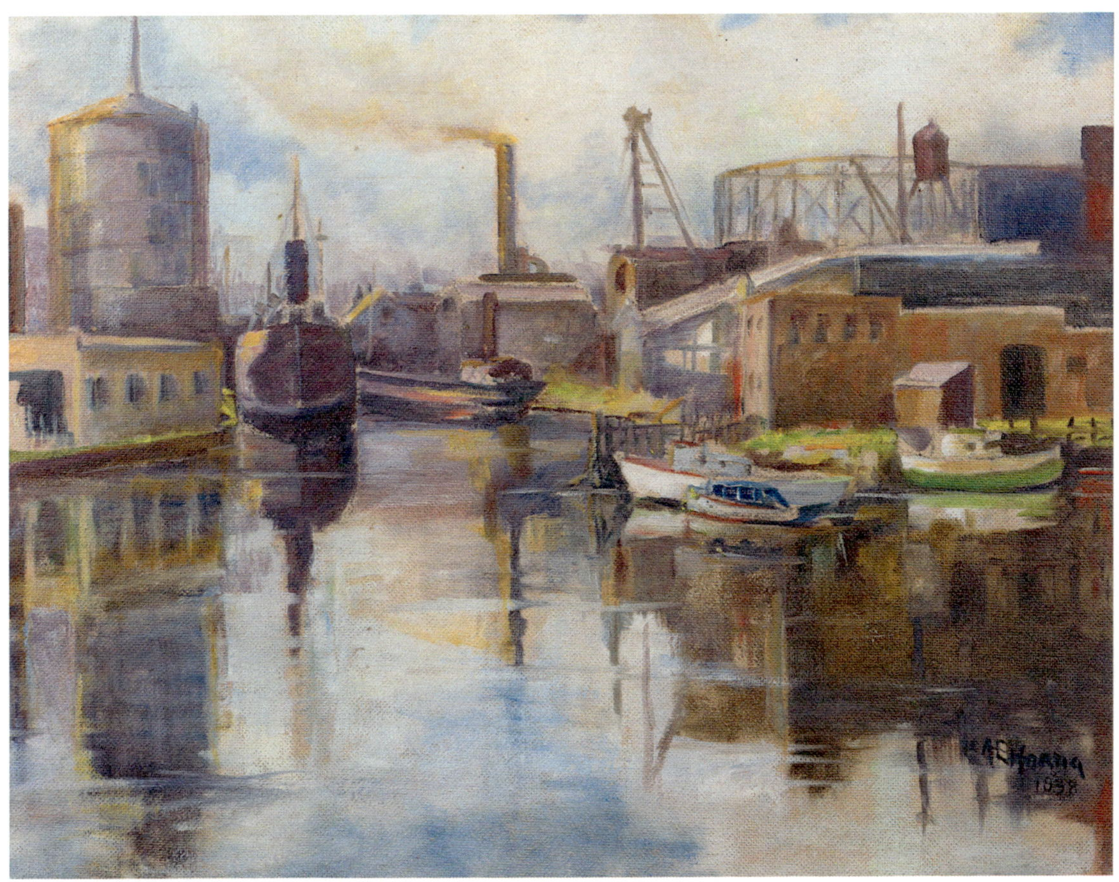

Arthur E. Hartig, *Harbor.*

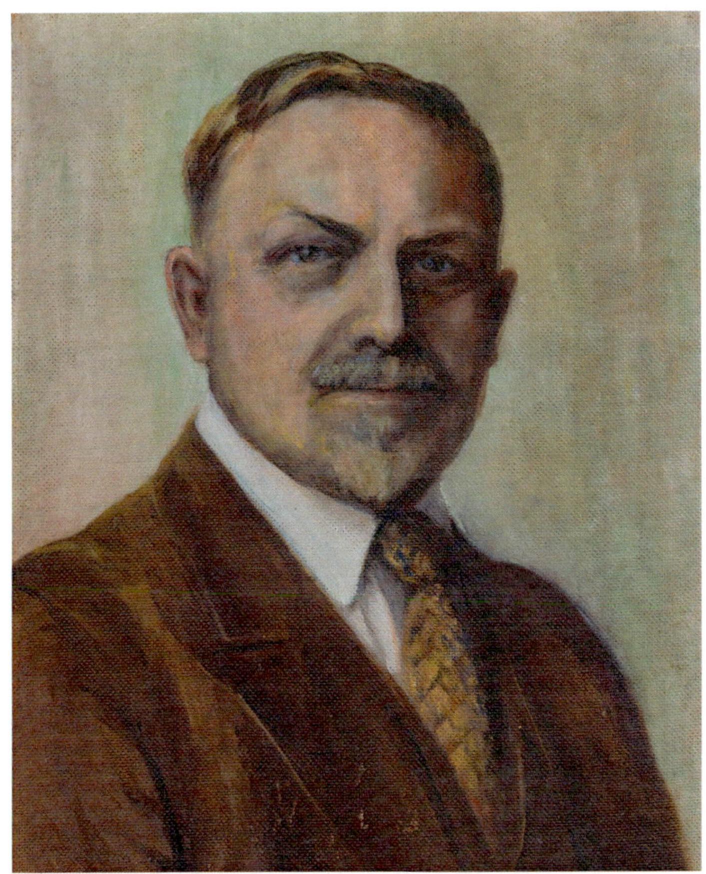

Arthur E. Hartig, *Portrait of Emile Jacques.*

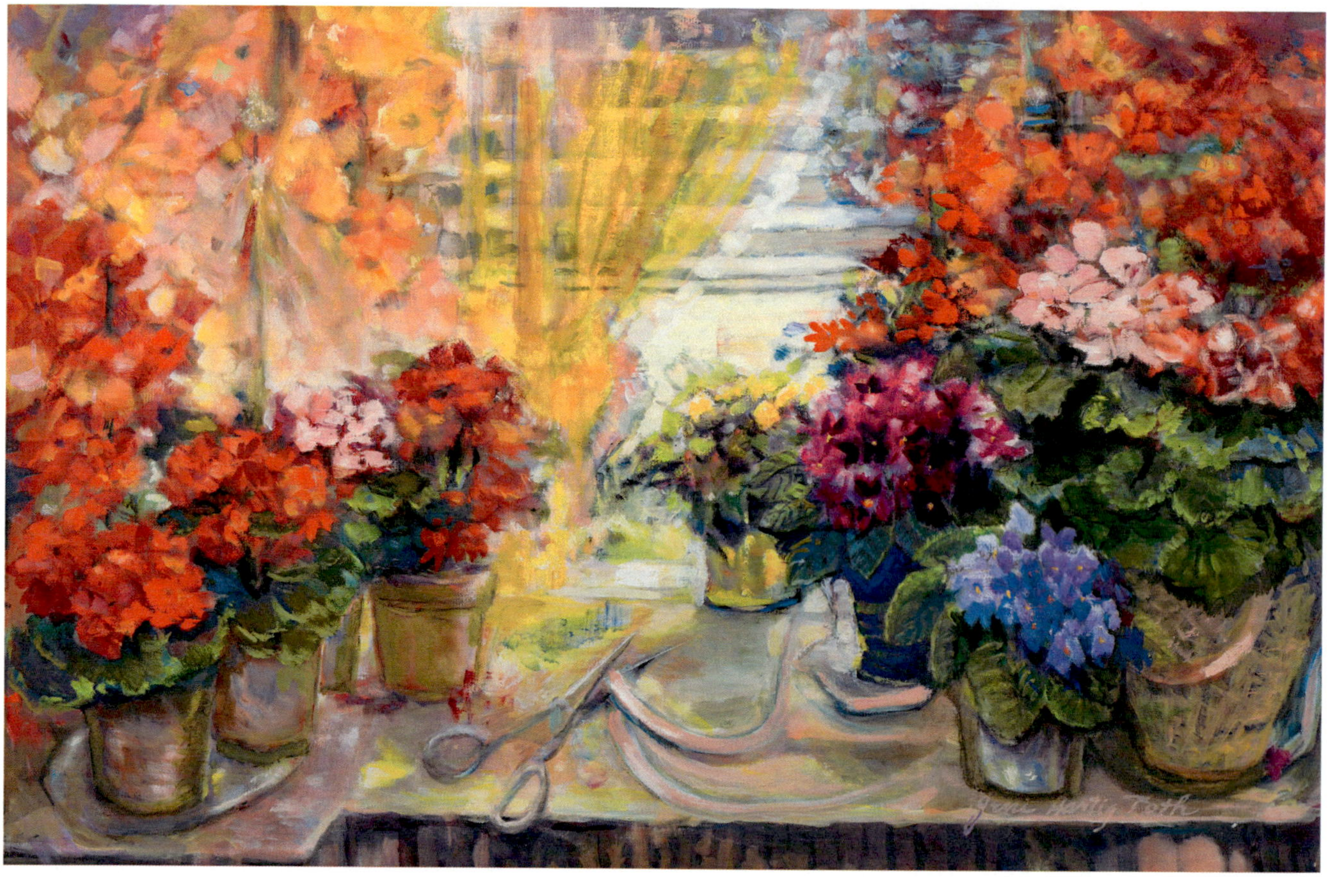

Genevieve Hartig-Toth, *Flower Still Life*.

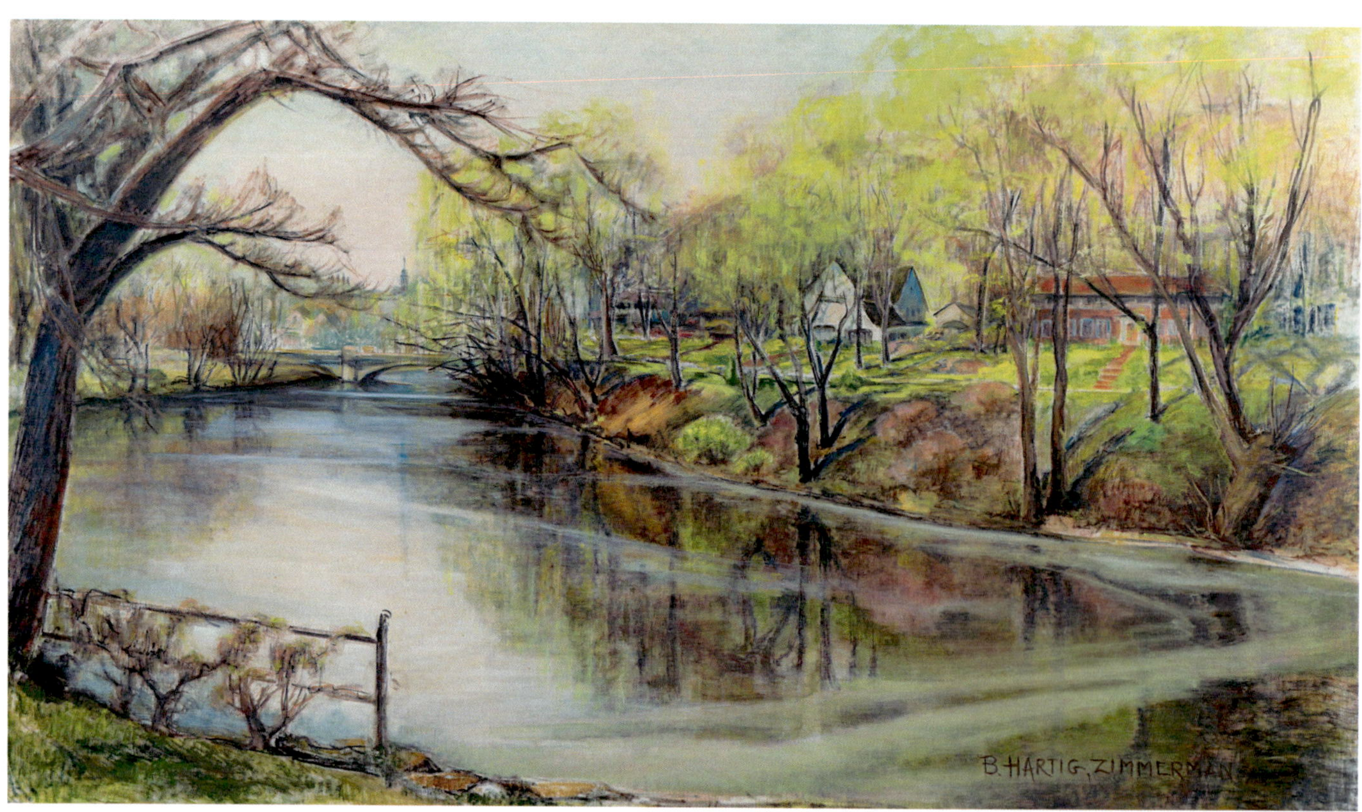

Beatrice Hartig-Zimmerman, *Landscape* (*St. Joseph River, Mishawaka, Indiana*).

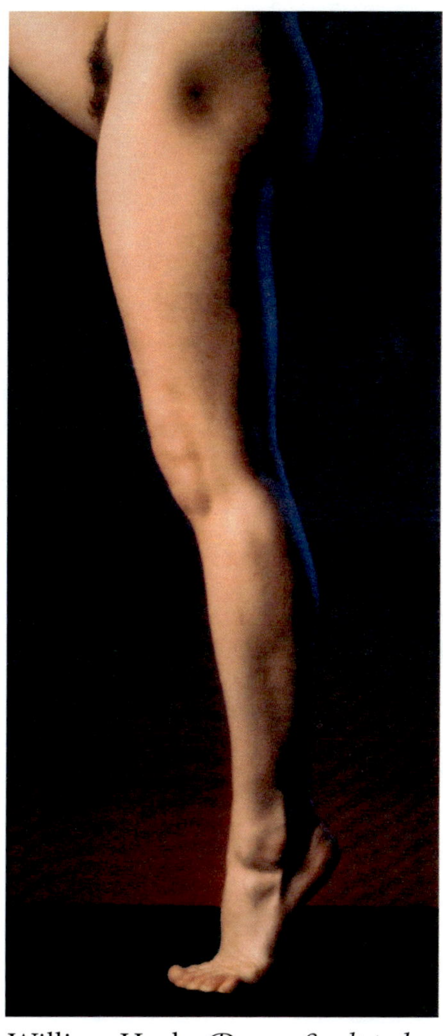
William Healy, *Dance Sculpted*.

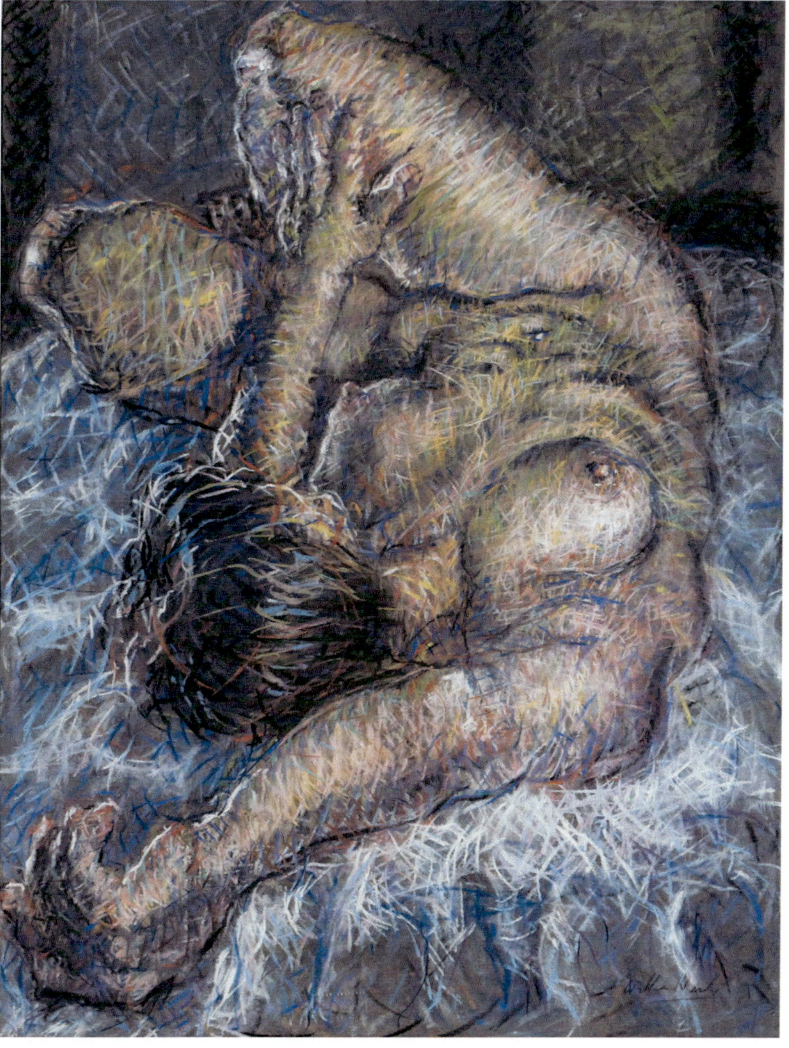
William Healy, *Sara Reclining*.

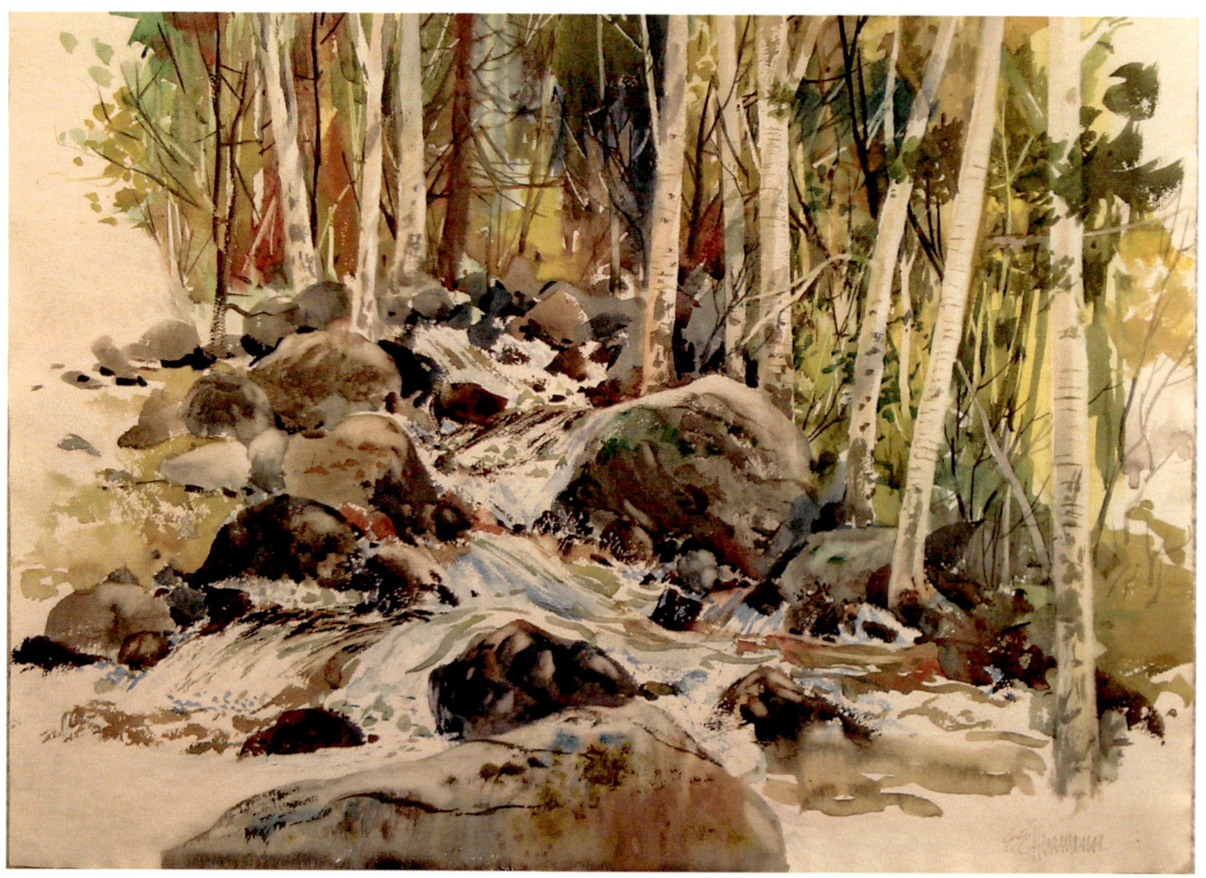

Edward E. Hermann, *Song of the Roaring River.*

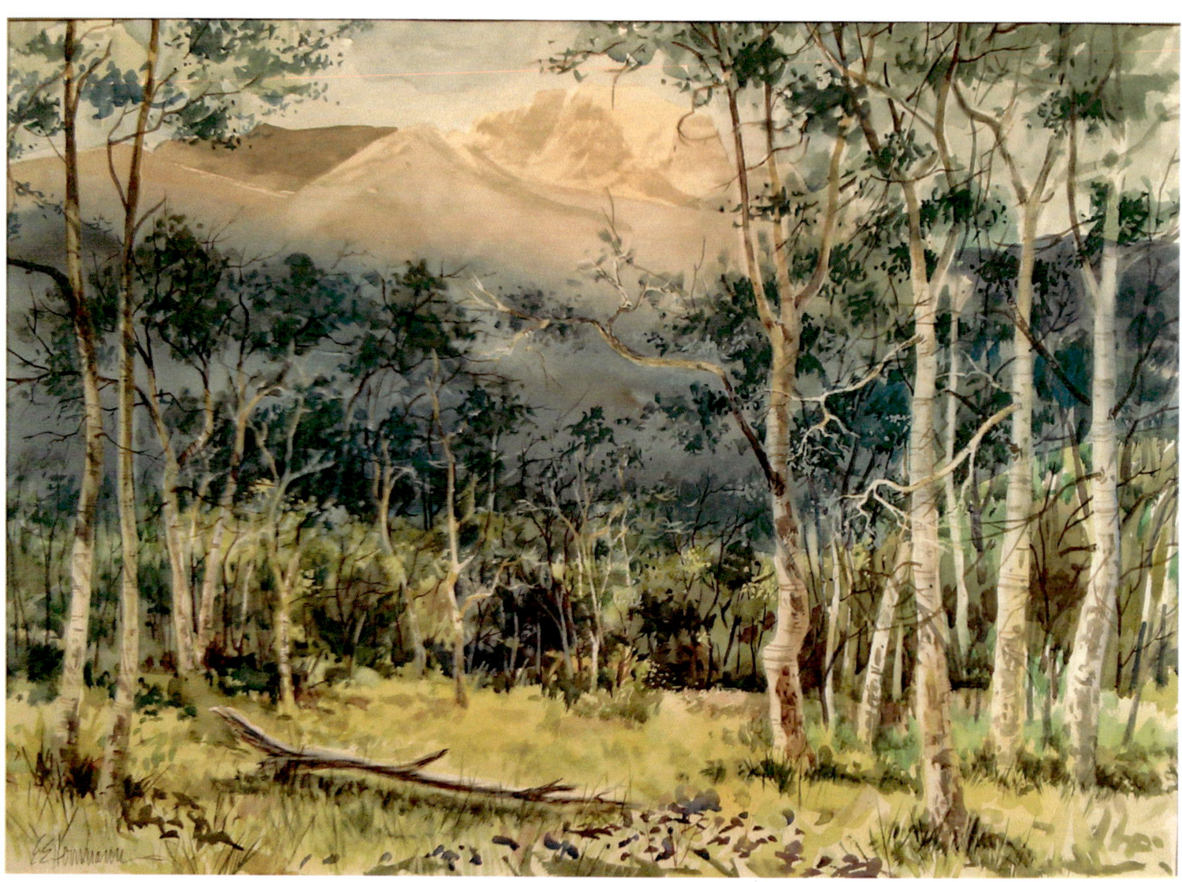

Edward E. Hermann, *Spring Aspen with Long Peak.*

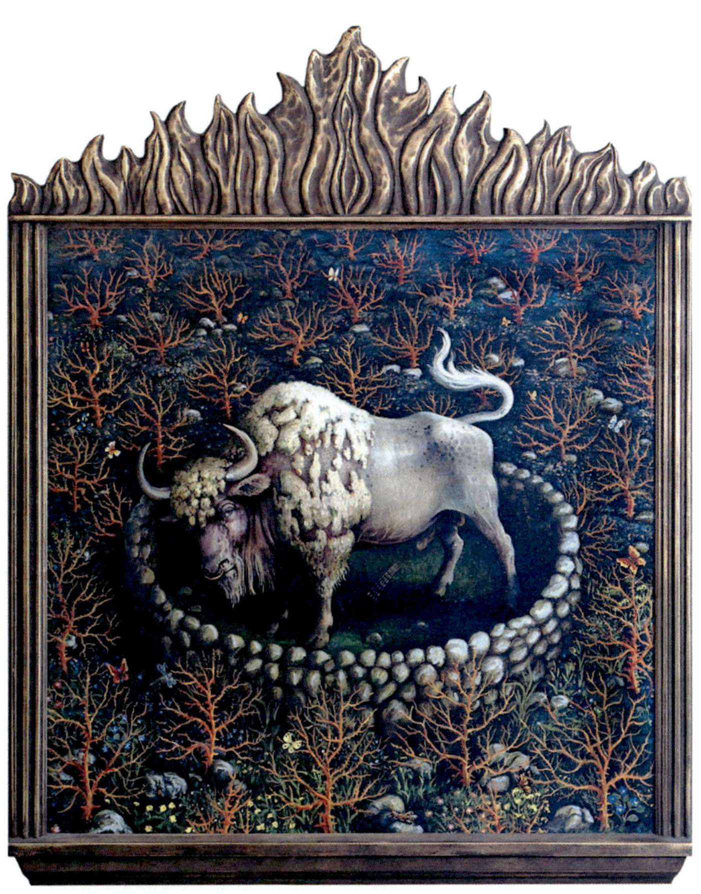

Kim Hoffmann, *The Gold Ring.*

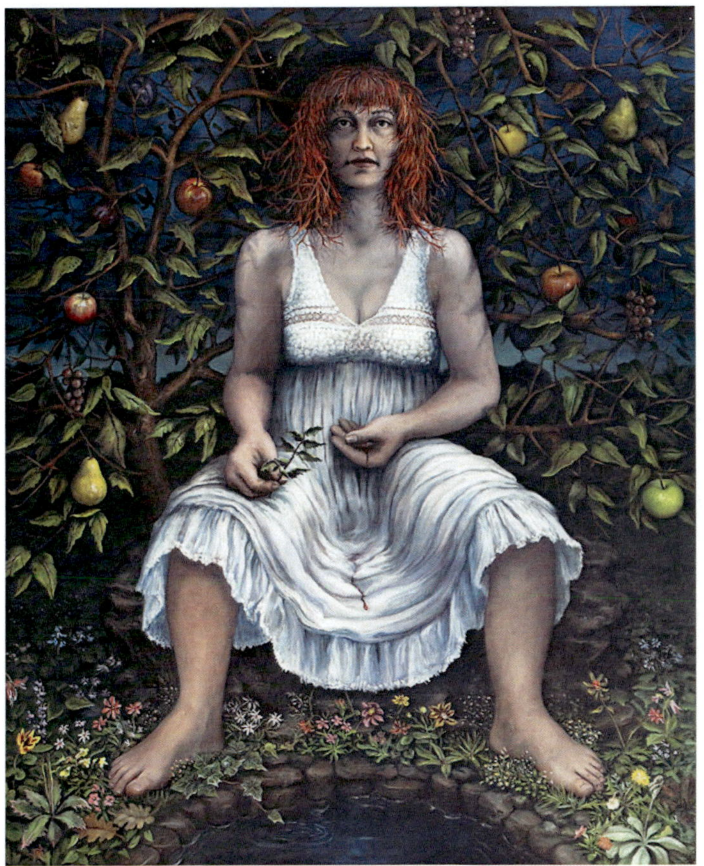

Kim Hoffmann, *Brigid's Well.*

University of Notre Dame as well as Andrews University, Indiana University South Bend, and Southwestern Michigan College. During the '60s he also made a shift in his artistic style. Instead of continuing his naturalist art style, Herrmann began allowing the paint to run, resulting in more abstract and expressionist paintings. He also opened Herrmann Studio Gallery in 1969 and maintained it until moving to Colorado in 1975. In Estes Park he operated the Hermann Gallery from 1975-1985, featuring his own paintings. Despite moving away from the Indiana art scene, he continued to paint and exhibit artwork, with his final exhibit taking place in 2002. Herrmann recently passed away on February 8, 2012 at 97 years old.

Kim Hoffmann studied at Indiana University South Bend during the 1980s with Harold Zisla. Hoffmann regularly creates oil paintings, and uses this medium to explore the relationship between mythology and organized religion, and she has also used her art to contend with roles of femininity and her Irish heritage. Her works have been on display and in the collections at many museums, including the South Bend Museum of Art. In addition to her artwork, Hoffmann has taught painting and has served as curator of the permanent collection for the South Bend Museum of Art and has juried many shows. On a larger scale, Hoffmann has been a member of the board of trustees for the Association of Indiana Museums. In 2000, she was an Indiana Arts Commission Individual Artist Grant Winner and even earlier, in 1993, Hoffmann was recognized locally for her art and community involvement by being nominated for the Woman of the Year in the Arts by the South Bend YWCA. Visual art isn't her only passion, however, as she also moves in Irish music circles, is a Midwest Irish music champion, and has competed in Ireland many times. She lives in South Bend.

Emile (Emil) Jacques, born in Moorslede in Belgium in 1864, spent the latter part of his life in America. Before moving to the United States he taught at the Royal Academy of Fine Arts at Antwerp where he won many awards including the Grand Prix offered by Antwerp and second prize in Grand Concours of Rome. However, World War I was not kind to Jacques as he lost friends and family. These loses prompted him to move to America in 1923 where he took a position teaching at Columbia University in Portland, Oregon. After teaching there for several years, he moved on to the University of Notre Dame in 1929 where he eventually became the director of the School of Arts. In addition to teaching at the university Jacques continued painting and he won a few awards. While in Europe his focus had been on religious figures but while in Indiana he took advantage of the beautiful scenery and moved towards regionalist landscape paintings. This was not a permanent shift, however. While teaching at Notre Dame he began painting a nine-part art cycle of murals that focused on the Virgin Mary and her life. The murals took 6 years to finish and included *The Queen of Heaven*, *The Immaculate Conception* and *The Homage of the Simple*. Unfortunately Jacques suffered an untimely death in 1937 from a heart attack while swimming in Central Lake near Petoskey, Michigan.

Zygmund Jankowski, not quite a realist but also not an abstract expressionist, evades definition by traditional styles. Zygmund was born in South Bend in 1925 and joined the navy in 1945. He attended the California College of Arts and Crafts with Dewilde, Otis Oldfield, and Georg Post (who was a huge influence on Zygmund's style) for a period of time but would return to South Bend to settle into his artistic career. There he opened a commercial art studio, taught at several locations such as the Barn School of Art, Indiana University South Bend, as well as Southwestern Michigan College, and Hilton Leech School of Art in Sarasota, Florida, He continued to exhibit across the nation. One of Zygmund's famous pieces, *Pink Seas in Gloucester Harbor*, demonstrates his consistent use of color and a mixture of styles. He often painted thematically or returned to erotica, self-portraits, floral, jazz themed images, and harbor scenes throughout his career. Zygmund moved to Gloucester, Massachusetts, with Beryl, his wife, and dedicated the remainder of his life to art. He passed away in 2009 after a lengthy career.

Sister Cecilia Ann Kelly, CSC, joined the congregation not long after completing her bachelor of arts at St. Mary's College. She came to South Bend from her hometown of Akron, Ohio. She spent a lot of time, even after earning her bachelor's, studying art; she spent one year and two summers at Ohio State University, some time at the Otis Institute of Art in Los Angeles, and finally earned her master of arts from St. Mary's-of-the-Wasatch in Utah. Additionally, Sister Cecilia Ann spent some time both studying and teaching in Florence and Rome. Most often, she would paint oil and acrylic, but sometimes used watercolors as well to create portraits and for figure work. While at St. Mary's, she taught many of the art students, traveled with them on trips, and helped set up a two week long art-based camping trip for students every summer. She also played an integral role in getting the art program at the college accredited. Sister Cecilia Ann has an honorary PhD from King's College, and currently resides in South Bend at St. Mary's College.

Douglas Kinsey, born in 1939, uses many abstract expressionist techniques, but is primarily a figurative painter. He received his bachelor's from Oberlin College in Ohio and went on to earn a master of fine arts from the University of Minnesota. Kinsey also gained artistic experience working around Berkley, California, before moving to the Michiana area, where he joined the art department at the University of Notre Dame in 1968. Kinsey also taught at the University of North Dakota, Berea College in Kentucky, and Oberlin College. The farthest from Michiana, however, was Kobe College in Japan, where he taught for a very short time. As he taught, Kinsey continued to paint and exhibit; in 1992 he painted a mural centered around the Orpheus myth in South Bend resident Jeff Gibney's home that was open to the public. His most recent exhibit took place locally at the South Bend Museum of Art in 2012.

Emma Kirwan, CSC, also known as **Sister Kirwan** and **Mother M. Aquina**, was born in Ottawa, Illinois in 1852. She joined the congregation in August of 1878 from Chicago and received the Habit on December 8th of that year. A short time later she made Final Profession at St. Mary's in Notre Dame, Indiana. She was sent to several different schools to teach art, from St. Cecilia's Academy in Washington, D.C. to Sacred Heart Academy

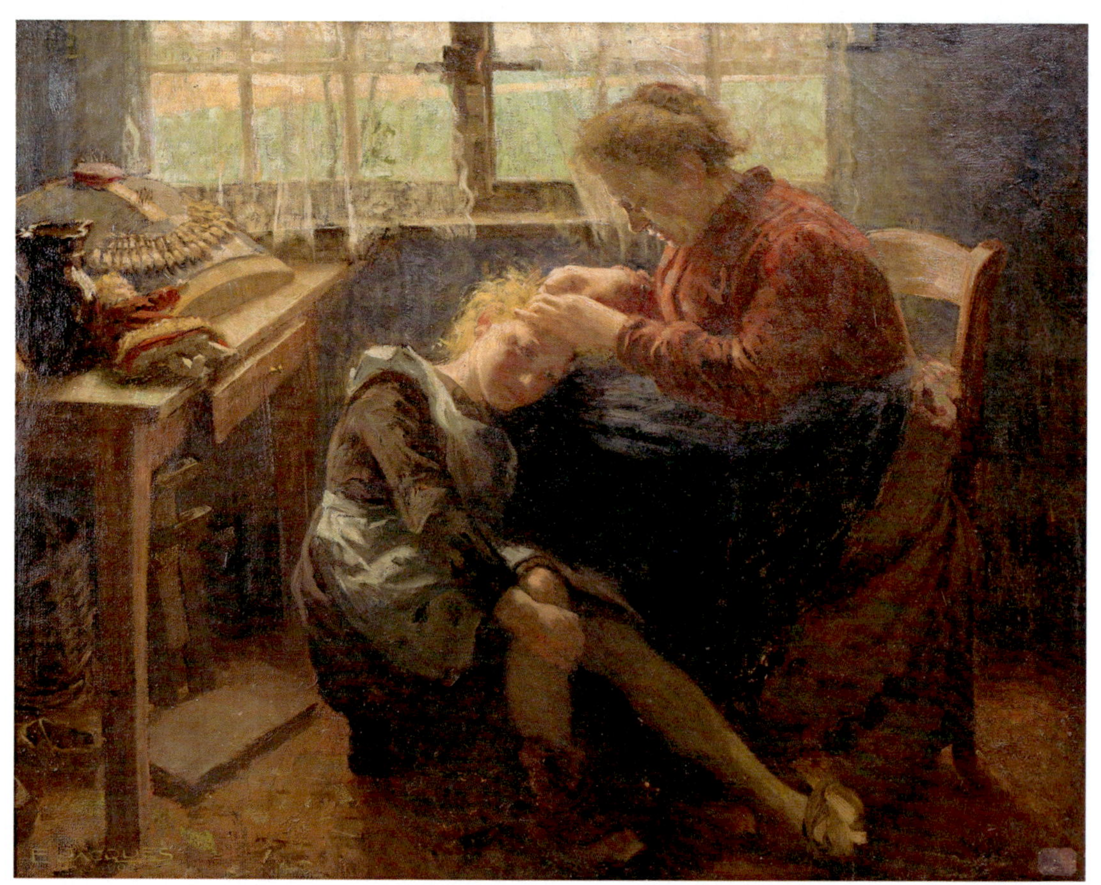

Emile Jacques, *A Mother's Care.*

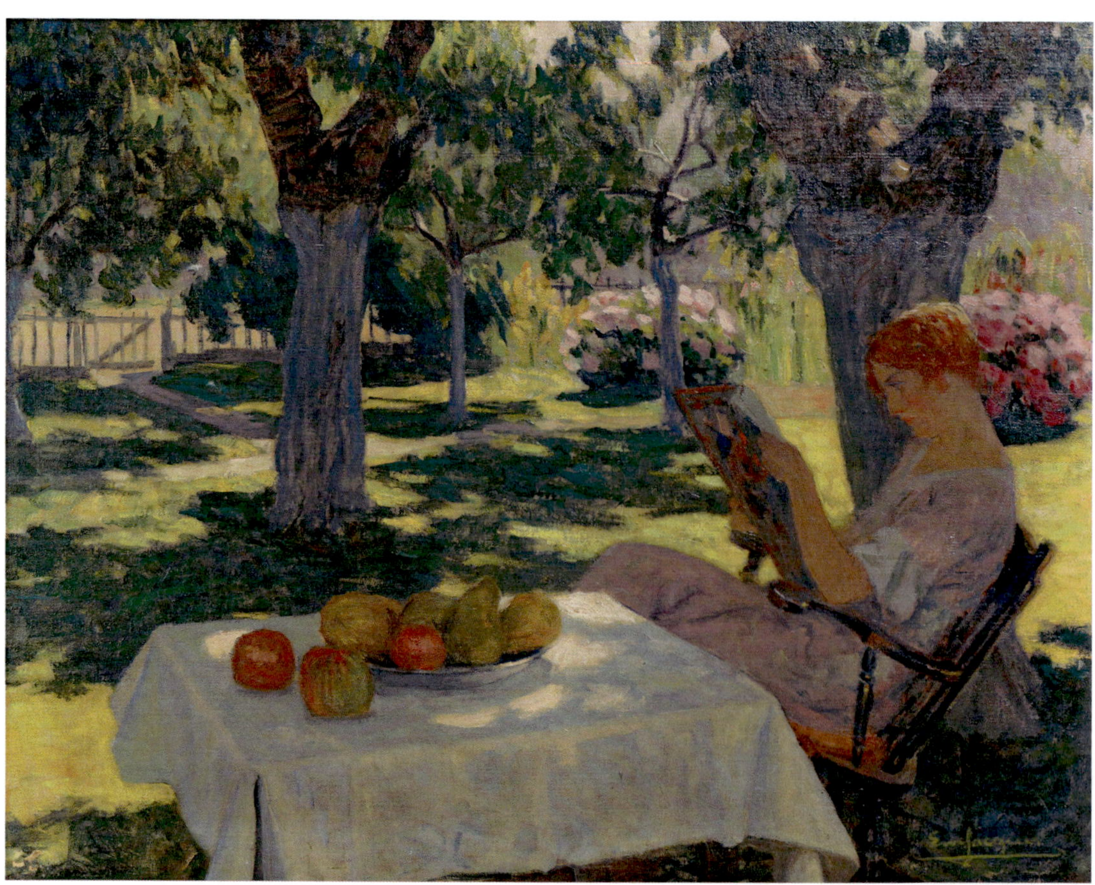

Emile Jacques, *Under the Fruit Trees.*

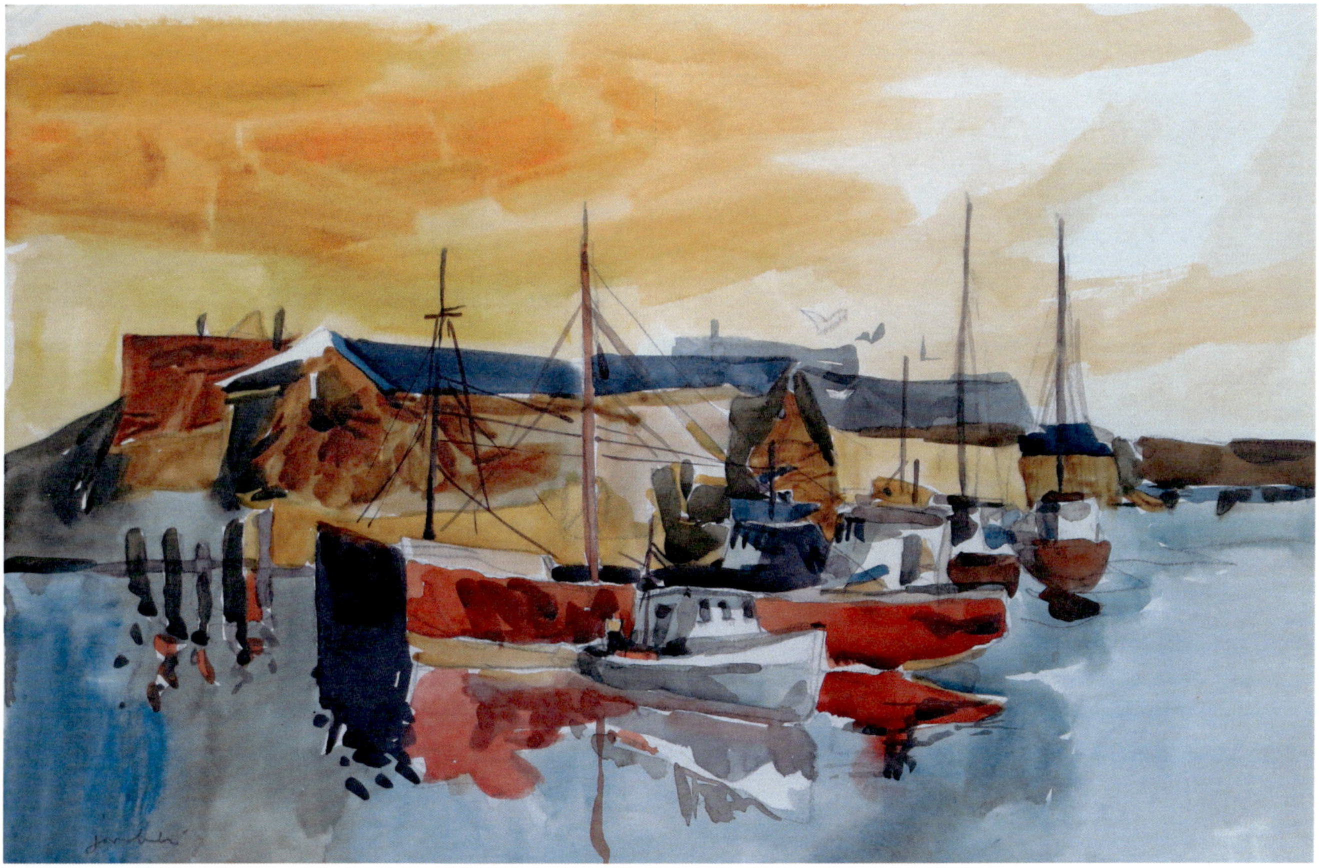

Zygmund Jankowski, *Gloucester Harbor.*

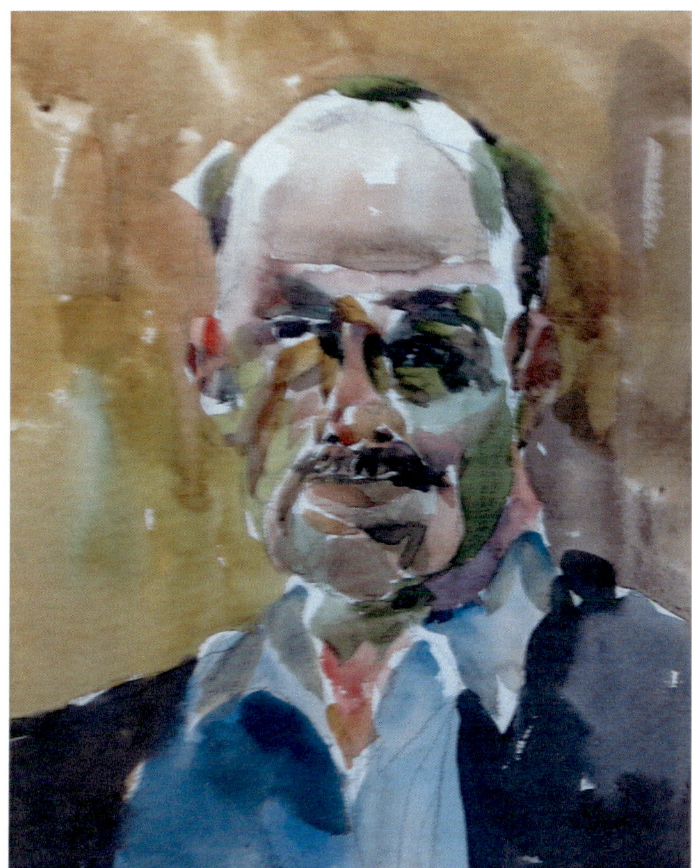

Zygmund Jankowski, *Self Portrait.*

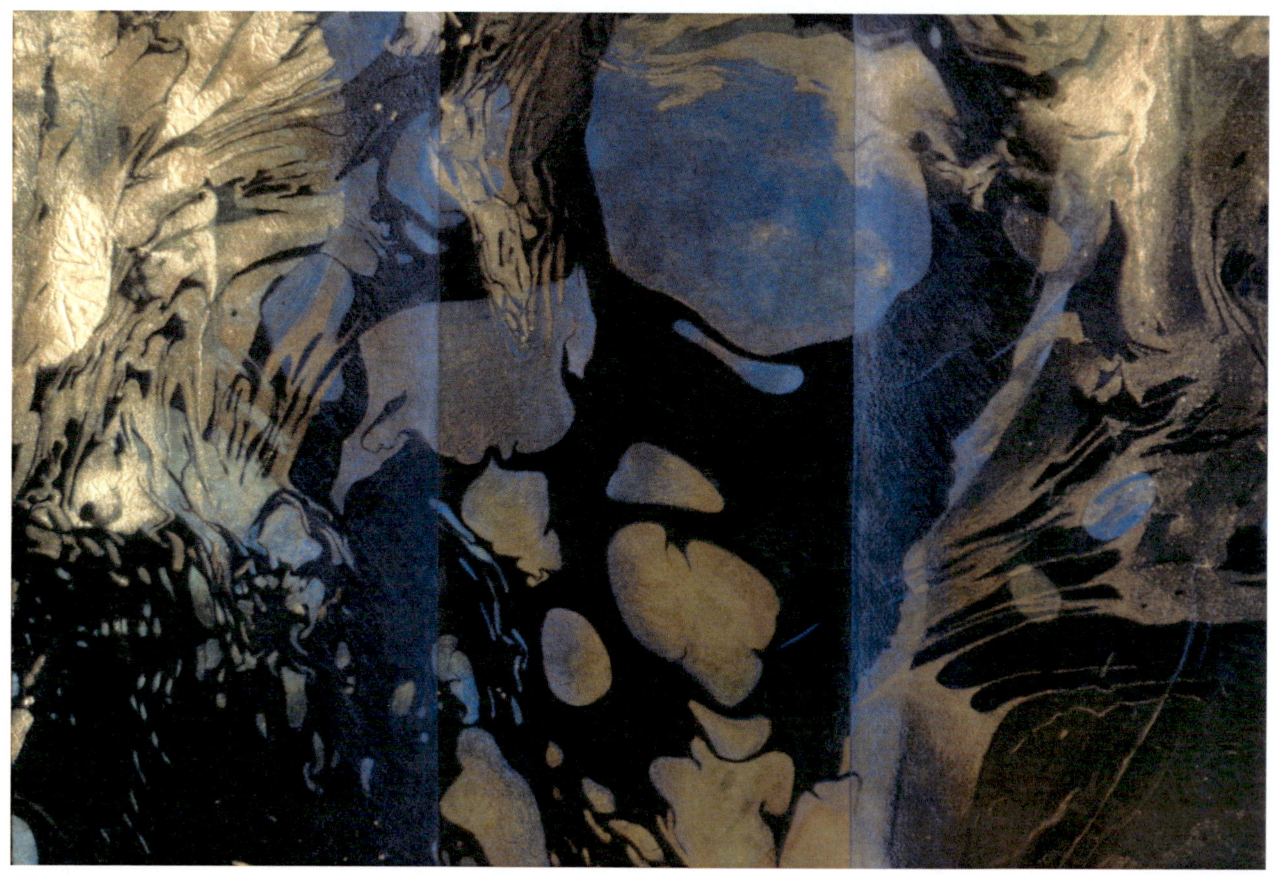

Sister Cecilia Ann Kelly, CSC, *Blue Lagoon*.

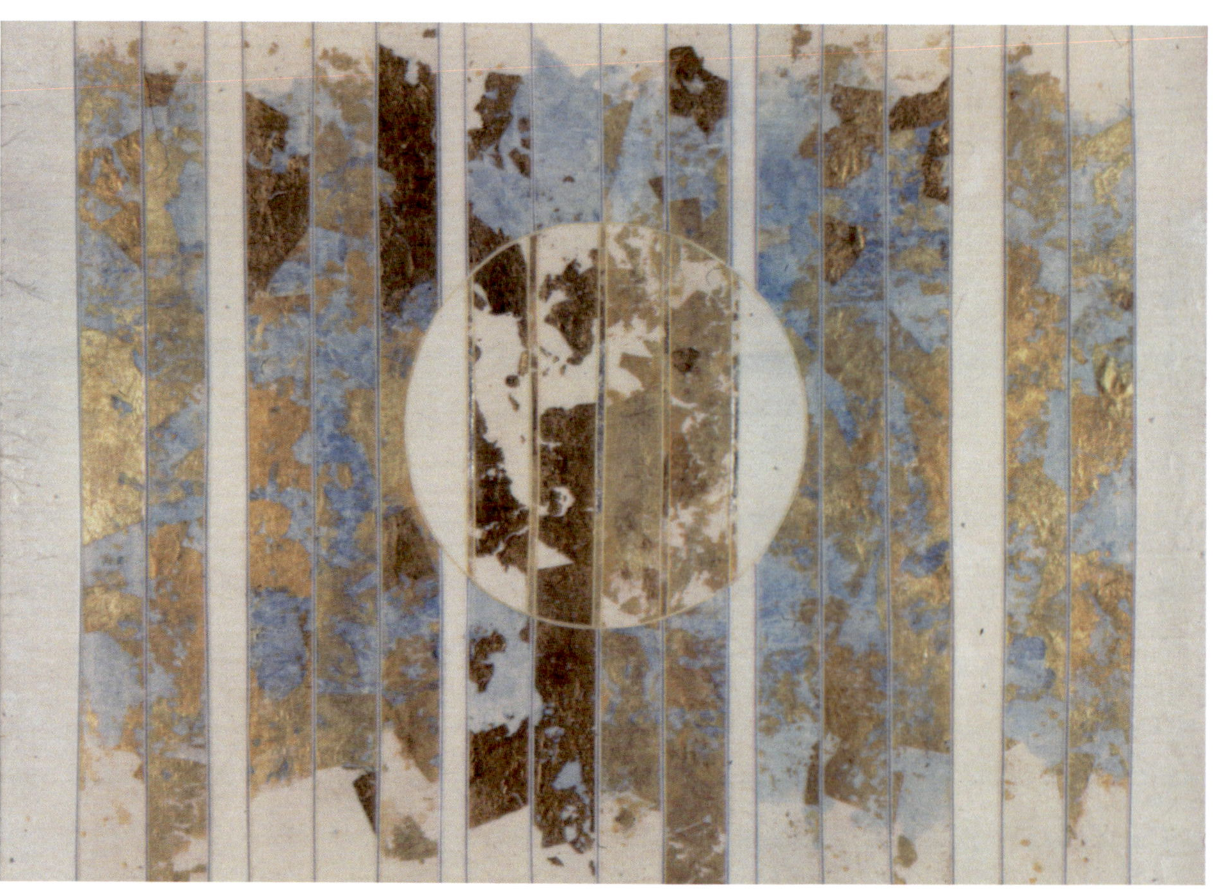

Sister Cecilia Ann Kelly, CSC, *Untitled*.

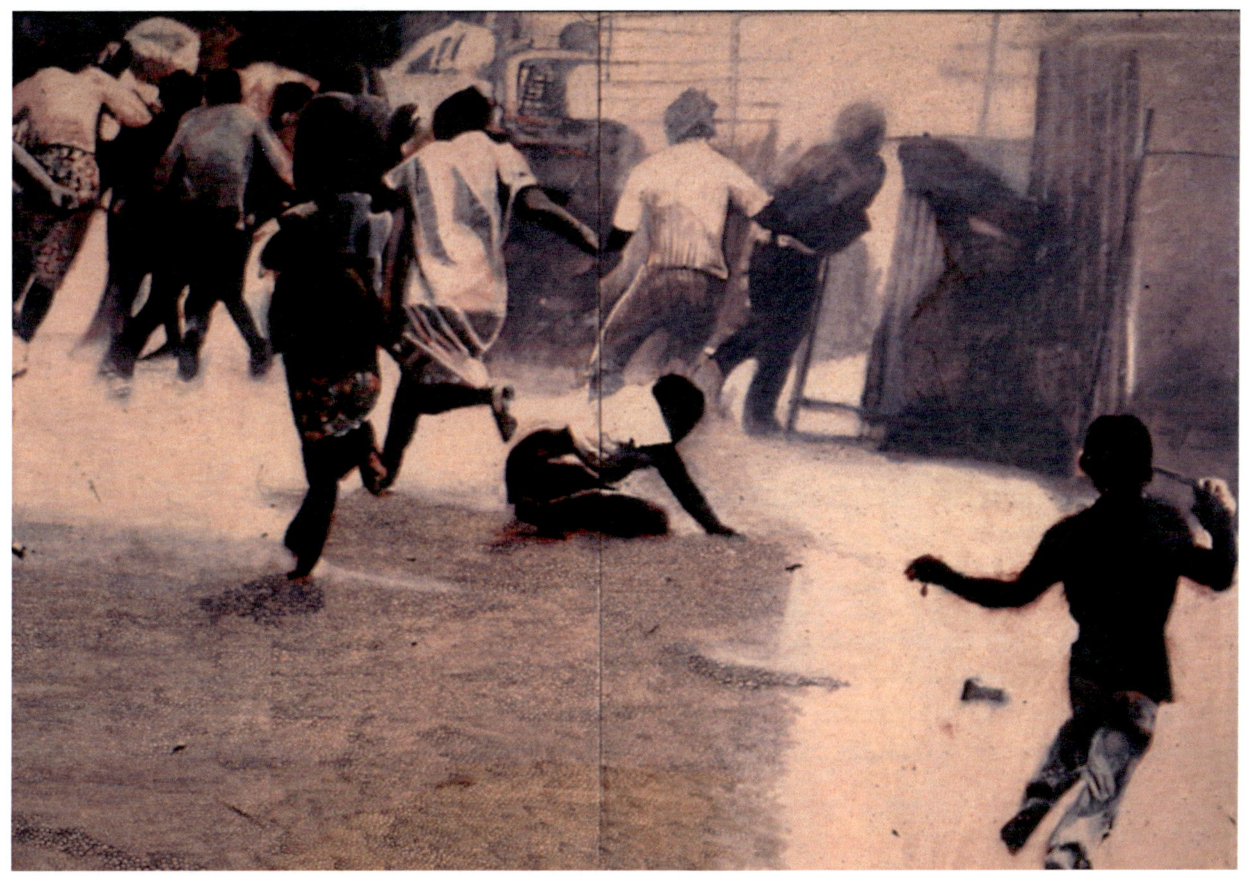

Douglas Kinsey, *Flight*, Diptych.

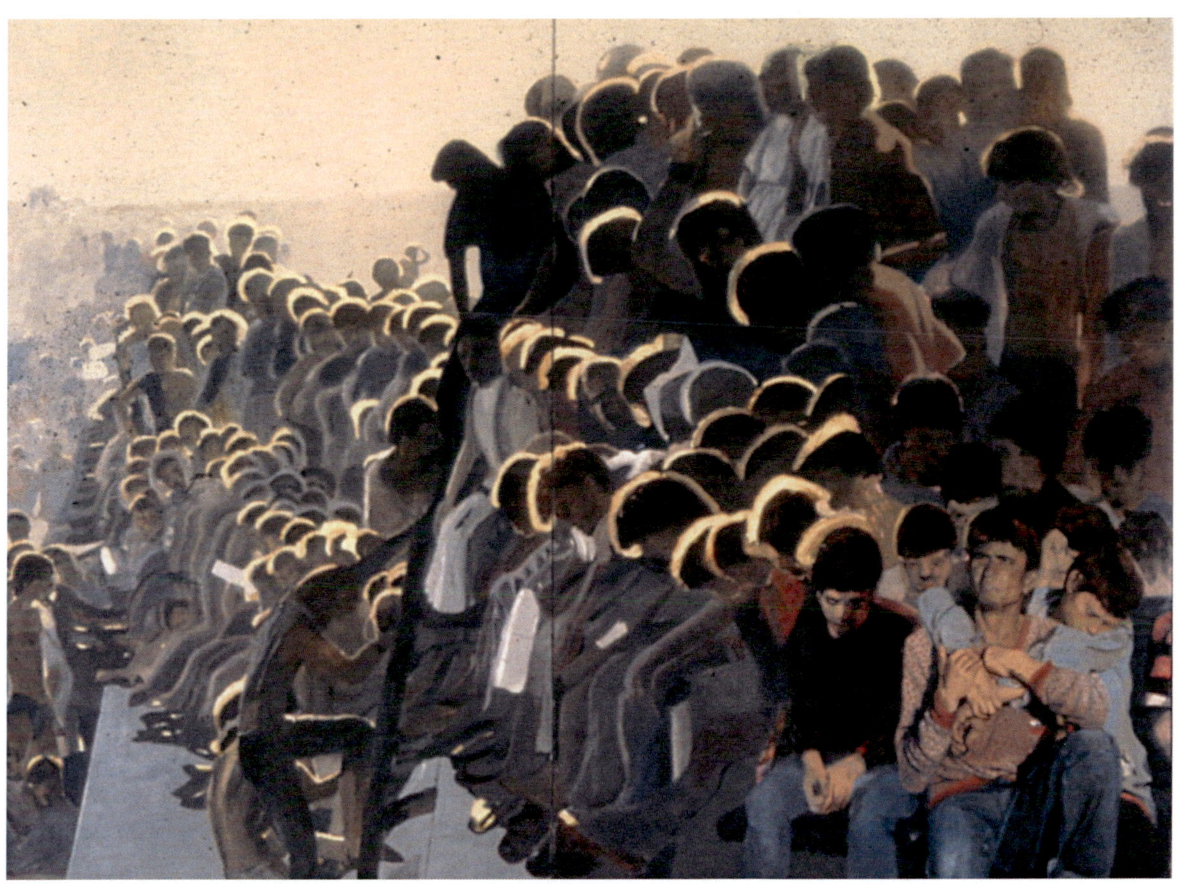

Douglas Kinsey, *Angels At the Gate*, Diptych.

in Fort Wayne, Indiana, where she served as the Superior. Sister Kirwan also served as the director of the art department at St. Mary's Academy (later at St. Mary's College) in South Bend. She passed away at St. Mary's Convent in Notre Dame, Indiana, near South Bend, in 1927. She spent little time creating art in the final years of her life and unfortunately very little of her artwork survives.

Eugene and **Elizabeth Kormendi** were both born and spent much of their young lives in Budapest, Hungary, around the turn of the twentieth century. They met at the Art Academy in Hungary, where each was very active with the Fine Arts Society in Budapest. Despite their similar backgrounds, however, Elizabeth created ceramic pottery, easel paintings, murals, and religious statuary, while Eugene focused on bronze and wood statues. Both artists derived their methods of representing their subjects from realist and naturalist schools. Following their marriage, the couple continued their artistic education in Rome, Paris, and Berlin. Shortly before the outbreak of World War I, the couple was visiting the United States but found themselves unable to return to Hungary. As a result, Eugene and Elizabeth took teaching jobs; Eugene began teaching at the University of Notre Dame in 1941 while Elizabeth taught at Dunbarton College, St. Mary's, and sometimes at Notre Dame for summer semesters. While here both artists continued to create; Eugene crafted a stone sculpture of St. Thomas Moore that still stands on Notre Dame's campus and Elizabeth's artwork can still be found across the Midwest. The couple remained in the United States until their deaths in 1959 and 1980, respectively, in Washington, D.C.

Daniel and **David Kotz** were born to German emigrants who moved to the Mishawaka area in 1846. Daniel was born in 1848 just a short time after his parents immigrated to America, while David was born in 1865. Despite this great age gap, both brothers were fantastic landscape painters. Unfortunately, David passed away at thirty-one in 1895 after several medical misfortunes but it was widely speculated that he was the greater artist between the brothers. David, on the other hand, lived a long life. At age 16, he began working in H. F. Spread's studio at Crosby's Opera House in Chicago. When the Great Fire broke out in 1871 he began studying art in college in at Northwestern University in Naperville, Illinois. While there he wrote the small monthly publication *Kotz's Mite*. After returning to South Bend in 1874, Daniel opened a small studio but promptly returned to Chicago where he entered H. A. Elkins's studio before opening his own Chicago-based atelier a few months later. Although he spent much of his life in Chicago, Daniel also visited other areas around the Midwest, including Grand Rapids where he painted his most famous painting, *Monarch of the Meadows*. At some point, Daniel relocated to New Jersey, where he passed away in 1933.

Bill Kremer and his ceramic artwork have been integral to the University of Notre Dame's art department since his arrival in 1973. He took a position with the university following his time studying art, first at the University of Wisconsin in Superior, where he received a bachelor of fine arts in 1969. As an undergrad, Bill found himself split between painting and pottery; as a painter he primarily painted abstract figure motifs.

Upon entering graduate school at the University of Wisconsin in Milwaukee, he chose pottery and ceramics as his focus and soon after received both a master of arts as well as a master of fine arts from the University of Wisconsin in Milwaukee in 1970 and 1971, respectively. He was hired to teach ceramics and sculpture at Nicholls State University in Thibodaux, Louisiana (1971-1973). A few years later, he joined Notre Dame to help establish a ceramics program. As the program developed, he found himself moving between both sculpture and pottery and although they developed separately, he soon began to meld the two into a unique style of ceramic sculptures. He also experimented with casting clay into plaster molds, which had equally unique results. The Notre Dame program has gained much recognition, and in 1998 the installation of an anagama kiln for the ceramics program began. Bill currently acts as the chair of the Ceramics Department at Notre Dame, but he continues to exhibit across the nation.

Robert Kuntz (b. July 12, 1925, in South Bend) has always been a member of the area, from his high school days at Riley in South Bend to his teaching at St. Mary's College. He did spend some time studying art in Chicago at the School of the Art Institute and the Contemporary Art Workshop, but South Bend has always been his home. Robert initially began his art career as a painter, but found that he preferred sculpting which he moved on to in the 1950s. He was initially influenced by British sculptors Henry Moore and Kenneth Armitage, and locally by Jim Paradis and Marion Pilarski who created an interest in sculpting. Local artist John Bednar taught Robert how to carve stone and was his greatest influence in establishing his career. Since his time as a student, Robert has worked as a designer of church furnishings, and as a clay modeler for Raymond Loewy and Associates at the Studebaker Corporation, which he credits as a highlight of his life. He currently owns Model Tech Display Studio, a woodworking shop in South Bend. His metal and wood sculptures can be found around the area from St. Patrick's Park to outside the Morris Civic, and even adorning the Mishawaka Riverwalk.

Norman Laliberté was born in Worcester, Massachusetts, in 1925 and moved to Montreal while he was young. He began his artistic education at the Montreal Museum of Fine Art and Design. He was there for one year but continued to study at the Institute of Design in Chicago where he earned a bachelor of science degree in visual design and served a fellowship at Cranbrook Academy of Art. Although he was primarily an illustrator and designer, he was also occasionally a printmaker, painter, and sculptor. While Laliberté labeled himself as a contemporary artist, he was always reluctant to name a more specific style and preferred "experimentation" to traditional classifications. He began teaching at St. Mary's College in 1958; previously he had been a faculty member at Kansas City Art Institute and School of Design. In 1964, he received international recognition for his work with the Vatican Pavilion at the World's Fair in New York, for whom he designed eighty-eight large cloth banners. Laliberté also created over 500 unique art books that serve as diary collections of his work by using found books and layering his illustrations over the pre-existing pages. In addition to these accomplishments, Laliberté holds

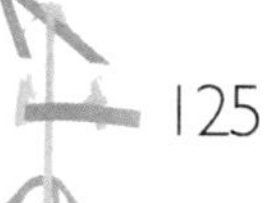

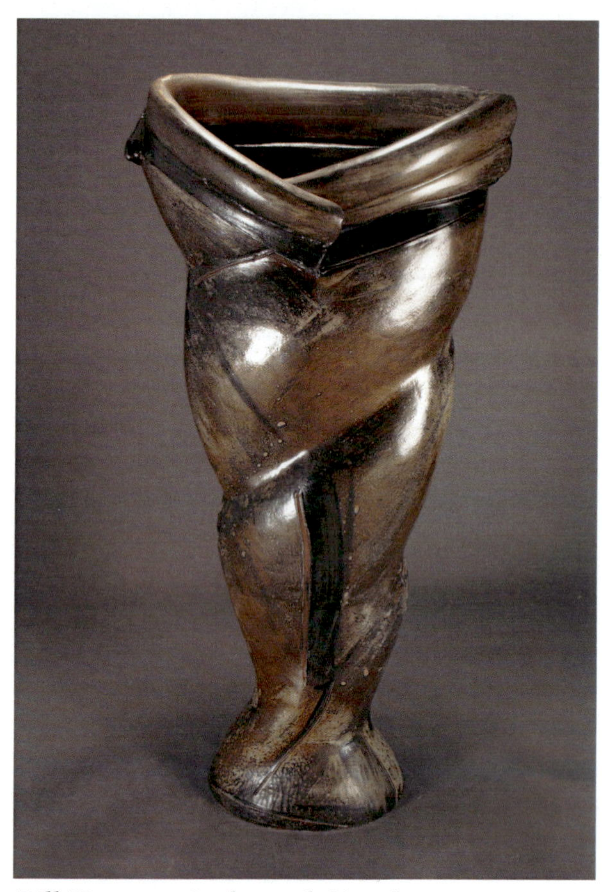
Bill Kremer, *Sculptural Vessel.*

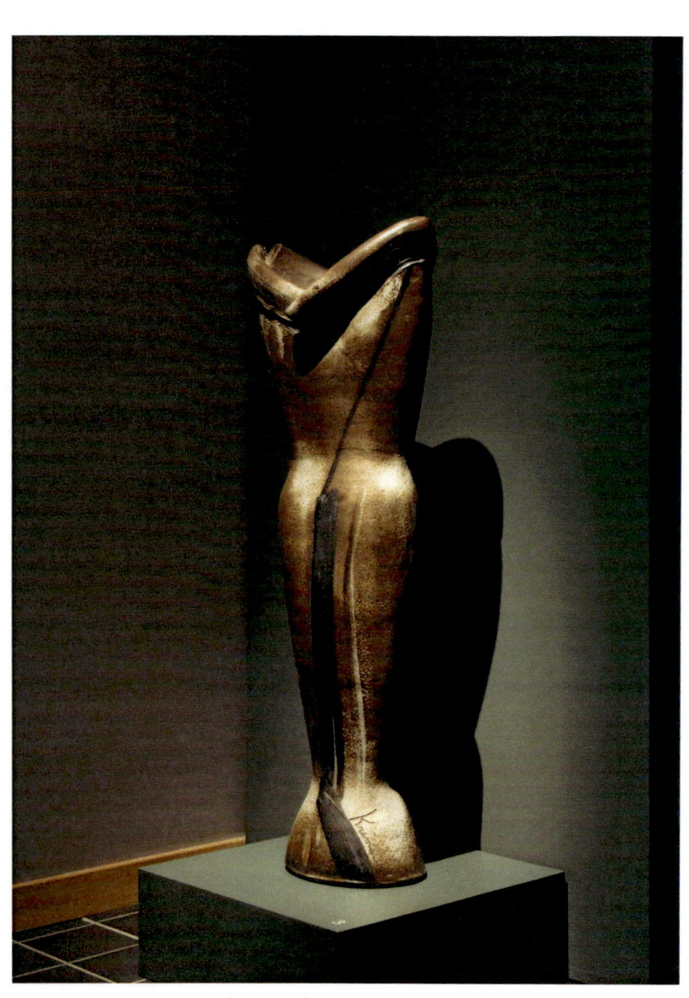
Bill Kremer, *Sculptural Vessel.*

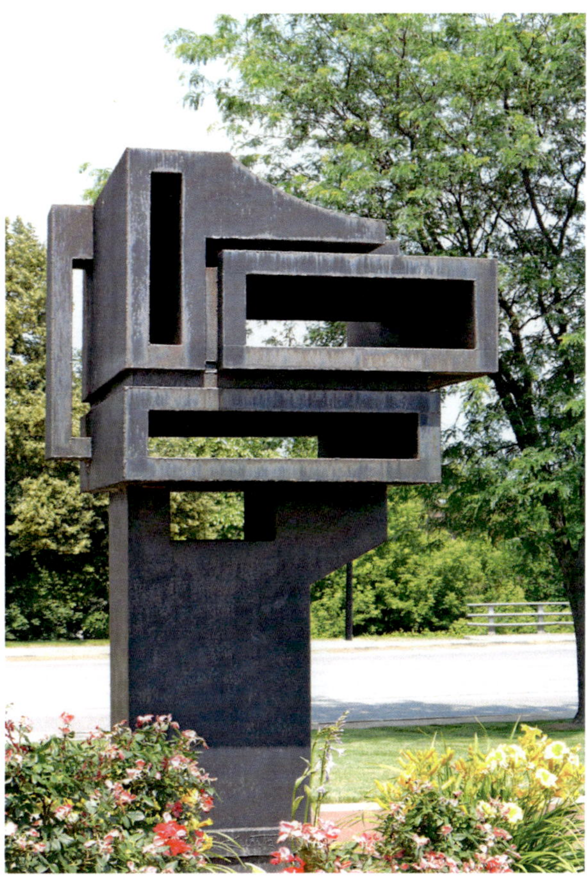
Robert Kuntz, *Triathalon.*

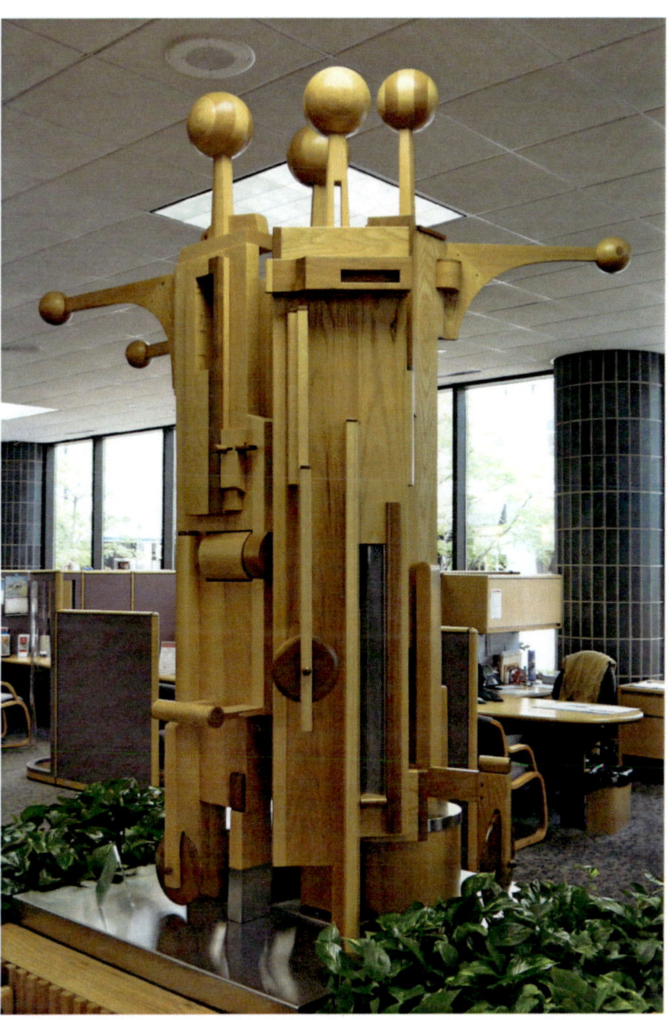
Robert Kuntz, *Membership.*

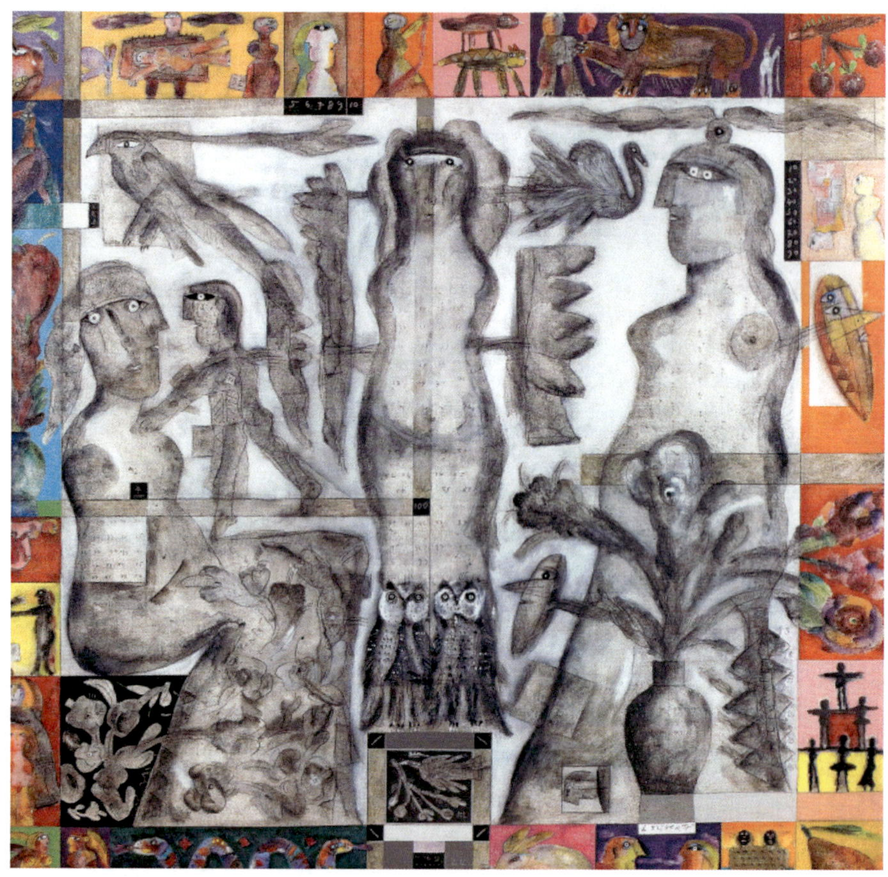

Norman Laliberté, *Adam's First Wife (Lilith).*

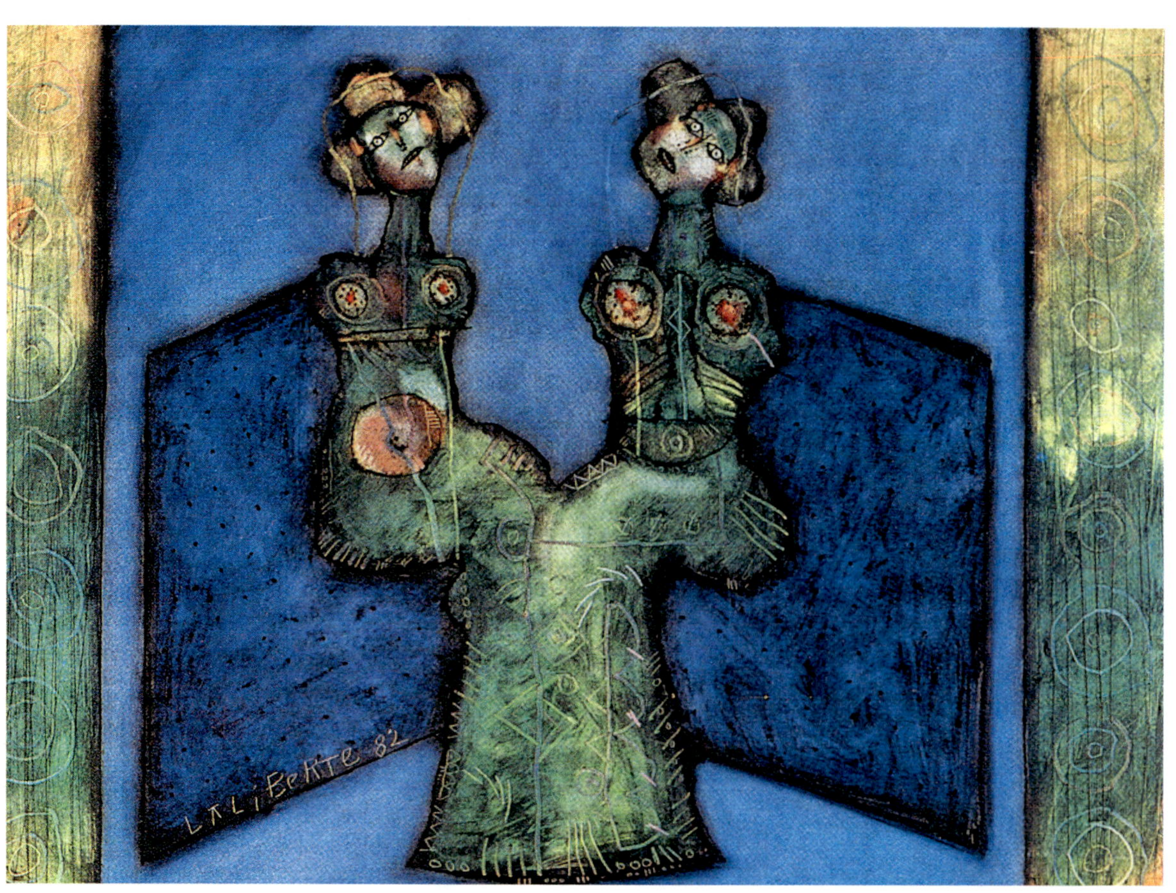

Norman Laliberté, *Gemini.*

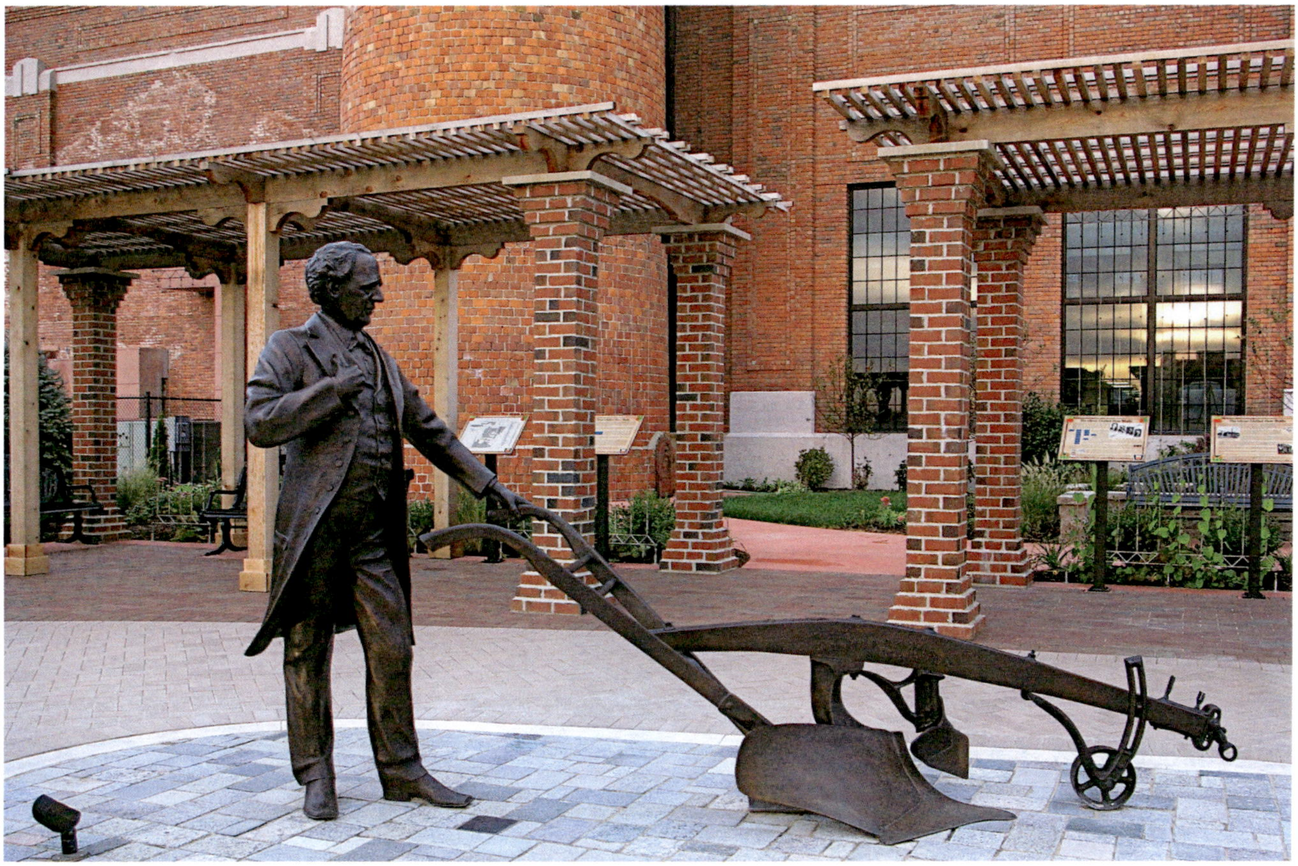

Harold "Tuck" Langland, *James Oliver Memorial.*

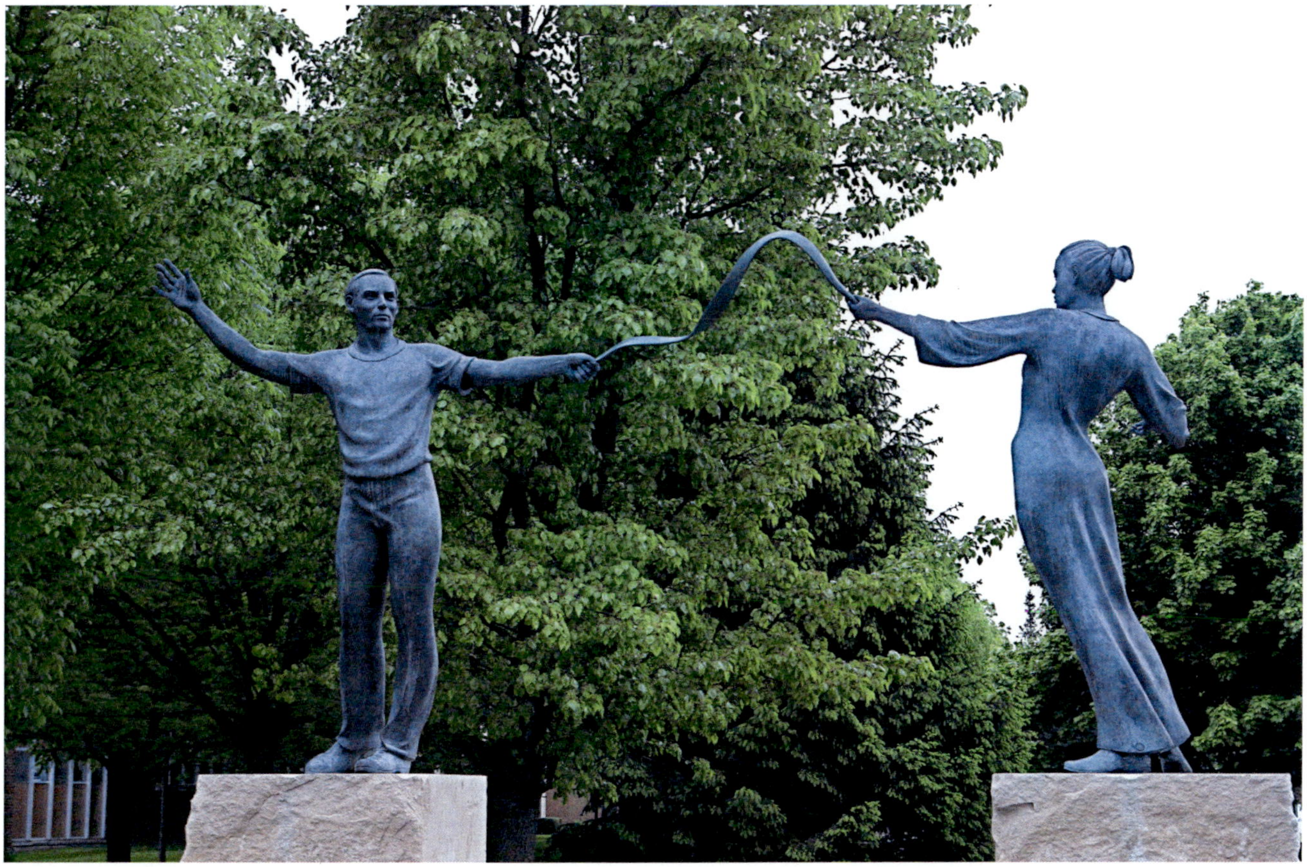

Harold "Tuck" Langland, *Crossroads.*

an honorary doctorate from St. Mary's College, Notre Dame, and has held more than 100 solo exhibitions in the United States and Canada.

Harold "Tuck" Langland was born in Minneapolis in 1939. He studied art and sculpture at the University of Minnesota, receiving his MFA in 1964. Highlights of a long and fruitful career creating figurative bronze works include sixteen solo shows in this region in thirty years, many large-scale commissions here and across the nation, solo shows in England, election as a Fellow in the National Sculpture Society, and inclusion of his works in the permanent collection of numerous museums. He taught for many years at IU South Bend, built the sculpture program, and retired as professor emeritus in 2003. His guides to the process of creating bronze sculpture remain touchstones in the field.

Alan Larkin came to Indiana University South Bend in 1977 as a professor of drawing and printmaking, and has been more than an asset to the university since. Born in Minnesota in 1953, Larkin graduated with a bachelor of arts from Carleton College in Northfield Minnesota in 1975, and shortly after received his master of fine arts in printmaking from Pennsylvania State University in 1977. He took the position at IU South Bend immediately after graduation and for his first thirteen years here focused primarily upon printmaking and especially on lithography. Over time, he began to shift and in 1991, Larkin found himself creating more pastel drawings and oil paintings, predominantly realistic portraits. Although he considers himself a printmaker first, he is more known for these later works. In 1997, his work *Gold Robe* won the award for Outstanding Work at the Seventy-Third Annual Hoosier Salon Fine Arts Exhibition and has won several awards there since. In 1998, he also had the honor of being commissioned to create nostalgic, 1920s-style advertising posters for the South Shore Train Line, of which *Neighborhood Sentinel*, depicting Gary's historic water tower, is most popular. Larkin currently resides in South Bend.

Anthony J. Lauck, CSC, also known as Father Tony, was born in Indianapolis on Dec. 30, 1908. Much of his adult life was spent at the University of Notre Dame, where he graduated in 1942. He also spent time studying sculpture at Corcoran School of Art, Columbia University, the State University of New York, and Cranbrook Academy, in addition to spending a short amount of time studying European art museums. In 1946, four years after graduating, Lauck was ordained and he became the director of Notre Dame's art gallery in 1962, a position he held until 1974, in addition to acting as the head of the Art Department from 1960-1967. Father Tony was widely considered the father of art at Notre Dame because of the works and artists he brought to the university. One of his most popular sculptures, *Our Lady of the University*, welcomes visitors and many new students to the campus, and still remains at the main circle. Several of his other works are also scattered around campus. Following his retirement, Father Tony was unable to sculpt and took up watercolor painting in order to continue creating art. He continued to live at Notre Dame until 2001, when he died at age ninety-two only a few weeks before his birthday.

Robert Leader, born in Cambridge, Massachusetts in 1924, spent much of his young life on the East Coast before moving to the area in 1953. He studied painting and stained glass art while at the Boston Institute of Fine Arts and also served as a marine during World War II before going back to school to receive his bachelor of fine arts from Yale and his master of fine arts from the University of Illinois in 1952. Upon graduating, he was offered a position at Clark College in Dubuque, Iowa and was there for a short period of time before taking a position with the Art Department at the University of Notre Dame. He remained there for several decades and taught Art Traditions, which was one of the most popular art courses taught at the campus for years. He also lectured extensively on stained glass and liturgical art during the '50s and '60s while at the university. However, his most prolific accomplishment was supervising and designing the stained glass at the Notre Dame de France Center in Jerusalem as part of the redecoration effort. Much of his work remains in place at Notre Dame's campus, as well as in Jerusalem and England. In 1985, he left Notre Dame, but remained in the area until he passed away on April 11, 2006, at Holy Cross Village in Notre Dame. He was eighty-one at the time.

Thomas R. Lias used his extensive art education to enhance his effectiveness as director of the South Bend Art Association, a position he took in 1952. He was born in Dayton, Pennsylvania, in 1903. He studied art at the Carnegie Institute of Technology from 1928 until 1936, when he graduated with a bachelor of arts. While taking classes, he taught art with Pittsburgh schools until 1942. Lias went on to establish himself as an oil abstract modernist painter as he continued to attend schools such as the State University of Iowa where he would receive both a master of arts and a master of fine arts in 1946 and 1947. He spent one summer at the Escuela Universitaria de Bellas Artes during the summer of 1947 studying wood sculptures before taking a teaching position with Florida State University from 1947-1949. He returned to the State University of Iowa 1950 and stuck around there until 1952. Following his time there he moved to South Bend and began working with the South Bend Art Association. His time there was limited, as he retired in 1956 and passed away a short time after in 1960 in his hometown.

Leon and **Theodora Makielski** were related by marriage and shared artistic ability. Leon was born in Morris Run, Pennsylvania, in 1885 while Theodora Doktor was born in Poland on November 29, 1890. Leon's art career began as a child; his skill was recognized by renowned artist L. Clarence Ball. He studied at many schools beginning with the Chicago Art Institute and after winning the John Quincy Adams Foreign Traveling Scholarship he spent four years in Paris, studying at both the Académie Julian and the Académie Grande Chauviere. Upon returning to America he painted primarily portraits and landscapes in an impressionist style before taking teaching positions with the University of Michigan and the Meinsinger Art School in Detroit. Theodora, after moving to America, also spent some time at the Chicago Art Institute, where she also focused on impressionism and painted primarily landscapes and portraits. In 1916 she married Leon's brother Joseph Jacob Makielski, Sr. and joined the artistic family.

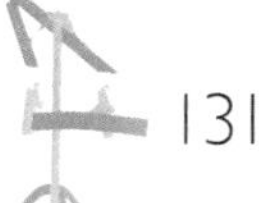

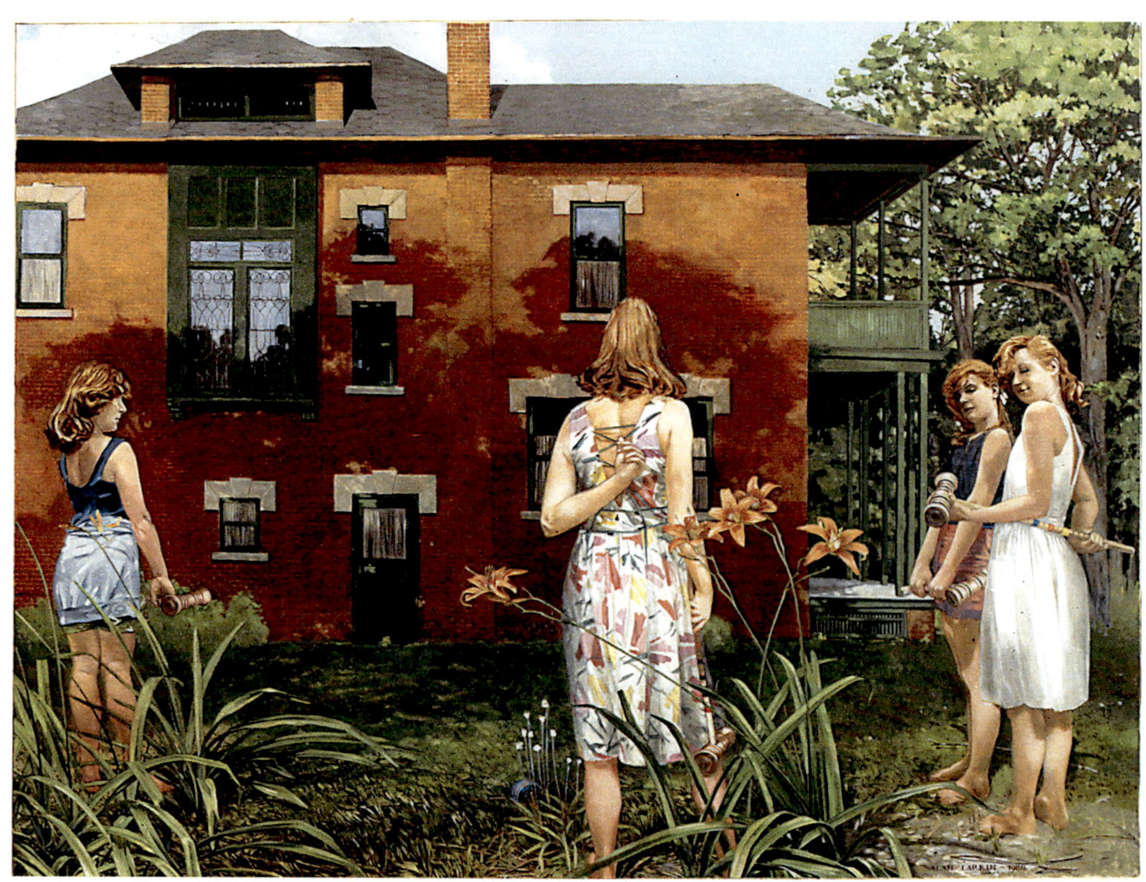

Alan Larkin, *Daylilies.*

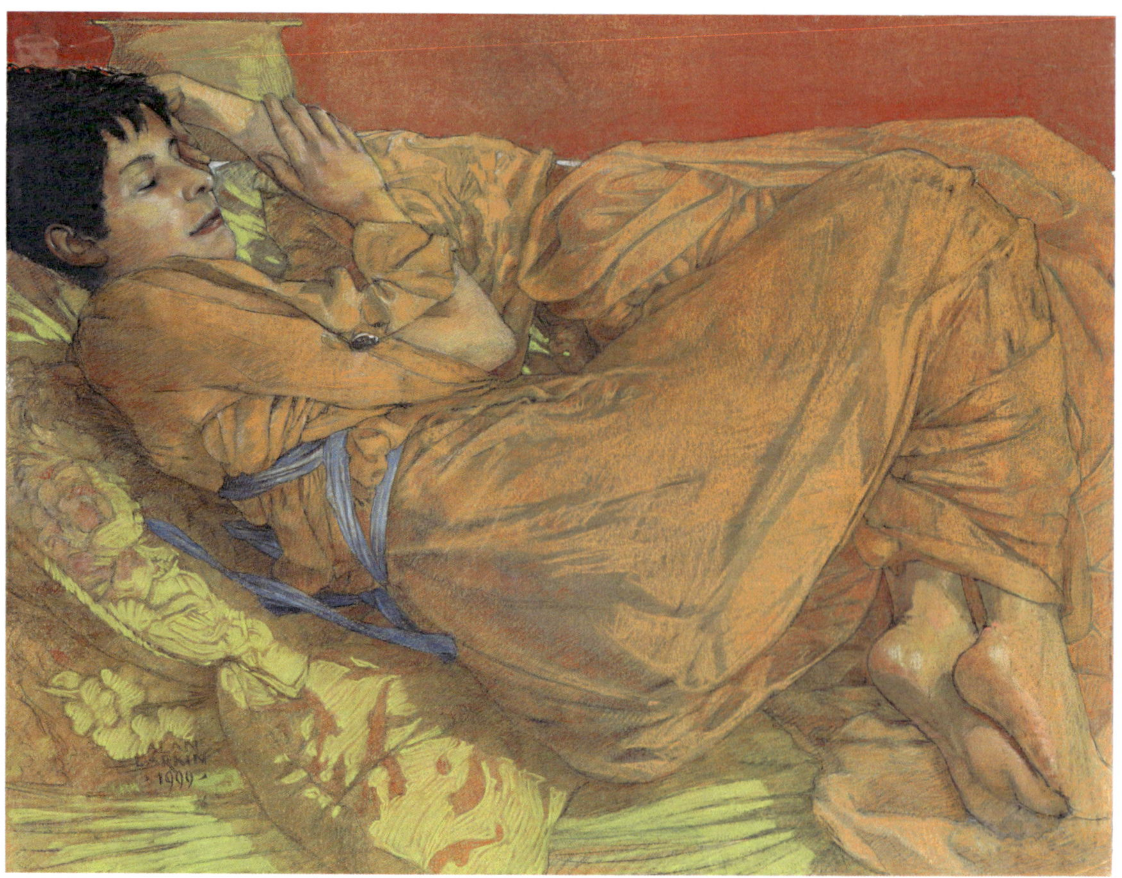

Alan Larkin, *The Orange Robe.*

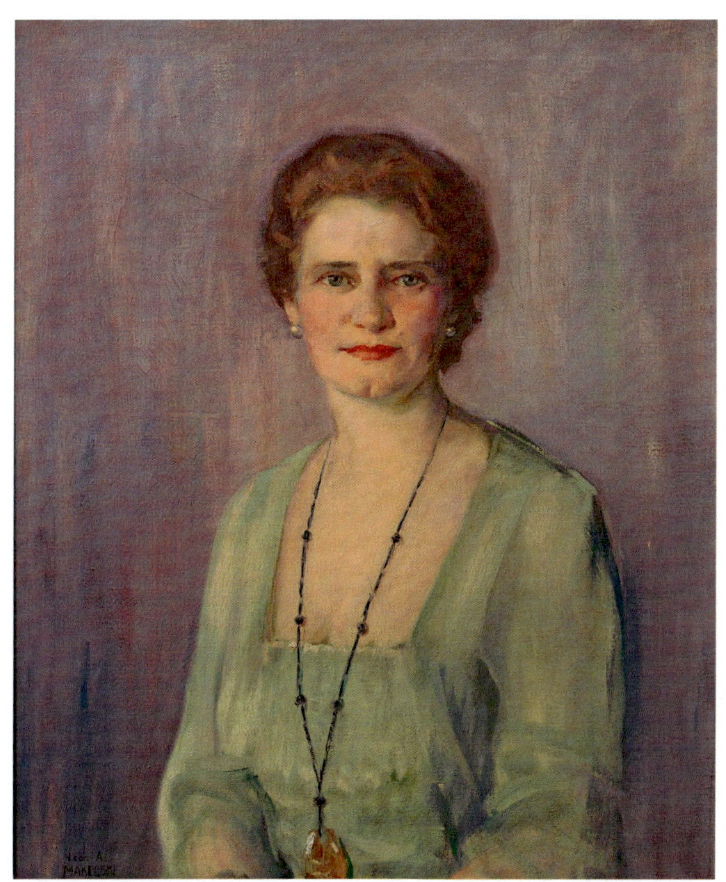

Leon Makielski, *Portrait of Mrs. Warren H. Miller.*

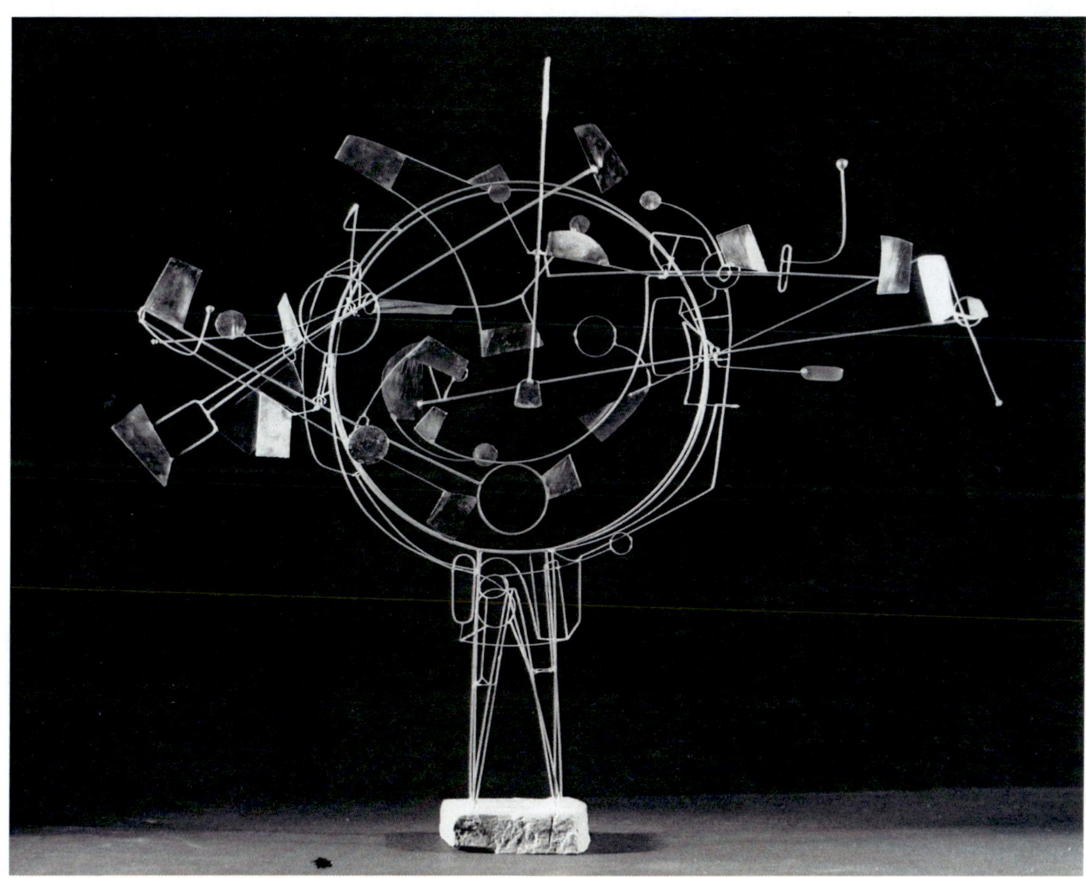

Konstantin Milonadis, *Elipsoid II.*

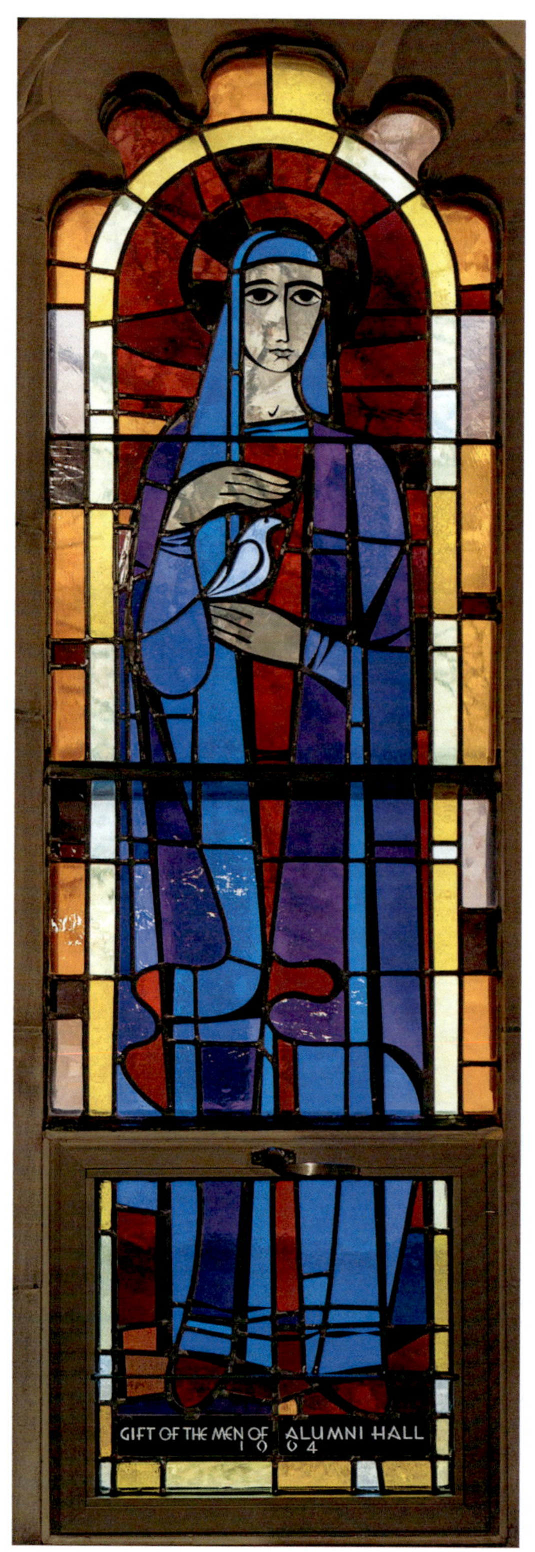

Robert Leader, *Madonna*.

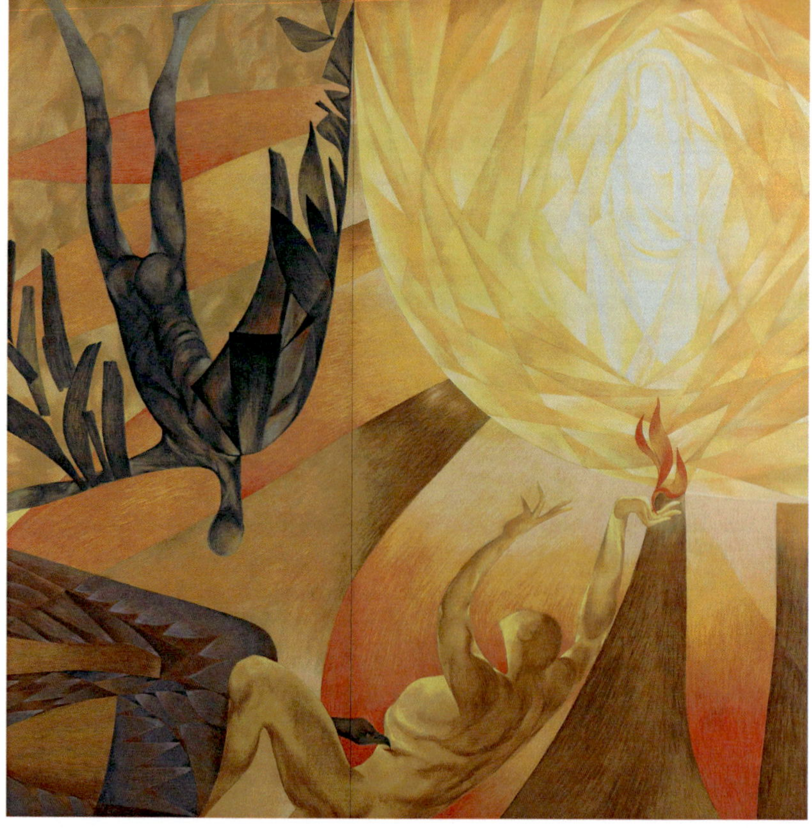

Robert Leader, *Icarus*.

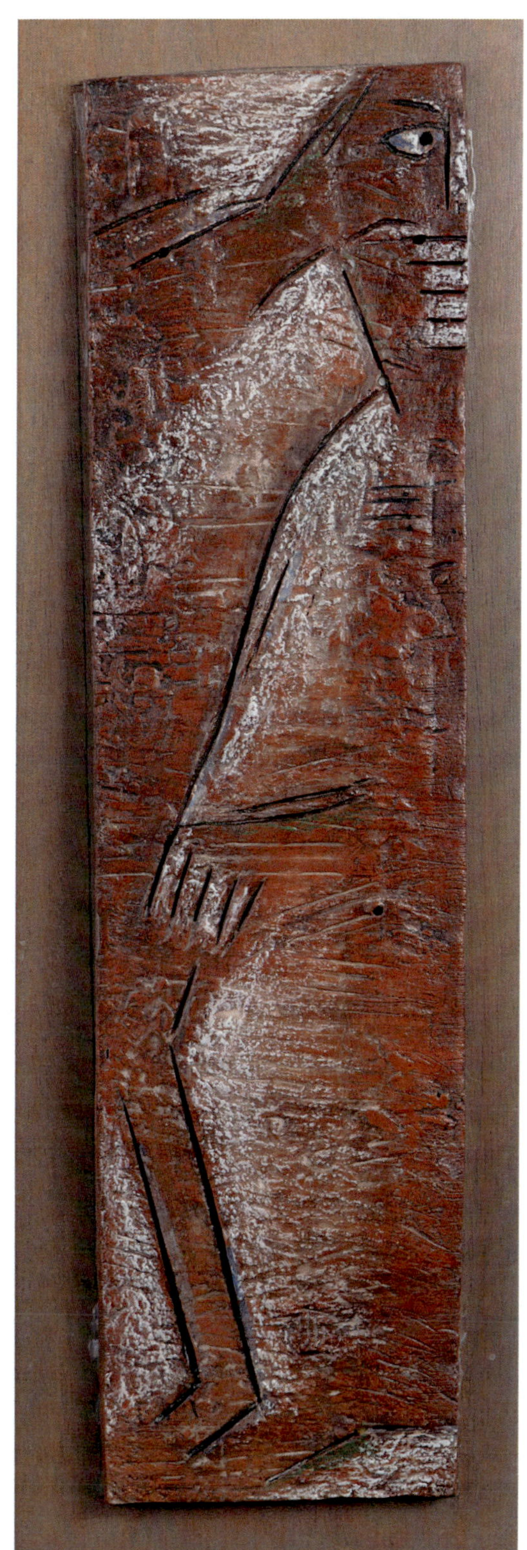

Anthony J. Lauck, CSC, *The Prophet*.

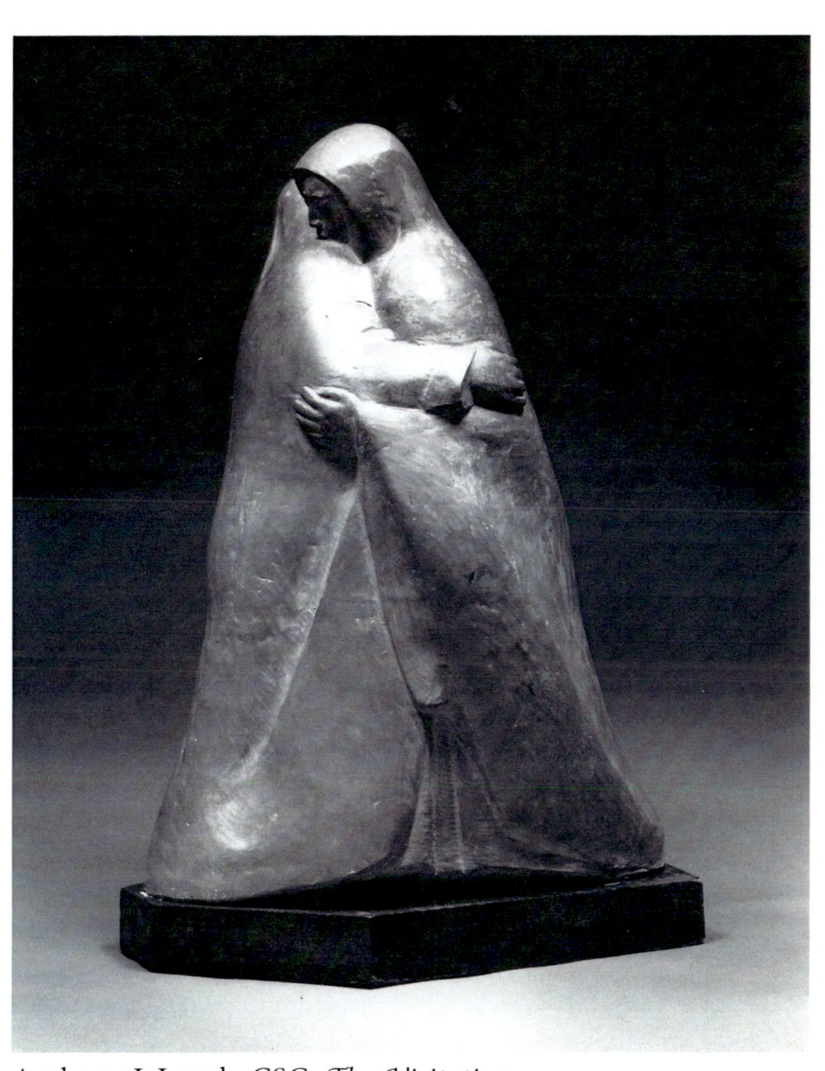

Anthony J. Lauck, CSC, *The Visitation*.

Included in her circle of friends were many prolific artists such as George Ames Aldrich, Emile Jacques, and Harold Zisla. She was a founder of Northern Indiana Artists and the shop she opened with her husband, Makielski Art Shop, served as the group's first meeting place. Both artists received several awards and took part in many exhibitions. Leon passed away in 1974, only a few years before his sister-in-law. However, even after her death in 1979, Theodora was the center of many exhibitions as late as 1991 and 1999.

Catherine McCormick, pastel artist, grew up in Wisconsin, and received a Bachelor of Science in Education from the University of Wisconsin-Whitewater. She worked as an editor and designer for newspapers in Wisconsin, Colorado and Arizona for 25 years. In Arizona, she attended workshops at the Scottsdale Artists School and taught at the Phoenix Center for Community Arts from 1989 to 2000, and the Shemer Arts Center from 1997 to 2000. Cathy moved to South Bend in 2000, and began teaching pastels and drawing at the South Bend Museum of Art, Studio Art Center, and Battell Community Center. She served as a docent at the Snite Museum at Notre Dame and South Bend Museum of Art. She also spent two years as the artist in residence at Prairie Vista Elementary School, Granger. In 2006 she started the Northern Indiana Pastel Society, a network of more than 250 artists in three states. She also served on the board of Northern Indiana Artists for 10 years. In 2007 her art was selected for the Celebration of Hoosier Women Artists Competition at the office of Lt. Gov. Becky Skillman at the State Capitol, Indianapolis, and in 2008 she won the Glenna Hartmann Memorial Award from Plein Air Painters of America. Her art is in the collections of University of Notre Dame London Program, Southwestern Michigan College, Lerner Theater, Lake City Bank, and Lakeland Hospital. In 2012 she was editor of *An Art Journey*, a book on the life and art of Dr. Faye Magneson. Cathy continues to live, teach and create in the area.

Reverend A. Merine, known only by that name, lived in the Michiana area beginning around the early 1840s. He came from Warsaw and almost immediately began posting advertisements for his artwork in the *South Bend Free Press*. A. Merine remained in the area for a period of time, but little more is known about his artistic history.

Ivan Meštrović, known around the University of Notre Dame as "The Maestro," was born in Vroplje, Croatia (former Yugoslavia). He began his artistic career during mid-life as an apprentice in Harald Bilinic's stonemason's shop at Split, Croatia, in 1900, before attending the Academy of Fine Arts in Vienna, where he matriculated from 1901 to 1906. However, it was in 1903 that his true ability began to show and a short time later he had earned an international reputation. He traveled the world, exhibiting his many sculptures of religious themes which he adopted during World War I. As a result of his artistic ability and continuous traveling, the Independent State of Croatia detained Meštrović until he was able to escape to Switzerland in 1943. Due to the political upheaval and rise of Communism in Croatia, Meštrović was unable to return to his home country and in 1946 he immigrated to the United States to teach at Syracuse University in New York. In 1955, the University of Notre Dame offered him a teaching position and artist-in-resident status, which he accepted in the hopes that his work would be received favorably amongst a Catholic audience. Meštrović eventually returned to Croatia to visit his homeland and deceased loved ones. Before his death, Meštrović finished a series of four clay sculptures to commemorate his children, who had all passed away before he did himself, in early 1962 in South Bend, Indiana.

Tom Meuninck is a true artist of the Michiana area; he grew up in Mishawaka and has spent most of his life teaching art at Washington High School in the South Bend Community School Corporation (SBCSC). He left the area to study at Ball State University with Marvin Reichle. There, he focused on drawing and printmaking, even though he would eventually be most well-known for his clay wildlife sculptures and ceramics. Meuninck also began teaching ceramics at the South Bend Regional Art Museum. Always a teacher first, he consistently put his students ahead of even his own artwork and artistic ambitions, and sometimes found himself learning alongside his pupils. Although he retired from the SBCSC in the early 2000s, he has continued exhibiting both individually and with other artists, with his most recent exhibition taking place at the Indianapolis Art Center with his son Tyler, a painter.

Muriel Miller, born in Eaton, Ohio in 1887, was an impressionist painter with an extensive artistic background; she was very well known throughout the Michiana area for her landscapes. By the 1920s Muriel was already married and widely known for her art as Mrs. Warren H. Miller. She took art appreciation classes at the Chicago Art Institute as well as private coursework. She continued her art education by taking classes taught by muralist J. E. McBurney and studying at the Mid-Western Art Colony in Paw Paw, Michigan under Audubon Tyler. In 1927, she spent a short amount of time studying in Europe. Back in South Bend, where she married her husband, Muriel became the chairwoman of the South Bend Woman's Club art department. While there she helped to establish the annual spring exhibit of South Bend artists. She also exhibited throughout the area and had two joint exhibits with fellow painter O. W. Fackert and represented South Bend in the Hoosier Art Salon in Chicago along with Alexis Fournier. Muriel passed away in 1975.

Konstantin "Mickey" Milonadis, another local artist from a faraway nation, was born in 1926 in the small town of Kremenchuck in the Ukraine. As a child, he spent a lot of time doing what children do—doodling in textbooks. This doodling became a larger artistic ambition but had to be put on hold when he was drafted into the Ukrainian army as a teenager during the 1940s. Although he never finished his Ukrainian schooling, he found his way through Europe and into Germany, where he lived as a refugee until 1951 when he was admitted into the United States. Almost immediately after, he was drafted for the Korean War where he trained as an engineer alongside learning English. In 1953 he found himself in Chicago, where he completed his GED before being accepted into the School of the Art Institute with the intention of becoming a sculptor. He received his bachelor's in 1957 before going on to earn a master of fine arts from Tulane University in New Orleans. Before too much longer

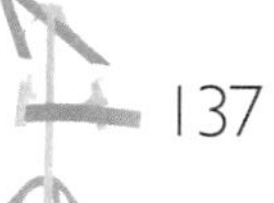

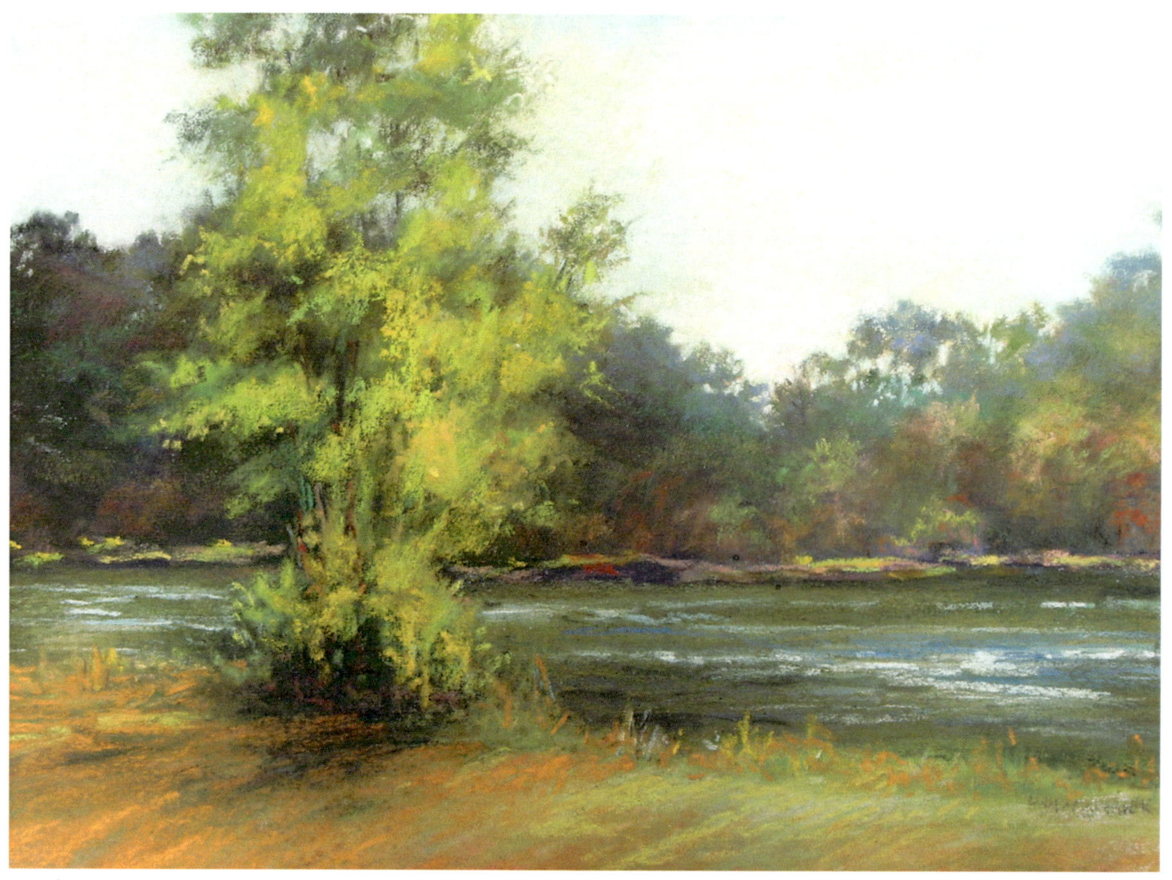

Catherine McCormick, *Trees at Pinhook Park.*

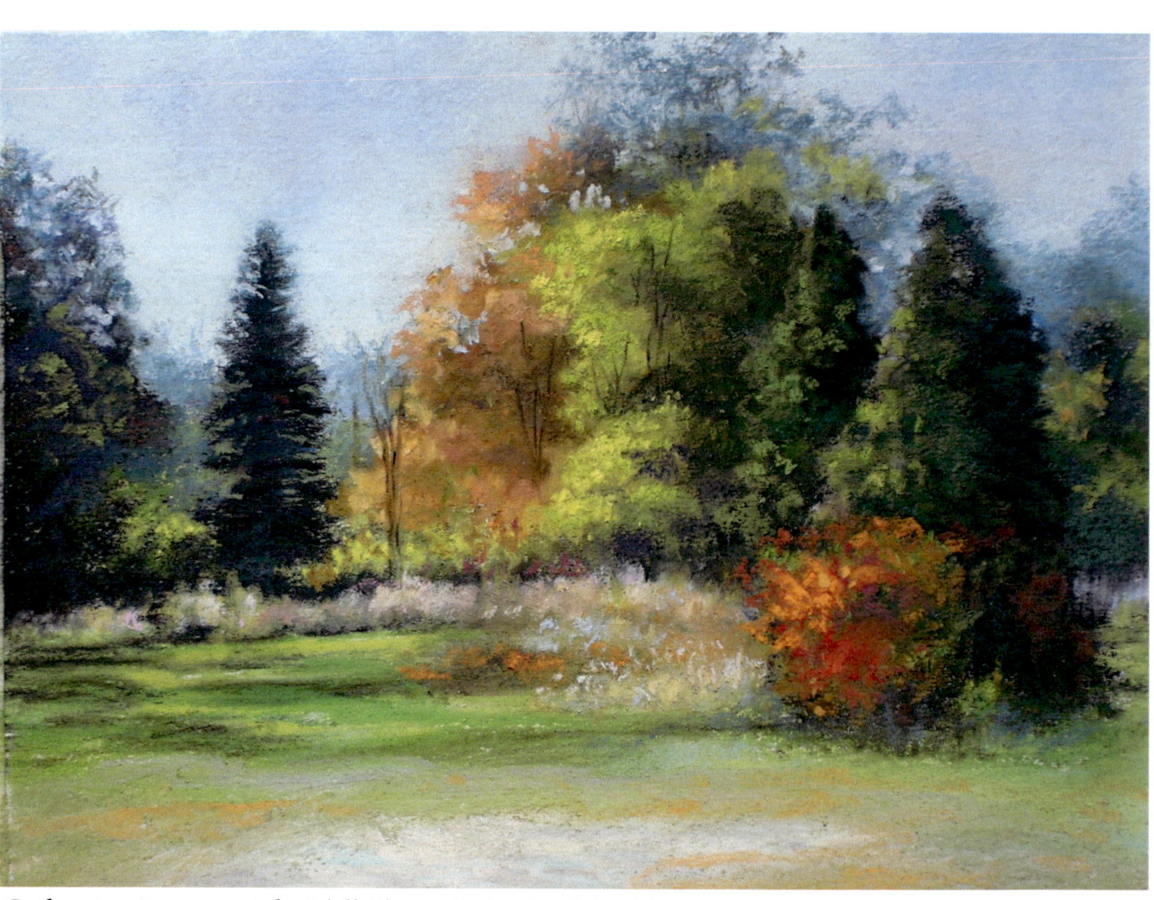

Catherine McCormick, *Fall Trees at St. Patrick's Park.*

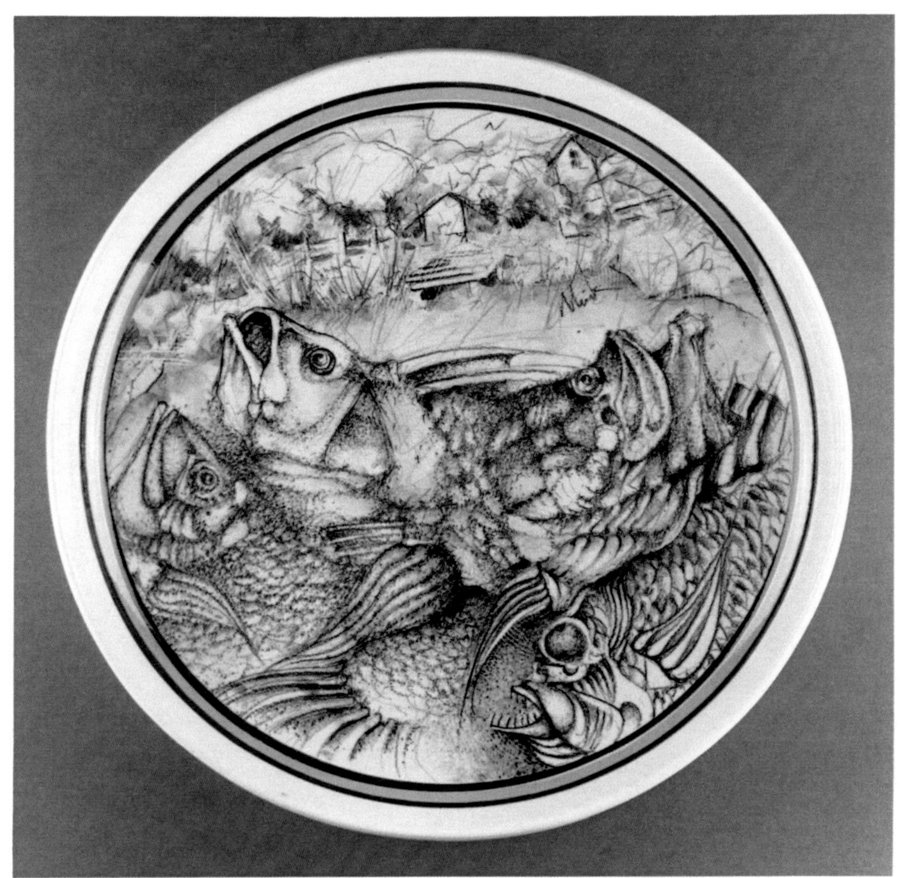

Tom Meunink, *Big Fish Pond*.

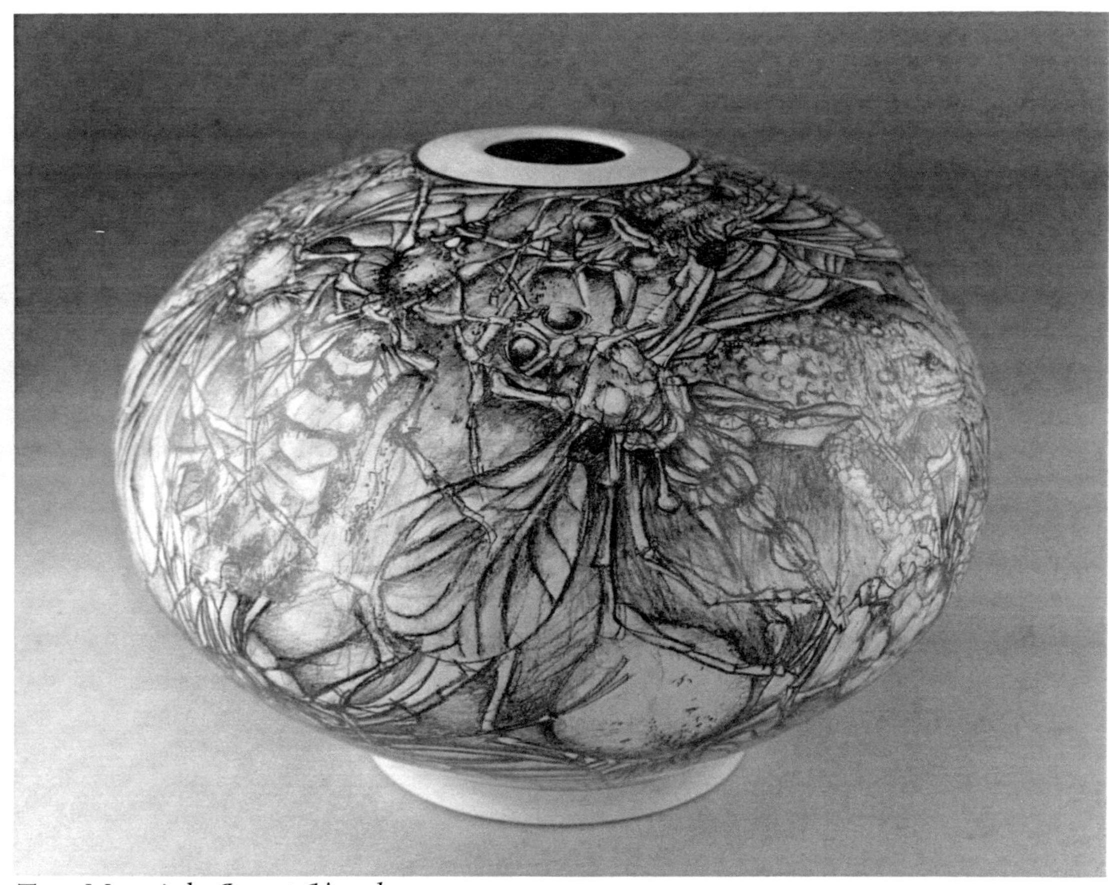

Tom Meunink, *Insect Vessel*.

he found himself in South Bend, teaching sculpture at the University of Notre Dame, where he would remain until 1973. In addition to these colleges, Milonadis was integral in the founding of the Ukrainian Institute of Modern Art in Chicago in 1971. He returned to teaching during the '80s and continues to sculpt and exhibit across the nation.

Ron Monsma, born in Columbus, Ohio, but brought to Michiana by his parents at age seven, began studying art while he was at Riley High School. Before too long he was studying at Indiana University South Bend with Tony Droege. Monsma was very influenced by American artist George Inness, and drew from the Dutch masters just as Inness had. He primarily used pastels to create still lifes and landscapes, but Monsma was also interested in nudes and the human form. As an artist, Monsma often shied away from overtly presenting politics and emotions in his work and instead wanted to focus on creating a mood and presenting the drama within the portrait. Monsma has been on the faculty at IU South Bend since 1997, acting as an assistant professor of drawing and painting; he also acted as a visiting artist for Hillsdale College.

Harriet Monteith, born on February 23, 1903, in Wakarusa, Indiana, was another early member of the Northern Indiana Artists community. As an artist she painted many oils, pastels, and water colors, largely portraits and still-lifes. Monteith wasn't always attached to the area, however. She attended Asbury College in Wilmore, Kentucky as well as Fort Wayne Art School and the Art Institute of Chicago. Two of her most notable teachers were the Russian portrait artist Robert Brackman and Notre Dame art professor Emile Jacques. As her technique grew, she began to exhibit her paintings at the South Bend Art Center (currently South Bend Museum of Art), the Hoosier Salon, as well as in thirteen solo shows across northern Indiana and southern Michigan. She also began to teach, and hosted her classes in her back yard. Montetih also joined alliances of artists, such as the Elkhart Art League and the Brown County Art Guild; she was a member of the American Professional League of New York and involved with the Palette and Chisel Academy of Fine Arts in Chicago. Throughout, the hub of her life was always Indiana, and she passed away here in September for 1975.

Phil Monteith was born in Elkhart, Indiana, in 1927. He studied at Transylvania College in Kentucky and Indiana University, Bloomington, graduating there with a master's degree in music education in 1952. He taught music to all grade levels in the Elkhart public schools for thirty-five years. Early in life he studied art with Harriet Monteith and Konstantin Milonadis, and he continued to study life drawing and pastels for many years as well. He is a self-taught wood-cut artist and a pastelist, and he has work in collections in twelve states. He exhibits locally, regionally, and nationally, is a distinguished member of several arts societies, and has served as president of the Elkhart Art League.

Stephen Moriarty graduated from the University of Notre Dame in 1969 with a bachelor of science in theology and continued on with schooling. A short time afterwards, he studied at the Art Institute of Chicago, and eventually returned to Notre Dame for a master of fine arts. He works primarily as a documentary photographer, and is nationally recognized for his works. For his works, Moriarty sometimes travels abroad, such as with his series on El Salvador. He spent six years abroad working on the series and eventually had an exhibit of the results at the Snite Museum of Art at Notre Dame. He also worked with the South Bend Museum of Art as the Milly and Fritz Kaeser Curator of Photography. Moriarty created the archive in addition to the accompanying exhibition and catalogue. He also taught a course on the history of photography that was exceptionally popular. Although Moriarty has retired from his position at the Snite Museum, he is continuing his photography career.

Rose Ellen CSC (Morrissey), born Rosemary Morrissey on March 31, 1921 in Oak Park, Illinois, graduated from St. Mary's College in 1943 after majoring in art with minors in philosophy and French. Art played a large role in her life, and even as a child its importance shone through as she began carving with soap, and later moved towards various medias such as clay, wood, metal, painting, and photography. A short time after her graduation from St. Mary's, she applied for admission into the congregation there and was accepted the following February. In 1946, she professed her vows and was fully accepted into the congregation. However, Sister Rose Ellen didn't let this slow down her artistic career. She began teaching 4th grade and art classes at St. Joseph's School in South Bend, as well as ceramics at St. Mary's. In 1961, Sister Rose Ellen became the esteemed head of the art department and held the position until 1975. She also found time in her busy schedule to pursue an additional bachelor's degree and a master's degree from the School of the Art Institute in Chicago, in addition to taking classes at Loyola in Chicago, New York University, and the University of Chicago. She was also an active board member of the National Association of Schools of Art and Design and served as the Director at Large from 1976-1978. She accomplished all of this even while teaching and creating and exhibiting her own artwork. She passed away in 1995 while living with the congregation at St. Mary's.

Reginald Neal, born in 1909 in Leicester, England, came to South Bend later in life to serve as the first director of the South Bend Art Association and to offer accredited adult art courses. Before coming to Michiana, Neal majored in art at Bradley University in Peoria, Illinois and studied at Yale University. He completed a few years of graduate work at both the University of Chicago and Colorado Springs Fine Arts Center. Perhaps best known for his work with lithography, Neal also used oil and watercolor paintings, as well as gouaches and drawings in both the realistic and the abstract styles. He began his teaching career as the head of the art department at a high school in Moline, Illinois, before moving on to head the Milikin University Art Department. He'd eventually become an instructor of lithography at Colorado Springs Fine Art Center and the Escuela des Bellas Arts in San Miguel de Allende in Mexico. On top of his teaching accomplishments, Neal won several prizes and participated in many exhibitions. From 1949-1951, he served as the director at the South Bend Art Association. Following his tenure there, he worked as the director of the master of fine arts programs

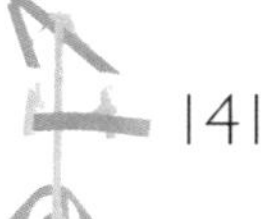

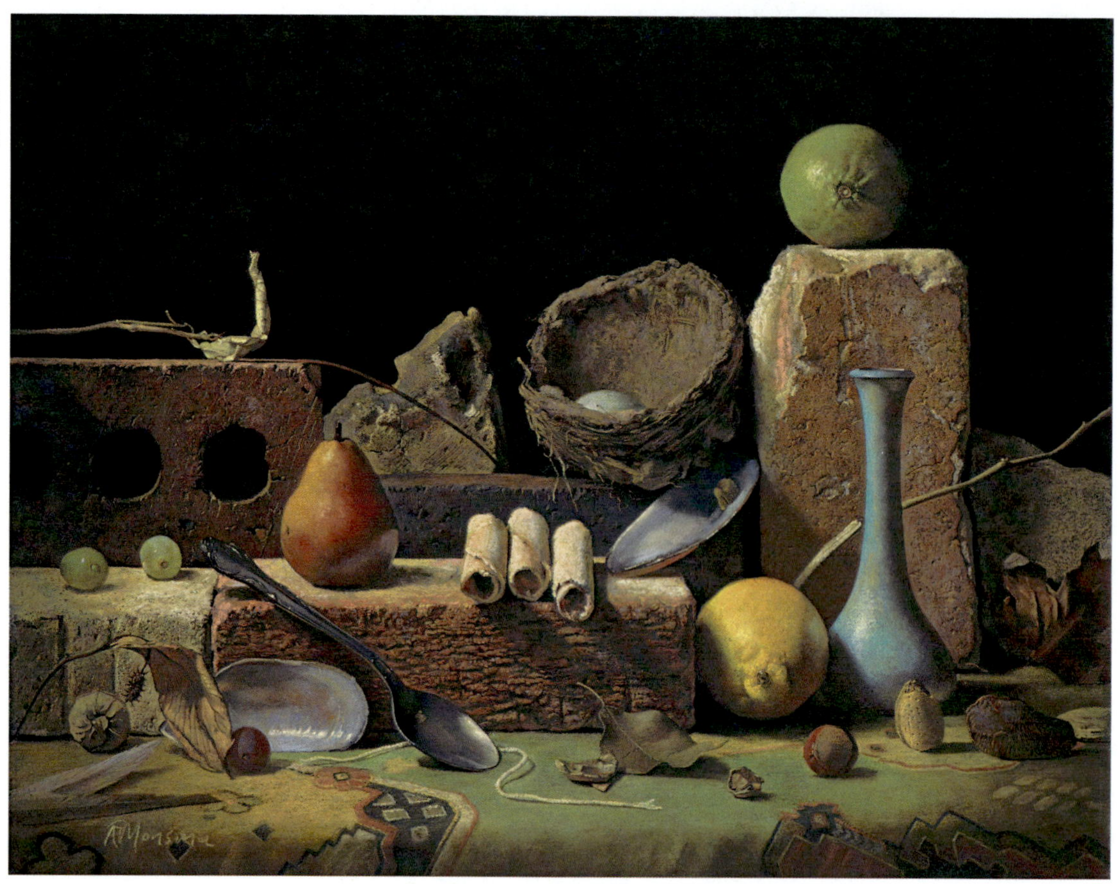

Ron Monsma, *Composition with Nest and Bricks.*

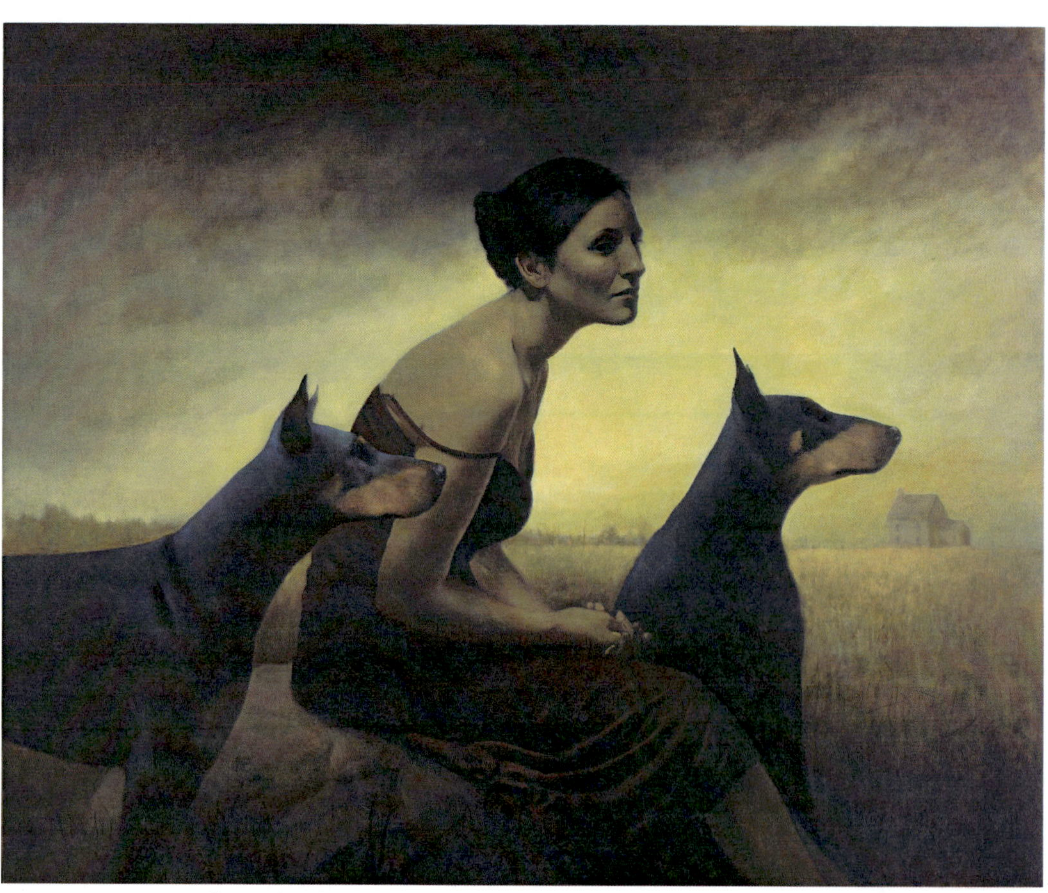

Ron Monsma, *The Weight.*

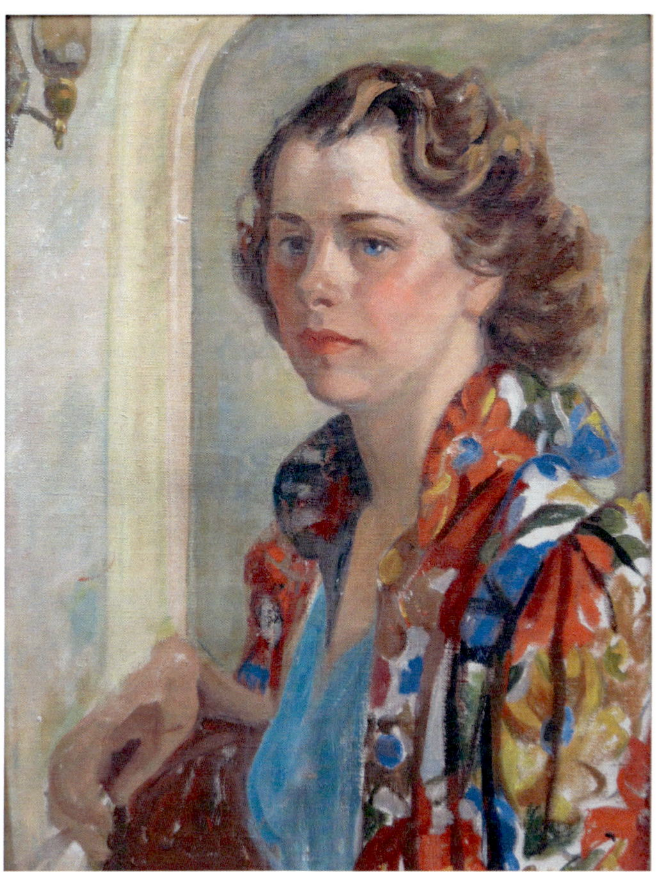

Harriet E. Monteith, *Self Portrait.*

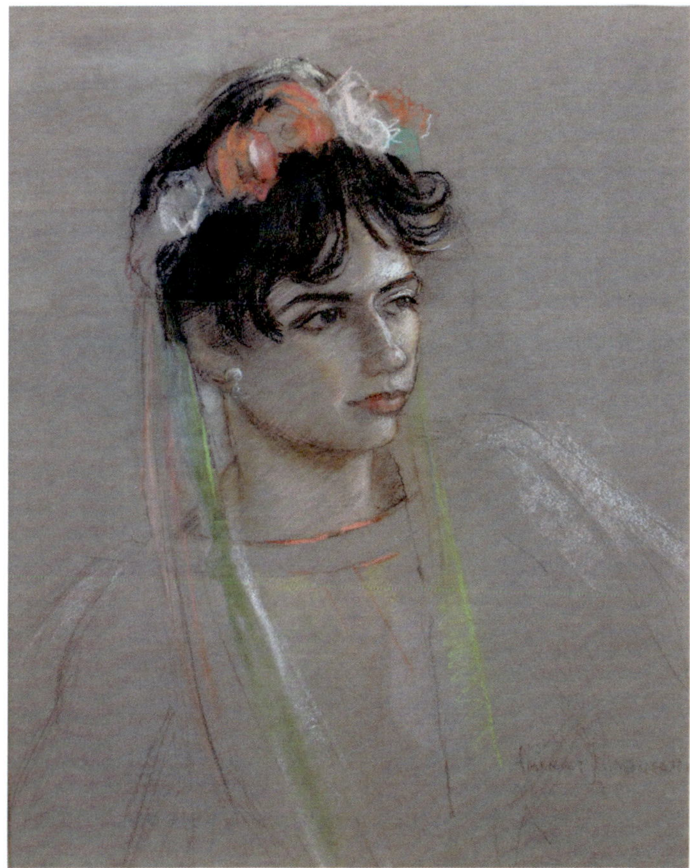

Harriet E. Monteith, *Portrait.*

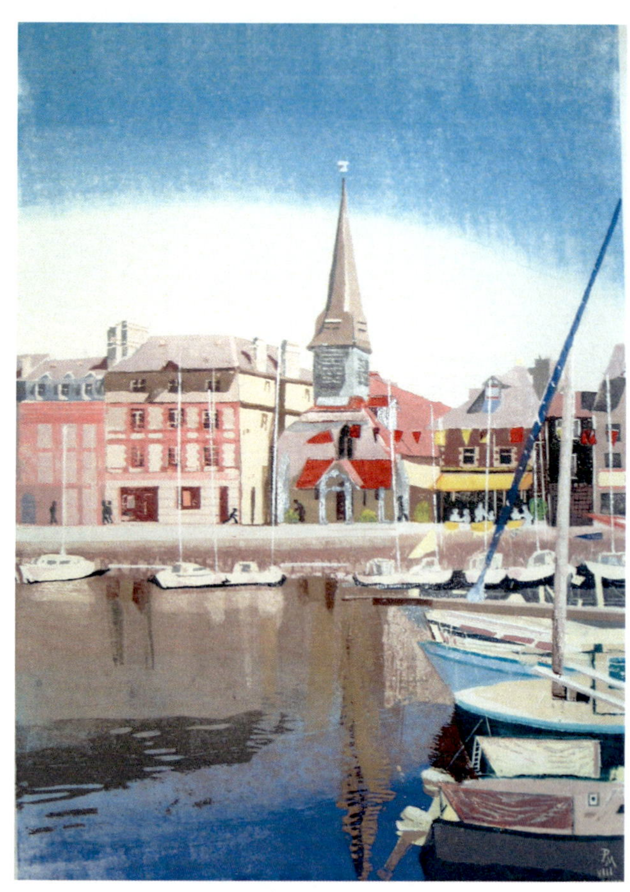

Phillip Monteith, *Honfleur Harbor Scene.*

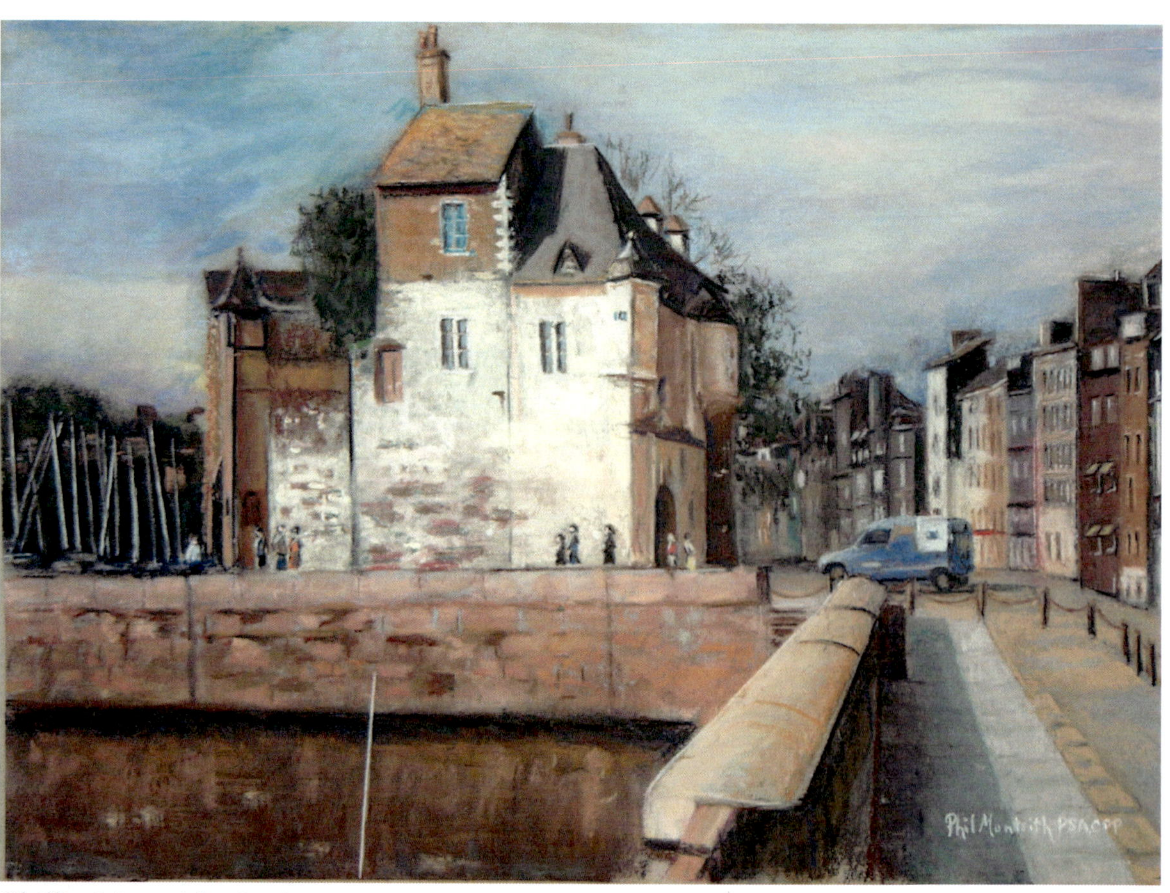

Phillip Monteith, *Le Lieutenance.*

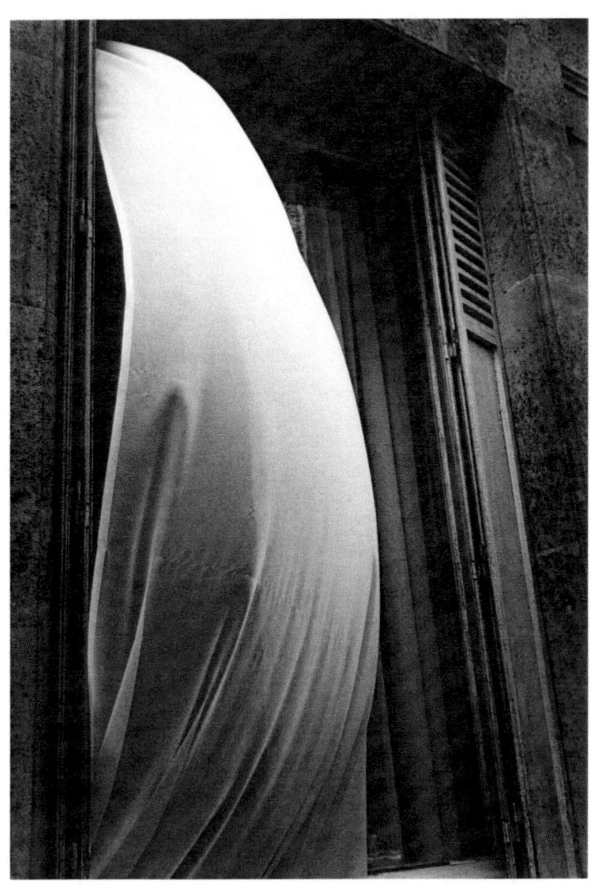

Steve Moriarty, *Curtain, Window, Paris.*

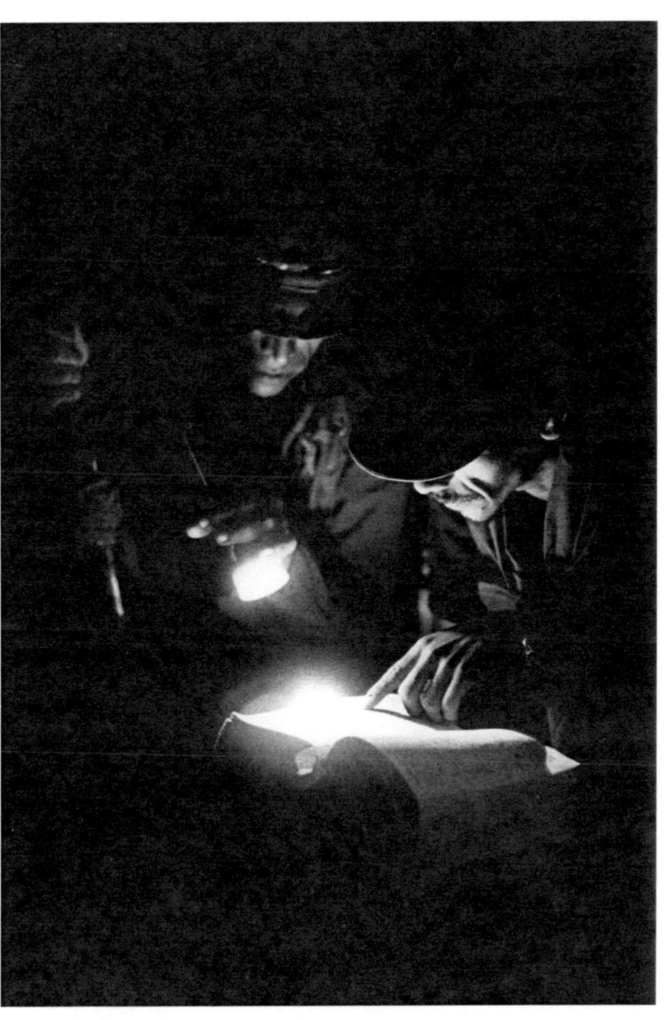

Steve Moriarty, *El Salvador Image.*

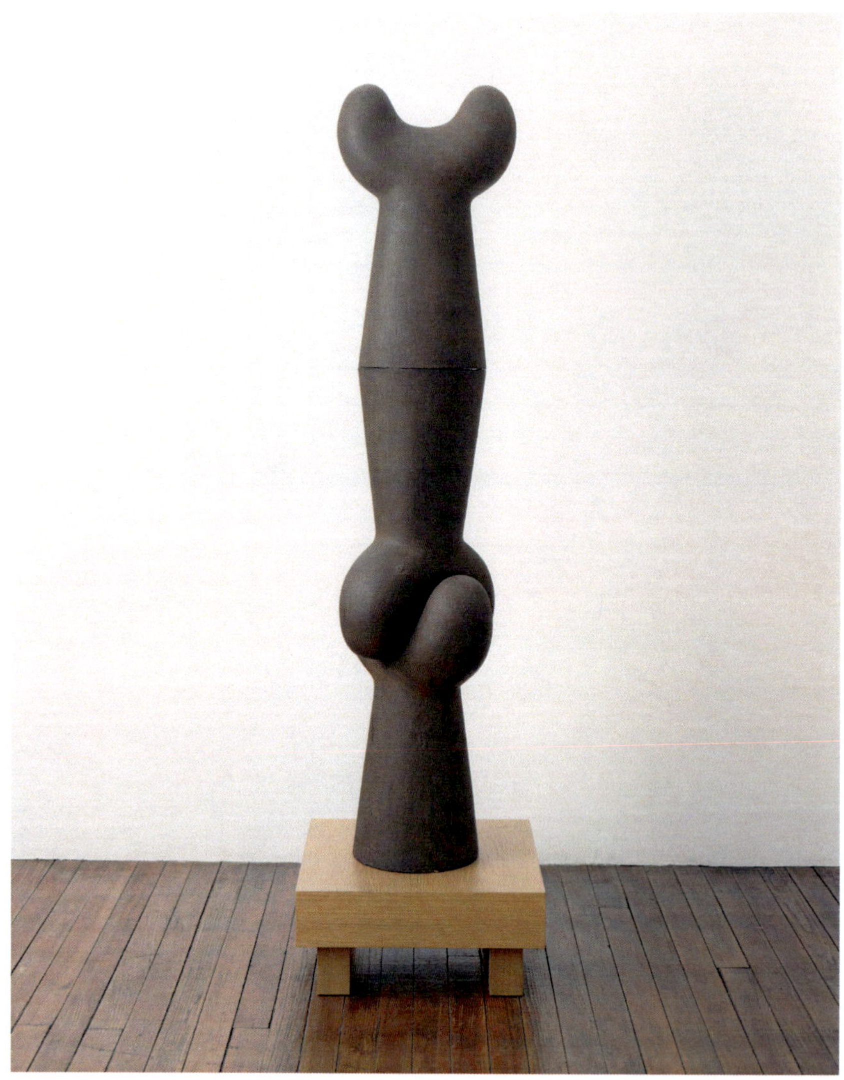

Isamu Noguchi, *Endless Coupling.*

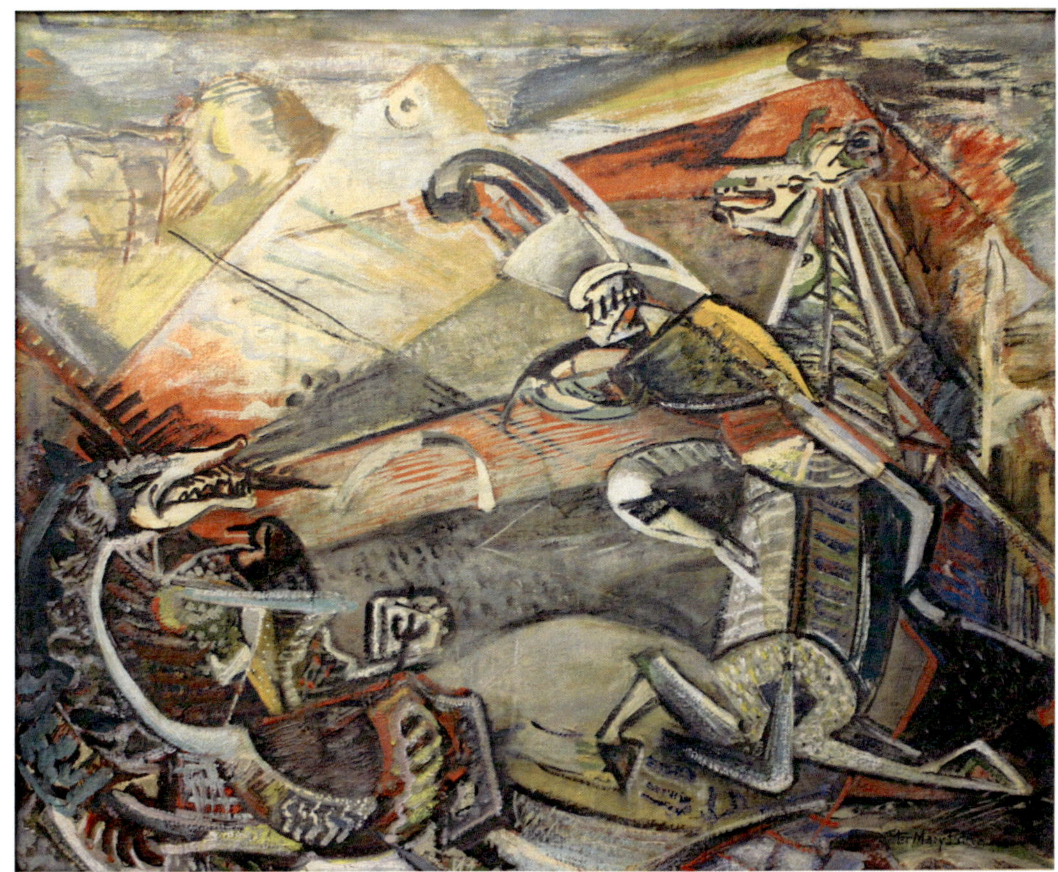

Sister Mary Edna Orzechowska, CSC, *Untitled.*

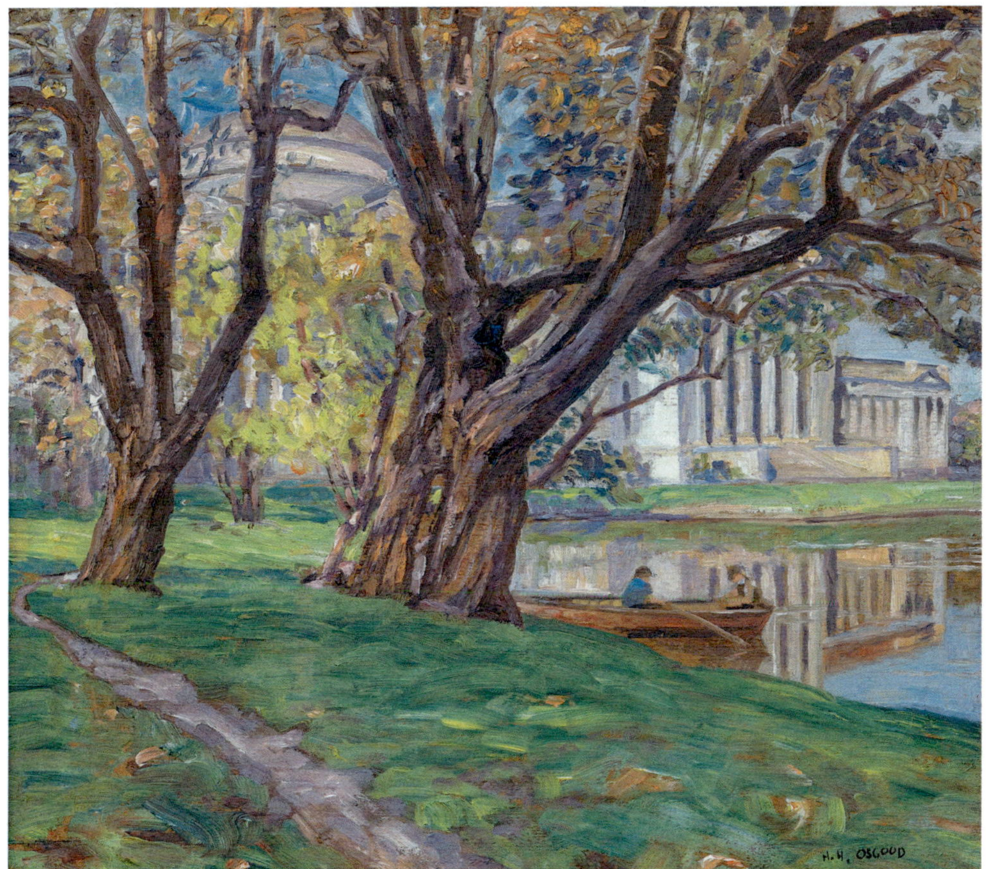

H. H. Osgood, *Rowers, Chicago Science and Industry Museum.*

at both Douglas College and Rutgers University before his death in 1992.

Isamu Noguchi was born in California in 1904. He lived in Japan until the age of thirteen, then in La Porte, Indiana, before moving as a young adult to New York and then Paris, where he studied under the sculptor Constantin Brancusi. His work ranged widely over the course of a lifetime, including stage sets for noted choreographers, a now-classic mass-produced glass-top table, sculpture, and public gardens. He drew upon art traditions he encountered in travel on three continents and responded to social issues of the day in some of his work. Before he died in 1988, Noguchi received many honors for a lifetime of achievement. Many of his works are preserved and displayed in the Noguchi Museum in Long Island City, New York.

Sister Mary Edna Orzechowska, CSC, born as Helen Orzechowska on June 6, 1892, joined the Congregation of the Sisters of the Holy Cross at St. Mary's in 1910. Although she joined the sisterhood and took her final vows on August 15, 1912, Sister Mary Edna became a successful artist. She received her bachelor of arts from St. Mary's and also studied at the Art Institute of Chicago, the Catholic University in Washington, D.C., and the Cincinnati Art Institute. She primarily used oil and watercolor paints to create fresco murals. From the day she took her final vows, Sister Mary Edna was a member of the St. Mary's art department and she continued to work with them until 1968 when she was named Associate Professor Emeritus of St. Mary's College. From that point on, she resided in St. Mary's Convent until 1973, when she passed away at the age of 80 following a short illness.

Harry Haviland Osgood was a painter and etcher born in LaSalle County, in north central Illinois in 1875; he died in South Bend in 1960. He studied at the Art Institute of Chicago from 1905-1919, where he also exhibited, and at the Académie Julian and the Académie Colarossi, both in Paris.

Harry James Paradis worked individually from ceramics and sculpture, painting and collage to focus on how the various forms of media could express emotions and ideas. He spent some of his life in Italy, both studying and teaching; but before his first trip there he found himself in the United States Marine Corps. After leaving the service, he began taking classes at Indiana University Bloomington, where he would received a bachelor of science before moving on to study fine art for one year at the University of California in Los Angeles. He later found himself back at IU Bloomington for a master of fine arts, during which time he also spent one year studying art history abroad in Florence and Rome. His artwork was heavily influenced by the abstract expressionists of the 1940s and 1950s, and his experiences with them. Upon finishing his schooling, Paradis settled down in South Bend, where he taught art at Washington High School, and ceramics at the South Bend Art Association as well as Indiana University South Bend and the Barn School of Art. He also began teaching at Saint Mary's College and at Notre Dame, where he remained for twenty-eight years, fifteen of which were spent acting as the chairman of the art department at St. Mary's. His earlier experiences abroad led him into the St. Mary's summer abroad program, with which he was involved for eight years. Paradis was also honored at the

Artist in Residence at Dunbarton College in Washington, D.C.

Marion Pilarski, another lifelong resident of the area, was born on October 13, 1928. As a printmaker and watercolor painter, he spent several years studying art at Indiana University Bloomington and received his bachelor of arts in 1956; he received a master of arts from the University of Notre Dame in 1962. Following his time as a student, Pilarski began teaching with the South Bend School Corporation. He spent much of his career there based at Washington High School, where he helped to establish a more prominent art program. Pilarski also took time to teach at Notre Dame and St. Mary's, Indiana University South Bend, and the South Bend Museum of Art. His works were also the subject of exhibits across the nation, due in part to his experiments with style and media. Pilarski's style tended towards the abstract with a variety of different subjects, anything from city scenes to still lifes. Although it is not readily apparent in his paintings, he often experimented with the media in his works using wood and metals. Pilarski continued to work with the SBCSC for thirty-four years. He passed away in 2002 at the age of seventy-three.

Dean Porter was born in a small town in northern New York State on June 13, 1939. His art career began when Kenneth Linday, a professor at Harpur College in New York, encouraged him to focus on art for his major. At the end of his freshman year at the State University of New York at Binghamton, he declared his major and never looked back. The following year he studied with Irving Zupnick, and developed into a printmaker and oil painter. He received his bachelor of arts a few years later, followed by his master of arts, also from the State University of New York at Binghamton, in 1966. Following graduation, Dean took a position with the University of Notre Dame as curator of the Snite Museum of Art, an office he held until 1974 when he followed Reverend Lauck and became the director of the Notre Dame Art Gallery. He held this position until 1999 but continued teaching until 2001. He was also integral in the designing and the opening, in 1980, of the new Snite Museum of Art. He has taken part in many exhibitions, including over forty solo shows.

Roman J. Radecki, born in South Bend in 1914, worked as a sculptor and art collector while the owner of Radecki Galleries, which he and his wife opened in 1957. Even before opening the gallery, though, Radecki had acquired an impressive collection, which he began at age nineteen. Radecki and his family worked intimately with the Snite Museum of Art, as well as the South Bend Art Center and the South Bend Center for History, on painting restorations. Since his death, his family has taken over the gallery.

Patty Reddy and **Kathy Reddy White** (twin sisters) have been engaged with art in the Michiana area for much of their lives. The pair attended Holy Cross Grade School and graduated from St. Joseph's High School in 1975. They remained together through the bachelors degrees from St. Mary's College, but split up for a short time afterwards—Patty studied graphic design at Ivy Tech and Kathy went to Notre Dame for a master of fine arts. They continued to progress separately for a

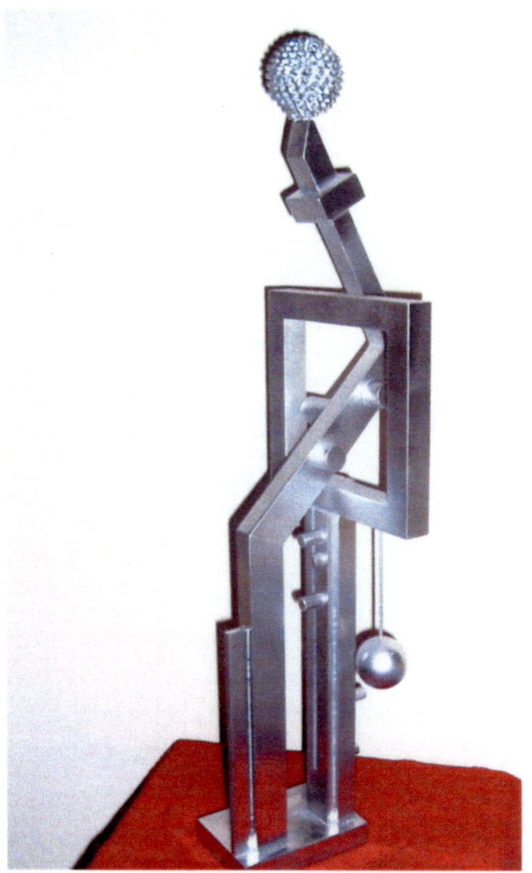

Harry James Paradis, *Challenge.*

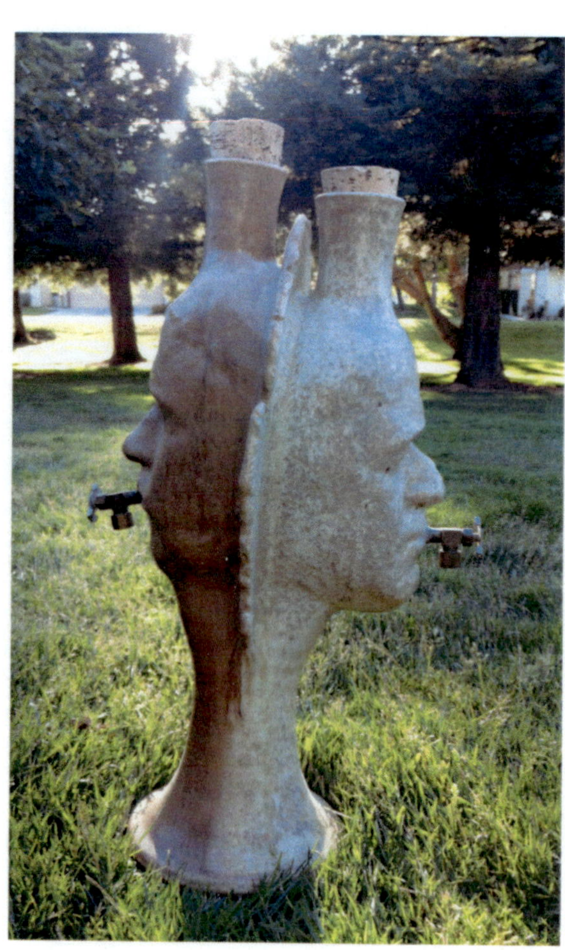

Harry James Paradis, *Janus.*

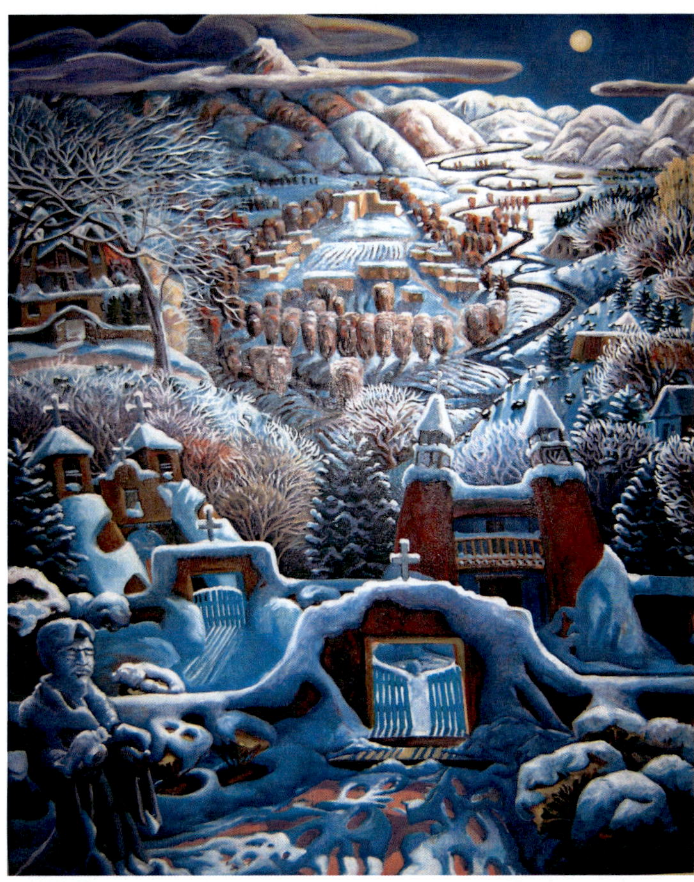

Dean Porter, *Southwest Fantasy.*

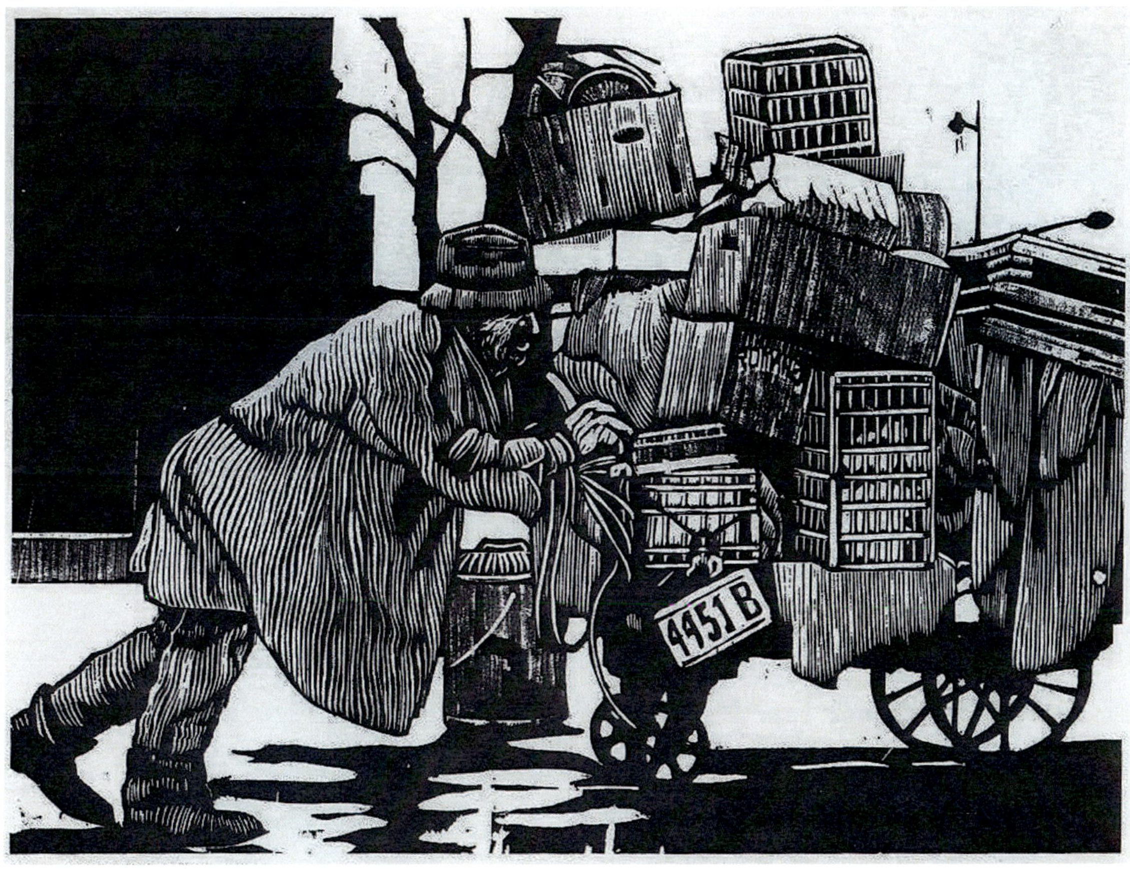

Dean Porter, *Junk for Some.*

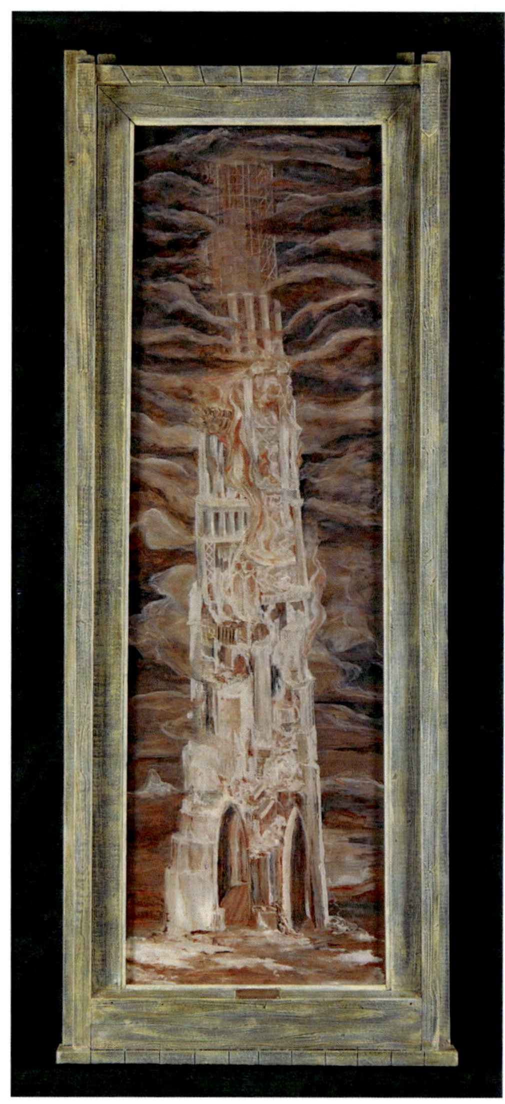

Roman Radecki, *Tradition.*

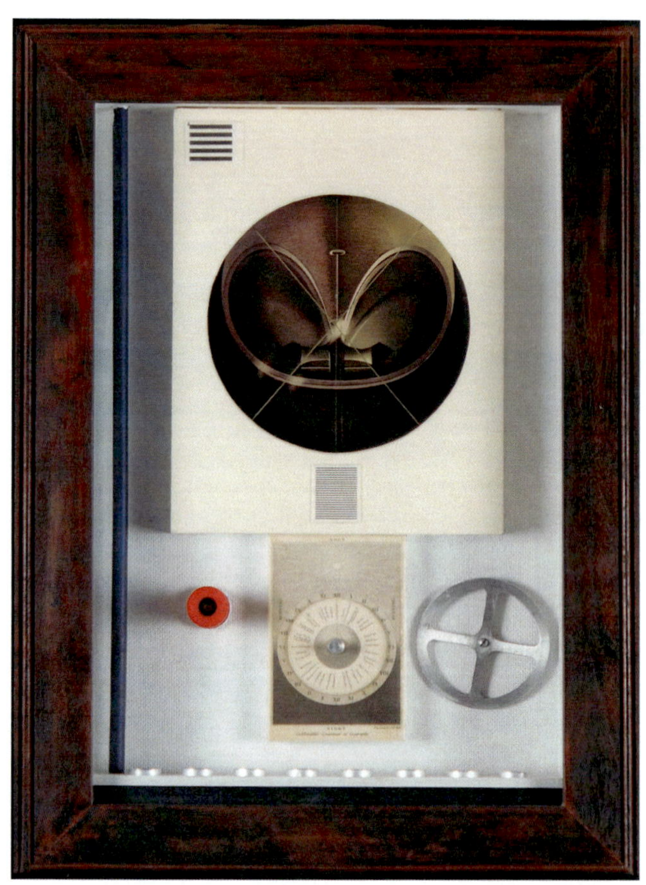

Roman Radecki, *Voyager #2.*

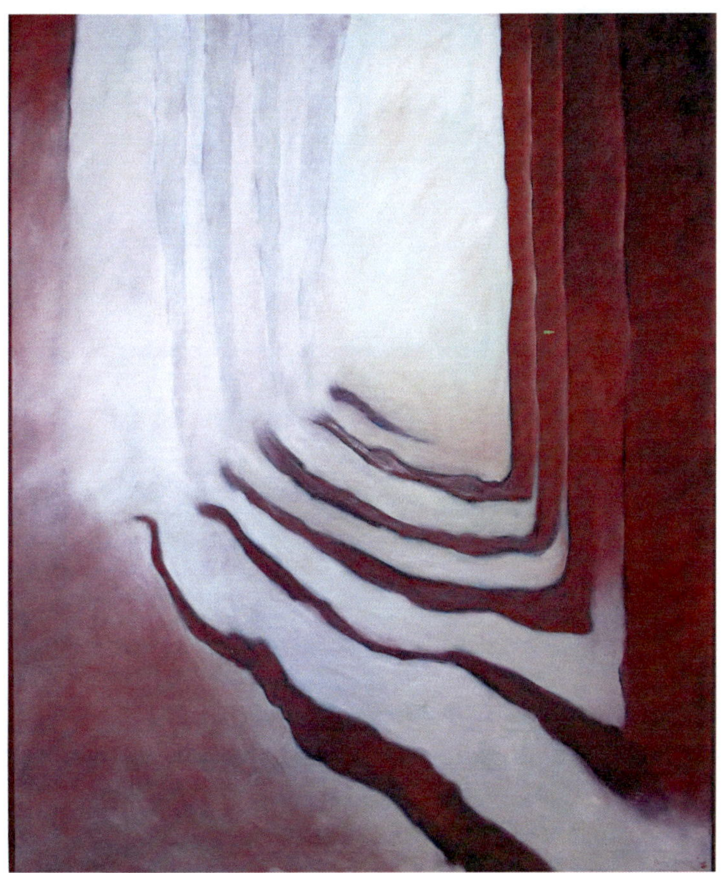

Patty Reddy, *Forest.*

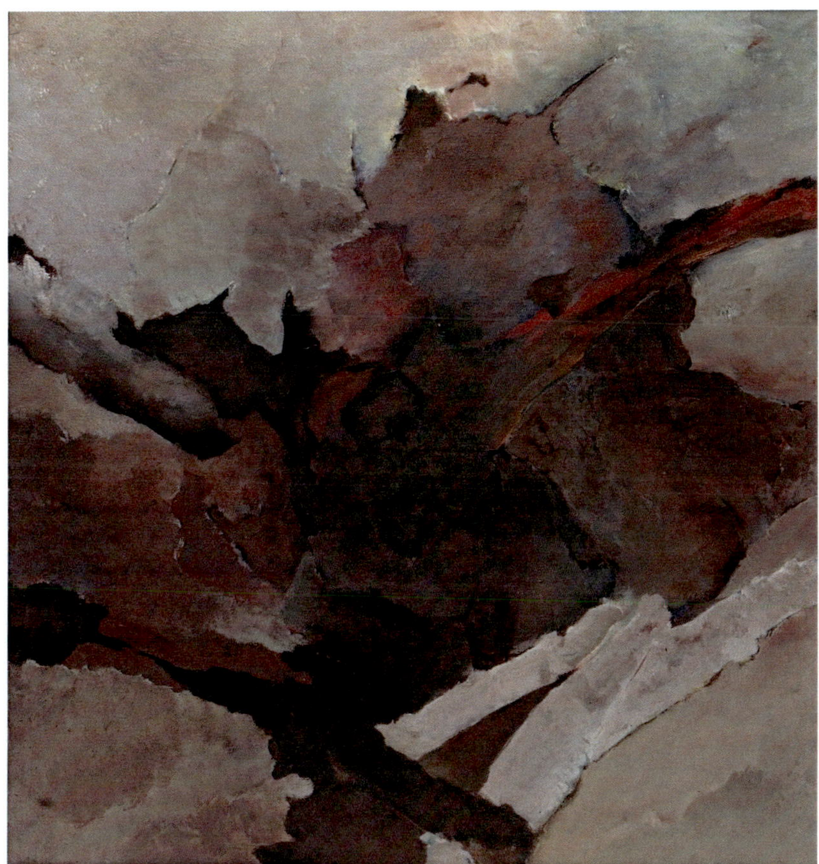

Patty Reddy, *Tornado.*

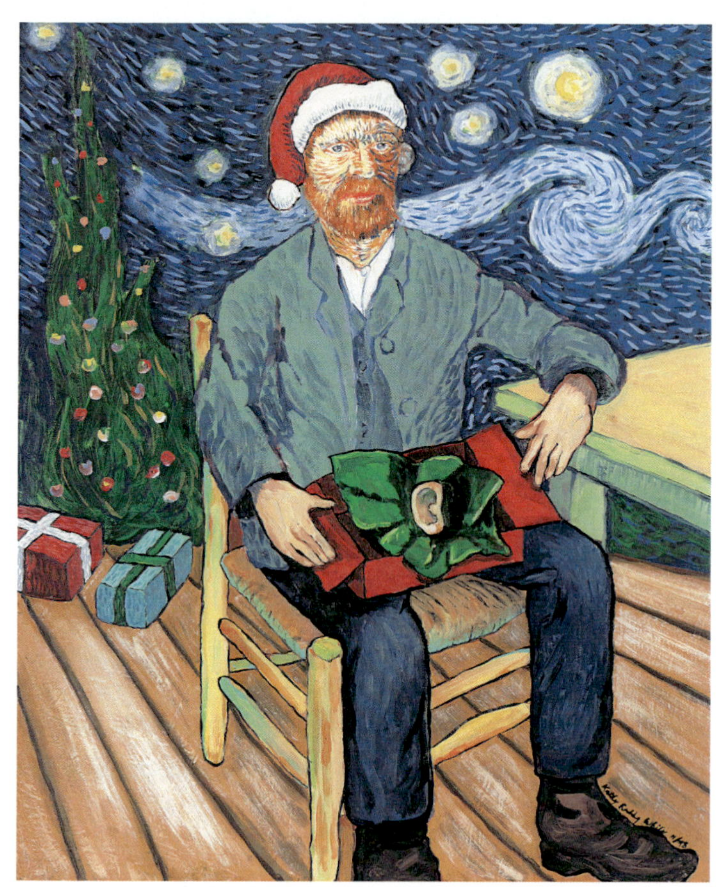
Kathy Reddy-White, *Van Gogh Christmas.*

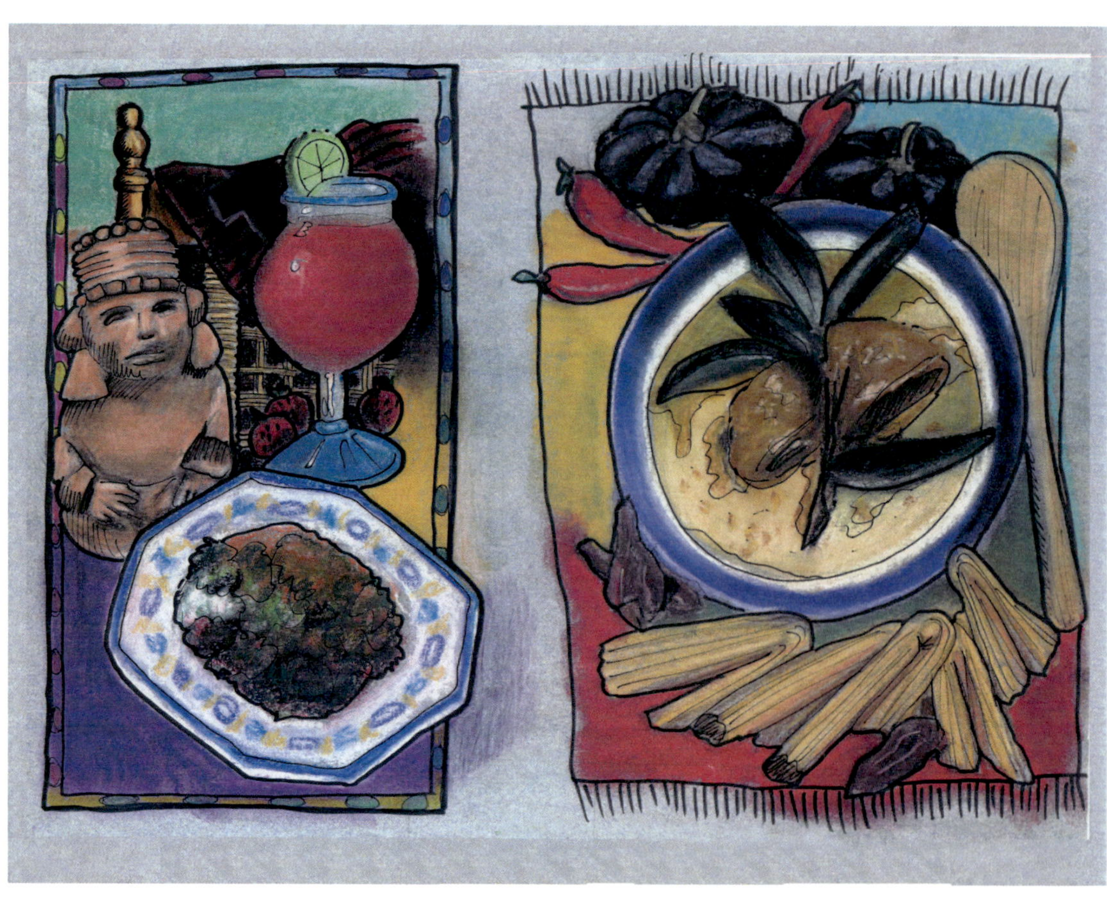
Kathy Reddy-White, *Celebration of Mexican Cuisine.*

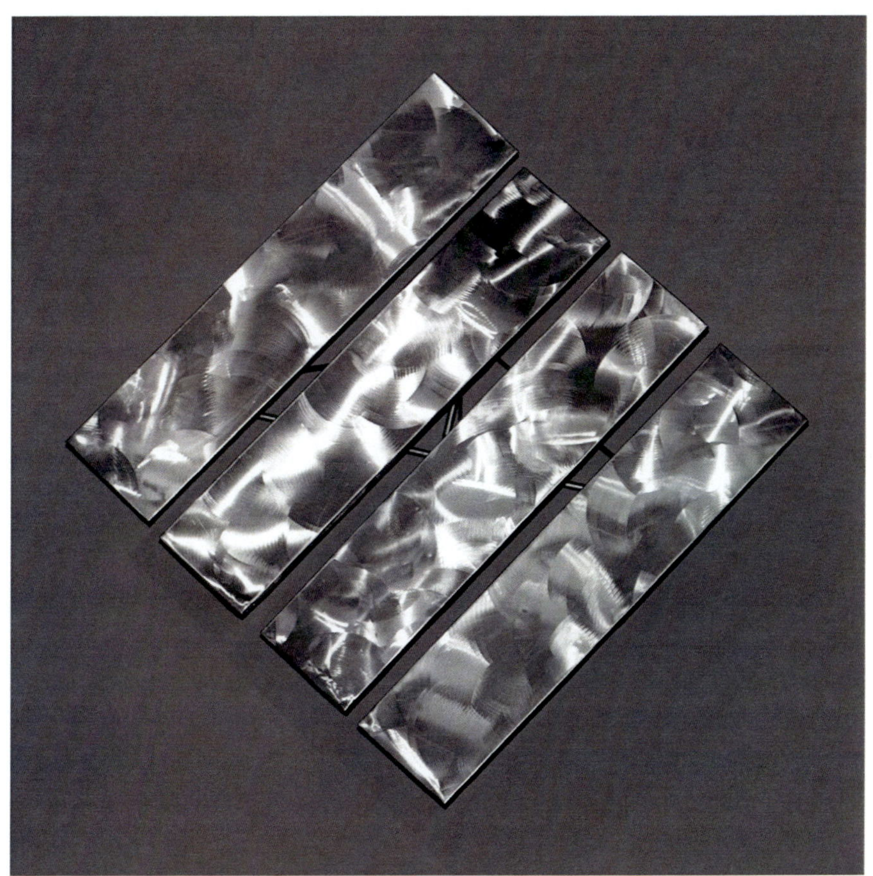

George Rickey, *Four Rectangles Oblique.*

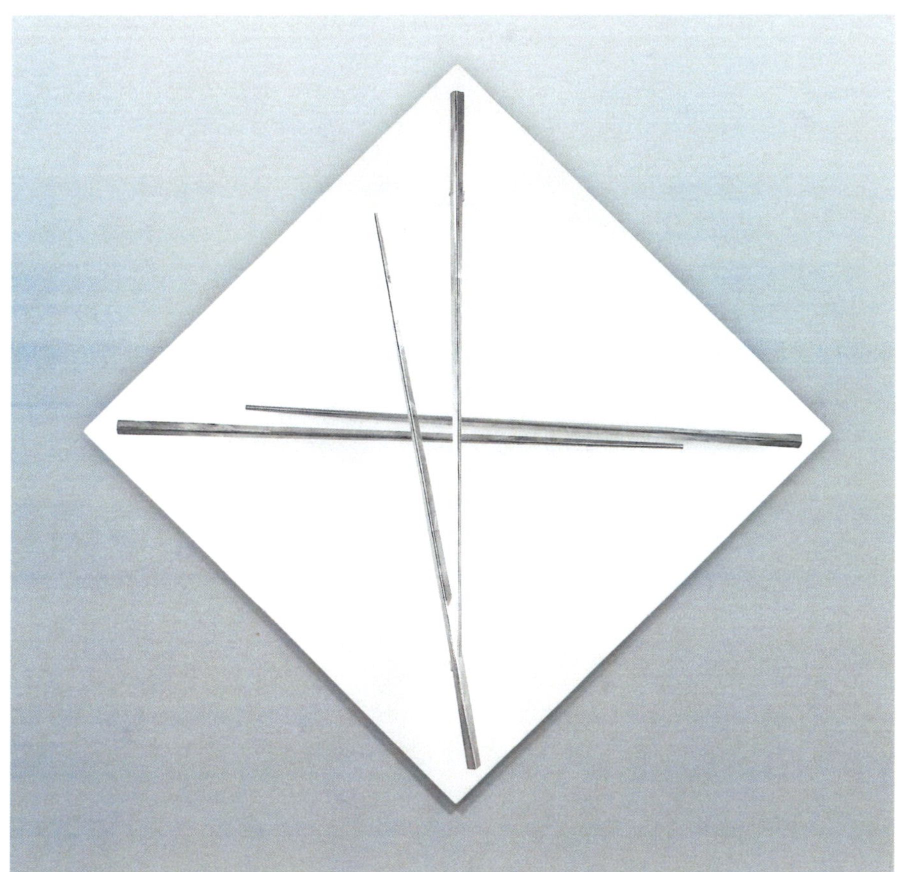

George Rickey, *Two Verticle Two Horizontal Lines.*

while; Patty moved away for a short time but eventually returned. Patty created cartoons and illustrations while also painting and working commercially on graphic design for commercial greeting cards and brochures. She is currently an art therapist for Lakeland Healthcare in Dowagiac, Michigan. Kathy, on the other hand, focused on tile-making and painting. She owns the CircaArts Gallery, established in 2001. Together, the sisters work for their passions as well as for the community: Patty helped organize the Holiday Art Walk in South Bend's northwest neighborhoods, and Kathy worked to help create ArtBeat, a day-long event that gives local visual, performing, and culinary artists an outlet to share their work with the community. She also helped establish ArtWalk, which is a walking tour of the galleries and studios scattered around downtown South Bend. Kathy is strongly influenced by water and life on the Lake Michigan Coastline. Patty and Kathy remain active in the area both individually and jointly.

George Rickey, born in the United States but raised in Scotland, had a very interesting childhood. He was born in South Bend in 1907 as the third of six children and resided there with his family until 1913 when at age five his father took a job in Scotland with the Singer Sewing Machine Company. He grew up there with his family and was initially inspired by his two older sisters who could paint and draw. He was in awe of their ability and this stimulated his young curiosity. Rickey went on to study history at Balliol College and painting at the Ruskin School of Drawing at Oxford University. In 1930, he returned to the United States to teach history and cubist painting at several different schools across the nation. In 1942, Rickey joined the U. S. Army where he worked as an engineer. The experiences gained from this occupation led him towards kinetic sculptures, where he would eventually find his fame. After being released from the army, he used his G. I. Bill to return to school at the New York University Institute of Fine Arts and later the Chicago Institute of Design. He continued to teach and eventually ended up at Indiana University South Bend, where he met and was motivated by David Smith and his kinetic sculptures. His first solo exhibit of this period was in 1953 at the John Herron Art Museum. His fame continued to grow as a result of his large kinetic sculptures that focused on movement. Rickey moved around, but returned to his hometown once more in 1984 with his show, *The Return of the Native*, where his sculptures and re-creations of his sculptures were placed in several venues across the city including the South Bend Art Center, St. Mary's College, IU South Bend and the Snite Museum at Notre Dame. Rickey traveled often, never fully settled into life in South Bend, but returned to his boyhood home from time to time until his death in 2002.

Sister Emily Rivard, CSC, was one of the first painting instructors at Saint Mary's College, then Saint Mary's Academy. Sister Emily was born in Canada, and although no one knows for certain when she arrived in the area, it is recorded that in January of 1851 she and another sister were invited by Mother Superior of the Sisters of Loretto in Kentucky to study artistic pursuits; in Sister Emily's case it was drawing. Her education continued to expand when in 1853 Father Moreau of the University of Notre Dame sent her to France where she studied painting and illustrating. Upon her return to America, Sister Emily taught at Saint Mary's Academy for several years.

Ramiro Rodriguez, born in 1965 in Michigan, is a painter turned printmaker. He studied at Kendall College of Art and Design, where he earned a bachelor of fine arts, and also at the University of Cincinnati, where he received his master of fine arts. Rodriguez remained in Cincinnati for several years after completing his degree, teaching at the University of Cincinnati, acting as a gallery director at 840 Gallery based in the University of Cincinnati, and as an installation assistant at the Contemporary Arts Center. He worked at the Cincinnati Art Museum for a short time as well, first as an art handler then as an exhibition preparator before moving to South Bend to take a position with the Snite Museum in 1998. In 2007, Rodriguez stepped up to become the exhibition coordinator for the Snite and currently holds this position. He has participated in many art shows, both solo and group, and has won several awards for his artwork.

Mitzi B. Sabato, born and raised in the Chicago, Illinois, suburb of Highland Park, has lived and worked in this area since 1984. Sabato was educated at Washington University, St. Louis, Missouri, (AB in psychology and philosophy), and the Art Institute of Chicago, (MFA). She also served as artist-in-residence at the University of Arizona, Tucson, and Saint Mary's College, in addition to a long career as guest lecturer in art at various local and regional institutions, including the Art Institute of Chicago. Sabato's early training and focus was in ceramics, fiber, and photography. She is recognized for her sculptural work and conceptually based assemblage. The work has been reviewed in numerous publications, and shown in solo exhibitions locally and throughout the Midwest. Sabato has been a strong advocate for visual and musical arts in the South Bend area, particularly through her service to the South Bend Museum of Art, South Bend Symphony Orchestra, and support of the Fischoff National Chamber Music Association. Sabato's background, as the daughter of a prominent Chicago psychoanalyst, combined with her psychiatric fellowships, and outdoor lifestyle in Indiana and Montana, inform a wide range of themes in her art. She is known for her unique blend of concept and materials, often incorporating unexpected found elements in her work. She has returned to her ceramic roots, working in porcelain work for the last half dozen years.

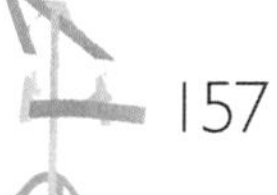

Billy Ray Sandusky's inspiration for art came from the Italian Renaissance masters; an influence that is apparent in his paintings. He received a bachelor of fine arts from the John Herron Art School of Indiana University, followed by a master of fine arts from Tulane University in New Orleans. Following his education, he moved to Italy, where he taught etching, lithography and drawing at the Santa Reparata Graphic Art Centre in Florence, Italy, from 1973 to 1980. While he held this position, he became the principle printer for other professionals involved there. During this time, he also began teaching for study abroad programs of American colleges and universities, and in 1976-1977 he taught printmaking in Florence for Loyola University's graduate program. Bill also taught painting for the St. Mary's Rome Program from 1977-1980.

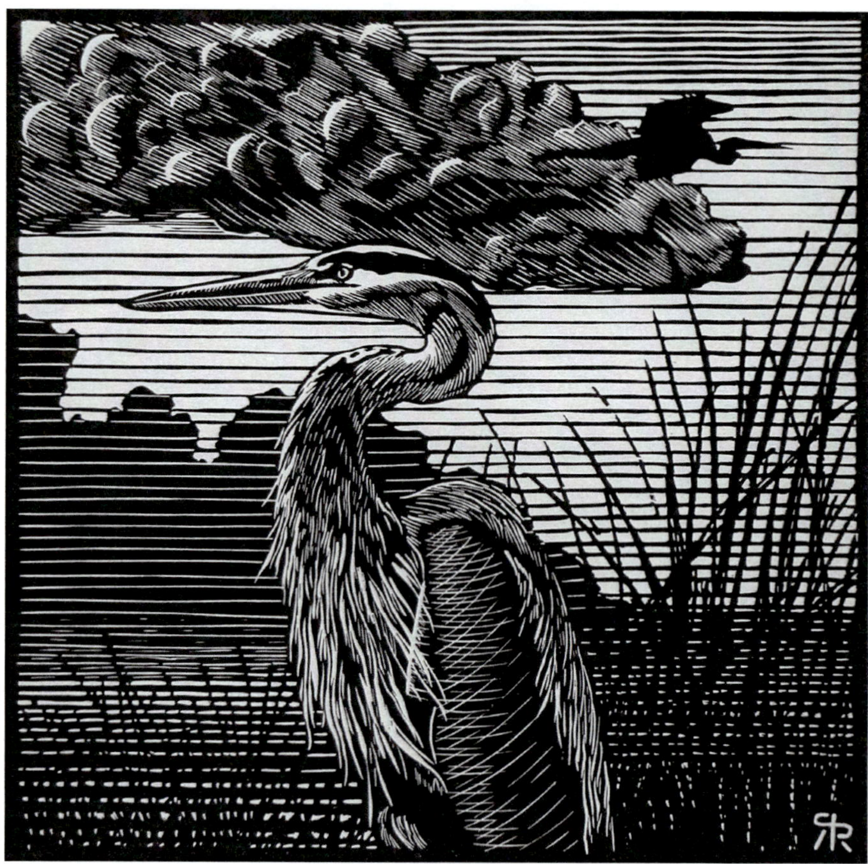
Ramiro Rodriguez, *Great Blue*.

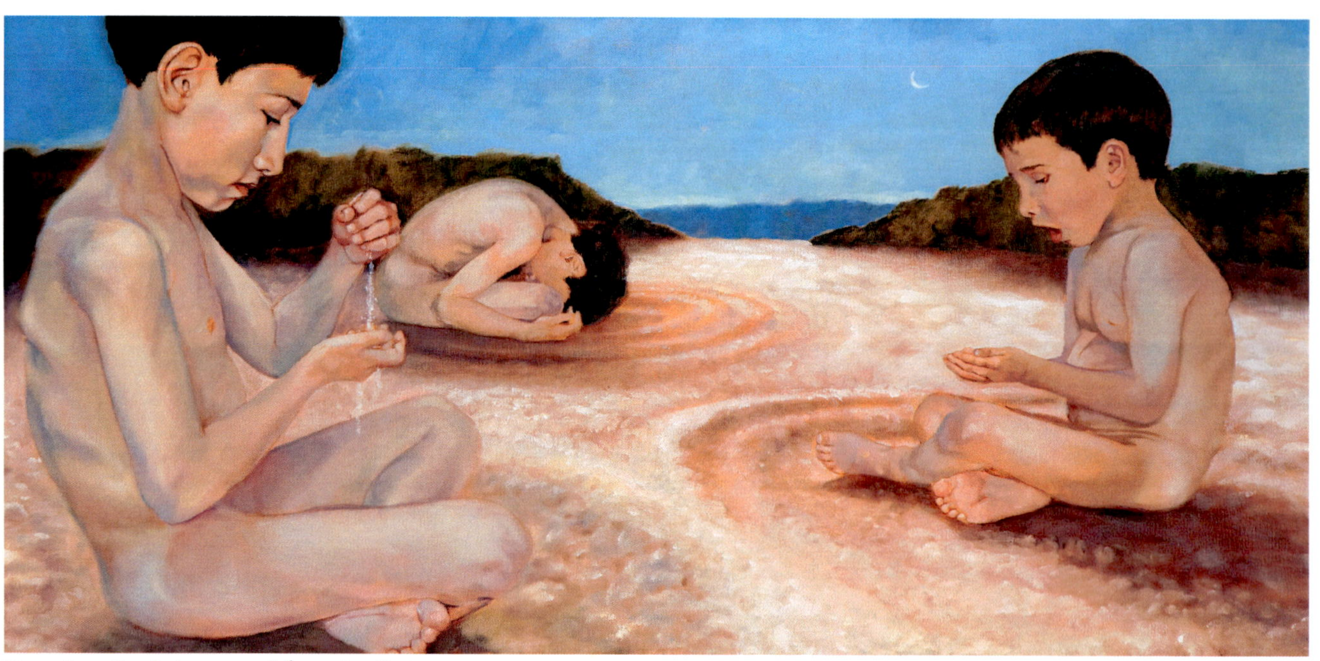
Ramiro Rodriguez, *Materia Prima*.

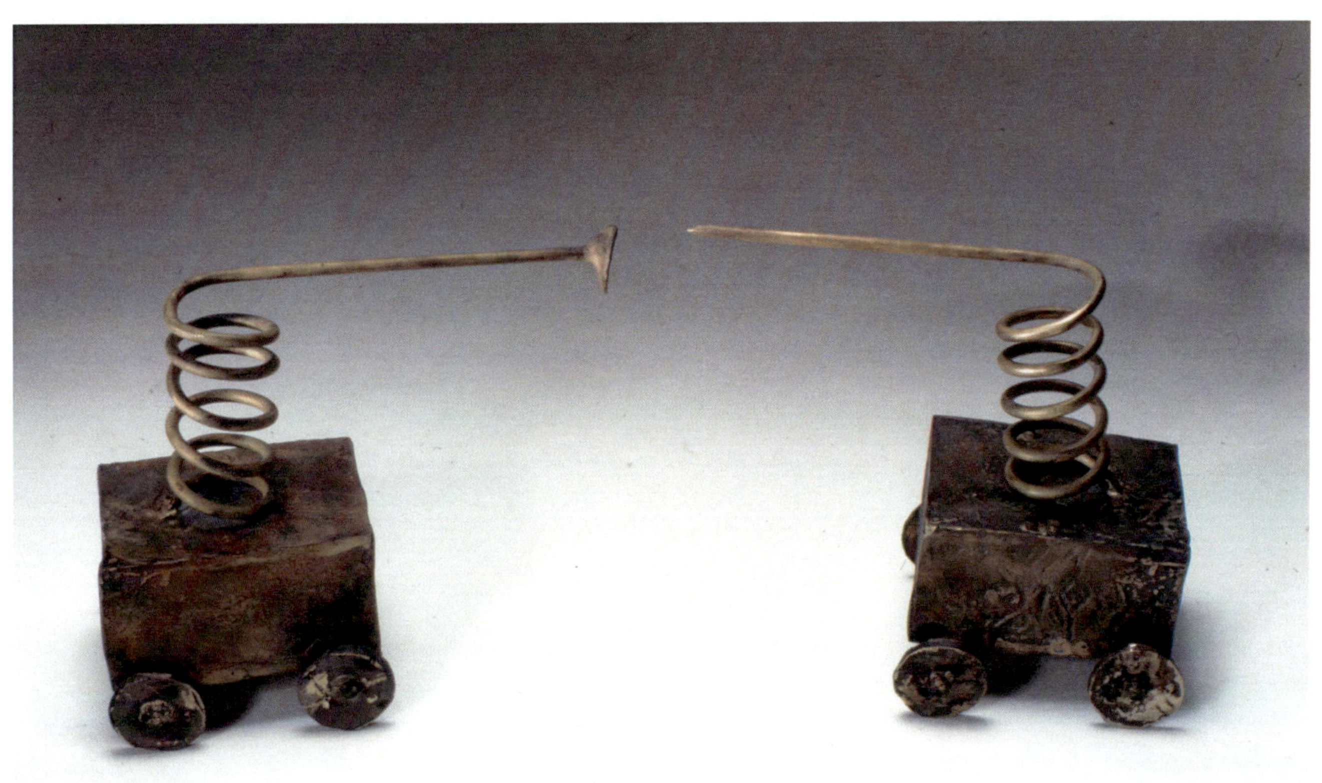

Mitzi Sabato, *Untitled.*

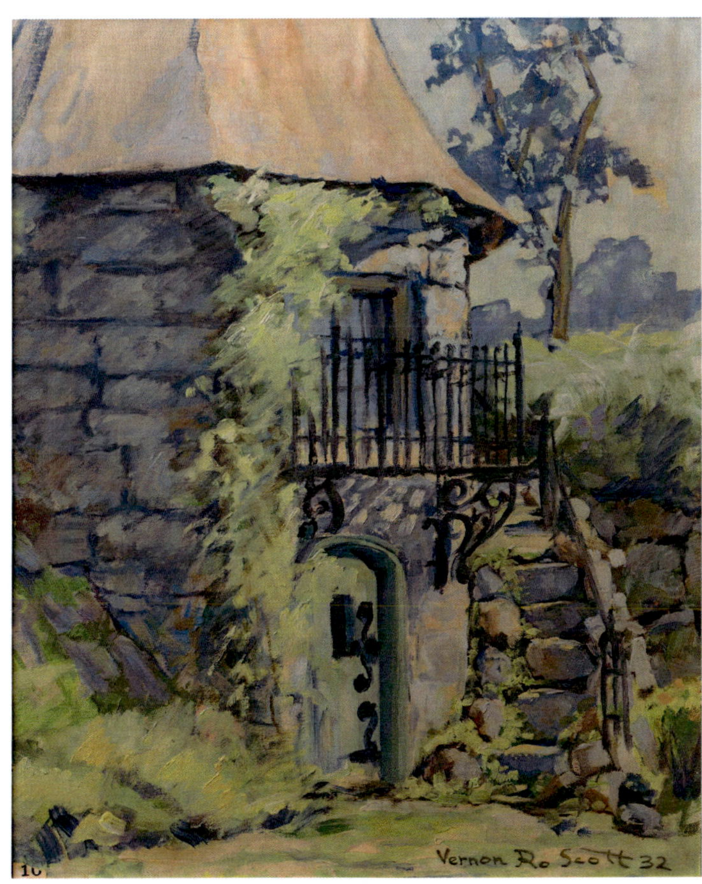

Vernon R. Scott, *La Tour Tranqille.*

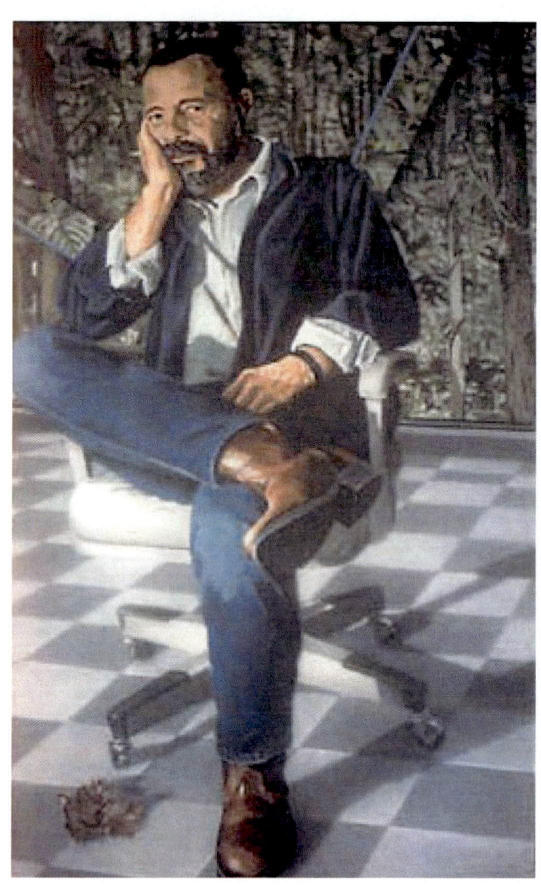

Billy Ray Sandusky, *Self Portrait*.

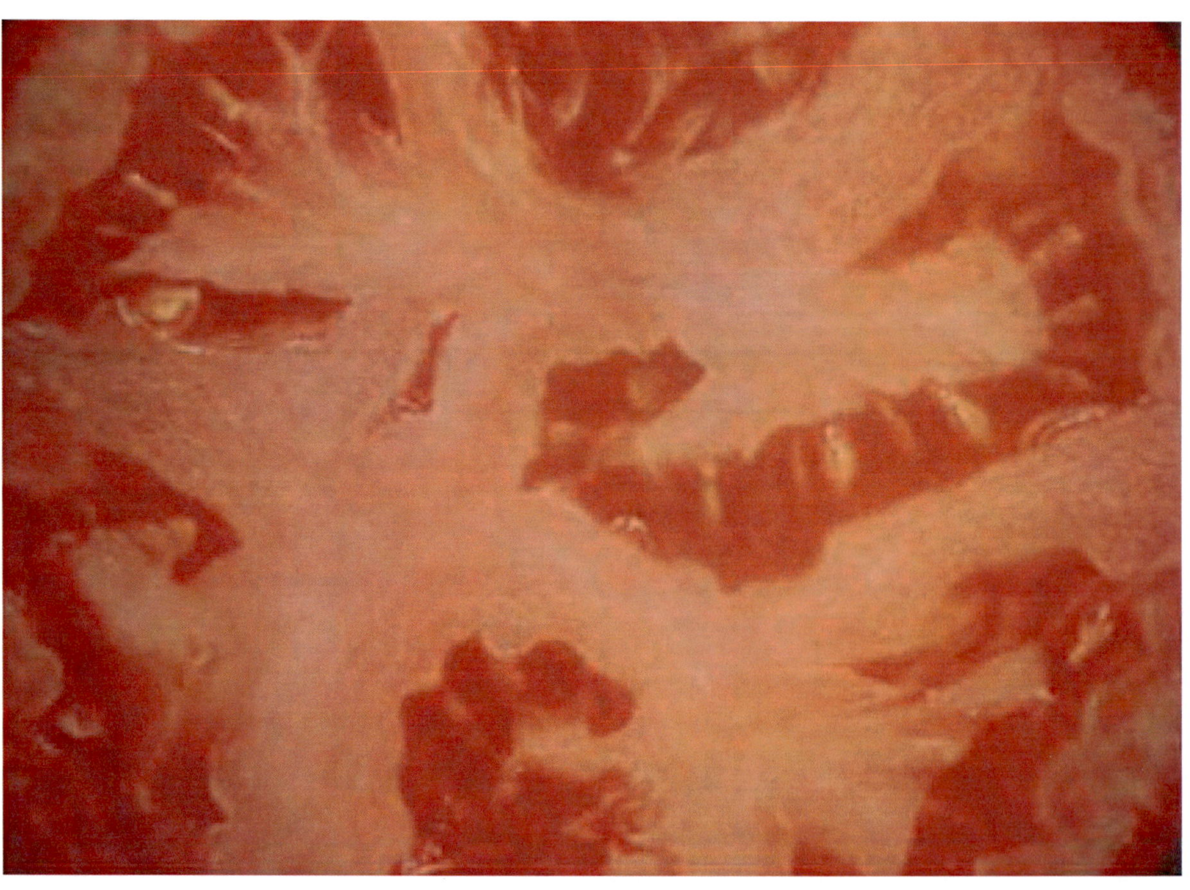

Billy Ray Sandusky, *Tomato*.

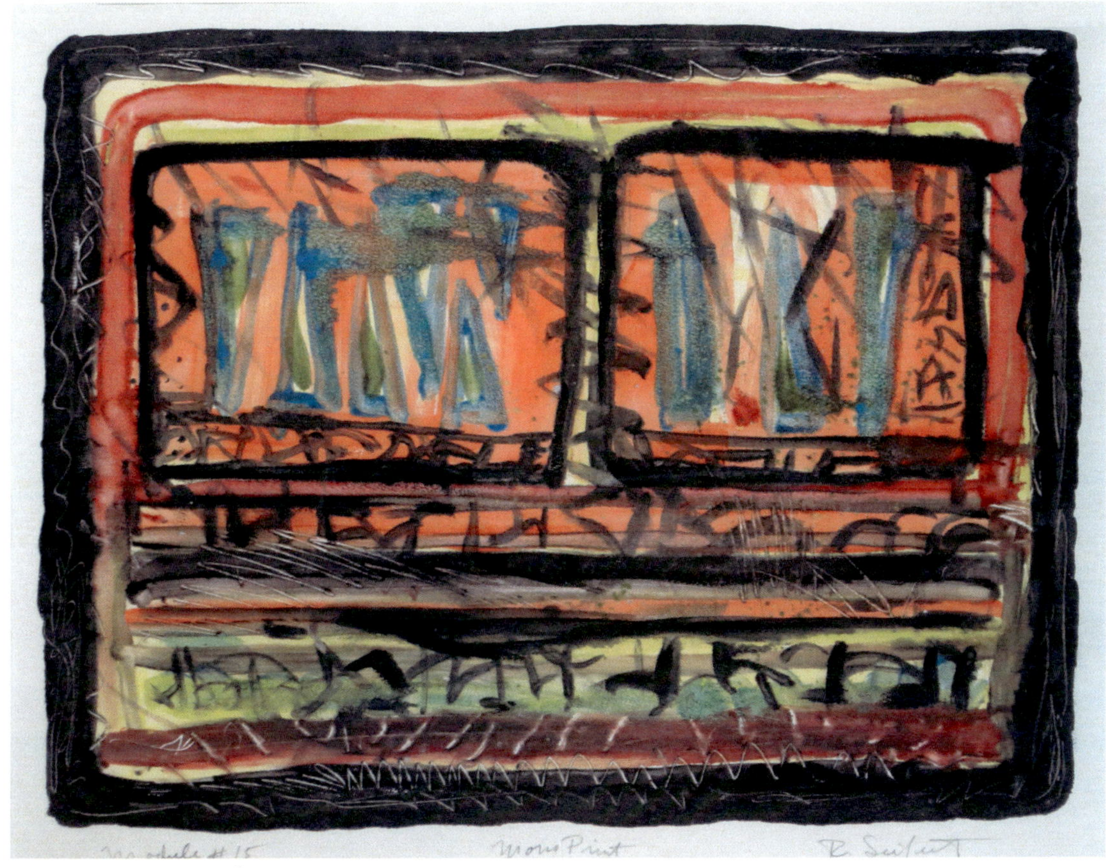

Robert Seifert, *Module # 15*.

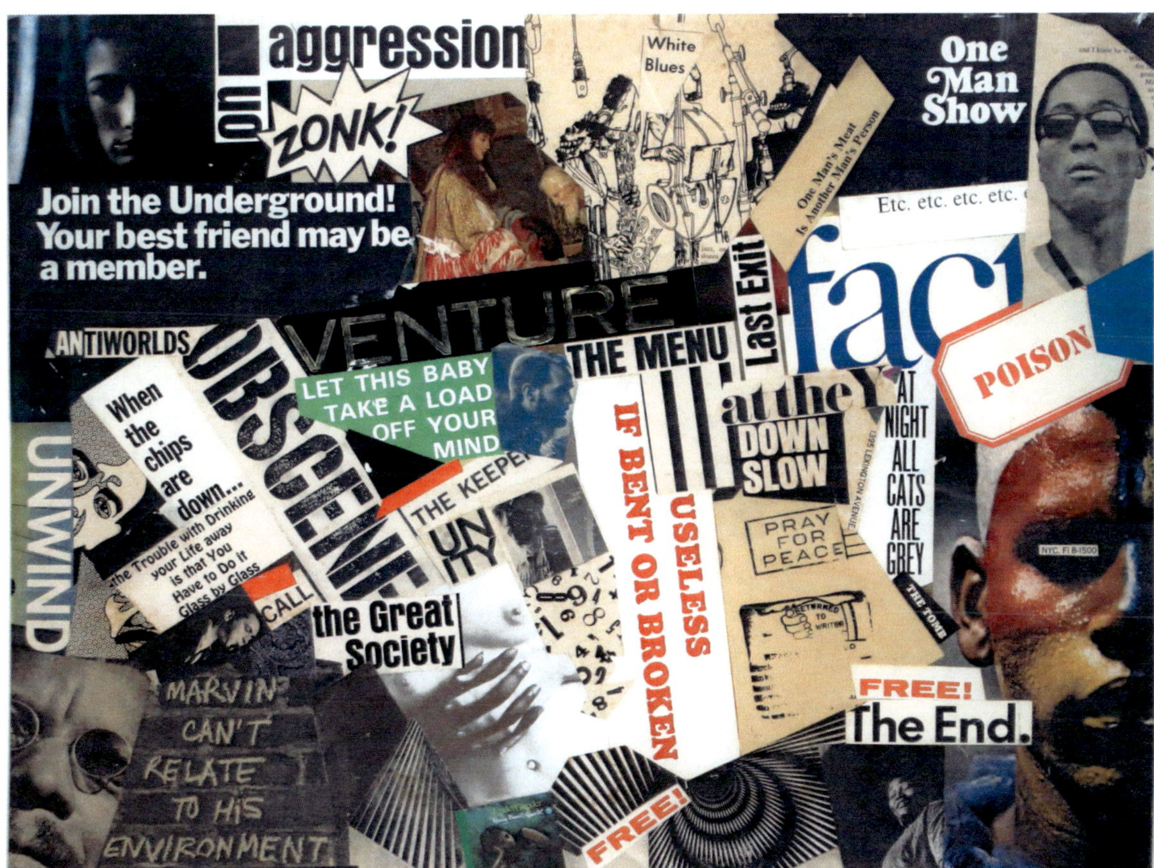

Robert Seifert, *Collage*.

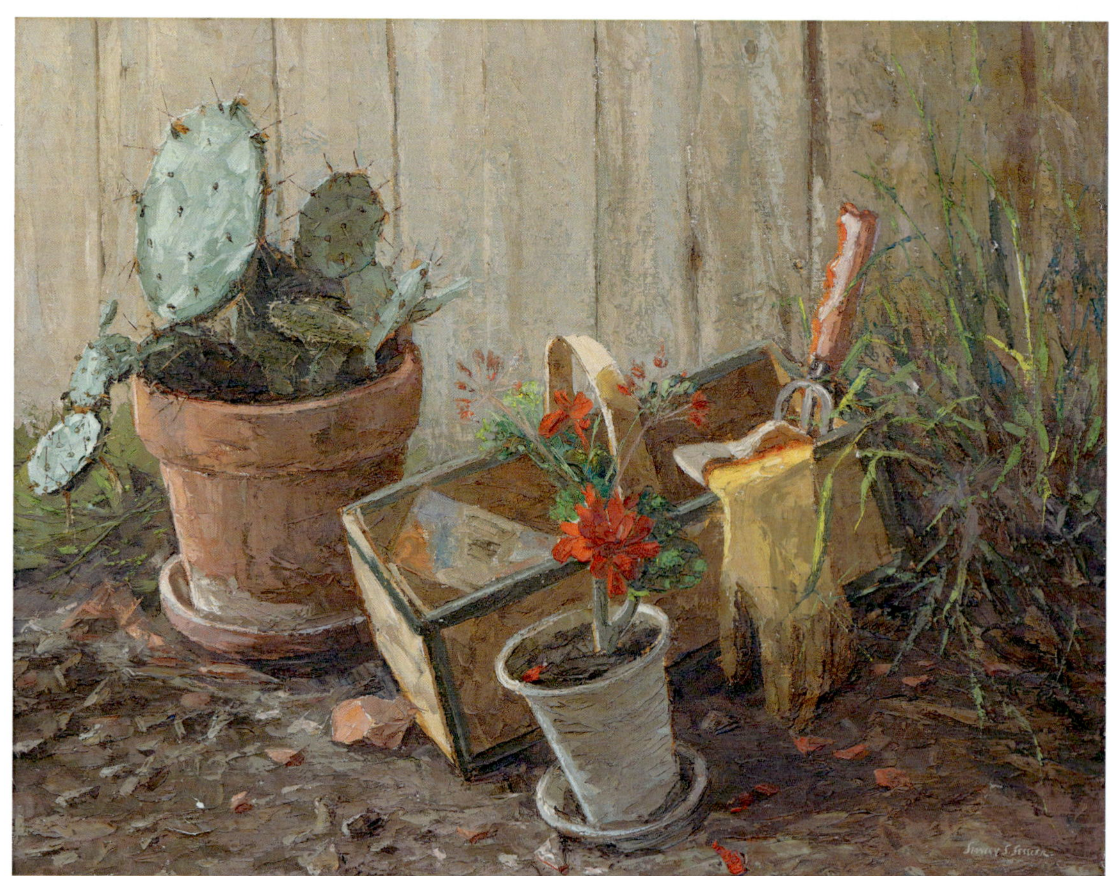

Stanley S. Sessler, *Backyard Rendesvous.*

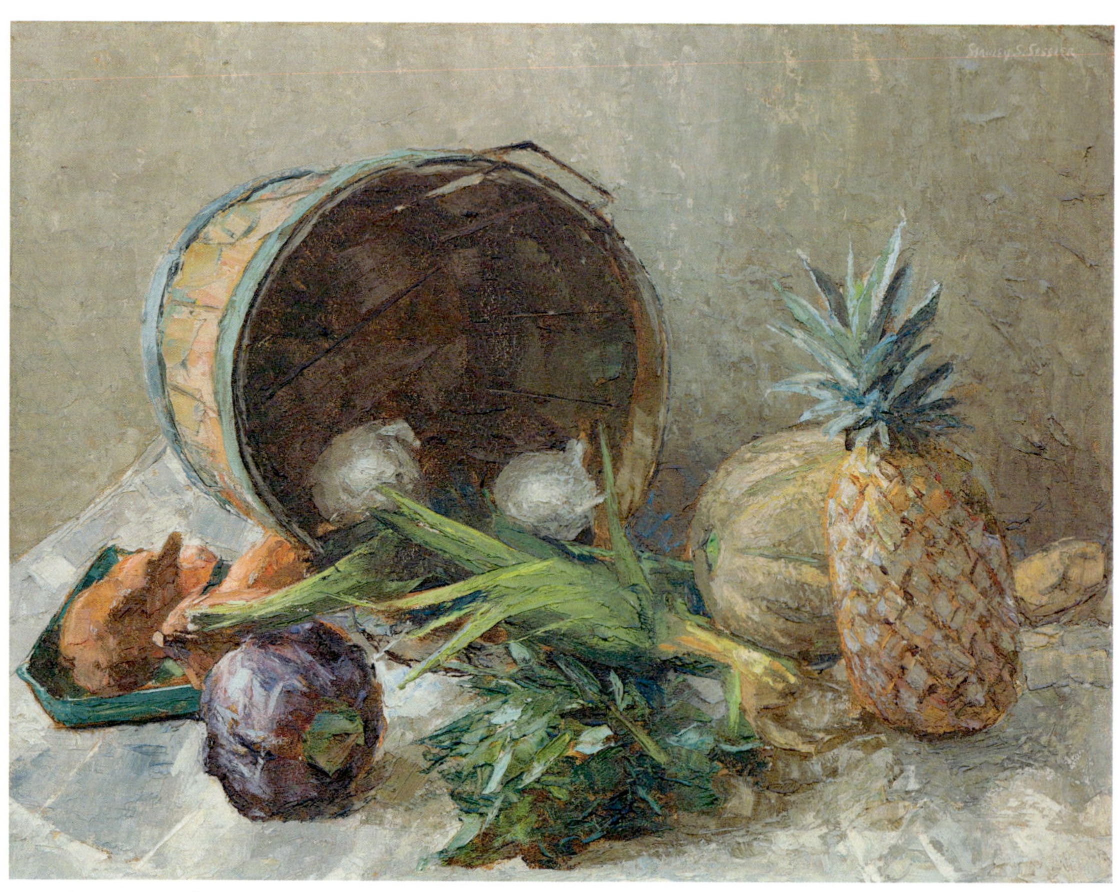

Stanley S. Sessler, *Cornucopia.*

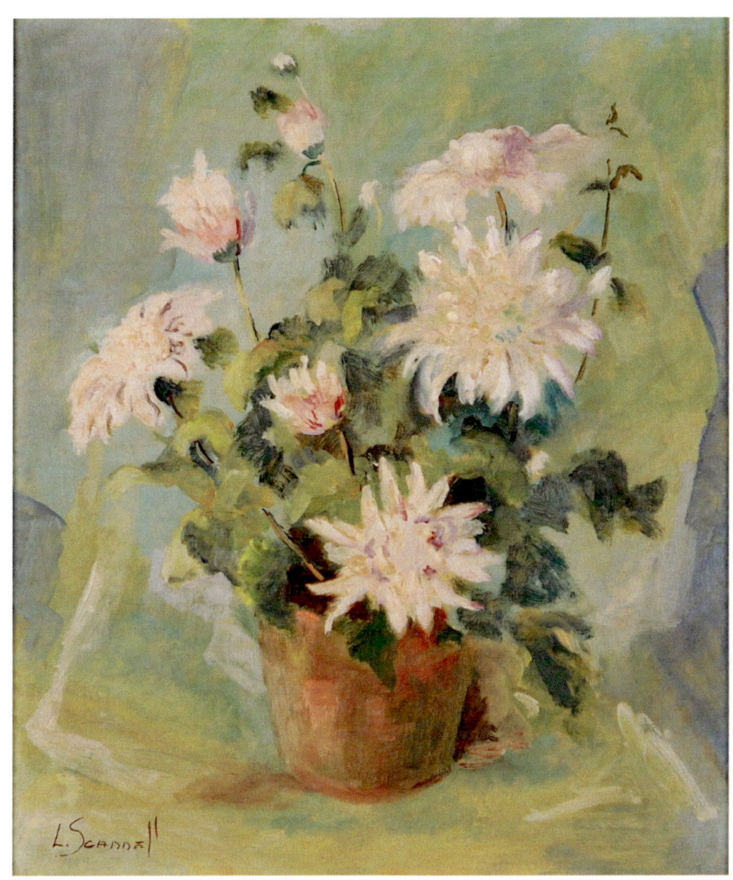
Lois Scannell, *Floral Still Life.*

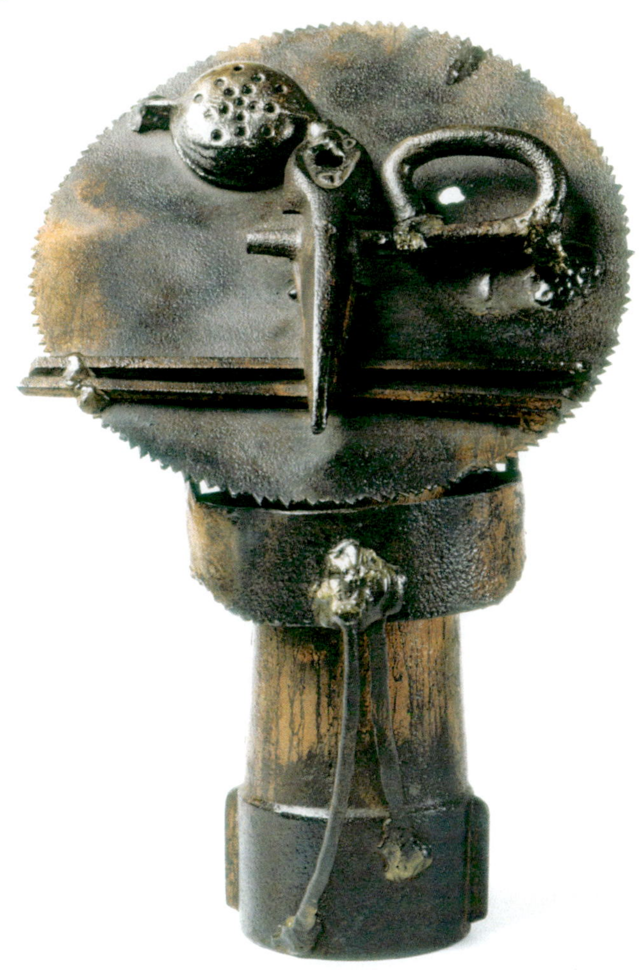
David Smith, *Saw Head.*

Upon return to the United States, he joined the faculty at St. Mary's College and it is here that one of his most ambitious projects took place. Bill supervised a reinterpretation of the fifteenth-century paintings that adorn the Brancacci Chapel in the Church of Santa Maria del Carmine in Italy. Bill and two students worked together for a short time on the project that began in 2004. Phase one was shown in the Snite Museum at the University of Notre Dame in 2005. Bill is working on phase two of the project that is still ongoing.

Lois Scannell began her art career at a time that most people are retiring, but she refused to let her age slow her down. Born in 1904, Scannell moved to the area in 1928 with her husband, who had just taken a job with the University of Notre Dame. She initially began painting during the 1940s but had to give it up to take care of her children. Once they had aged, she resumed painting in 1957. Not only did Scannell return to painting, but she also learned teaching and sharing her artistic abilities with others. At sixty-one, she offered landscape painting classes out of Pinhook Park for the South Bend Recreation Department as well as teaching at the Forever Learning Institute and the YWCA. Her warm personality and supportive spirit made her very popular with all of her students from beginning painters to seasoned artists. Scannell lived a long and creative life; she passed away in South Bend in 2001.

Vernon Scott was born in Portland, Indiana, south of Fort Wayne, on December 3, 1912. As an artist, Scott created realistic urban landscapes of South Bend that act as a historic record of the city during his time here from around the 1930s onward. In addition to his landscapes, he worked as a commercial artist and partner with Advertising Artists in South Bend, which was established in 1830. Concurrently, he worked as the first president at the Midland Academy of Art in 1933. He also exhibited regularly; in 1934 he displayed the painting *Sunny Side Church* in 1934, and a variety of paintings in the 1944 Hoosier Salon. He continued to live in the area. He passed away in the spring of 1980.

Robert Seifert was born in 1943 in South Bend and graduated from South Bend Central High School in 1962. Then off to Florida where he studied at the Florida Keys Junior College until 1972, followed by Florida Atlantic University where he received his bachelor of fine arts and teaching certification in 1976. Seifert then spent some time on the west coast before returning to his hometown. Here he took a job with Framer's Workshop and remained with them for 33 years. He also helped in the position of exhibit preparer at Colfax Cultural Center, a position he retied from in 2007. As an artist, Seifert was primarily a printmaker, but also worked in cutwork paper, collage, watercolor, and mixed media. He taught printmaking at the South Bend Museum of Art, and also participated in many local exhibits that often resulted in a prize for his artwork. Seifert passed away in February in 2011.

Stanley S. Sessler, Born in 1905 in St. Petersburg—later Petrograd, then Leningrad—Russia, came to South Bend in 1928 to become a faculty member at the University of Notre Dame's Art Department. Prior to then, he studied at the Massachusetts School of Art in Boston, where he received a master's degree, as well as at the Courtauld Institute at the University of London. In 1937, he became the Chairman of Notre Dame's Art Department, a post which he held until 1960. While there he managed to develop the graduate student program as well as to expand the department's curriculum. His oil paintings of realistic landscapes and portraits won him several awards throughout the United States. Sessler was voted a fellow of the Royal Society of Arts in London in 1951 in addition to his memberships in Chicago Galleries Association and the International Institution of Arts and Letters. He also served as an intelligence officer during World War II during which he created a system to identify enemy vessels and planes. Sessler passed away in 1986.

Frederick Simper is one of the few artists in the area that was for the most part self-taught; but that never restricted his opportunities as an artist. He was born in Mishawaka in 1914, and although he spent much of his artistic career in Detroit, Simper was also involved with the Michigan Watercolor Society and was the first vice-president of the Midland Academy of Art, as well as a charter member of the Northern Indiana Artists association. He also taught watercolor painting with the Bloomfield Art Association in Birmingham, Michigan, from 1968 to 1970 in addition to his time as the Art Director at the D'Arcy-MacManus advertising agency from 1949 to 1980. Simper also worked for the Detroit Institute of Arts, the South Bend Art Museum and the U.S. Embassies Collection.

David Smith, on March 9, 1906, was born in Decatur, Indiana and he remained in the area until 1926. His art career began with a correspondence cartooning course from Cleveland Art School. During this time, he took a job as a riveter and welder for the Studebaker Corporation to pay for schooling at the University of Notre Dame before leaving to attend college at Ohio University in Athens for a short time. Eventually, Smith ended up back at Studebaker but this time as a member of the finance department in New York. Under the influence of his soon-to-be wife, he began taking classes at the Art Students League where he learned from cubist Jan Matulka and surrealist painter Richard Leahy. Although both were significant in developing Smith's style, Matulka's experimental tendencies played a much larger role in Smith's long-term career. Smith began experimenting with found object sculptures, sometimes combining canvas with items such as coral and wood. Eventually he would grow to begin constructing large-scale steel sculptures inspired by Pablo Picasso's paintings. His work varied however, and displayed strong anti-war messages, but this did not stop Smith from supporting the war effort by working at American Locomotive Company as a welder. Following the war he had over 30 solo exhibitions throughout America and Europe, many of which continued with anti-war themes. His most famous piece is also one of his most recent, titled *Cubis*, which consists of three separate sculptures, *Cubi XVII* (1963), *Cubi XVIII* (1964), and *Cubi XIX* (1964), was completed only a short time before his death in 1965 following a car accident.

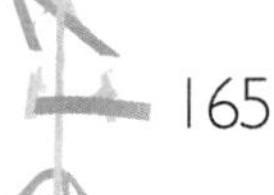

John Henry Striebel is best known for his illustrations on the comic "Dixie Dugan" about a showgirl named Dixie. Striebel was born in Bertrand, Michigan on September 14, 1891, and moved to South Bend with his family at a young age. At the age of 14 he was

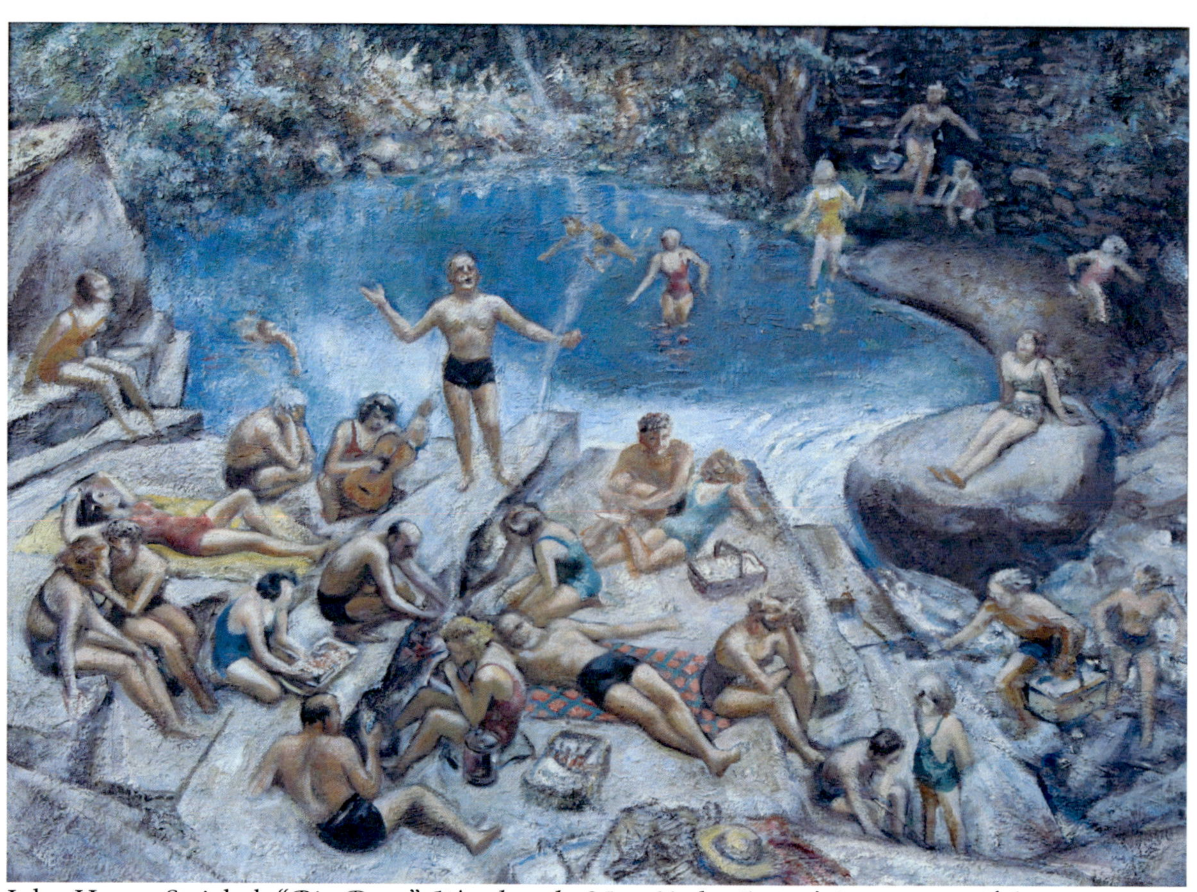

John Henry Striebel, *"Big Deep" Woodstock, New York, Artists' Swimming Hole.*

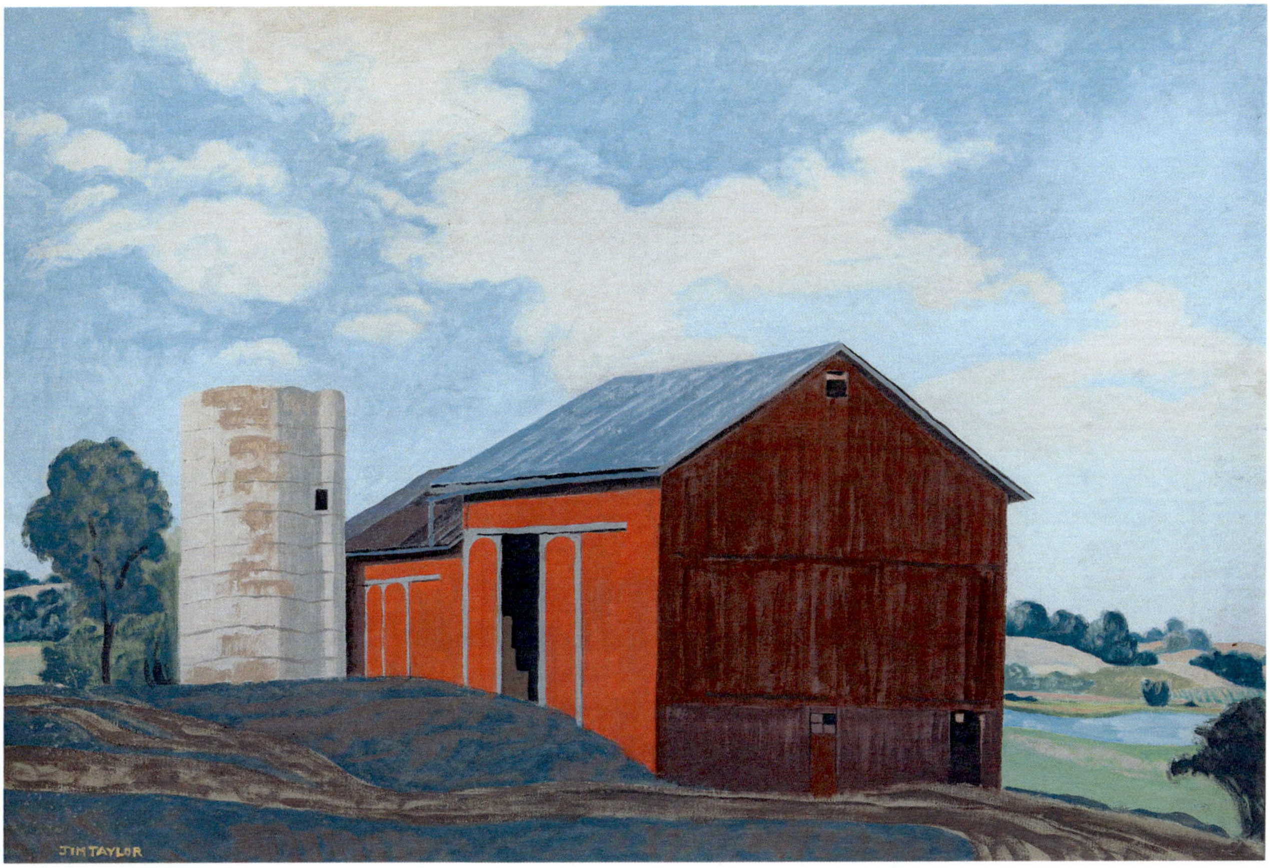

James Taylor, *Red Barn.*

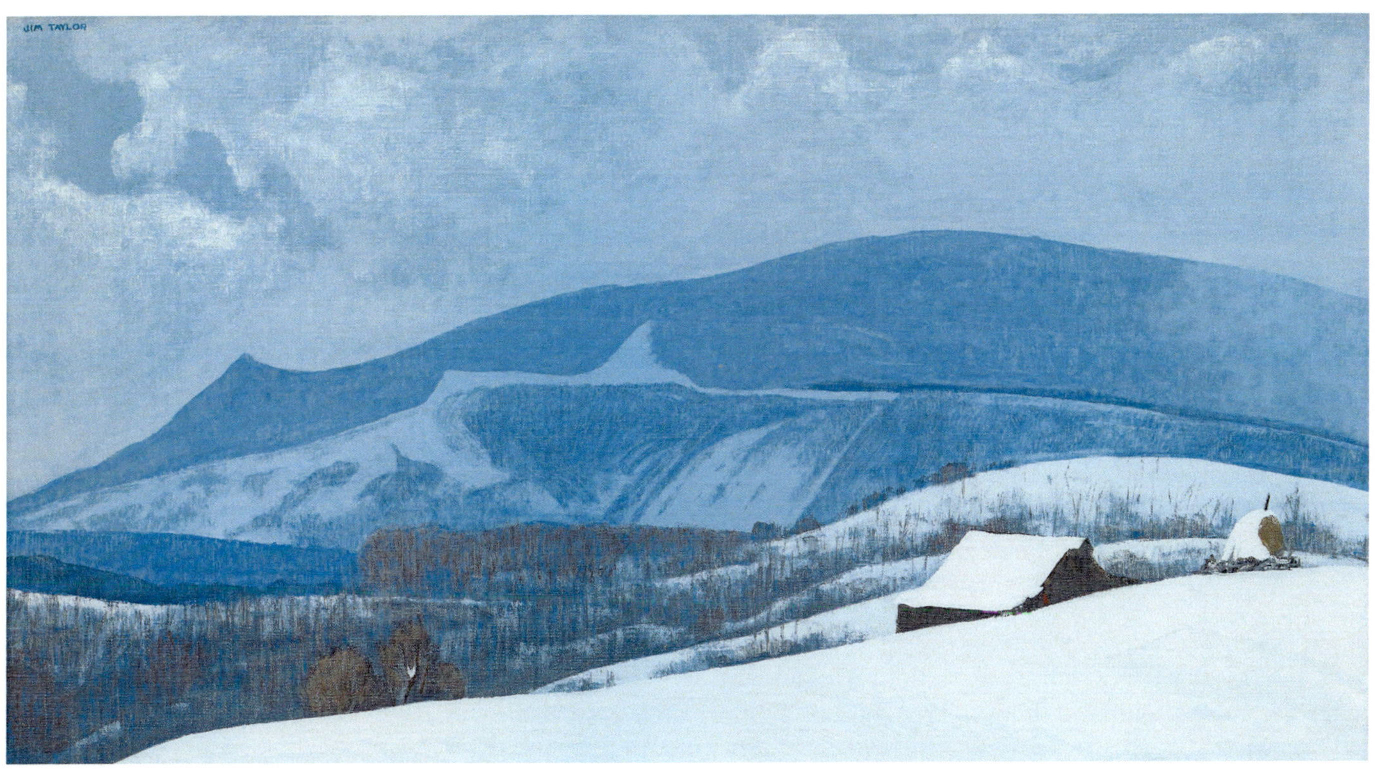

James Taylor, *Allegheny Mountains.*

already doodling political cartoons for the *South Bend Daily Times* and using his earnings to attend school at the University of Notre Dame. At nineteen he ran off to Chicago where he found work with the *Chicago Tribune* as an advertising and fashion illustrator. He also worked for the *Chicago Tribune* and spent much of his time working on side projects such as *The Potter Family*, with J. P. Mc Evoy as well as Robert Quillen's *Aunt Het*. Two other popular works of his include *Pantomime*, and Mc Evoy's *Show Girl* serial. In 1923 he moved to New York to study painting with Henry Lee McFee and Andrew Dasburg. Only six years later, Striebel was working with McEvoy again, this time producing his famous work, *Dixie Dugan*, which drew inspiration from the team's earlier work on *Show Girl*. This endeavor lasted over thirty years, with the strip concluding in the early '60s and syndication continuing from McNaught Syndication until 1966. Striebel passed away on May 22, 1962, in Woodstock, New York after fighting prolonged illness.

Curran Swaim, portrait artist, was born in 1826 in Randolph County, Virginia. At a young age, he moved to a farm near Fountain City, Indiana. He first came to South Bend around the age of thirty, but left to study art in New York. There, he met his wife and studied passionately until he returned to South Bend to work on his professional career. His artwork was well known and very well received by the general public and in the mid-1860s Curran's influence from photography began to show in his paintings, specifically in his portraits. In 1869, he and his family moved to Illinois. Curran would continue painting for around ten years before finally ending up in Jasper County, Missouri in 1878 where he would live out the remainder of his life until 1897.

James W. Taylor was born and raised in South Bend, Indiana; he attended South Bend Central High School and later Dartmouth College in Hanover, New Hampshire. During the 1940s his career took off beginning with the Hoosier Salon Show in January 1943, where he won first prize. His first solo show, in 1947, was at the Hoosier Salon Gallery in Indianapolis and displayed 18 oil landscapes. Taylor was also a founding member and former director of the South Bend Art Center who later also served on the board of trustees. He later moved towards photography and many of his photos were featured in magazines and newspapers.

Maria Tomasula, the eldest of three children, grew up in Chicago and northwestern Indiana neighborhoods where her father worked in steel manufacturing. She was heavily influenced by her family's Latino heritage. Maria studied at the University of Illinois at Chicago, where she received a bachelor of fine arts, followed by a master of fine arts from Northwestern University. She adopted a style characterized by a high articulation of form, saturated color, and a shallow, theatrical space for her still life paintings. She often uses combinations of fruits and flowers to resemble and stand in for the human figure. Her work has been widely exhibited since the the early 1990s, including in over 20 solo exhibitions. She divides her time between Chicago and South Bend, where she teaches painting and drawing at the University of Notre Dame.

Julie and William Tourtillotte are a printmaking power couple. Both work with printmaking, but branch out in separate directions from time to time—Julie also engages with mixed media such as using stitching, embroidery, dyed fabric, and photography to create small pieces while William also creates illustrations. They met at Cranbrook Academy of Art in Detroit, where Julie had already pursued her bachelor of fine arts and was going for a master's in printmaking. William had received his bachelor's from the Cleveland School of Art, and was also seeking his master's from Cranbrook. Together they came to South Bend. Julie works as an associate professor of art; William was a curator at the South Bend Museum of Art, and also does work with St. Mary's College, Notre Dame, and IU South Bend.

Douglas E. Tyler began as a muralist, but that changed as he began experimenting in new media and a new art form known as holography. He studied communications at Michigan State University, where he received a bachelor of arts in 1970 as well as a master of arts in art history in 1973. A few years later Tyler attended the Cranbrook Academy of Art for printmaking and graduated in 1977. Following this graduation he immediately began teaching photo media and new media at St. Mary's College. It was while teaching here that he began to experiment with the relatively new art form of holography. Holography is a technique of using lasers and light to create three dimensional-images. His mastery of the form was publicly recognized when he received the first European Holography Prize. Additionally, he has received several fellowships from the National Endowment for the Arts. Experiments with this art form led Tyler to found Dimensional Imaging Consultants, Inc., and he has taken to teaching screen printing and holography to his students at St. Mary's.

Van Sanden is an man of whom very little is known, except that he painted portraits of Native Americans. The most notable work attributed to him is a portrait of Chief Leopold Pokagon, leader of the Pottawatomi Indian Tribe. The portrait is thought to have been completed around the time of the Fort Dearborn Massacre.

Adolphus Van Sickle was born in Ohio in 1835 to portrait and panorama artist Selah Van Sickle. It is easy to imagine that Adolphus Van Sickle would have a keen eye for framing figures within his artwork. He is most known for his portraits, primarily of important figures within society at the time. He remained in the area until the 1870s, but very little is known about his personal life. Adolphus is widely considered to be third known artist in the area.

Donald Vogl works primarily in painting, with some printmaking and mixed media. He was born in 1929 in Milwaukee, and studied at the Art Institute of Chicago and the University of Chicago, earning a bachelor's in art education; the University of Wisconsin-Milwaukee, earning a master's in art education, and classes at the Cleveland Institute of Art and the California College of Arts and Crafts in Oakland, California. Before his arrival in South Bend, he taught art in the Milwaukee school system from 1958-1961, and at Marygrove College in Detroit from 1961-1963. He began teaching at the University of Notre Dame in 1963 and

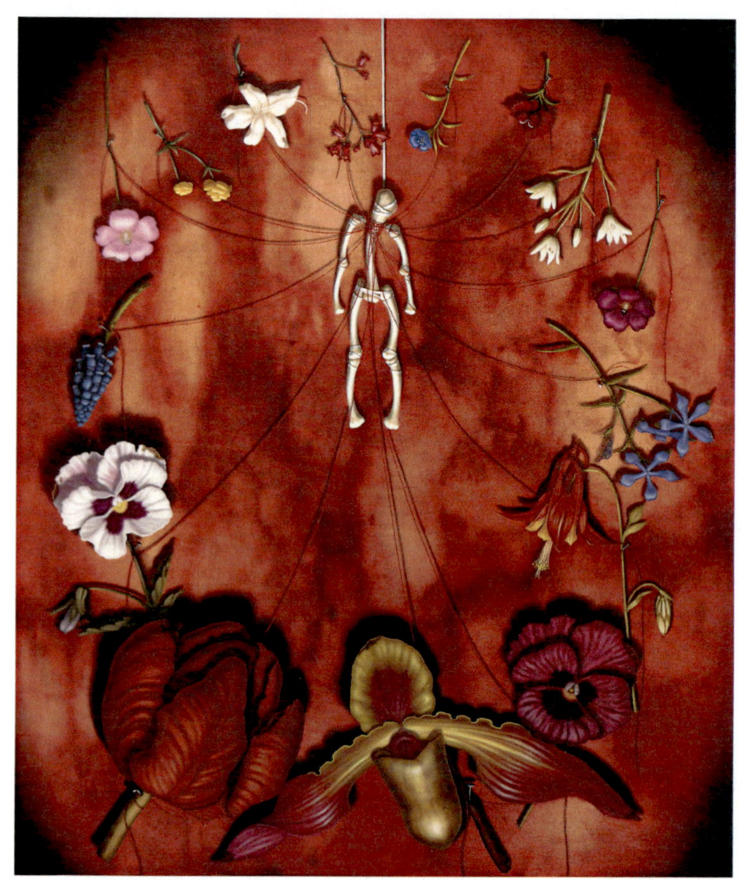

Maria Tomasula, *Burden of Memory.*

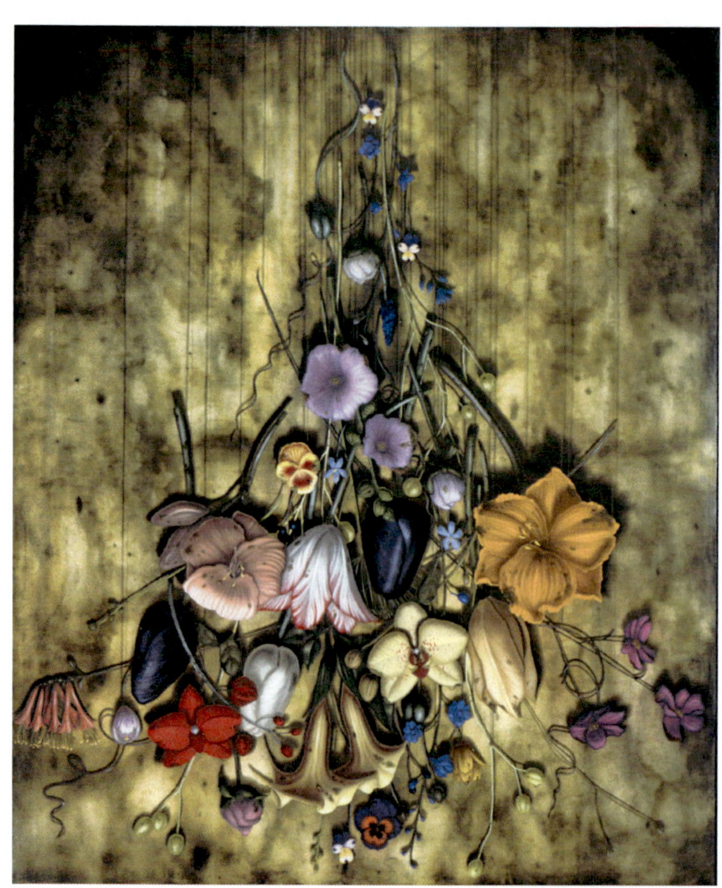

Maria Tomasula, *Origin.*

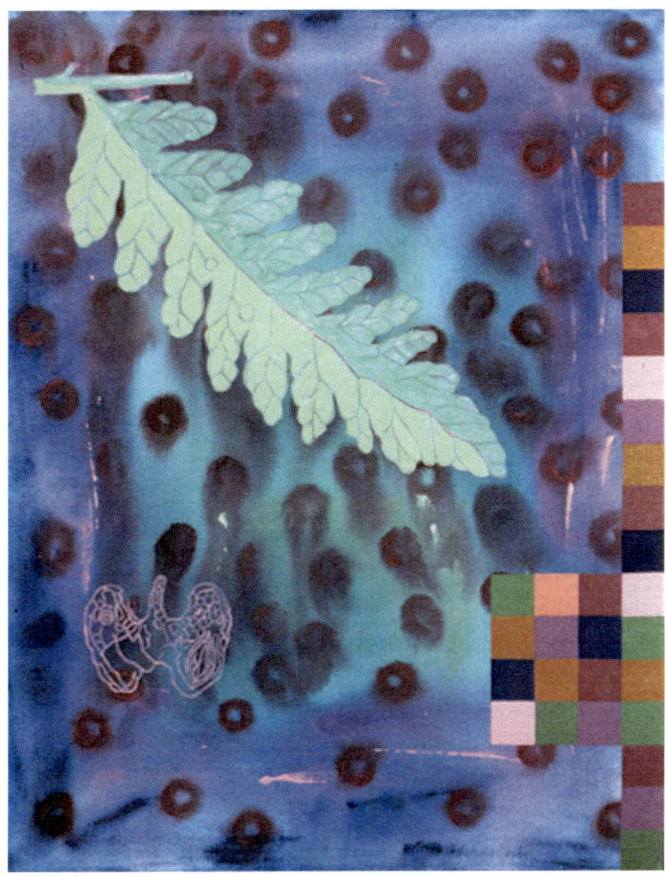

William Tourtillotte, *Gene Genie.*

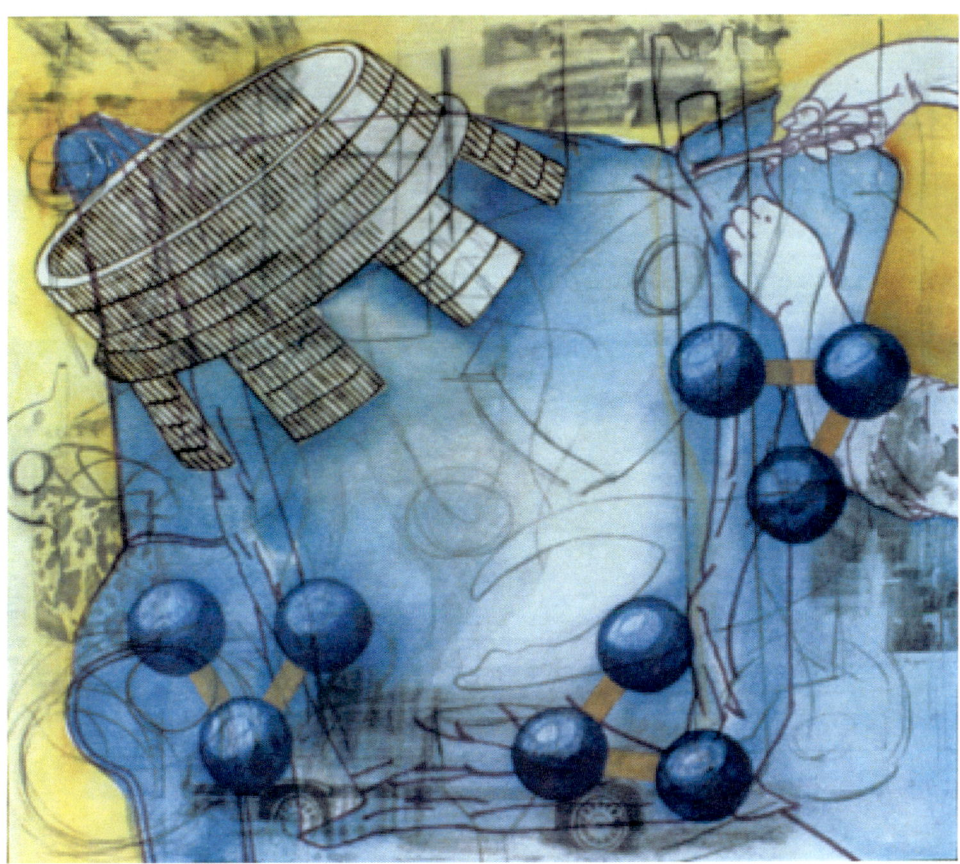

William Tourtillotte, *Fade Away.*

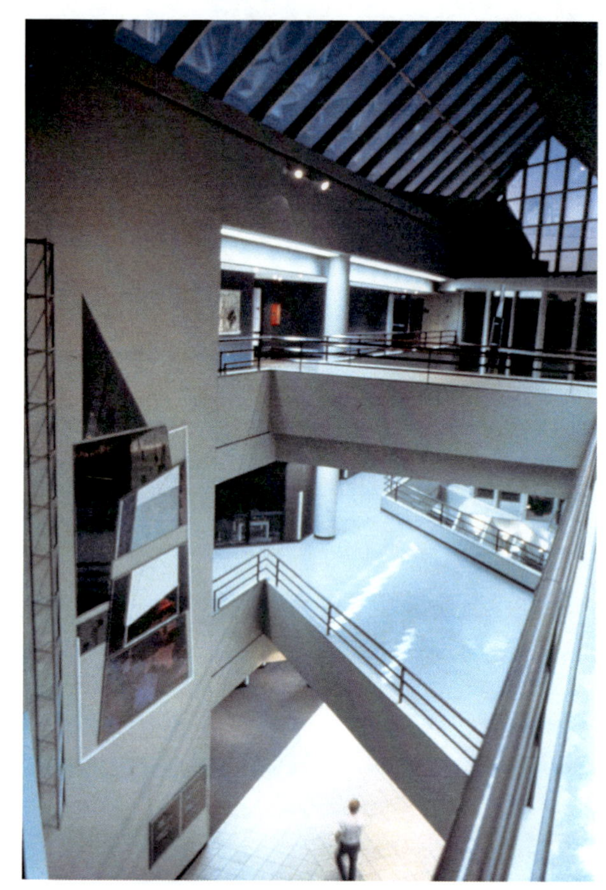

Douglas E. Tyler, *Uno Installation.*

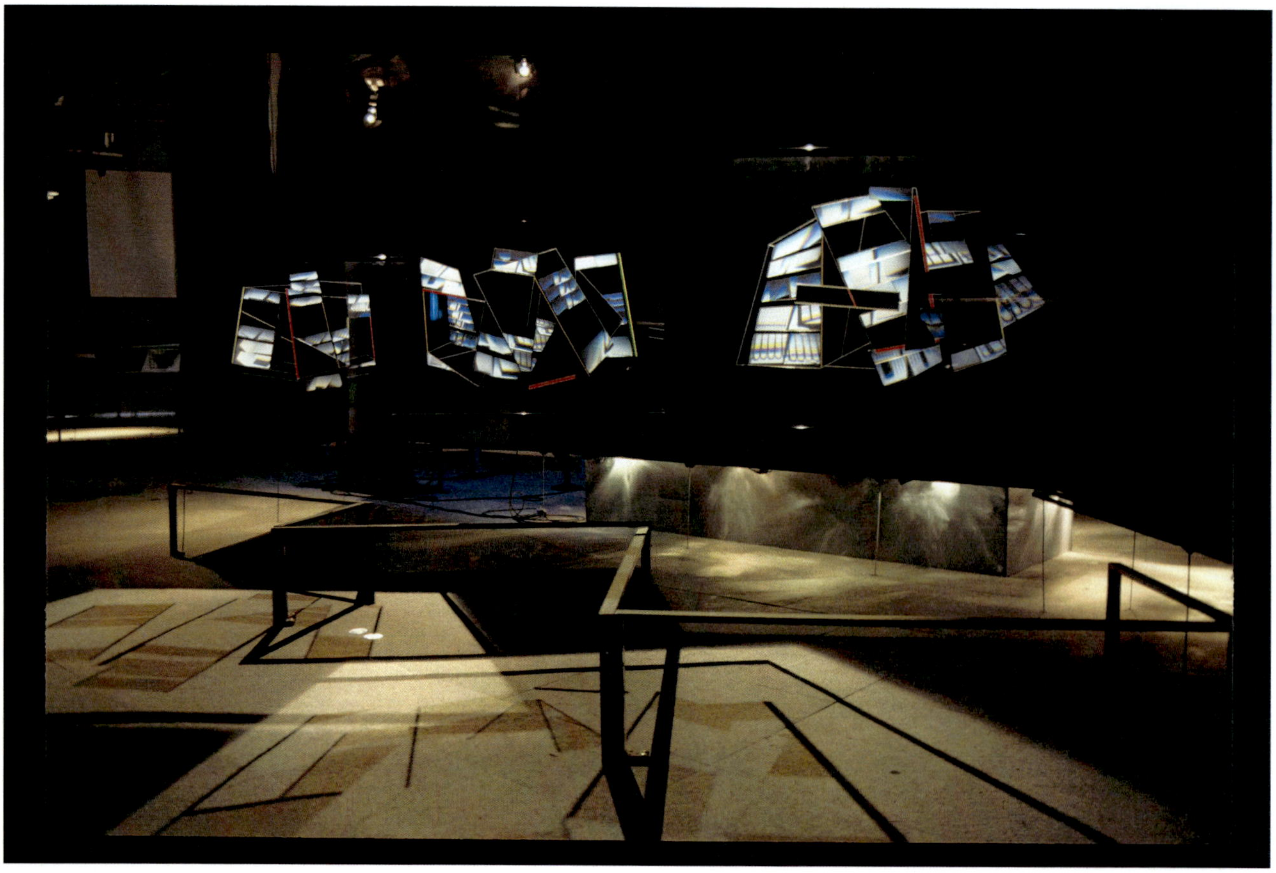

Douglas E. Tyler, *Dream Passages.*

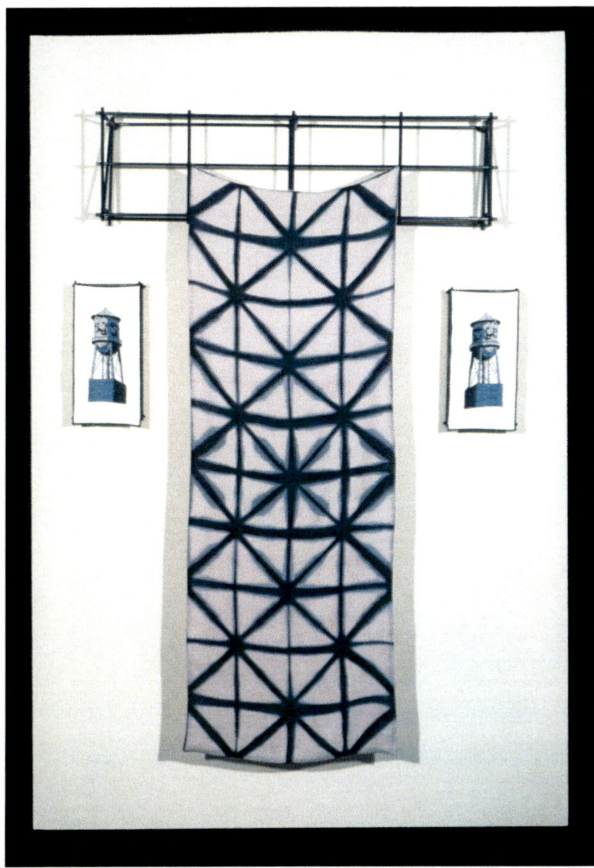
Julie Tourtillotte, *Remnant: Water Tower.*

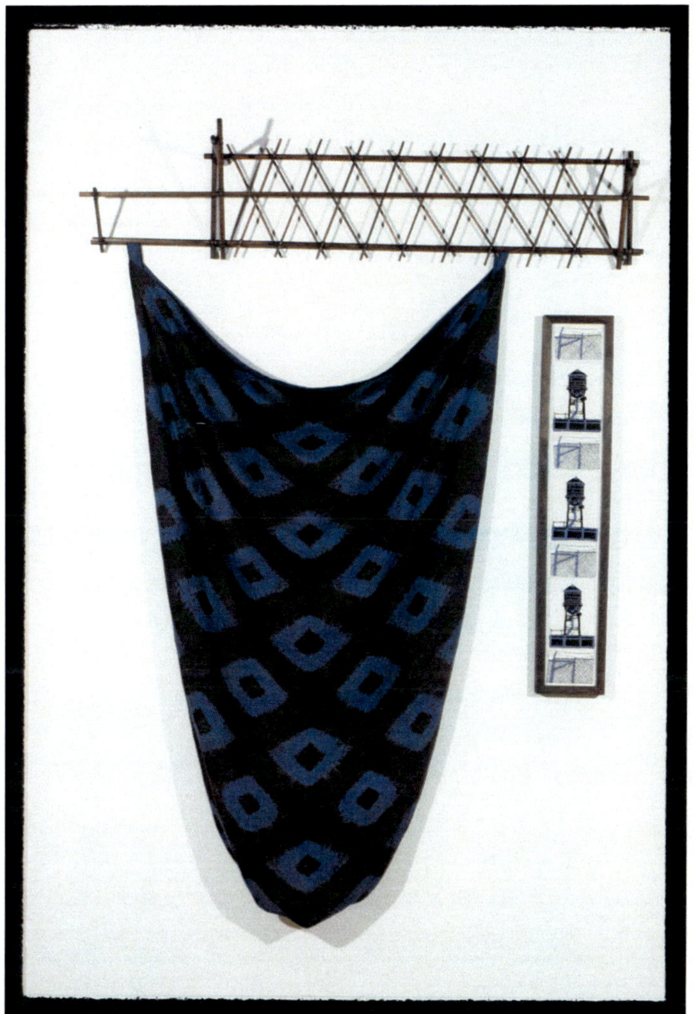
Julie Tourtillotte, *Remnant IV: Studebaker Water Tower.*

was an associate professor of painting and printmaking . He became emeritus professor of art in 1994. In addition to his teaching responsibilities, he acted for ten years as designer for the Notre Dame Art Gallery, which is now known as the Snite Museum. Locally, he participated in many exhibitions at the Snite Museum, the South Bend Museum of Art, the Midwest Museum of Art, and the Hoosier Art Salon. He won five Best of Show awards in competitions in Indiana, Michigan, and Illinois, plus twelve awards in other categories. A mural he did at Purdue University, Lafayette, *Clouds Rolling*, was commissioned for the university's eleventh annual Art in the Classroom Competition for Indiana artists. In 2003 he moved to Fort Collins, Colorado, where five of his six children and six of his nine grandchildren live. He enjoys painting the landscapes there, and continues to exhibit with art organizations there. His web site is www.donvogl.com.

James "Jake" Webster and **Kay Westhues** are another successful artistic couple from the Michiana area. Jake creates oil paintings and sculptures, while Kay is a photographer. Together, they opened the Art Post Gallery in downtown South Bend in 2009. Both have impressive educational backgrounds; Jake enrolled at the Art Students League in New York where he studied stone sculpture, as well as studying at Mississippi Valley State University. While there, he was able to travel abroad to Italy, Greece and France to expand his skills. He also taught with the South Bend Community School Corporation as an adult basic education teacher, and as a special education instructor at Logan Center in South Bend. Kay focused—literally—on photography at the Rhode Island School of Design and at Indiana University where she completed a specialized degree program centered around the theme of photography and ethnocentrism. Kay also worked with the South Bend Museum of Art for some time. Together, they reside in South Bend and continue to create art and run the Art Post Gallery.

Jacqueline H. Welsh focuses on the community just as much as her artwork. Her small, intimate pastels often depict various landscapes and landmarks around the area, but this is only the beginning of her work with the community. She worked with the Snite Museum at Notre Dame as the Curator of Education and Public Programs. In fulfilling this role, she worked with artist Bernard Williams on the mural outside the Robinson Community Learning Center as well as implementing the JumpstART program for elementary school aged children and a summer apprentice program for area high school students to work with the professional artists and the university. Her work extended beyond her position at Notre Dame, however, as she put together for the South Bend Museum of Art educational guides for the exhibitions so children could enjoy them with their parents while learning about the artwork. She also acted as a volunteer artist for the Northeast Neighborhood Association's after-school art program. In recognition of her many accomplishments, she was awarded the YWCA's *Women of the Year* award for the Arts, Letters and Humanities Division in 1998. On top of these achievements, she joined artists Michael Slaski and David Allen in co-founding Studio Arts Center in 2002 for aspiring child and adult artists. She continued to work for the community both through Notre Dame and on her own until

2010, when she retired from the University of Notre Dame.

Wilbur Warne West, born in 1912, grew up in Indiana and began his art career in the Michiana area. While in the area, he participated in the 1935 and 1936 Hoosier Salon exhibitions, where he showed *Eden*, *Barn in Brown County*, and *Scherazade*. West was also a member of the St. Joseph Valley Chapter of the American Artists Professional League as well as the first president of the Northern Indiana Artists in 1942. He attended Ohio State University in Columbus, where he received his bachelor of science and studied under Arthur Baggs and Edgar Littlefield. He also studied at the Art Institute of Chicago and received a master of arts from Columbia University in New York. In 1948, West took a position with Cornell College, where he acted as the Head of the Art Department and the Gallery Director. He also acted as a coordinator of the Foreign Study Program, where he lectured on art and architecture. West remained with Cornell until 1974.

E. E. Whitehill, with his Rockwell-esque paintings, was often overlooked by the larger art community outside of South Bend. Whitehill was born in Peru, Indiana on May 16, 1890, and as a child he broke both his kneecaps in a fall. This tragic incident led to his first drawings, which were completed on those plaster casts. Not too long after, he received his first payment for art by creating woodcut posters for the Ringling Brothers Circus whose winter home was in Peru. After a short time in Chicago to study at the Chicago Art Institute, Whitehill relocated to South Bend where he would continue to study under George Ames Aldrich, whom he met in Chicago. In 1920, Whitehill was a founding member of the Northern Indiana Artists group and would go on to open a studio with fellow artists. He also worked with John H. Streibel to illustrate many children's books. Although he never established a large following outside of Indiana, his art was widely accepted and enjoyed throughout the community, as was his genial nature. Whitehill always put the community and others first and often worked to help college students through their schooling with an agreement for repayment "when possible." This nature made him well loved in the area and although it was always his dream to permanently move to Brown County and paint, his dream was never fulfilled and he passed away in 1966.

Guy Brown Wiser and his younger sister **Miriam Gertrude Wiser Butcher** were born in Marion, Indiana in 1895 and 1898 respectively. As a child Guy gained experience with portraiture by focusing on his little sister Gertrude, whom he often claimed was his favorite subject. He began studying architecture at Cornell University but had to abandon his studies due to World War I. The war did little to slow him down, as during internment he spent much of his time sketching fellow soldiers. Following the war he received employment with Austin and Shambleau Architects as well as the art department for the Studebaker Corporation in South Bend. In 1924 he began studying under Jean Despujols and August F. M. Gorguet at Fontainebleau and would eventually study at the Pennsylvania Academy of fine Arts, the Hawthorne Cape Cod School of Art, and at Ohio State beneath James R. Hopkins. Beyond portraiture, Guy taught charcoal at Ohio State and illustrated more than 80 books for children on top of designing sets for the RKO, Universal and Columbia studios. He passed away in Fallbrook, California in 1983. Gertrude, on the other hand, largely remained close to home, although she studied in many schools such as Columbia, the University of Chicago and the University of Colorado. She was a member of the Northern Indiana Artists as well as the St. Joseph Valley Chapter of the American Artists Professional League and taught art in the South Bend School Corporation in addition to classes at the South Bend Art Center until her death in October of 1997.

Joseph Wrobel was in and out of the commercial art world for much of his life. He was born in Wieprz, Poland in 1907, but immigrated to South Bend, Indiana, in 1915. His first job was at the Studebaker Corporation, which he abandoned after a short time to study art. He was in and out of northern Indiana for many years and attended several American art schools including the Chicago Academy of Fine Arts, the Chicago Art Institute, John Herron School of Art, and the Art Institute in New Orleans to study watercolor painting. On one of his return trips to the area, Wrobel was employed at Studebaker once more before quitting to open his own studio. In 1950 he began once more working as a commercial artist, illustrating technical manuals for Boeing and various publications for the *Saturday Evening Post*. In 1959, Wrobel founded the Saint Joseph Valley Watercolor Society in South Bend, an organization that still exists today, and founded the Leeper Park Art Fair in South Bend. He also taught classes at the South Bend Art Center and helped to establish a commercial art program at Ivy Tech Community College with Joseph E. Schultz and Harlan Bourdon. Wrobel passed away in South Bend in 1984.

Harold Zisla's influence extends through much of northern Indiana, despite being born in Cleveland, Ohio in 1925. He began his relationship with the Michiana area as a designer at UniRoyal before moving on to become the director of the South Bend Art Center (now the South Bend Museum of Art) from 1957-1966. Following his time there, he became the first art department chair at IU South Bend. Zisla studied at several schools himself, including the University of Notre Dame, the Cleveland Institute of Art, where he graduated with a major in painting, and bachelor of science in art education as well as a master of art in art history from Case-Western Reserve University. He was initially trained as a traditional representational artist, a form he most recently combines with abstract expressionism to create unique representations of his subjects. However, Zisla also embraces abstract art without portraiture as seen in *Springtime Wispings*, which is currently owned and on display by the IU South Bend Schurz Library. Although he retired in 1989, Zisla's final exhibition in 2008 entitled *Exit: Final Destinies,* worked to help establish the Harold and Doreen Zisla Scholarship. He currently resides in South Bend, Indiana.

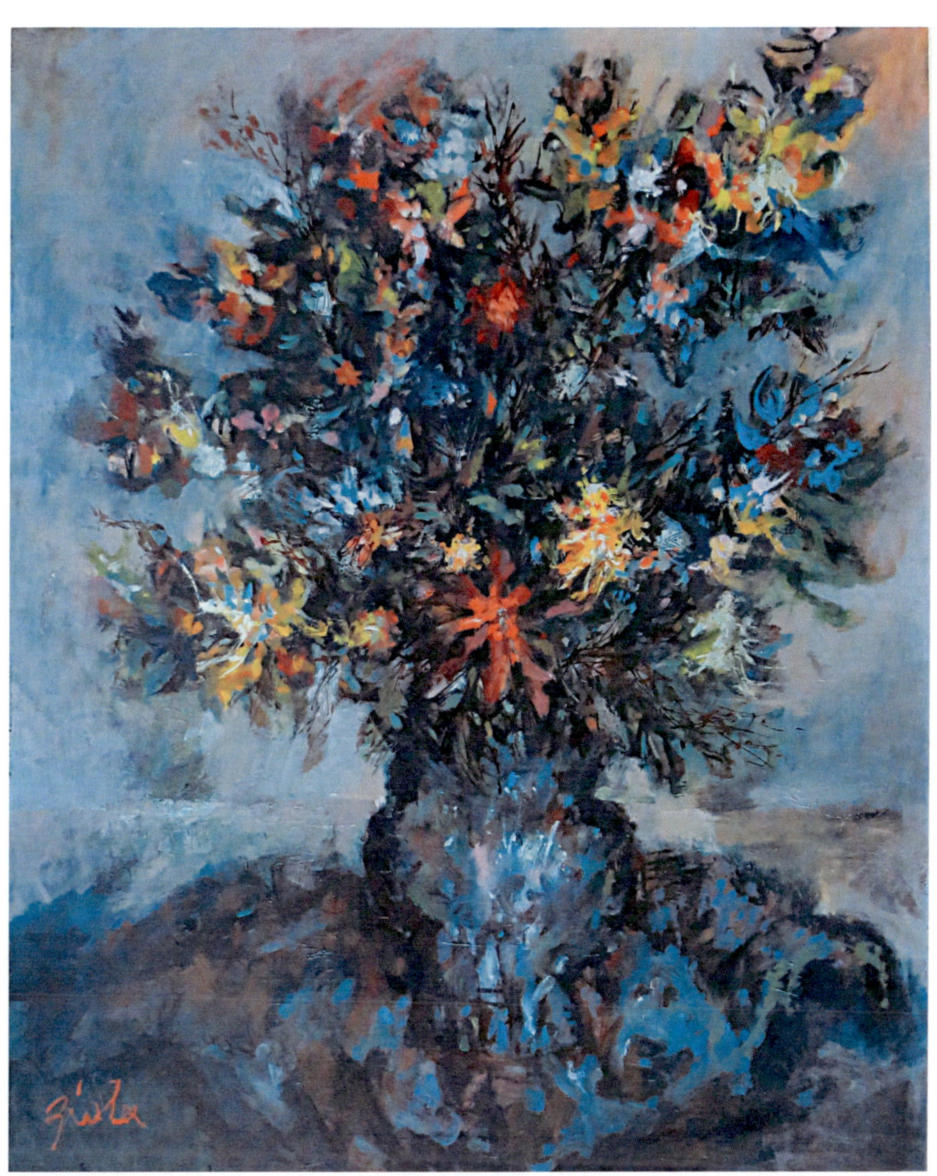

Harold Zisla, *Blue Bounty.*

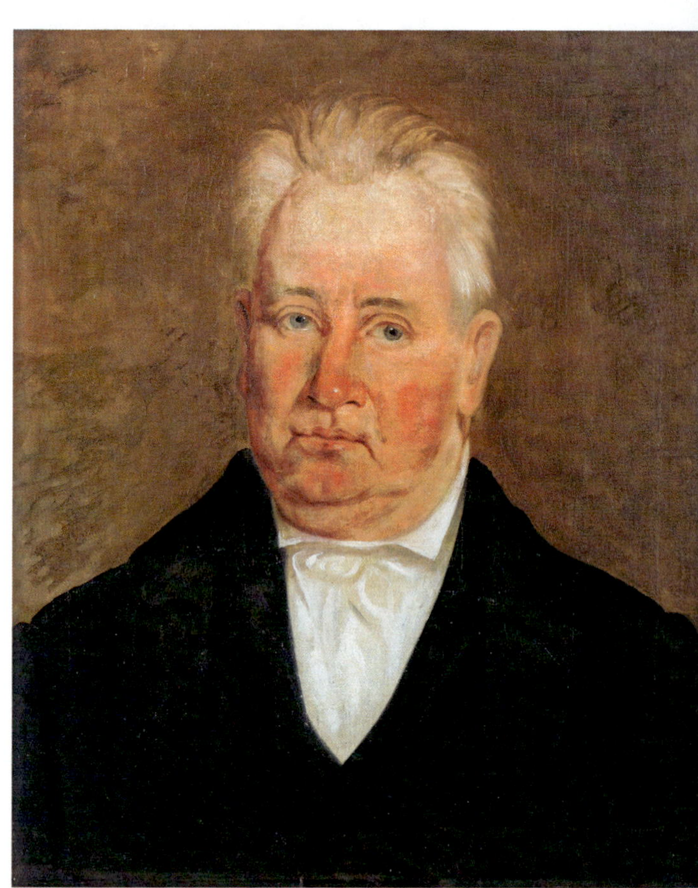

Van Sanden, *Self Portrait.*

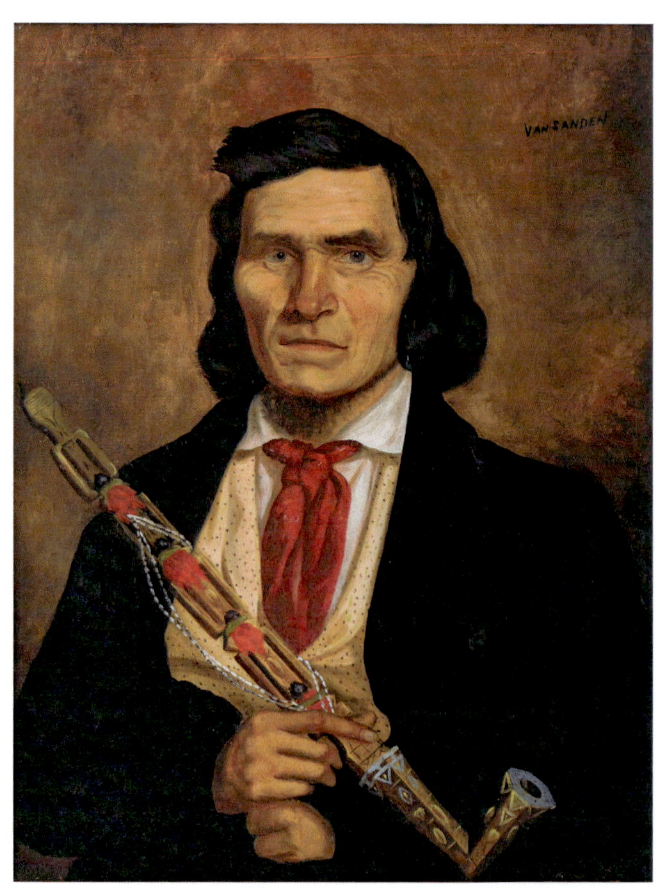

Van Sanden, *Chief Topinabee.*

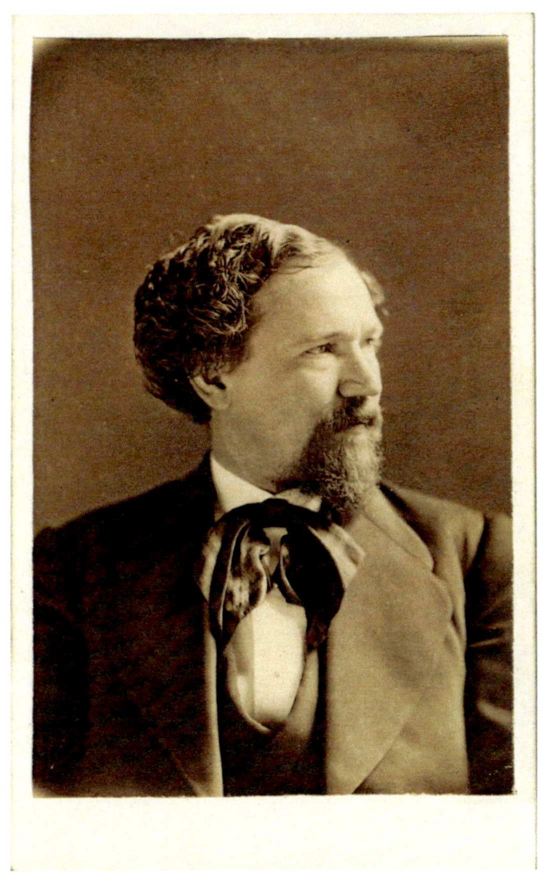
Adolphus Van Sickle, *Self Portrait.*

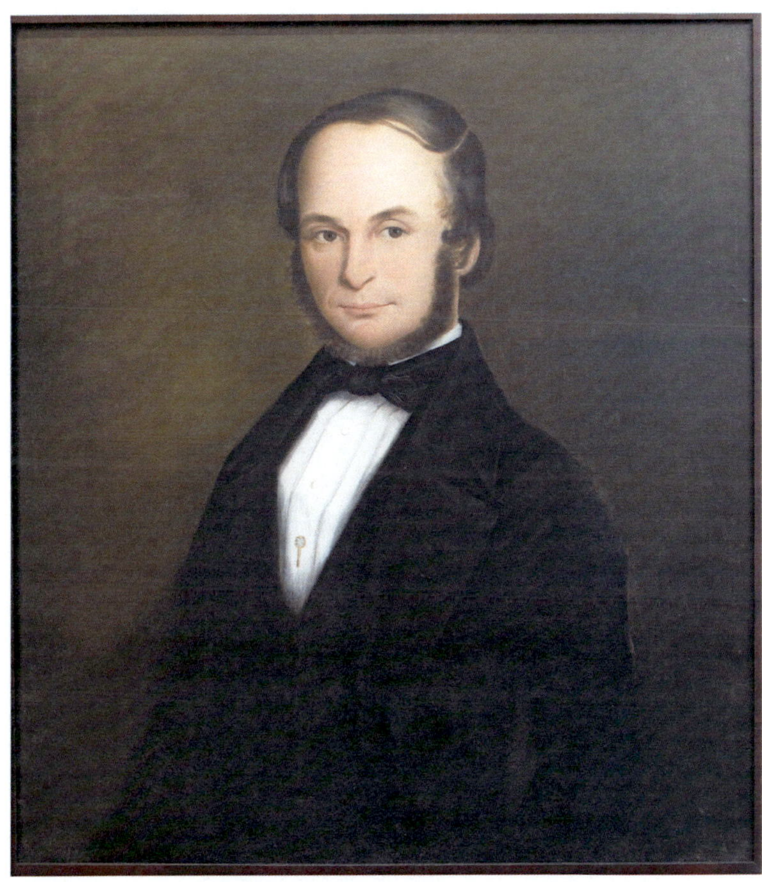
Adolphus Van Sickle, *Portrait.*

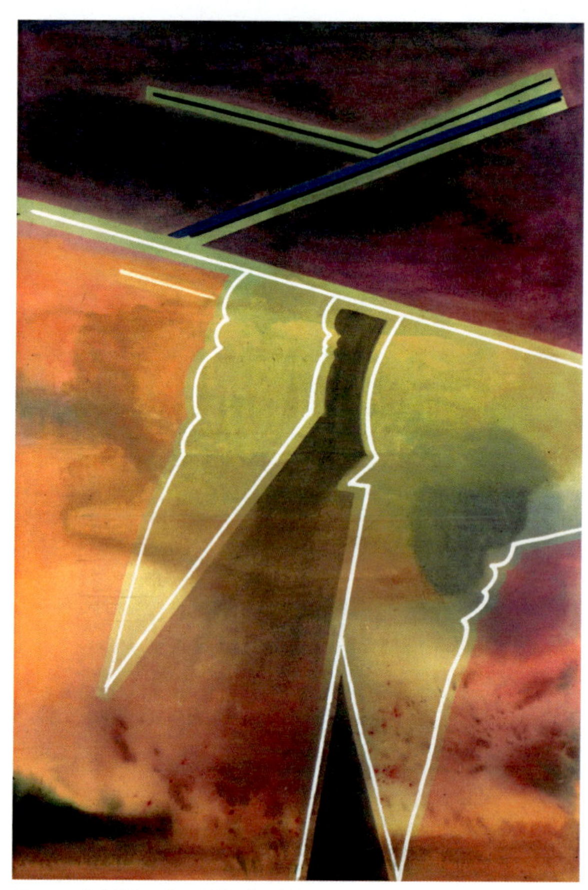

Donald Vogl, *Flight II*.

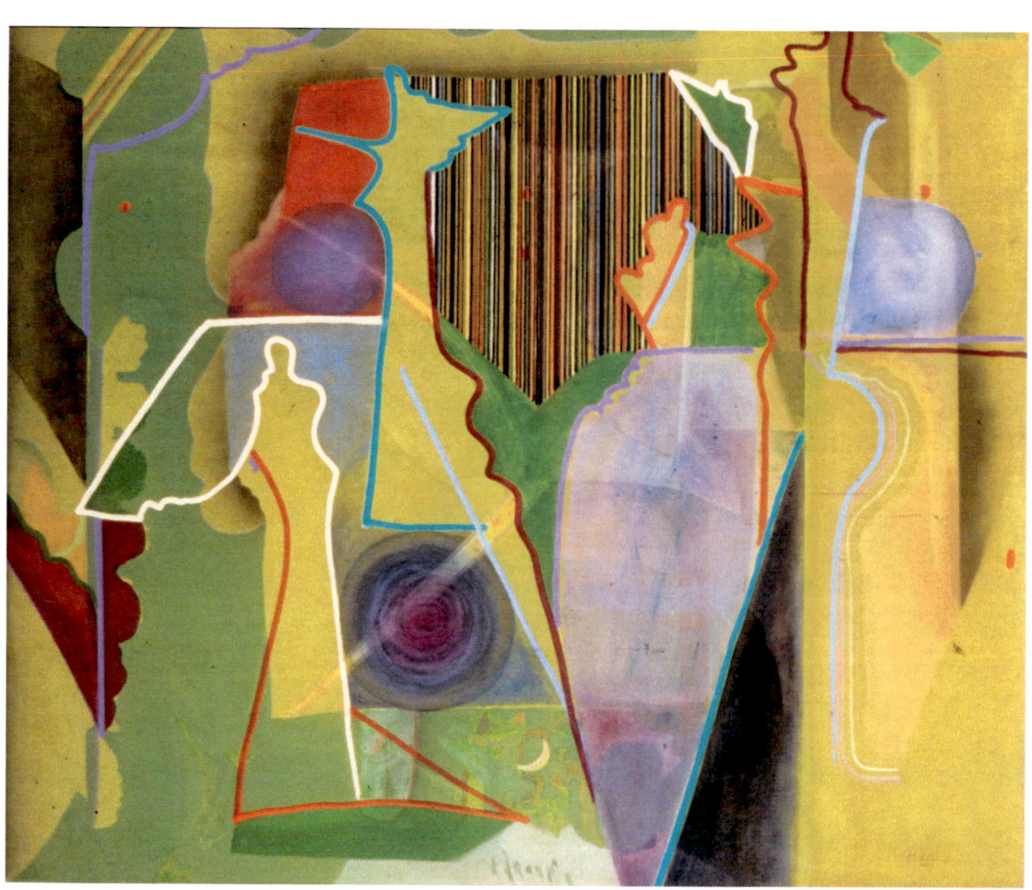

Donald Vogl, *Elysian Shield*.

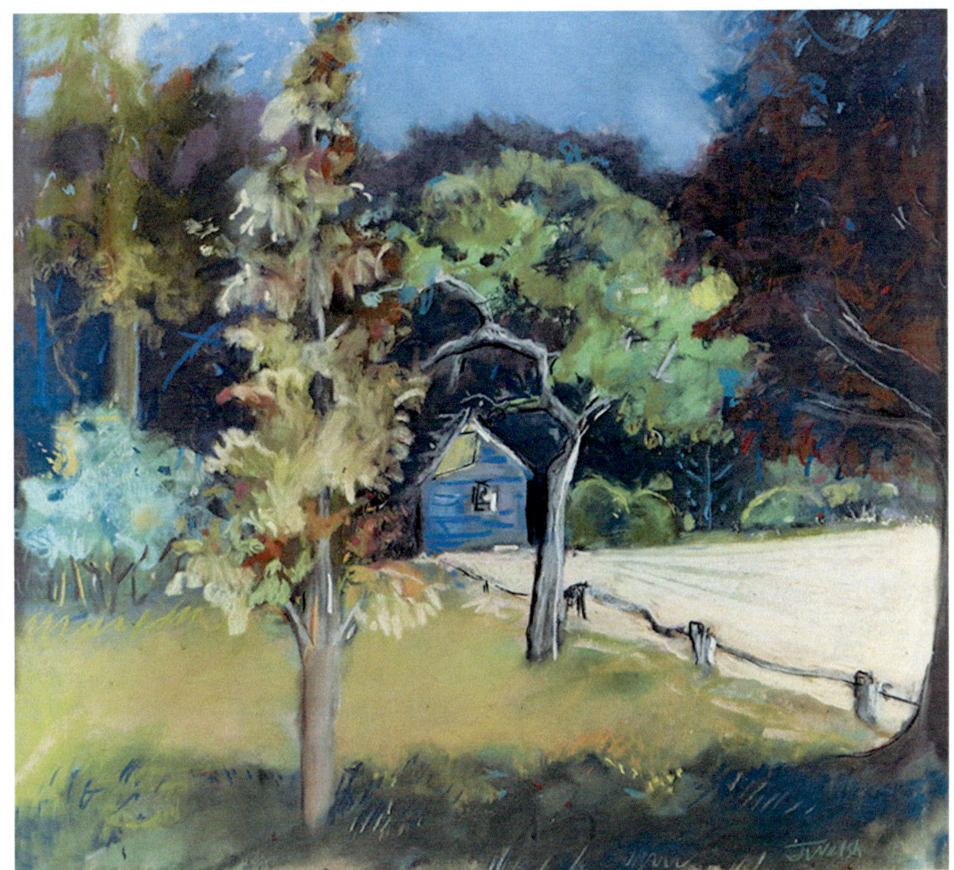

Jacqueline H. Welsh, *The Blue Cabin at Oxbow.*

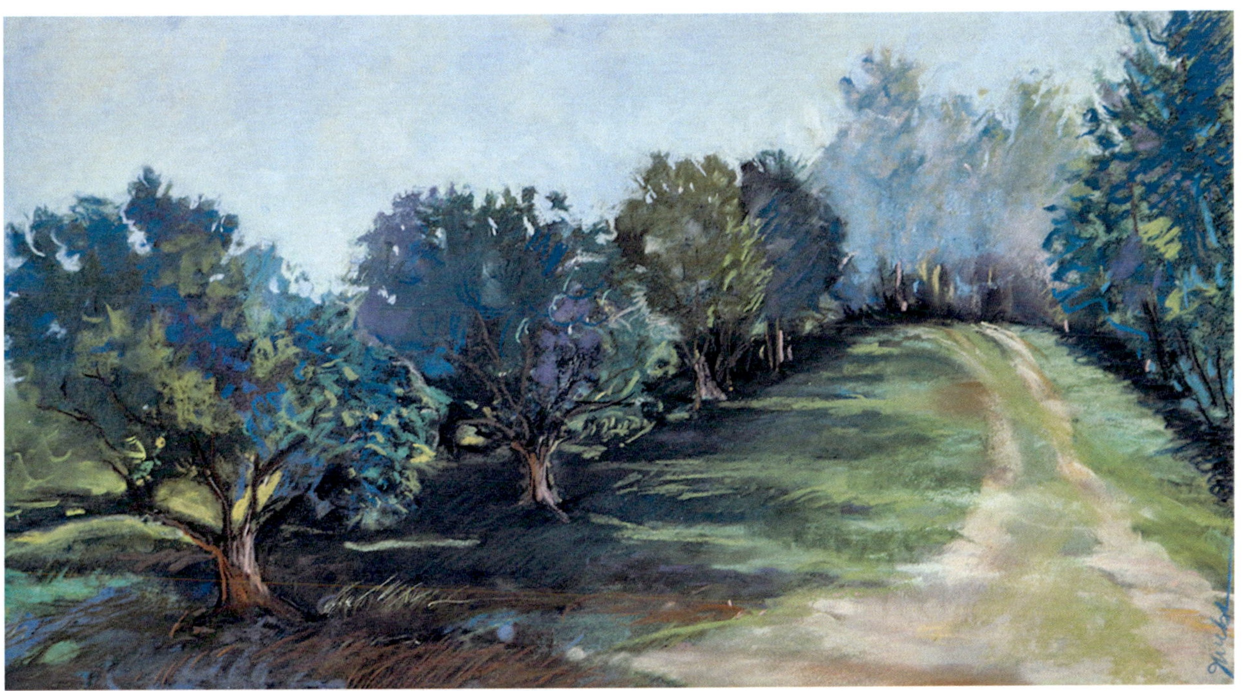

Jacqueline H. Welsh, *Orchard.*

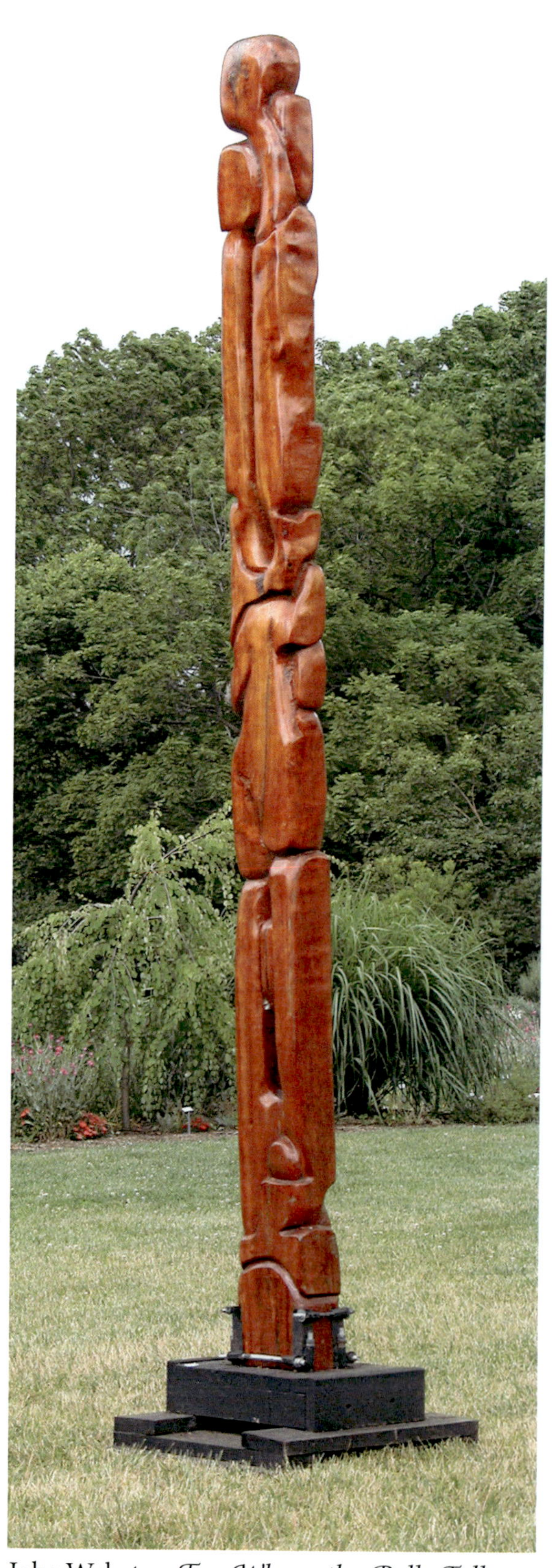

Jake Webster, *For Whom the Bells Toll.*

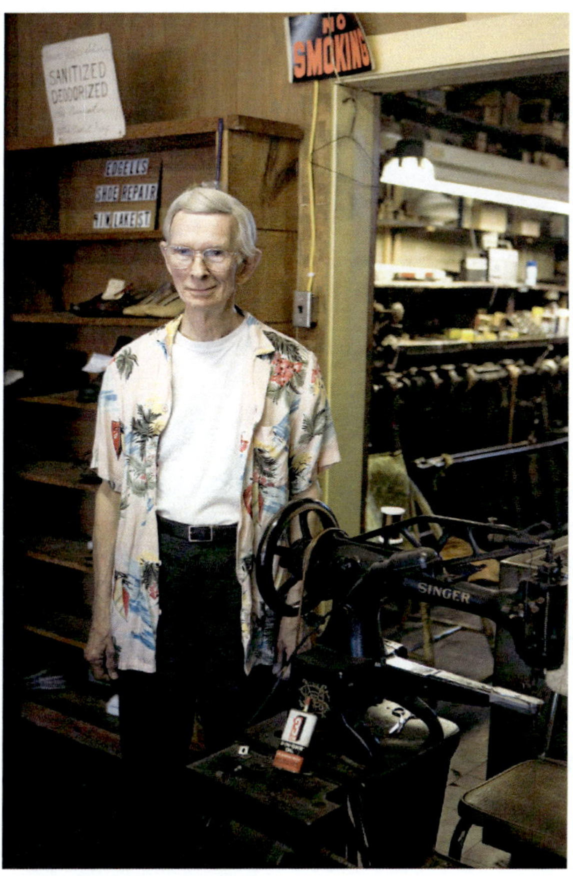

Kay Westhues, *Bob Edgell.*

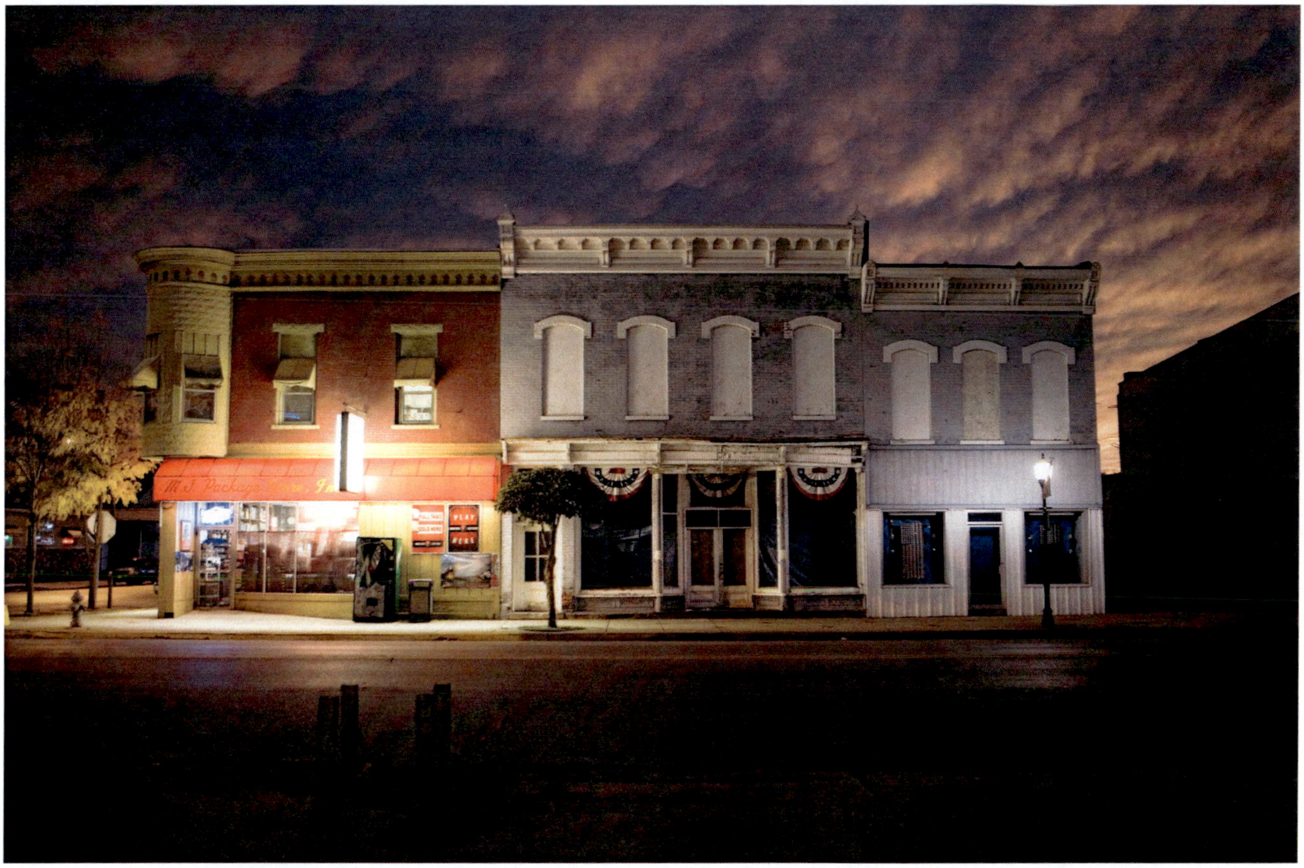

Kay Westhues, *Walkerton Sunset.*

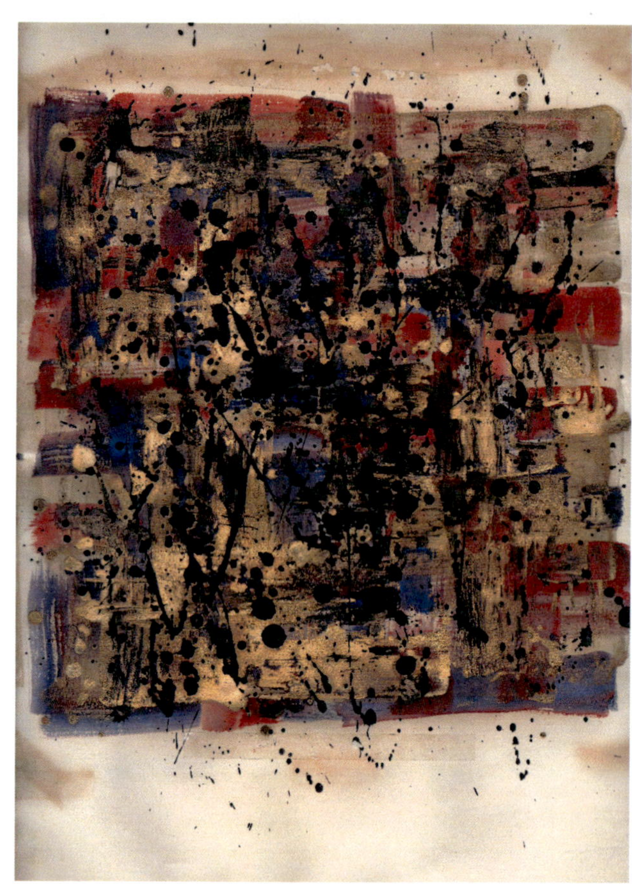

Wilbur Warne West, *Il Penseroso.*

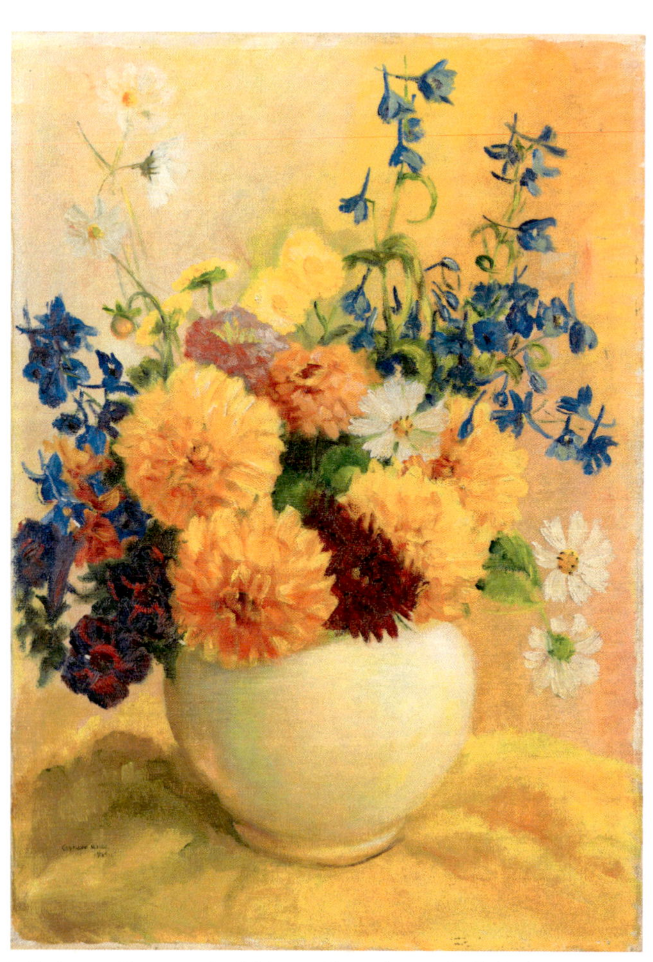

Miriam Gertrude Wiser-Butcher, *Still Life.*

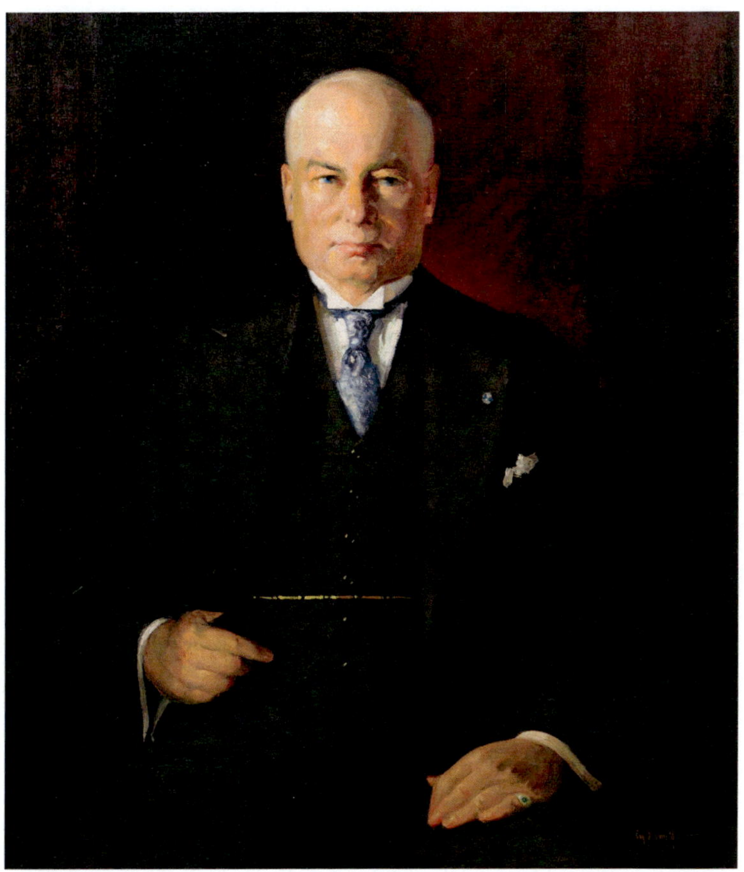

Guy Brown Wiser, *Portrait of Mr. Charles Arthur Carlisle.*

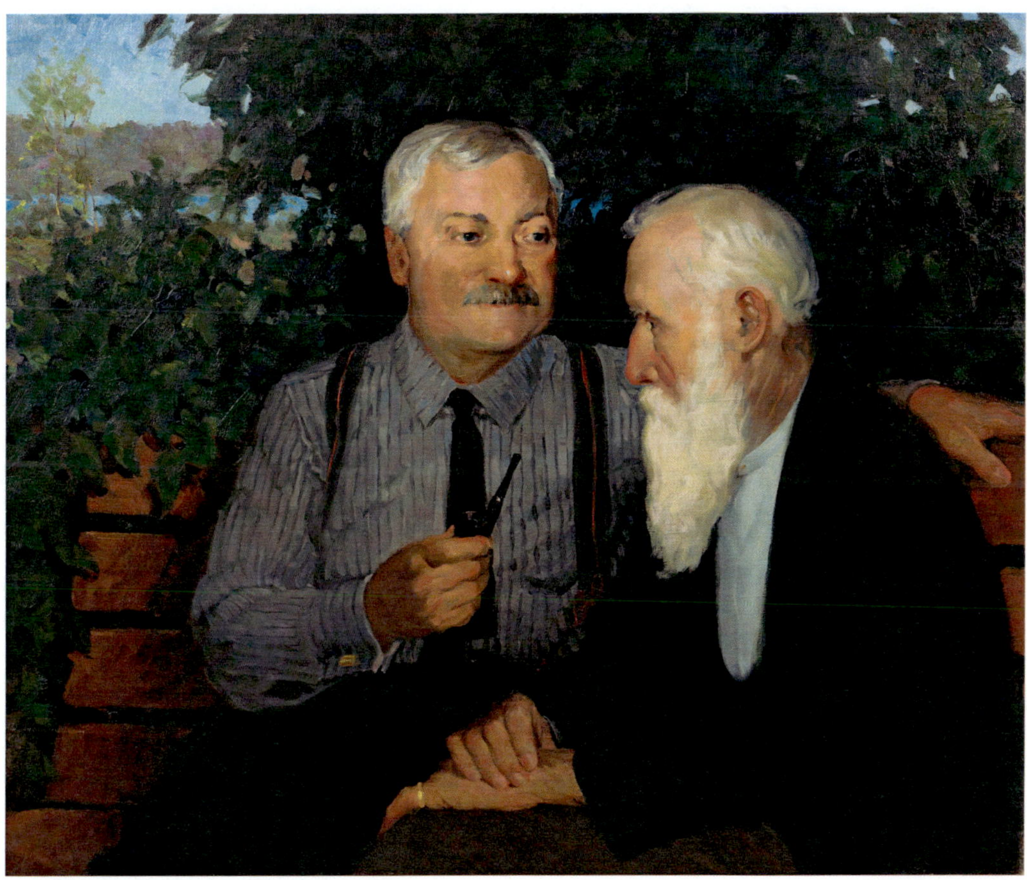

Guy Brown Wiser, *Cronies.*

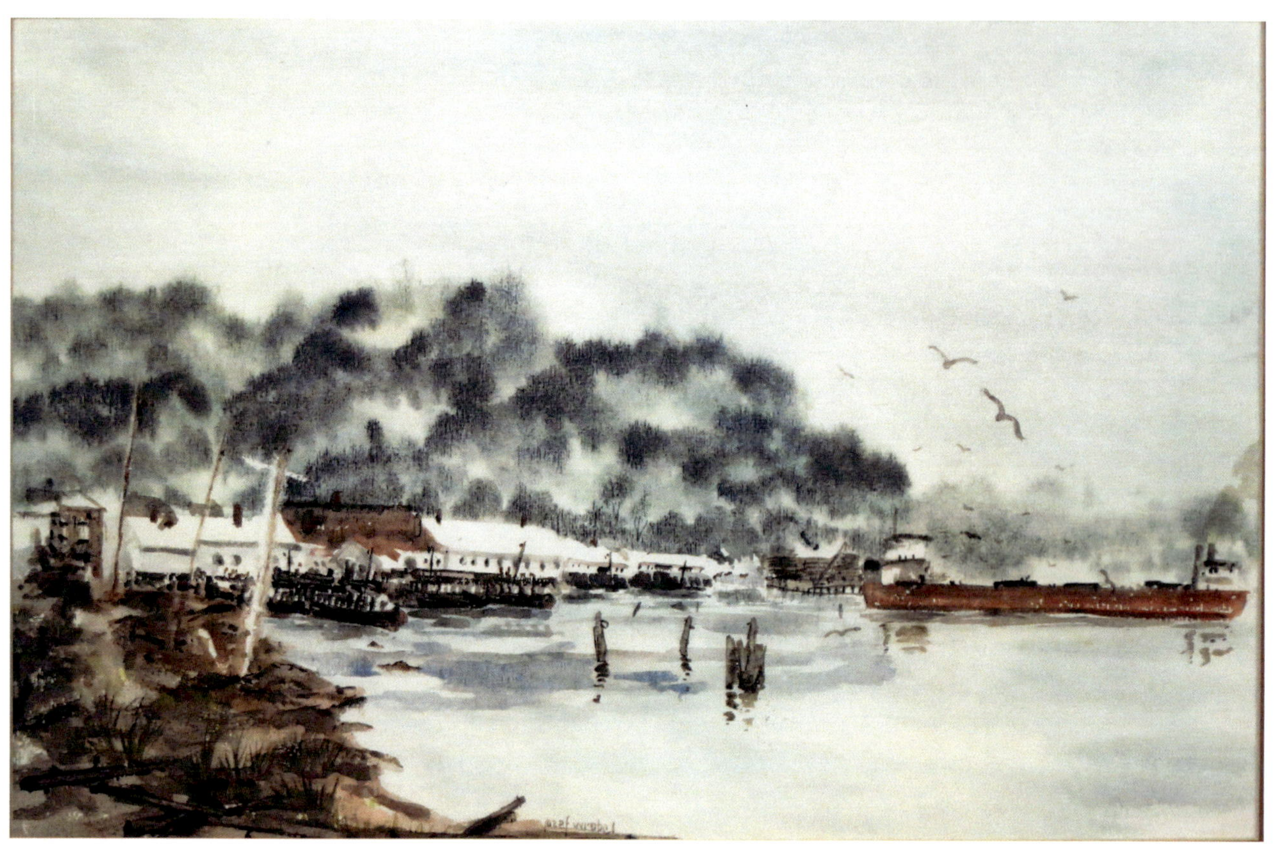

Joseph Wrobel, *Shipyard Motif*.

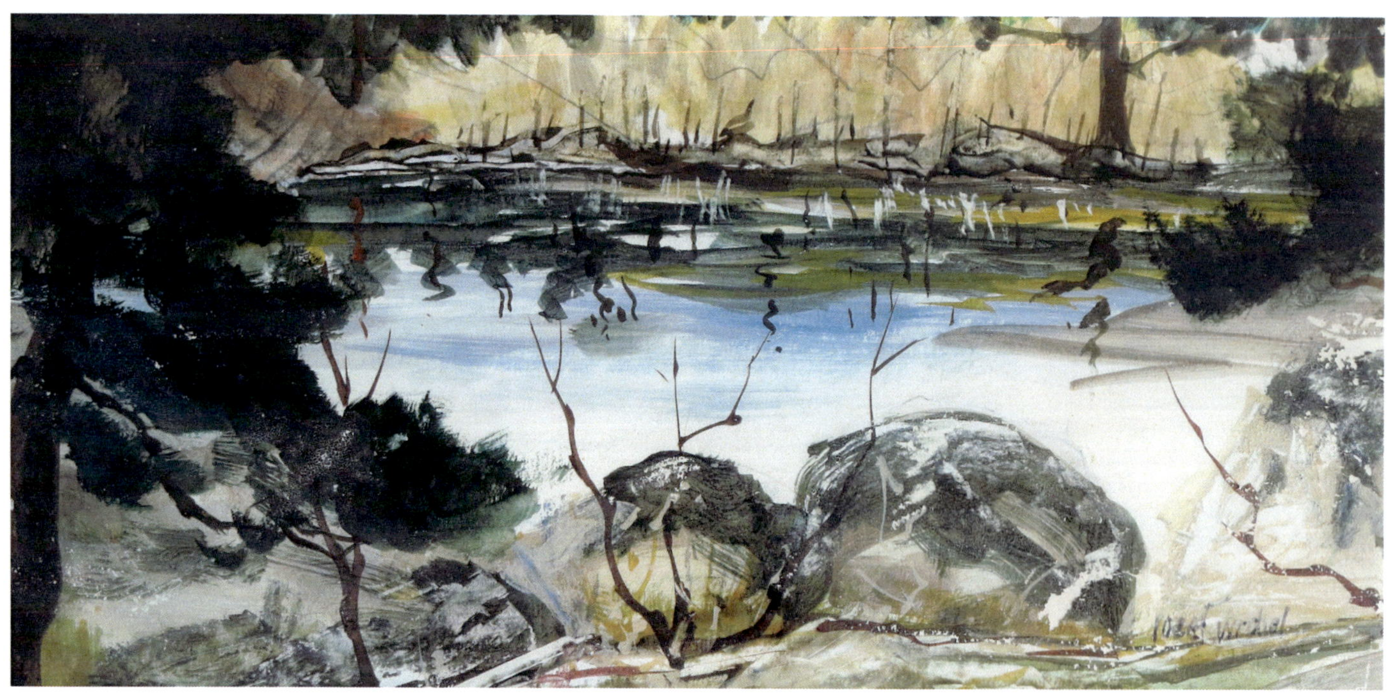

Joseph Wrobel, *Aspens on Lookout Mountain*.